To the memory of my parents,
Bill and Doreen Stedman Jones

# Durkheim Reconsidered

*Susan Stedman Jones*

The right of Susan Stedman Jones to be identified as author of this work has been asserted in accordance with the Copyright, Designs and Patents Act 1988.

First published in 2001 by Polity Press in association with Blackwell Publishers Ltd

*Editorial office*:
Polity Press
65 Bridge Street
Cambridge CB2 1UR, UK

*Marketing and production*:
Blackwell Publishers Ltd
108 Cowley Road
Oxford OX4 1JF, UK

*Published in the USA by*
Blackwell Publishers Inc.
350 Main Street
Malden, MA 02148, USA

ISBN 0-7456-1615-1 ISBN 0-7456-1616-X (pbk)

A catalogue record for this book is available from the British Library.

**Library of Congress Cataloging-in-Publication Data**
Jones, Susan Stedman.
    Durkheim reconsidered / Susan Stedman Jones.
      p. cm.
    Includes bibliographical references and index.
    ISBN 0-7456-1615-1 — ISBN 0-7456-1616-X (pbk.)
      1. Durkheimian school of sociology. 2. Durkheim, Emile 1858–1917. I. Title.

  HM465 h.J65 2001
  301 — dc21

                            00-060615

Typeset in 10 on 12 pt Times
by SetSystems Ltd, Saffron Walden, Essex
Printed in Great Britain by MPG Books Ltd, Bodmin, Cornwall

This book is printed on acid-free paper.

# Contents

# Preface

Why does Durkheim need a reconsideration? There is certainly always a gap between a thinker and what is made of him or her subsequently; but when this gap becomes unbridgeable, then something must be done. The gap between Durkheim's thought and what has been made of him subsequently in the social sciences is the reason for this reconsideration. This book is a response to the puzzles I have encountered in the way he has been interpreted and the research that inspired me to attempt to unravel them. Unlike many sociologists or anthropologists, I read Durkheim before I read those thinkers or movements by whom he has been interpreted – this at least allows the possibility of a fresh view of an important thinker. I discovered that the interpretation of Durkheim has a feature which characterizes prejudice everywhere: if something is repeated long and often enough, it acquires the patina of truth. These difficulties which I encountered in the interpretation he has received in the social sciences have led to questions which are germane to the understanding of his thought and which serve to underpin the reflections in this book.

I first encountered Durkheim through anthropology, when between my degrees in philosophy, I buried myself for a while in the study of 'other cultures', and it was here that my suspicions were initially aroused. Here through his identification with Radcliffe-Brown's structural functionalism, he was a characterized as a thinker interested above all in rigid structures and functions as sustaining them: he was associated with 'closed' and 'unchanging' societies whose only dynamic, it would appear, is to stay still. This early colouring has remained as an accepted feature of his view of society. But I could not square this with the picture I got when I read his actual texts: did he not insist on the changing dynamic quality of social relations? But how did he account for these?

Durkheim's vision is so much larger than that of Radcliffe-Brown: he employed a language in his description of the social that is so much more complex and nuanced than that encapsulated simply by 'structure' and 'function'. Indeed, the more I read and reflected, the more it became clear that there was another language which seemed more theoretically profound than the first, and even to be the basis for it. I recognized certain terms of this consistent language, which, while put to a different use, were distinctly philosophical – in fact were Kantian in origin – where else could all that talk about representations and categories come from? Here, then, is a another question: how do representations relate to structure and function?

Then I encountered another Durkheim in anthropology; here he had became source and justification for a kind of determinist collectivism *outré* in questions of knowledge; again, this has clung to his name. So he was held to authenticate reference to the group and its structural and symbolic activity as sufficient to answer all questions about knowledge in society. Certainly Durkheim put society and the collective centre stage in terms of epistemology, but what is, and what is not, entailed by this position? How is it that he uses the concept of 'reason' as part of his account of the human being (1925a: 95/113)? How does this relate to the collectivity? And having just read *Le Suicide*, I was inspired to ask how he could then hold 'free thought' to be a constant aspect of 'the history of the human mind' (1897a: 430/375) These might not be very interesting questions for anthropological accounts of specific societies, but they are crucial when it comes to the interpretation of a thinker, especially in evaluating his notorious 'sociologism'. So how do these fit in here? The answer I received was that they don't, and that this is not authentic Durkheim! So – and this has remained a feature of the interpretations imposed on him – those features that do not fit each passing 'dominant ideology' are swept under the carpet in the interest of sustaining each cherished interpretation, or one that is easier on the mind theoretically.

It was whilst teaching the philosophy of social science that I noticed that students arrived at university with their minds made up about Durkheim, and that their views were confirmed not only by what they were taught subsequently, but also by student texts which continue to exercise a baleful influence. Durkheim appears peculiarly easy to parody and reject, particularly when certain philosophical and historical issues are left out of account. It was also whilst teaching that I encountered yet another Durkheim – this was the sociologists' Durkheim. Unlike the sociologists, I became acquainted with Parsons only through my interest in Durkheim; whereas they, it would appear, were acquainted with Durkheim through Parsons. Thereafter, Durkheimianism and Parsonianism were identified. But again I could see that Durkheim's theoretical interest or language was not adequately expressed by Parsonianism. The result of this identification was a Durkheim concerned above all with order and normative integration. But what does Durkheim mean by order and the normative?

I was now becoming aware of the peculiar fate Durkheim had suffered: he was treated as a kind of badge of foreign authority for theories which only encapsulate a small aspect of his thinking, but with which he was identified and through which he was interpreted. This fate is the contrary of the old adage that a rolling stone gathers no moss. The Durkheim stone had rolled between different theories, and was thick with moss – consisting of the set of interpretations and criticisms attached to his name. The Durkheim stone has travelled widely: it was rolled all the way from France to the United States and from there to Britain and elsewhere.

Although previously he was positively attached to theories which claimed to represent him, now a new phenomenon occurred. With the swing away from structural functionalism, he became the bogeyman of sociology – this is particularly clear in Gouldner's *The Coming Crisis of Western Sociology*, where Durkheim is blamed for structural functionalism's ahistorical, uncritical thinking. Of course, he was also by now the archetypal conservative as interpreted by Nisbet, Coser and Parsons. But this raises further questions: in what sense is Durkheim a structural functionalist, and what is entailed by the functionalism he does espouse? In what sense is he a conservative? By now the moss on the Durkheim stone was thick with all the attachments, positive and negative, that clung to the concept 'Durkheimian'.

There was a further movement in sociology which added significantly to this and which I was uniquely placed to observe. This was the swing away from science and the move towards questions of interpretation and meaning as dominant in theory. Durkheim now became the straw man of the phenomenological movement for his scientism and positivism. Odd that he was originally held to be mystical for his strange concept of the conscience collective! Now there is another question: what does Durkheim mean by 'science'? Why did Durkheim think there was a science which adequately accounted for social reality? What was its nature, and what is and is not entailed by it? This concept of 'science' had become a political football amongst the competing schools of sociology. I stubbornly refused to believe both the critics of his science and his supporters who wanted to turn him into the hard man of science who ignored all 'soft' philosophical issues. I was convinced that he was using a scientific language, but with a unique philosophical nature. How else can his science be connected with 'rationalism' (1895a: ix/33)?

A distinct feature of many of the critiques of Durkheim is their philosophical inspiration. Since he had acquired the reputation for both scientism and conservatism, he was now the butt for both Marxist and phenomenological critiques. But did he never consider the type of questions raised here? Did he not know about meaning and the question of how things appear to consciousness (the problem of phenomenalism)? But here is another question: what is the relation of meaning to structural conditions? Are social worlds built up out of the rational pursuit of meaning? Further, for Marxists – through the static, moralizing aura that clung to his name – he failed to acknowledge conflict or historical development. But had he not heard about Hegel and dialectical views of history, or questioned the problem of materialism? Now another question emerges for the radicalism that has so consistently opposed Durkheim: why is it, given the degree of conflict (industrial and gender) in society, that it hasn't quite fallen apart? What is it about social worlds that has such a tenacity? Uniquely, Durkheim underlines this, but how?

Whatever the critiques of his actual sociology, Durkheim has been treated as though extraordinarily philosophically naïve. But there is an unusual feature of this: those educated as sociologists were using concepts derived from philosophy to attack Durkheim, but here was a thinker educated as a philosopher, who taught it before turning to found his sociology. The peculiarity of Durkheim is that he does not overtly reflect on the philosophical aspect of methodologies, but advances a distinct theoretical language as a means of accessing the social world. Was it possible that this was like the tip of an iceberg, whose concealed mass might, if brought to the surface, begin to answer some of these philosophically inspired critiques?

It has been stated correctly that Durkheim is well known, but not known well. With significant exceptions, he has been taken out of context theoretically and politically – particularly through the critiques addressed to him. The world he lived in was swept away by the horrors of the 1914–18 war – and it is to significant features of this that we must return to understand the full complexity of his thought. Given the current state of the social sciences, a reconsideration of Durkheim is timely, and even necessary. What follows can only contribute to this, by revealing certain misunderstood or neglected aspects of the original vision, and by clearing away the thicket of interpretations that obscure the view. It is with these that we must begin.

# 1

# Questions of Interpretation: Sociology contra Durkheim

Durkheim, who died in Paris in 1917, was a republican philosopher, a self-proclaimed rationalist and socialist; yet he is taken as the apostle of conservative thought as well as the most unphilosophical scientism, empiricism and positivism in the social sciences. Of the triumvirate of thinkers who are regarded as the founding fathers of sociology, neither Marx nor Weber has received more opprobrium than Durkheim. He has, it would appear, committed every sociological sin: he is concerned with consensus, and has no theory of conflict or of power; he has a static view of society, with no theory of social change; he has no theory of agency and no conception of the problems of meaning and interpretation; he has little or no conception of the individual and individual consciousness; and, as the architect of sociological positivism, he is the principal author of what has been characterized as a crisis of irrationalism in the human sciences. The name 'Durkheim' now evokes all that must be avoided in sociology, and has become like a billboard which is so pelted with missiles that the original message is obscured. The attempt to uncover this is my task in this book.

Sociology has its own oral tradition, and it is in this that Durkheim's name has been particularly blackened. The process is fed by pre-university courses and by introductory texts. An example of this is Bilton et al. (1981), where Durkheim is presented as an 'organicist positivist' whose view of science, which is 'crudely positivistic', comes from Comte (Bilton et al. 1981: 691, 702). Organicism, based on an analogy with a living organism, is held to be tied to functionalist explanation, where the elements are explained by the role they play in the functioning of the whole (ibid. 704). Functionalist explanations alway require equilibrium mechanisms; in this way Durkheim, like other functionalists, avoids historical explanations and stresses order and integration (ibid. 713–15). So organicism leads directly to social order, for conflict cannot be allowed between component parts, and a high degree of integration and co-ordination is regarded as 'normal'. The primacy of value consensus 'cannot be overemphasized' for, like other organicists, Durkheim considers society as primarily a 'moral order', that is constituted by institutionalized norms and values (ibid. 701).

In another textbook, the external and constraining nature of social facts for Durkheim is held to confirm his organicism and holism; his concept of constraint is said to be central to his functionalism, and is opposed to conflict theory. His view of structure is viewed as opposed to action, meaning and, for Giddens, agency (1989: 720–3). This continues a long-standing criticism that Durkheim's objectivism – seen in the externality of social facts – rejects the subjectivity of the individual (Tosti 1898).

It is not only textbooks which express such views; we find them also in recent commentaries. Lehmann's *Deconstructing Durkheim* sees him as a conservative patriarch whose conservatism is tied to his positivism and whose 'uncompromising' organicism (1993: 8) is central to his social ontology and entails his determinism (ibid. 45). His view of constraint is evidence of holistic determinism (ibid. 55), as are his concepts of external-ity, force and thing. In maintaining that for Durkheim the individual is 'impotent' in face of society as a 'natural entity', Lehmann continues the critiques that have stemmed from Gehlke (1915) and continued through ethnomethodology that he ignored the role of the individual as an active cause of social phenomena. His most distinguished commentator claims that Durkheim has 'an absolutist conception of knowledge' which misses the 'essentially meaningful character of social interaction' (Lukes and Scull 1984: 23). Further, in books focusing on other topics, asides are thrown at Durkheim which are equally condemnatory: 'Durkheim mod-elled his sociology on the natural sciences, thus violating hermeneutics' (Meadwell 1995: 189).

These criticisms circulate widely, and form the basis of a thinking about Durkheim that can be called 'vulgar Durkheimianism', which is the distillation or worst-case analysis of what has been said about him in the history of sociology. It combines the concepts of system, order, morality, holism, functionalism and science. With this conglomeration of unrecon-structed concepts, the main accusations against Durkheim have been made: he is a thinker who adapted the methods of the natural sciences to the study of society; he is a conservative in his concern for social order and moral integration in society; and his functionalism confirms his scientism and conservatism, just as his view of society is taken to deny the individual.

Is there anything wrong with these views? Are they not a fair distillation of his failures, and an accurate final judgement on the founder of the subject? Whilst I will show in the next two chapters how various views that have been ascribed to Durkheim are contradicted by his own statements, and in the subsequent chapters offer new light on Durkheim's theoretical positions, here I will just indicate some of the problems with these views. Accusations centring on his organicism ignore his rejection of biological explanations in sociology: to call society an 'organism' is 'an aphorism' which alone does not establish a science (Durkheim 1885a: 1.373). And why should an unreconstructed organicist argue that, with society, the organism 'spiritualises' itself (1893b: 338/284)? If society is really a 'natural entity' which renders us impotent, why is it 'irreducible' and how can Durkheim argue that through social forces 'we rise above things' to deprive them of their 'fortuitous, absurd and amoral character' (ibid. 381/321)? If his holism is really incompatible with freedom, agency and the individual, why does he reject those views which overemphasize cohesion to the exclusion of liberty (1892a: 14), argue that the individual is the only active element of society (1898b: 43n./29), and hold that 'freedom of thought is the first of freedoms' (1898c: 269/49)?

If his view of externality really is incompatible with the subjective nature of social reality, why does he hold that externality 'is only apparent', and argue for internality (*le dedans*) (1895a: 28/70)? If social facts really are 'hard data' which exist without reference to meaning, why does he hold that social life is made 'entirely of representations' and that this indicates the role of mind (ibid. xi/34)? If constraint is central to a functionalism which denies conflict, why does he characterize the constraining division of labour by the 'war of the classes'?[1] And if his functionalism ignores the historical and change, why does he deal with 'historical development' (ibid. 94/123) and talk of the 'free currents' of social life (ibid. 14/58)? And if he really ignores all questions of hermeneutics, why does he argue that interpretation is possible and associate it with type and 'species' (*espèces*) (ibid. 89/119)?

Interpretations are complex, they consist not only of what has been said, but also of what has not been said. Lukes in his magisterial intellectual biography has done much to set the record straight. And other commentators (Giddens, La Capra, Tiryakian and Pickering, amongst others) have demonstrated the rich complexity of his thought, and have insisted on the centrality of the conscience collective and of collective representation to his thought. But however much the sociological reading of Durkheim has improved, there are certain theoretical lacunae in these accounts which leave certain fundamental critiques unchallenged, and this remains the case despite new and interesting readings of Durkheim (by Gane, Pearce, Schmaus and Meštrović).

The continuing accusations show that there is still a deep confusion about his theoretical language, particularly over 'force', 'thing' and 'externality'. This is one of the reasons why vulgar Durkheimianism remains *theoretically*, if not sociologically, fundamentally unchallenged. This is composed of the concepts of holism, positivism and scientism, functional-ism, and determinism. The interrelation and apparent mutual implication of these is aided and abetted by the neglect of other concepts which affect their interpretation. This allows the development of a mythology wherein Durkheim has become a kind of monster who rules over a dead world of facts and things, the point of whose thought is to nail persons to social structure, to found a science on untransformable fact, and to endorse any order as morally right and authoritative. But, like Frankenstein's monster, this Durkheim is constructed out of parts which come from diverse sources.

A fundamental source of misinterpretation is a tendency to read him through different and later theories. So the over-identification with Comte leaves Durkheim sharing his anti-individualism, authoritarianism and pos-itivism. His overwhelming concern for order and moral consensus comes from reading him through Parsons. (Bilton et al. show the consequences of reading Durkheim through both Comte and Parsons.) The overly scientistic view of structure and function comes from equating Durkheim with Radcliffe-Brown and Malinowski. And of course there has been an enthusiastic structuralist reading of Durkheim which may entail as many pitfalls as a Parsonian reading. So in general we can say that Durkheim is judged by the company he is said to keep; in the history of the subject he founded, the great patriarch of the social sciences has found (like many a young girl) that it is easy to acquire a reputation, and very hard to lose it.

This dismal picture is reinforced by the particular location of Durkheim within what are seen as the antitheses of sociological thought: consensus versus conflict, holism versus individualism, structure versus agency, causal versus meaning-type accounts, and those based on transformative histori-cal interest versus static functionalist accounts. In some cases these actually falsify Durkheim's position; in others they obliterate the originality or complexity of his position. As a result of this, every retrogressive move-ment in sociology seems to claim Durkheim as its own, whilst every progressive movement claims him as its enemy.

However, these views can be directly contradicted by Durkheim's own statements. An examination of these is the basis of the 'critique of critiques' which forms the kernel of these first two chapters. The way in which I propose to unravel the problems of interpretation is, first, to examine Durkheim's location in types of sociological theory. This will not only call into question the established forms of classification of Durkheim's thought, together with the dangers of reading him through later theories, but will also reveal those concepts which require examination together with certain problems in translation. Secondly, in chapter 2, I will pursue this question of interpretation by examining the concepts of order and of science which seem to sum up the 'vulgar' Durkheim.

The division of types of theory within the present conscience collective of sociology and its teaching practices is inimical to a proper understanding of Durkheim: he is identified with theories with which he has significant differences, and he is contrasted with those with which he has more similarity than is apparent.

## The theories Durkheim is compared with: the differences

### Structural functionalism

It is important to remember that Durkheim wrote before Parsons; but from the way Durkheim is viewed in sociology's oral tradition, we have to conclude that although formally it is recognized that he died in France in 1917, he suffered a veritable rebirth in America! Paradoxically for a French thinker, this has become the dominant culture in the interpretation of Durkheim. Here he becomes a born-again conservative, not only by the perceived identification of him with the concerns of a particular form of structural functionalism, but also by the characterization of him imposed by significant thinkers within this movement.

Lukes has warned us that the sociologists' Durkheim is strongly coloured by Parsons; consequently, for many sociologists the success or failure of Durkheim's thought is judged in terms of that of Parsons and American functionalism. For this to be fair, there would have to be an identity between the central concepts of the two systems that I suggest is fundamentally lacking. Just as Parsons has no theory of conscience, conscience collective or collective representation, so Durkheim lacks the Parsonian conception of the functional prerequisites of a system, a concern with latency, equilibrium and the problem of social control, and the study of actors in terms of deviance and conformity – yet Parsons associates these terms with Durkheim (Parsons 1937: 376). Is Durkheim's view of constraint and sanction the same as social control? To identify them is to presuppose the meaning of sanction, to gloss over the distinction between legitimate and illegitimate constraint, and to ignore the possibility of a dialectical tension between structure and agency in Durkheim's conception of sanction.

Durkheim might well agree with Parsons that society is 'essentially a network of interactive relationships' (Parsons 1951: 51). However, whatever his intentions were, Parsons's stress on 'the system' makes it sound like an invisible fish tank in whose transcendent interests the fish swim. In so doing, he has bypassed what for Durkheim is the crucial logical access to society – representation. The conformity with role expectations and the integration of a common value system is the dynamic of a social system for Parsons (ibid. 42), whilst the search for justice and the need to make a morality are central to the dynamic of modern society for Durkheim (1893b: 406/340). But, according to Gouldner (1970), morality means integration and conformity for Parsons, a view he also ascribes to Durkheim.

For Parsons there is no theory of solidarity in the same sense as there is for Durkheim; his minimal reference to solidarity is subordinate to 'the collective orientation of roles' (1951: 96–101). Solidarity for Durkheim is not necessarily the same as value consensus is for Parsons, and rather than integration being his dominant problematic, he is clear that it is only possible through the full realization of solidarity – which is compromised by injustice and inequality. Reading Durkheim through Parsons (or a particular view of him) has had the effect of passing over his concern with questions of individuality, sociality and moral relatedness in historical forms of solidarity, and thereby replacing them with questions of systems, stability and integration. This is to turn what for Durkheim is achievable into the achieved, and the concern for the social and historical possibility of morality and social relations into the concern for normative integration within the present system.

Gouldner (1970) blamed Durkheim for the pall cast over sociology through the concepts of function, system, order and integration, which are central to structural functionalism. Durkheim is the source of its obsession with unitariness, for 'The parts only take on significance in relation to the whole' (ibid. 198). On the contrary, for Durkheim, 'A whole can only be defined in relation to the parts which form it' (Durkheim 1912a: 49/33). He rejects precisely the kind of holism ascribed to him by Gouldner. There is no 'objective unity' to such a 'heterogeneous whole' (1903c: 1.132). There is both 'unity and diversity' in social life (1912a: 591/417). Unlike Comte, Durkheim insisted that diversity is not pathological, but an essential part of modern society (1928a: 222/237). There is a tension in his thought between individuality and sociality, which is expressed in the relation between different forms of individualized and collectivized con- sciousness – *conscience particulière* and *conscience collective* – both of which are states of mind, but with different roots.

Because of this 'unitarianism', Gouldner believes that Durkheim cannot deal with the potency and functional autonomy of the individual: he obliterates the individual (who is a 'tool' of the *conscience collective*) in his concern for social order (1970: 196). This neglects, first, Durkheim's argument that 'as societies become more vast ... a psychic life of a new sort appears. Individual diversities become conspicuous ... individuals become a source of spontaneous activity' (Durkheim 1893b: 339/285). Secondly, it overlooks Durkheim's logical pluralism, which is central to all wholes: wholes are not *logically* prior to persons in the way Gouldner suggests. 'One cannot following idealist and theological metaphysics derive the part from the whole, since the whole is nothing without the parts which form it and cannot draw its vital necessities from the void' (1898b: 44/29). These considerations make a difference to the type of integration which is ascribed to him, for this implies a conception of unity. Alpert argues that Durkheim's conception of social integration centres on unity – for Durkheim society is a unity, and 'not a mere plurality of individuals' (Alpert 1941: 2.29). But for Durkheim wholes are relational and founded on pluralism. 'All of social life is constituted by a system of facts which derive from positive and lasting relations established between a *plurality* of individuals' (1893b: 329/277).[2] How can there be a unity which is compatible with logical pluralism? A positive answer to this question means that there can be a real interdependence at the social level which is incompatible neither with the heterogeneity and 'difference' of phenomena nor with the autonomy of the agent: thereby integration does not require subordination for Durkheim.

So, thirdly, Gouldner overlooks Durkheim's insistence on the plural nature of the conscience collective, and that it cannot be 'hypostatised' (1895a: 103/145). Durkheim argues that we have two 'consciences', and whilst one is collective in type, the other represents our personality (1893b: 74/61). We are not 'tools' of the *conscience collective* – for, as we will see, the latter is compatible with the freedom and individuation of the 'particular conscience' (*conscience particulière*).

This dismal picture of the consequences of Durkheim's holism is compounded when it is combined with a particular view of functionalism: static, overly scientistic and anti-epistemological, obsessed with integration at all costs, subservient to the needs of the system, anti-individual and deterministic. Structural functionalism can be defined as the view that elements of a culture or society are explained by their functional contribution to the overall coherence and stability of the social system: cultural/ social systems are homeostatic functioning units. This definition implicitly introduces the teleological assumption that the point of any part is to contribute to the overall stability, continuity and functional unity of the whole.[3] However, Durkheim opposes teleology as explanation (1893b: 330/288), and does so through the idea of function (1895a: 95/123).

The sense of function Durkheim uses is dynamic, not static. Its original introduction in nineteenth-century thought stressed relations, activities, transformation and dynamism, as against the fixed and unchanging – static form and fixed organization (Kallen 1935: 523). 'To remain adapted, the function itself therefore must be always ready to change, to accommodate itself to new situations. . . . nothing immobilises a function more than to be tied to a too defined structure' (Durkheim 1893b: 323/272–3).

He rejects the static view of function of Comte and Spencer, which assumes that 'society will have an arrested form, where each organ, each individual, will have a definite function and will no longer change' (ibid. 322/271). This must cast doubt on the accusation that Durkheim's functionalism is inherently conservative because it is committed to maintaining the *status quo* (Gouldner 1970: 335). Gouldner similarly accuses Durkheim of 'opposing a future perspective', and thereby consolidating sociology to the stasis of the 'synchronic present' (ibid. 119). This overlooks the following: 'If men have learned to hope, they have formed the habit of orientating themselves to the future' (Durkheim 1893b: 225/190).

Function for Durkheim is a relation of correspondence to the needs of the organism (ibid. 11/11). For Pierce, Radcliffe Brown (1952: 178) eradicated the dynamism of Durkheim's account by identifying 'needs' with the conditions necessary for the existence of society (Pierce 1960: 158). The real function of the division of labour for Durkheim is to create solidarity, and solidarity is a 'completely moral phenomenon' (Durkheim 1893b: 28/24). He held that present society was passing through 'an appalling crisis' of morality (ibid. 405/339). His functionalism thus must have a dynamic moral interest that has been lost through its identification with later static conceptions of function.

There are of course many definitions of 'function' (Pierce 1960: 167; Nagel 1968: 522). For Durkheim it is associated wtih differentation of family tasks (1893b: 92/78), with activity (ibid. 416)[4] and the repetition of ways of acting (ibid. 357/302), and thus with the 'habit of certain practices' (ibid. 321/271); functions and relations mutually imply each other (ibid. 92/78). So, as for Merton later, function for Durkheim also means reciprocal relation and mutually dependent variation. None of these meanings can, without deformation, be annexed and subordinated to function as meaning the equilibrium of a homeostatic system.

Yet there are other conceptions of function which are crucial to the interpretation of Durkheim, which have either been ignored or mistranslated. First, there are 'the speculative function' (1912a: 614/432) and the 'cognitive and intellectual functions' (ibid. 613/431). The 'higher intellectual functions' are effective in action, and this is shown in the role of 'attention', which can interrupt, stop or facilitate action (1898b: 31/17).[5] Function here thus has a clear epistemological sense, and this is seen in its identification with the 'psychic' and with representation: 'Judicial, governmental, scientific and industrial functions, in a word all the special functions belong to the psychic order (*sont d'ordre psychique*) because they consist in representations and actions' (1893b: 46/39).[6] What is the psychic? Durkheimian authorities are tellingly quiet about this term – probably because it is an odd term for a man of science to use! But it significantly affects the meaning of his organicism – for 'the essential characteristic of psychic life' is that 'it is more free, more complex and more independent of the organs which support it' (ibid. 338/284).[7]

Secondly, he connects function to conscience: 'Conscience, like the organism, is a system of functions' (ibid. 217/183).[8] We have to know more about conscience and its functions, and how it is related to the set of relations of which it is a part, before any implications about its necessary subservience to the functional needs of systems are drawn. Conscience is the crucial intermediary factor between function and system: conscience is the necessary medium for adaptation (ibid. 14/14).

Thirdly, Durkheim talks of 'representative functions' (*fonctions repré-sentatives*) (ibid. 270/228), which are more developed in 'the most culti-vated societies . . .' (1897a: 45/76). I will show that these are crucial to thought, action and transformation – yet they have been largely obliter-ated through translation. Further, 'spirituality' is the distinctive feature of 'representative life' (1898b: 49/33).[9] Psychic functions are connected with 'representative faculties' (1925a: 34/39). Again, translation has falsified this concept, and this is partly the reason for the lack of commentary on their significance.[10] The representative faculties are connected to practical functions (*les fonctions pratiques*) (1893b: 270/228). The latter are con-nected with the ideal. 'We diminish society when we see it simply as a body organised in view of certain vital functions. In this body lives a soul: it is an aggregate of collective ideals' (1911b: 116/93). The ideal is central to action and to transformative potential–ideals are 'forces' (ibid. 117/93): 'The ideal is not there in the service of the real' (ibid. 111/88).[11] Most importantly it is volition which enacts ideals (ibid. 112/89).

So function, in addition to being relational and dynamic, is both cognitive and evaluative, and has critical and transformative aspects. But, through the neglect of these distinct meanings Durkheim's functionalism is presented in introductory texts as opposed to phenomenological or interpretive sociology, and is identified with the later functionalist move-ment and its lack of critical, transformational logic or theory of the ideal.

So Nisbet (1952: 170) cites the concept of function as evidence of Durkheim's conservatism, and this is reinforced by Coser, who saw Durkheim's conservatism as the desire to 'maintain the existing order of things' (1960: 212). For Gouldner, functionalism assumes that social order can be maintained 'regardless of the level and distribution of economic gratification' (1970: 343). The opposite is the case for Durkheim: 'Equality in the external conditions of conflict is not only necessary to attach each individual to his function, but also to link functions to one another' (1893b: 374/316). For Lockwood, Durkheim's interest in consensus over-rides questions of inequality (Lockwood 1992: 23). This overlooks how 'a moral equality – that is an equality of rights and powers' is for Durkheim

essential to contemporary moral consciousness and therefore to questions
of consensus (1910b: 2.375/67).

Durkheim is compromised neither morally nor politically by the concepts of function or the whole: neither the conceptions of function nor
those of system that I have outlined imply that there is an automatic and
inevitable subordination of the person to the needs of the system. This
would be incompatible with Durkheim's democratic pluralism and individualism; the latter, however, are compatible with his relational holism. The
reconciliation of these centres on the theory of logical pluralism, which
will be examined in chapter 4. It follows that the 'irreducibility' of society
need not imply an ontologism of system.

Irreducibility, I suggest, indicates, first, the impossibility of reducing
social thinking conceptually, characterized by a 'meaning holism' (shown
in collective representations) to individual thinking; they have different
foundations (1895a: 105/131). This is made structural and institutional by
being repeatedly acted upon – that is, by becoming habitual. Secondly, it
indicates a type of social being – which is not ontological, but 'psychic'
and relational, and thus is independent of the individual level, even though
this is 'composed' of individuals.

Through these false views of the whole and of function, a picture of
Durkheim's view of society is built up which he would condemn as
'ontologist' or 'realist' (ibid. xi/34), which is logically anti-individualist, and
has more to do with Comte and the later Hegel than with Durkheim.
There is, for Durkheim, no 'unrepresentable absolute' (1897e: 250/171).
Wholes are plural and relational, and function is dynamic, relational,
cognitive and active. He might stress the importance of the consolidation
of social functions, but he also stresses creation and the development of
solidarity, and these do not imply an automatic subservience to the needs
of unity and stability in a system. As Bouglé reminds us, Durkheim
insisted that 'Society is not a system of organs and functions . . . it is the
foyer of moral life'; against materialism and organicism, his spiritualist
tendencies must be recognized (Durkheim 1924a: 10/xl).

## Structuralism

The decline of interest in Durkheim's thought has been reinforced through
the identification of him with structuralism. But does this mean that he
thereby stands accused, through the critiques of post-structuralism, with
its ahistoricism, anti-humanism and thus with the problems that structuralism has with self, individuation, agency, pluralism and difference?

Althusser's conception of structure is associated with the concept of the
whole, unity and domination: 'the complex whole possesses the unity of
an articulated structure in dominance' (1965: 208). In contradistinction to

the Althusserian view, for Durkheim, 'The general has no virtues of its own. It is only an extract of the particular. It can thus contain nothing more than the particular' (1910b 2.374/66).[12] The widespread structuralist interest in Durkheim must confront not only the question of the 'vacuums' (*vides*) which Durkheim sees as part of social reality (e.g. 1897a: 317/281), but also the compositional nature of social reality. The latter term is central to his account of the complex, compound nature of social reality. Whilst he uses 'composition' consistently, it is largely eradicated by translation,[13] and is overlooked theoretically by his major commentators.

For Durkheim, unlike Althusser, the concept of structure is identified not with the dominance of a whole but, first, with the habitual: 'Structure is consolidated function, it is action which has become habit and which is crystallised' (1888a: 105/66). The 'habit of living with each other' is central to 'ways of being' (consolidated 'ways of doing') and to the political structure of society (1895a: 13/58).[14] Structure is the consolidation of beliefs and practices through repetition, which in turn is central to habit (ibid. 8/54): 'They are the product of repetition, and from the habit which results they acquire a sort of ascendancy and authority' (ibid. 19/63). Secondly, action is central to structure: 'Structure is not only a way of acting, it is a way of being (*être*) which necessitates a certain way of acting' (1893b: 324/273). Such definitions of structure do not entail the thesis of over-determination and the denial *per se* of freedom of action of the Althusserian account. Much, as we will see, depends on the habitual – how it is understood and how overcome, for 'sooner or later custom and habit re-assert themselves' (1886a: 197).

In contrast with the monist tendencies of structuralism (the unity of the dominating structure of Althusser), Durkheim stresses the real diversity of social life (1920a: 2.320/84). The 'interdependence' of social facts (1903c: 1.157/205) is not incompatible with the difference that experience shows. The task of science, after the acknowledgement of differences, is to integrate them in an explanatory framework: 'beside the resemblances, the differences remain to be integrated' within representation (1893b: 355/ 300).

For Durkheim the forces, syntheses and combinations which make up social reality are developed through association. The latter operates on 'psychic forces', and thereby releases their energy together with a new 'psychic life' (1950a: 96/60); association is the determining condition of social phenomena. The 'properly human milieu' which is 'internal' and is the active factor in social life (1895a: 111/135) consists analytically of consciences in association. Collective representations which form the web of society are 'the product of the actions and reactions exchanged between the elementary consciences of which society is made' (1898b: 39/25).[15]

Association invokes a principle of combination – logical pluralism –

which differentiates Durkheim from the later movement: 'Combination presupposes plurality' (ibid. 28/14). Whilst the thesis of over-determination of the whole characterizes the later movement, Durkheim stresses an indetermination which is a factor of society that comes with complexity (1895a: 88/117).[16] And how are we attached to these plural totalities? – Is it through a thesis of unified conceptual domination of whole to part? On the contrary, for Durkheim, 'The links (*liens*) which attach us to society, derive from the community of beliefs and feelings' (1893b: 119/101).

Foucault's critique of continuity is central to post-structuralist thinking, and can be seen to oppose holism diachronically. Although Durkheim stresses the importance of social continuity, it does not follow that he embraces a philosophical continuum. Indeed, he criticizes Comte's philosophy of history for fallaciously unifying historical events, for it 'introduces a unity and continuity which they lack' (1903c: 1.128). For Durkheim the rejection of continuity has a practical importance: it shows where human agency can insert itself in the historical process (1895a: 91/120).

Amongst the critiques levelled by post-structuralism is the accusation that structuralism is the enemy of a dynamic, changeful world. This cannot apply to Durkheim: 'Structure . . . forms and decomposes itself (*se décompose*) ceaselessly, it is life come to a certain degree of consolidation' (1900c: 1.22/362). He insists that a static vision contradicts science (1898b: 16/4). Derrida's critique of structuralism focuses on the 'metaphysics of presence' in form-thinking which is static and Apollonian. Against this, he embraces force-thinking, which recognizes difference and becoming; in this he could be drawing on Durkheim, who sees society as a system of 'acting forces' (*forces agissantes*) (1912a: 638/448).[17] Force is central to the meaning of causality for 'humanity has always seen causality in dynamic terms' (ibid. 519/367). And just as Durkheim recognizes 'difference', he also recognizes becoming: 'Structure is found in becoming (*devenir*) and it can only be made evident on condition of taking account of the process of becoming' (1900c: 1.22/362).

It is a constant complaint against both structuralism and post-structuralism that their theoretical terms allow no active subjects at all. For Althusser, there is no subjectivity of action in history: 'the true subjects' are 'the definers and distributors: the relations of production' (Althusser and Balibar 1970: 180). Durkheim specifically repudiates the accusation that he denies that 'Historical persons are factors of history' (Durkheim 1913a(4): 674). Durkheim's interest in the structural and the general does not require the denial of agency or of the activity of the subject in society. That the reality of society exists in the whole (*le tout*) and not in the parts is not incompatible with the claim that 'Individuals are the only active element of it' (1895a: xvi/46). The way in which the whole is defined is central to the possibility of this.

Whilst Althusser's social formations are deterministic, Durkheim's conception of determinate law and structural causality is compatible with agency and freedom of will (1893b: xxxvii/xxv). Individuals do not fit automatically and unreflectively into structures. 'An agent endowed with conscience does not conduct himself as a being whose activities can be reduced to a system of reflexes: s/he hesitates, makes attempts, deliberates and it is by these distinctive characteristics that it is recognised . . . this relative indetermination does not exist where there is no conscience and it grows with conscience' (1898b: 15/3).[18]

Even when he is concentrating on social physiology, he identifies collective will and intelligence as involved in the deepest level of structure (1900c: 1.30/369).[19] Unlike the later movement, Durkheim – both early and later in his thought – recognizes action, autonomy and individuality. 'To be a person is to be a source of autonomous action. Man acquires this quality only in so far as there is something in him which is his alone and which individualises him' (1893b: 399/335). He identifies the 'personal ideal' with autonomy of action (1912a: 605/425). We individualize structural relations (1895a: xxiii/47): there is no social uniformity which denies 'individual gradations' (1900c: 1.29/367). And whilst the later movement is characterized by an impersonality, Durkheim stresses both the personal and the impersonal (1914a: 318/152). 'The very materials of conscience must have a personal character' (1893b: 399/335). 'The more complex a state of conscience is, the more personal it is' (ibid. 298/251). Indeed, is not the idea of 'a personal being' (*être personnel*) (1925a: 40/46)[20] an awkward element for a structuralist reading of Durkheim – as is his science of morality for a science of structures?

One of the main arguments against structuralism is that it lacks an account of agency: the lacuna of Althusserian structuralism is not only the absence of a concept of will, and therefore of the possibility of agency, from the theoretical terms of structuralist science, but the elevation of this lacuna into a theoretical advantage. Althusser's conception of the 'author-less theatre' and the radical negation of the subject are important features of his rejection of humanism and the establishment of a science of social formations. Hirst (1975) gives an Althusserian reading of Durkheim, and praises Durkheim for his theoretical anti-humanism and for not conceiving the world as a cosy conspiracy of human subjects.

Of course, the collective is the primary *explanans* for Durkheim, but this does entail eradicating the theoretical possibility of the agent/subject. Similarly, his theoretical account must acknowledge the individual, otherwise it lacks the means to explain moral individualism where 'The centre of moral life has been transported from without to within and the individual has been exalted as the sovereign judge of their own conduct' (Durkheim 1898c: 273/52). The theoretical description of neither individualism nor humanism are undermined by science for Durkheim.

The concepts of sign and of signification are central to Durkheim's thought, and were clearly influential on the later movement: thought is expressed through signs for Durkheim (1895a: 4/51). And words represent ideas: 'the affinities of ideas communicate themselves to words which represent them' (1893b: 51/42). The dominance of the linguistic method, which characterized the later movement, does not follow for Durkheim: language is not the key to understanding religion, for example, for this implies a complex interrelation between belief, representation and action (1912a: 116/79). Language expresses representation: 'What it expresses is the way society ... represents objects of experience to itself' (ibid. 620/436).[21] So Durkheim does not hold that linguistic structures underlie all cultural phenomena: it is not by the logic of the mind that the study of culture must proceed – the individuality of each culture 'depends only partly on general human faculties' (1920a: 2.320/84).

### The theories that Durkheim is contrasted with: the similarities

Weber's action perspective is contrasted to Durkheim's structural approach, just as his methodological individualism and *verstehen* approach is contrasted with Durkheim's holist, positivistic approach; explanation by the ideal type is contrasted to Durkheim's functionalist, empiricist method which treats social phenomena as facts and things. But this radical contrast between Durkheim and Weber is false. For example, both hold to an objectivist, causal approach as the final criterion of the scientific – Durkheim, like Weber, holds that all questions of interpretation cannot alone be sufficient explanations, and must be supported by causal analysis (1895a: 89/119). This false opposition has begun to be questioned (Coenen-Huther and Hirschorn 1994). The following reflections add to this reconsideration of their theoretical relation.

Does not Durkheim's conception of the 'the psychic type of society' (1893b: 46/39) show an affinity to Weber's 'ideal type'?[22] 'Types of thought' and of 'action' are central to society (1912a: 620/436), and that much maligned concept of 'health', Durkheim says, is an 'ideal type' which is nowhere entirely realized (1893b: 330/278). Even the concept of charisma is not absent from Durkheim: the man who speaks to the crowd draws on a plethora of forces which come from the crowd and incite 'the demon of oratorical inspiration' (1912a: 300/212).

To oppose the structural to the action perspective blurs just how much Durkheim is concerned with action. He questions 'this logic by which law would exclude action' (quoted, Lukes 1973: 653), and insists that 'Every idea, when it is warmed by feeling, tends to action' (Durkheim 1885c: 1.376). Action is central to his definition of society. 'It is through common action that it becomes conscious (*conscience*) of and establishes itself: it is above all an active co-operation' (1912a: 598/421). Indeed, as we have seen, 'structure . . . is action which has become habitual and is crystallised' (1888a: 105/66). Social facts stem 'from collective activity' (1900c: 1.32/ 371); ways of beings are actually ways of acting which are 'consolidated' (1895a: 13/58).

So, like Weber, Durkheim can claim that his method deals with thought and action (1895a: 74/104); however, unlike Weber, he claims that 'The passions are the motivating forces of conduct' (1925a: 80/94).[23] And, 'The springs of our activity are internal to us, they can only be activated by us and from inside' (ibid. 149/178). But his account of action includes that of *tendances* (1895a: 92/121). And although he rejects the psychological finalism of Comte and Spencer, he does admit that there is a 'finalism' which 'existence implies' (ibid. 96n./144). The neglect of these two concepts, together with 'passion' and the logic of internality, has fuelled misunderstandings on this point. Indeed, for Durkheim there is a profound and radical view of the relation between thought and action: 'The imperatives of thought are probably only another aspect of the imperatives of will' (1912a: 527/373). But it is above all the 'ideal . . . which energetically solicits action' (1925a: 103/123).[24]

Durkheim's holism is contrasted with Weber's methodological individualism, yet he argues that the method of irreducibility does not eradicate the individual at the theoretical level. 'Here as elsewhere what exists is the individual and the particular: the general is only a schematic expression' (1893b: 1st edn 16/1933 trans. 419). 'Society can only exist in and through individuals' (1912a: 356/252) – that is 'through the individual consciences which compose it' (ibid. 317/223). Indeed, 'truth is only realised through individuals' (1955a: 196). Cuvillier said that although this will surprise those convinced of Durkheim's 'sociologism', this nevertheless represents the authentic Durkheim, and he cites 1924a 'At the same time as it [society] transcends us, it is interior to us, since it can only live in us and through us' (Cuvillier in Durkheim 1955a: 196). 'If individual life is not valued, however little this might be, the rest is worthless, and evil is without remedy' (1887c: 1.330). He argues that 'In conclusion social life is nothing other than the moral milieu or better, the collection of different moral milieux which surround the individual' (1900c: 1.28/367). And 'In qualifying them as moral we wish to say that these are milieu constituted by ideas' (ibid.).[25]

Clearly, what has not been recognized is the way in which he refers to the individual: if all is representation, how is the individual represented? It is connected with the concepts of the personal, the autonomous and, above all, the particular conscience (*conscience particulière/individuelle*). It is through this that individualization occurs. 'The impersonal forces which are released from the collectivity cannot constitute themselves without incarnating in individual consciences where they individualise themselves' (1912a: 382/269). As a result of overlooking this logic, in contrast to Weber, who extols the autonomy of value, Durkheim is regarded not only as incapable of accounting for the individual, but also as an apologist for the customary and as an advocate of conformism. Recognition of his view of the diversity and pluralism of the modern world, together with his view of the autonomy of the person must correct this characterization. Indeed, for Durkheim, this intellectual conformism occurs only under specific conditions: 'As long as mythological truth reigns, conformism is the rule. But intellectual individualism appears with the reign of scientific truth; and it is even that individualism which has made it necessary ... [thus] social unanimity cannot henceforth establish itself around mythological beliefs' (1955a: 185).

The radical opposition of Durkheim's scientific and positivist approach to Weber's '*verstehen*' and all consideration of hermeneutics is unhelpful. First, it is clear that the concept of understanding is central to Durkheim's view both of science and of social reality: good science is a product of the understanding for him (1895a: 34/74). He insists on the activity of cognitive and practical faculties in social development: as the social milieu becomes 'more complex and more undetermined', faculties of reflection develop which are 'indispensable' to societies and to individuals' (ibid. 96/124). It is true that he insists on the method of observation, but this reveals 'an order of phenomena called representations' (1898b: 16/4). Even that concept of constraint, viewed as central to his functionalism, is operated through the mind: 'It is through mental routes that social pressure is exercised' (1912a: 298/211).

Indeed, just as with his view of science, his functionalism includes the concept of understanding. 'The understanding (*l'entendement*) is only one of our psychic functions: beside the purely representative functions there are the active faculties' (1925a: 34/39). And we need to know more of what he means by the psychological before his sociologism can be radically contrasted to it. It is not the case that psychology is 'irrelevant for sociology' as is widely held (Lukes 1973: 228). All functional phenomena 'are psychological' for they are 'modes of thought and action' (1900c: 1.23–4/363). Sociology will culminate in a psychology, but a more concrete and complex one (1909d: 1.185/237). It is a 'purely' psychological explanation which he rejects (1895a: 106/131). He uses both the psychological and the psychic – but this can be obscured by translation. He claims that the association of particular consciences (*consciences particulières*) leads to a new kind of 'psychic individuality' (ibid. 103/129). The psychic (*psychique*), like the representative, is a constant of his thought. 'The degree of simplicity of *psychic* facts gives the measure of their transmissibility' (1893b: 297/251).[26] In fact, it is clear – against the positivist, functionalist interpretation of Durkheim – that meaning is central to all aspects of society – in the 'psychique' and in 'representation'. Just as he insists that 'social life is entirely made of representations' (1895a: ix/34), so he also claims that 'representations are conceptual' (1912a: 618/434).

So this opposition of the scientific and the functional to the interpretive and the phenomenological is particularly inimical to the understanding of Durkheim. His ethnomethodological critics treat him as a philosophical fool who had never understood the problem of meaning or of intentionality in social action. 'For a long time we have only recognised value in an action if it is intentional, that is if the agent represents in advance what the action consists in' (1925a: 101/120).[27] I suggest that Durkheim problematized social meaning, but did not exclude it.

So we need to know what Durkheim means by psychology, and most particularly by the psychic (*psychique*) before he can be convincingly radically opposed to the tradition of hermeneutic thought. Indeed, when interpretation is defined as grasping the meaning given to consciousness then the variables involved in this – consciousness, symbolization, signification, intelligibility and choice – are found not to be missing from Durkheim's account. The first four are aspects of mind and mental operation: all aspects of the mental are covered through conscience and its functions, and by representation in general. The fifth element, choice, is covered by freedom: he acknowledges 'a freedom of thought which we actually use (*jouissons*)' (1895a: 71/102).

## Marxism / Critical Theory

Durkheimian theory is of course contrasted with Marxism, and during the period when Marxism was more dominant in the universities than it is now, this was taken as equivalent to a rejection of socialism. Lukes outlines Durkheim's sympathy for socialism, and corrects the view that Durkheim 'always rejected socialism' (Coser 1960: 216); yet he agrees with Sorel's characterization of him as the 'theoretician of conservative democracy'. However, Sorel's brand of revolutionary syndicalism was opposed to Durkheim's democratic socialism. Lukes characterizes his position as 'strongly reformist and revisionist' (1973: 320–1); but the question of revisionism can only be determined in the historical context of the Third Republic and contemporary views of socialism. In fact, Durkheim's criticism of Marxism, rather than being either revisionist or a rejection of socialism, can be seen to be a critique subsequently made by socialists themselves: Gramsci's critique of Marxism for its historicism, materialism and determinism is matched in many respects by Durkheim's.

In Bottomore's view (1984) Durkheim emphasizes solidarity rather than conflict, order rather than change, and the ideational as opposed to the structural. But is it really the case that Durkheim underestimates or ignores conflict? He characterizes the 'constraining' division of labour by class conflict. Recognition of this is hampered by the unjustifiable exclusion of the original detailed table of contents from the 1984 translation of *De la Division du travail* (where 'constraint' (*contrainte*) is translated as 'forced'). Here it is clear that 'constraint' means all forms of inequality in 'the external conditions of struggle' (1893b: 415). He opposes class domination and economic inequality as unjust: 'If a class of society is obliged, in order to live, to accept any price for its services, whilst the other due to its own resources can avoid this . . . the second has an unjust domination of the first' (ibid. 378/319).[28] Further, 'There cannot be rich and poor at birth without there being unjust contracts' (ibid.). Like Marx, he criticizes the brutalizing of human nature by economic factors: 'one cannot remain indifferent to such a degradation of human nature' (ibid. 363/307).

The central difference, however, is that he does not view conflict as a means of provoking change. Rather than provoking class conflict, he wanted to turn socialism from 'the feelings of anger which the less favoured class has against the other to those feelings of pity for this society which is suffering in all its classes and all its organs' (1899e: 1.169/143). Although he has a clear critique of Marxism, the interests and sympathy of the early and the late Durkheim are supportive of socialism. His study of the division of labour should help with the long-held dream 'of realising in the facts the ideal of human fraternity' (1893b: 401/336). And in 1915, 'Our salvation lies in socialism discarding its out of date slogans or in the formation of a new socialism which goes back to the French tradition. I see so clearly what this might be' (quoted in Lukes 1973: 321). In his time the socialist students in Bordeaux planned to disrupt Espinas's classes to demand that Durkheim should be their teacher (Weisz 1983: 105). Now, after nearly a century of sociology, he is seen as the conservative enemy of socialism!

For Aaron, 'Durkheim was a sociologist and not a socialist' (1960: 6.76). Lukes held his socialism to be 'idealistic and non-political' (1973: 321). It is now clear that for Durkheim, in 1899 at least, what prevented his political engagement was the class-based character of socialism (Durkheim 1998a: 226). This is not an anti-socialist position, but is central to a distinct view of democratic socialism which became central to Jaurèsian socialist politics.

Saint-Simon was the father of French socialism, and Durkheim expresses the Saint-Simonian view that socialism began with the French Revolution (1905e: 289). Rather than socialism implying the mutual destruction of two opposing classes, it requires the development and extension of solidarity – and what renders this impossible is a 'moral egoism' (1898c: 267/48). Gouldner, when he says Durkheim opposed his moralism to Marxism, overlooks that at the time, 'Socialism is the philosophy and morality of solidarity' (Mouy 1927: 129).

## The concept of a critical science and the question of power

In Habermas's distinction among three types of enquiry in the humanities – empirical/analytic, historical/hermeneutic and critical sciences – Durkheim is clearly held to be an arch-representative of the first. But for him, 'The critical method alone suits science' (Durkheim 1890a: 217/35). Durkheim 'would not dream of denying that reflection is modificatory ... Conscience and scientific thinking, which is nothing other than the highest form of conscience, does not apply itself to phenomena without efficacity, but it puts us in the position to change through its illumination' (1907a(3): 572). The whole point of a social science is some practical transformation: the very act of knowing is itself to initiate change – because 'conscience is not epiphenomenal, without efficacity: it affects the reality that it illuminates. ... In acting on societies we transform them' (ibid. 579).

For Habermas, in an empirical/analytic science there is no identity between the aim/structure of the science and its subject matter. This is not the case for Durkheim: the central element of societies consists in the particular consciences (*consciences particulières*), which are the necessary part of their composition. And 'Science is nothing but conscience (*la conscience*) carried to its highest point of clarity' (1893b: 14/14). The point of a science is the enlightenment of conscience: 'The more a conscience is obscure, the more it is unwilling to change ... That is why it is necessary that intelligence guided by science should take a larger part in collective life' (ibid. 15/14).

What view does Durkheim have of practical transformation? He insists that 'critique and reflection are the supreme agents of all transformation' (1925a: 45/52). But against the characteristic categorical repudiation of institutions by revolutionary socialists, he advocates great caution in overturning them: moral and social phenomena are complex historical phenomena, and not our 'personal work' – they cannot be philosophically repudiated from a position which has no knowledge of their causes, interrelations and the needs to which they respond (1897d: 243/136).

He denies that positive sociology has a fetishism with fact and an indifference to the ideal: 'sociology is directly situated in the ideal; . . . it starts there. The ideal is its real domain' (1911b: 120/96). This points to a model of how the future is to be grasped, how action and practical reason are to be implemented, which is distinct from the Hegelian/Marxist model. The ideal and its relation to action encompasses the normative orientation which, for Habermas (1992), is crucial to critical science and the relationship between theory and practice: the function of ideals of value 'is to transfigure the reality to which they relate' (1950a: 120/96).

The aim of a critical science is to establish a freedom from illusion. In addressing 'the blind force of habit', Durkheim can be seen to be addressing one of the goals of a critical science, which is to establish a 'rationally satisfying existence' (Geuss 1981: 55). Habit must not be 'the sovereign mistress', says Durkheim. 'Only reflection allows the discovery of new practices' (Durkheim 1950a: 123/90). The problem is that 'sooner or later custom and habit re-assert themselves' (1886a: 197). Indeed, it was force of habit that led to the re-introduction of authoritarian regimes in nineteenth-century France 'more than we wished for' (ibid. 95/60).

Value-freedom is central to an empirical/analytic science for Habermas. But for Durkheim, 'There is not one way of thinking and judging to deal with existence and another for estimating value. All judgement sets ideals to work. There (is) . . . only one faculty of judgement' (1911b: 119/95). For Habermas this separation of value from fact leads to the 'complete elimination of questions of life from the horizons of the sciences' (Habermas 1976: 145). Science is not silent, Durkheim says, on the ultimate question of whether we should wish to live (Durkheim 1893b: xl/xxvii). Science can offer 'a new objective to the will' (ibid.) and helps with the orientation of action through clarification of the ideal (ibid. xxxix/xxvi). And this has a reflexive foundation: 'Every strong state of conscience is a source of life' (ibid. 64/53).

For the Frankfurt School, a critical free thinking requires freedom of mind and the ideal of autonomy of action. This is not missing in Durkheim's thought – he objects to certain forms of philosophical critique precisely because they do not give free thought sufficient room (1907a(3): 572). Indeed, he calls freedom of mind 'the first of freedoms' (1898c: 269/49), and claims that the modern moral consciousness requires a 'true and effective autonomy' (1925a: 96/114). 'It is science which is the source of our autonomy' (ibid. 98/116).

The orthodox view of Durkheim is that he shows no concern with the role of political power (Giddens 1995b: 107). It must not be concluded, however, that he has no account of power – he talks of 'the eminently personal power which is the human will' (1912a: 521/368). Adorno says, more strongly, 'The powerlessness of the individual in the face of society . . . for Durkheim was precisely the criterion for *faits sociaux*' (Adorno

1976: 120). It is surprising then that Durkheim identifies the person with autonomy (Durkheim 1893b: 399/335) – even in his reputedly early 'positivist' stage – and argues that '. . . individual consciences constantly affirm their autonomy' (1897a: 158/159)! He was aware of how society could both crush and emancipate: he acknowledges both 'the power of action and creation of social thought' (1910a(2): 1.193) and that 'every society is despotic if nothing comes from the exterior to contain its despotism' (1950a: 96/61). However, he claims that in history we see the individual becoming 'An autonomous foyer of activity, an imposing system of personal forces' (ibid. 93/57).

Power, for Durkheim, is involved in both the concepts of force and causality. 'Productive power', 'active force', is the first thing implied in the causal relation (1912a: 519/367). Force expresses power (ibid. 522/369), and initially comes from our 'internal experience' (ibid. 521/369).

# 2

# Durkheim as Theorist of Order and Science

A key source of the prejudice against Durkheim is the perceived narrowing of his thought to two key problematics: those of order and science. If we can compare the reading of an author's works to unravelling a sacred text, then the imposed readings we can call 'sins of commission', and the glosses and elisions of important theoretical terms 'sins of omission'. The former, imposed readings are clear in their identification of social order as his main concern; the latter are more evident in the characterization of Durkheim as the apostle of positivism and scientism.

## The concept of order

Although the characterization of Durkheim as a theorist of order has been questioned sociologically (Lukes 1973: 338; Mĕstrović 1988: 7), the persistence of this myth demands that something further be done: the sources of it should be identified, and the fallacious historical and philosophical analogies on which they are based unravelled. Of course, much depends on what is meant by 'order': there is a sociological and a political sense. Durkheim's interest in aspects of the former has been dominated by particular versions of the latter. There is a sense of order compatible with democracy and the concept of rights; there is another which is the interest in 'order at any price' at the expense of autonomy and diversity. Through two famous comparisons Durkheim has been condemned to the latter, without recognition of how he attempted to theorize the former in terms of modern society.

Parsons's identification of Durkheim with the Hobbesian problem of order is a distinct source of Durkheim's 'conservatism' and his 'authoritarianism' (Parsons 1937: 309). It is philosophically and historically misconceived, however; Durkheim does not share Hobbes's nominalism, materialism, deductive geometrical method or his theory of the state of nature; yet all of these are logically tied to Hobbes's account of the constitution of society and political authority.

Hobbes and Durkheim share neither a theoretical nor a political view of the social. Hobbes's political authoritarianism is rooted in seventeenth-century statism: for the monarchist Hobbes, as distinct from the republican Durkheim, order must be imposed from above by force. This imposition of unified state power is essential to his account, whereas for Durkheim unity and authority are consensual: 'What gives unity to organised societies . . . is the spontaneous consensus of the parts' (Durkheim 1893b: 351/297). Organic solidarity is only possible without violence: 'All external inequality compromises solidarity' (ibid. 373/314). Thus the full potentialities of modern society and its stability will occur only when certain moral requirements are satisfied;[1] for Hobbes, however, stability *per se* is the primary political virtue. So whereas Durkheim subjects modern society to a moral critique, there can be no moral critique of the state for Hobbes – this is essential to his political absolutism. Moral distinctions can be developed only after a central state authority has been established, thus there can be no morality independent of state authority.

For Hobbes, 'Leviathan' is the incarnation of absolutist authority; but for Durkheim authority is made 'entirely from respect' (1911c(1): 68). Whereas for Hobbes, Leviathan has *de facto* and *de jure* all the rights, for Durkheim, on the contrary, modern moral consciousness acknowledges a reciprocity of rights and duties; the concept of individual rights is central to his moral individualism (1925a: 17/20). Durkheim explicitly opposes his view of constraint to that of Hobbes (1895a: 122/146): constraint is only the external sign of society and not its whole nature (1912a: 298/210). He objects to Hobbes's conception that 'the individual is naturally resistant to social life' and can only accept it through force such that 'the object of society is to contain and constrict the individual' (1895a: 120/142).

For Hobbes the dominant passion which drives people is the fear of death, whereas for Durkheim human beings, although creatures of passion, must be primarily understood as cognitively orientated to the world. 'From the mental point of view [man] is nothing more than a system of representations' (1912a: 325/229). For Hobbes (and for Comte), since feelings dominate reason, it follows that an authority that controls feelings is required to establish order. But for Durkheim, 'My reason requires reasons before it bows before someone else's' (1898c: 269/49).

The second famous comparison is that imposed by Nisbet. This is the most influential, particularly in introductory sociology texts. It inspired Coser to argue for Durkheim's conservatism (1960: 212–13). Through this, Durkheim becomes an authoritarian supporter of order and the *status quo* interested in hierarchy and obedience, and thereby a deeply conservative gloss is put on his ideas of authority, duty and obligation.

Nisbet (1952) sees Durkheim as having scientifically confirmed the conservative view of society, and translated 'into the hard methodology of science, the ideas and values of Bonald and Maistre' (Nisbet 1965: 24). Traditionalist thinkers, called 'prophets of the past' by Comte and theorists of 'order at any price' by the socialists and republicans, wanted to reverse the effects of the revolutionary rupture of 1789. To read Durkheim through them is to identify him with post-revolutionary reactionary politics: whilst they wanted to turn the clock back to the *ancien régime*, Durkheim with Saint-Simon held that the revolution of 1789 had definitely destroyed it with a new system 'that was in harmony with the new order of things' (1900b: 115/6).

Whilst the republican, anticlerical Durkheim rejected both religion and royalty as bases of modern society, the Traditionalists extolled a principle of unity for society based on royalty, religious devotion and hierarchy. The Traditionalists opposed faith and revelation to reason, and instinct to the rational organization of society. Whilst Nisbet argued that Durkheim reacted against both rationalism and individualism (Nisbet 1952: 174; 1966: 83), Durkheim actually supported both of these, and thus supported precisely what the Traditionalists condemned: Bacon's critique of final causes and Cartesian methodical doubt, which was the 'ruin of France'. The main virtues of rationalism and individualism for Durkheim are that they 'combat intellectual servitude . . . and open conscience to new ideas' (Durkheim 1925a: 10/12). For the Traditionalists, the enemy of a settled order was anyone who believed in the free exercise of reason or will in political matters. Indeed, the very conditions for the development of sociology for Durkheim contradict Nisbet's comparison – for here traditionalism must 'have lost its domain', and 'a veritable faith in the power of reason' must be applied to social matters', and he held that France, through the revolution of 1789, satisfied these conditions (1915a: 1.117/ 383).

For the Traditionalists, the order of things was mystically sanctioned by God's will; whereas for Durkheim, institutions have their 'source in the intelligence and will of men' (1893b: 3/3). It follows that for the former 'homo faber' must be replaced by 'deus fabricator'; this, however, is the obverse of Durkheim's practical constructivism. For the Traditionalists, it was illegitimate to oppose the idea of justice to the established order; whereas for Durkheim, 'Injustice is unreasonable and absurd' (1925a: 10/ 12). 'The task of the most advanced societies is then a work of justice . . .' (1893b: 381/321).

Democracy for Durkheim requires exactly those qualities that posed such a threat to order for the Traditionalists: more reflection, will and deliberation, and therefore more change (1950a: 123/89). Durkheim is explicitly opposed to traditionalism and what he calls the spirit of routine

– he rejects its 'immobilism' (ibid. 75/38). Democracy is the opposite of feudalism, for the latter requires the maximum of obscurity and unconsciousness (ibid. 123/89). And whilst the Traditionalists admired the organization of feudalism and influenced Comte in this regard, for Durkheim, the moral superiority of democracy is that it liberates and individualizes thought (ibid. 125/91). Indeed, the value placed on individual personality in a democracy entails the rejection of authoritarian states (ibid. 124/90). Whilst Maistre condemned 'that stupid indifference called tolerance' (Berlin 1991: 104), Durkheim supported tolerance, which 'must rely on the idea of complexity, the necessary and efficacious diversity of opinions' (Durkheim 1955a: 187).

Although the Traditionalists raised the problem of authority, they solved it in a way that is anathema to Durkheim's thinking, by establishing what Berlin calls the 'terror of authority' (Berlin 1991: 118): the incurably corrupt nature of man entailed the need for authority understood as hierarchy and obedience understood as subjection. For Maistre, sovereignty is one and absolute because of its divine origin; he therefore opposes the democratic view of power which comes from 'below' (Beneton 1988: 35). But it is the latter which characterizes Durkheim's view of power and authority, as the force stemming from the conscience collective (1893b: 51/43). His advocacy of 'secondary groups' as forms of 'moral authority' to mediate between the state and the individual (ibid. xxxiii/liv) is more akin to the Proudhonian socialist vision of the decentralization of authority than to this monarchic, autocratic view. As will become clear, Durkheim's analysis of power and authority is undertaken within democratic terms.

So whilst the Traditionalists have an absolutist theory of sovereignty precisely because it requires obedience, for Durkheim authority must be founded 'rationally', for this is the only basis of respect (1898c: 269/49). The question of authority entails that of realism for the Traditionalists. Nisbet argues that realism and organicism are central to Durkheim's conservatism: he opposes the 'metaphysical reality of society . . . to individual agglomeration' (Nisbet 1952: 169). But Durkheim repudiates 'realism' (Durkheim 1895a: xi/34), and explicitly denies that society is 'a metaphysical entity'; rather, it is 'a collection of organised individuals' (1886a: 200).

For the Traditionalists, realism entails the logic of divine politics – for the power and force central to society must be superior/transcendent to individuals. For them, language has a divine origin, and thus truth, which depends on tradition and authority, is general and never individual. For Durkheim, the rationalist conception of truth is tied to individualism: as we have seen, 'truth is realised by individuals' (1955a: 196). Rather than society being a unified authoritarian structure which rightly subordinates the individual in the interests of unity and hierachy, there is for Durkheim a tension between authority and freedom, both in intellectual judgement as well as in social reality.

Parsons's and Nisbet's characterization of Durkheim as an unequivocal follower of Comte further reinforces his concern with 'order' and conservative values. Like the Traditionalists, Comte was profoundly anti-individualist: individualism was the deepest threat to order, and this is supported by science (Comte 1975: 2.183). For Durkheim, 'Society is a whole composed of parts . . . There is nothing in society but individuals . . . Of what is a milieu made if not individuals?' (1885c: 1.351–2). Beyond their biological expression, individuals were not real for Comte, and in this he continued the social realism of Bonald, and from this stems the politics of authoritarianism.

But for Durkheim, unlike Comte, individualism did not simply represent an aspect of the transition from medieval authoritarianism to the positive state: the ideal of a society of autonomous persons in a democratic community emerging in history cannot be overemphasized for Durkheim (Neyer 1960: 35). This development is 'normal': 'As societies become more vast, individual diversities multiply . . . personality is strengthened' (Durkheim 1893b: 339/285). Against the uniformity required in the interest of stability, Durkheim holds that 'Uniformity cannot be maintained by force . . . Functional diversity induces a moral diversity' (ibid. 352/298).

Durkheim does not share the admiration for the Middle Ages, its hierarchy and religious organization, which Comte acquired through Traditionalism. And unlike Comte, Durkheim did not condemn free thought, which for Comte acts merely as a dissolvent of the theological stage – as part of the metaphysical stage of society.[2] And he rejects Comte's doctrine that intellectual individualism leads to anarchy (1955a: 186), for, as a general rule, freedom entails anarchy – it spells a complete absence of intellectual rules (Comte 1975: 2.28). For Durkheim, 'The history of the human mind is the history of free thought itself. It is therefore puerile to wish to check a current which everything proves irresistible' (Durkheim 1897a: 430/375). Whilst Comte tolerates no corresponding theory of individual right, for Durkheim the sphere of individual rights grows through history (1950a: 103/69).

Society for Comte is the result of the instinct for sociability and its preponderance over egoism: individual life is characterized by the dominion of 'personal instincts' (Comte 1975: 2.176); whilst for Durkheim, 'The progress of conscience is in inverse relation to that of instinct' (Durkheim 1893b: 338/284). For Comte, the subjective principle of positivism means that the affective must dominate the intellectual; yet for Durkheim, the collectivity is engaged through its 'representations and volitions' (1950a: 86/50). For Comte and Saint-Simon, love is substituted for justice as the foundation of social relations, whereas Durkheim sees the task facing modern societies as the realization of justice (ibid. 381/321).

The family is the principal institution of society for Comte, and he extends the subordination and hierarchy that the family requires to society; discipline and hierarchy are thus linked (Comte 1975: 2.188). For Durkheim, the state is slowly taking over from the family (Durkheim 1925a: 63/74), and the moral role of the state is to realize 'progressive liberation . . . and individuation' (1950a: 103/69). Whilst Comte required the necessary obedience of the proletariat, Durkheim sympathized with the socialist 'ideal of human fraternity' (1893b: 402/336). And just as Comte ended up justifying inheritance and the social role of those who inherit and accumulate wealth (Richard 1914: 123), so Durkheim argued against the injustice and inequality involved in inheritance (Durkheim 1893b: 378/319).

So there is little evidence that order was Durkheim's central and dominant problematic – certainly not in the sense that has been ascribed to him. There is, however, a sense of order unacknowledged by his commentators, and this relates to science. 'If each science has its method, the order which it realises is entirely internal' (ibid. 359/303). Order for Renouvier meant simply any set of relations that presents itself to science; in this theoretical sense, order is politically neutral. Further, Renouvier, who was active in the revolution of 1848 and whose 'Manuel Républicain', (1848) was too radical for the short-lived Second Republic, argued against the liberals who rejected it: 'Liberty is divine, but liberty alone without heart, without reason, without order . . . is an idol fed on human blood' (Foucher 1927: 149). This showed a use of the word 'order' which was also used widely amongst nineteenth-century French socialists to mean the set of relations that should obtain in society or the proper form of social organization that serves the interest of humanity; neither sense entails the preservation of the *status quo*. It is used in this sense by Louis Blanc, Proudhon and Jaurès. 'Society cannot afford not to constitute an *order*, that is to say to give itself a government' (Proudhon 1967: 166).

The characterization of Durkheim as a conservative theorist of order must give way to Durkheim as a socialist interested in the organization of society. This is clear from a late publication recently brought to light, where Durkheim stresses the importance of the social organization of economic activity – a conception initiated by the revolution of 1789 and continued by the Saint-Simonians, and which he held to be central to all socialist doctrines (Durkheim 1917c).

If, sociologically, order means the 'normal' functioning of society and the regularity of social conditions and the stability of expectations that should obtain in society, then Durkheim does deal with order. Much then depends on that complex concept of the 'normal'. Order can also be associated with contract, but even this does not entail conservative implications. In a just contract, Durkheim argues, there is an 'equilibrium of things' such that there is equivalent social value. It consists in satisfied labour found in exchanged services where each receives what he or she desires; and it occurs in 'an equilibrium of wills which the contract states and consecrates' (1893b: 376/317).[3] 'The necessary and sufficient condition' for this equivalence is 'equality in external conditions' (ibid. 377/318). (The meaning of 'external', which I will discuss later, will affect the significance of this.)

The concept of order, particularly when identified with the *status quo*, is also associated with the widespread view that Durkheim has no theory of change. This was initiated by Parsons (1949: 448). However, Durkheim must have one: 'The more the milieu is subject to change, the greater the role of intelligence in life becomes' (Durkheim 1893a: 256/214).[4] Durkheim rejects Comtean and Hegelian/Marxist theories of change; his own conception logically centres on the concept of 'becoming'. 'It is a commonplace of science and philosophy that everything is subject to becoming (*devenir*). To change is to produce effects' (1898b: 16/3). The neglect of this concept by his commentators is the source of this misconception. But there are further concepts associated with change whose similar neglect reinforces this. First, his concept of mind and of indetermination: 'The more specialised (the) faculties . . . are more undetermined . . . and therefore can more easily change . . .' (1893b: 299/253). Secondly, the concept of difference: it is 'differences which provoke changes . . . If all is absolutely homogeneous, everything will stay immobile and at the same level' (1885c I: 351). And thirdly (until recently), the concept of habit: when groups are the 'prisoner of tradition . . . the conditions of life cannot change very much; habit thus has dominion over people and over things without any counterbalance and innovations in the end come to be dreaded' (1950a: 75/38). And habits 'are resistant to change precisely because they are obscure' (ibid. 117/84). We need to know what 'obscure' means for Durkheim, but this has also been overlooked. If habitual action is central to structure, then overcoming the 'obscurity' of habit is one answer to static structures and a way of provoking change.

## The concept of science and the question of positivism

So, whilst his apparent conservatism is established by the imposition of interpretations on his thought, the scientism and positivism of which he is accused in sociology's oral tradition are established by the theoretical neglect of central features of his account. Most commentators assume that

Durkheim drew either on Comte or on natural science for his conception of science and its methodology; however, it is not at all clear that either of these accurately reflects his view of science or how it applies to society.

His analogies with natural science must not be taken as conceptual identifications: analogies are made only in the 'birth pangs' of a science (1895a: 143/162). Science is not 'a fetish or an idol whose infallible oracles must be received on bended knee' (1895b: 3.433). Science 'is a *degree of knowledge*' which brings 'light', and is distinguishable only by 'clarity and distinction'; its principal object is 'to take us out of ourselves and to bring us nearer and nearer to things' (ibid.).

Durkheim has almost universally been characterized as a Comtean positivist (Tiryakian 1979: 204). His rationalism is identified with positivism by Parsons, Nisbet and even Lukes (1973: 421). But Durkheim argued that his 'so-called positivism' is a '*consequence*' of 'scientific rationalism', and that his position must not be confounded with 'the positivist *metaphysics* of Comte and Spencer' (Durkheim 1895a: ix/33). Indeed, he repudiated Comtean positivism for its lack of positivity, and claimed that it was 'essentially philosophical speculation' (1903c: 1.127, 129). I take Durkheim's statement about his 'so-called positivism' to mean that positive knowledge of phenomena requires conditions which scientific rationalism provides and which positivism does not.

Durkheim undeniably admired certain features of Comtean thinking: his application of science and the concept of law to society; the vivid sense of the reality of society and its historical nature; the comparative method; and the concern with solidarity and sociability, even though Durkheim criticizes this as 'philosophical meditation on human sociability in general' (1888a: 89/53).[5] Nevertheless, throughout his works there is evidence of a considerable theoretical disagreement, with Comte's characterization of both society and the nature of science.

Although Durkheim stresses the importance of a consciousness of the 'organic unity' of society (ibid. 109/69), is it the case that Durkheim was inspired by the Comtean vision of social reality as 'an indissoluble whole' (Tiryakian 1979: 203)? This tendency to identify his holism with that of Comte is paradoxically evident in Lukes's formulation of Durkheim's statement that the 'axiom that the whole *is greater* than the sum of its parts' was derived from Renouvier (Lukes 1973: 57). What Durkheim actually said is a little different. 'From Renouvier came the axiom that a *whole is not equal to the sum of its parts*', and that this is at the basis of his 'realism' (Durkheim 1913a(15): 326).

'Not equal to' is not equivalent to 'greater than'. 'The whole does not equal the sum of its parts: it is something different' (1895a: 102/128). This whole is formed through 'composition' and through 'association' (ibid.), and 'in such combination they become something else' (1898b: 40/26). For

Comte, society is indeed 'greater than' the individual, not only scientifically but also politically, for society is 'Great Being'. Whilst Durkheim's organicism has been understood through Comtean positivism and reactionary thought, there are other ways of understanding it. First, as we will see, it was precisely to avoid the oppressive and anti-individualist consequences exploited by Comte and others, that Renouvier developed the logical pluralism which underwrote his own form of holism and organicism. Secondly, Jaurès identified organicism with socialism, and held that Hegelian thought was the source of this (Jaurès 1892: 104); here organicism indicated the interdependence of reality.

Durkheim argued that sociology can only become positive by rejecting the Comtean vision of the whole (Durkheim 1915a: 1.113/380); Comte's 'great syntheses' are 'premature generalisations' (1893b: 353/298). He rejects Comte's unified vision of humanity and science – humanity for Durkheim is not 'a realised whole' (un tout réalisé) (1900b: 119/9). On the contrary, what exist are 'particular societies' (1895a: 20/64); social systems are 'heterogeneous wholes' which cannot be studied as though they have 'objective unity', for this implies 'an infinite world' of which we have only 'a truncated representation' (1903c: 1.132/184). Further, he rejects the objective unity of science, which for Littré and Comte was central to the positivist point of view: for Durkheim, since methods cannot be unified, neither can science (1893b: 354/299). 'Philosophy becomes more and more incapable of assuring the unity of science' (ibid. 353/298).

Durkheim breaks not only with this vision of science, but also with its theory of the genealogy and development of science. Like Renouvier, who argued that it was 'bizarre' of Comte to make sociology dependent on biology (Renouvier 1859: 526), Durkheim maintained that psychology (which Comte rejected) was the necessary propaedeutic for sociology (Durkheim 1895a: 110/135). For Durkheim, 'Science advances slowly and establishes only probabilities' (1908a(3): 1.206); yet Comte rejects probability as 'irrational and sophistic' (Comte 1975: 1.435). There can be no theory 'more radically irrational' than numerical probability for Comte (ibid. 2.168). Indeed, he argues that because all idea of number is forbidden in biology, so it must be banished from sociology; the concept of number, as we will see, is an important feature of Durkheim's logic of explanation.

He repudiates the central features of the Comtean account of synchronic holism and of the diachronic: he rejects Comte's unilinear conception of historical 'becoming', for each society has its own form of becoming (1906a(2): 1.198). There is no 'continuous series' (1895a: 20/64): such a linear conception of historical development makes comparison impossible (1906a(2): 1.198), and implies that a complete system of society can be constructed scientifically – which is impossible (1897d: 243/136). There is no one law which 'dominates the necessary and continuous movement of history' (1903c: 1.128). It follows that he rejects what for Comte is the true scientific subject, 'the continuous (and progressive) development of humanity' (Comte 1975: 2.123/127). For Comte, 'progress is the social fact par excellence' (Durkheim 1903c: 1.127/180); for Durkheim, 'The progress of humanity does not exist' (1895a: 20/64), and it involves a 'metaphysical entity' (ibid. 108/133). He criticizes the Comtean account of development and change (ibid. 98/125; 116/139) and, as we have seen, uses the logic of becoming to explain change (1898b: 16/3). Indeed, this is central to the dynamics of science itself: 'Science is always in perpetual becoming' (1908a(3): 1.206).

Thus he rejects both Comte's statics and his dynamics: whilst the first is merely 'reminiscent of political philosophy', the latter and its law of the three stages, 'which dominates the whole system', is no longer defensible (1900b: 119/9); it is simply 'a glance at history' (1895a: 117/140). Not only has Comte's supreme law no 'causal relation in it', he is wrong to define the third positive state of his law as the definitive state of humanity (ibid.). With it, Comte falsifies history (1888a: 89/53) and cannot explain how the new is possible (ibid. 90/54). Whilst for Durkheim, science is 'impersonal and collective reason' (1906b: 95/73); for Comte, science is the unification of the facts and laws established by the positive sciences. In fact, if Durkheim were following Comte, he could hardly argue that science is 'only a more perfect form of religious thought' (1912a: 613/431).

The issue of the real and the objective is far more complicated for Durkheim than for Comte: for both agents and theorists, reality is inter-penetrated by and grasped through representation and conscience. 'If wars, invasions and class struggles have an influence on the development of societies, it is by the condition of acting first on individual consciences. It is through them that everything proceeds, and it is from them in a word that everything emanates' (1885c: 1.352). Need it be stressed that there is no theoretical account of representation, nor of 'conscience particulière' and the conscience collective in Comte?

For Comte, to account for reality in terms of the discriminations of a conscience collective or collective representations would be to move from the subjective (the human mind) to the objective (the order of world) – which is banned from the spirit of positivism. But central to Durkheim's practical constructivism is a positive and constitutive role for thinking. 'Definitely it is thought which creates the real', for 'the primary role of collective representations is to make that superior reality which is society itself' (1955a: 174).

## Science and its concepts

The widespread belief that Durkheim's sociology is fundamentally under-mined by false scientism is fuelled by accusations of his materialism, which is clearly inappropriate for dealing with meaningful social phenomena (Walsh 1998: 191). But Durkheim's method in part follows 'spiritualism', according to which the 'psychic' cannot be derived from the organic (Durkheim 1895a: ix/32). For Hirst, Durkheim is a 'rationalist and a materialist' (Hirst 1975: 14). But Durkheim rejects materialism even in his early thought: 'This is what spiritualist philosophers have learned and the great service they have rendered science has been to combat doctrines which reduce psychic life (*la vie psychique*) to being merely an efflores-cence of physical life' (1893b: 340/286). He repeats this denial of material-ism in *Les Règles* (1895a: 90/120).[6]

Comparisons with materialist thinkers reinforce these false accusations: Hirst associates Durkheim with Bernard, for whom it is said that there is one fundamental and universal law – that the inferior is the condition of the superior (Janet 1872: 266). But is not the concept of irreducibility in opposition to the logic of materialism (Durkheim 1903c: 1.124)? Given Durkheim's insistence on the irreducible nature of social laws, an import-ant question is: why and how does he insist that they are natural?

Of all his terms, 'thing' is the most complicated and difficult: it inspired accusations of materialism, but also the characterization of the 'natural-ness' and hence of the determinism of social life for Durkheim (Alpert 1939). Social facts are not 'material', but they are nevertheless 'real things' (Durkheim 1895a: xxiii/46). Why does he use 'thing' in the way that he does, if he rejects materialism, 'realism and ontologism' (ibid. xi/34)? An examination of the significance of this term is crucial to this 'reconsidera-tion' of Durkheim.

But the above quotation (from 1893b: 3/286) is of the greatest import-ance, for it raises a central question in the interpretation and understand-ing of Durkheim: what view of science was influenced by spiritualist philosophy? Clearly, this was neither that of Comte, Claude Bernard nor of natural science. Indeed, if Durkheim really was a positivist, how could he use the term 'psychic', and how is science connected with it? 'Social facts are produced by a *sui generis* elaboration of psychic facts (*faits psychiques*)' (1895a: 110/134). Society is as a psychic being (*un être psychique*) (1925a: 56/65). The psychic is theoretically important for Durkheim – even though social facts must not be 'directly explained' by a psychic fact (1895a: 103/129). I suggest that it is through this concept of the psychic that the compatibility of science with morals, values and ideals can be understood: 'Law and morality only exist in the ideas of men, they are ideals' (1908c(1): 1.219/230).

The concepts of synthesis and force have appeared to further reinforce Durkheim's positivism and his scientism. The purported comparison with thermodynamics and electricity is held to support his sympathy for historical materialism (Lukes 1982: 8). But this overlooks the connection of synthesis with conscience and creation: the *conscience collective* is a 'synthesis *sui generis* of *consciences particulières*' (1912a: 605/426); 'all creation is the work of synthesis' (ibid. 637/447). Further, Durkheim explicitly denies that religious forces are physical forces.' Religious forces, I wrote, are human forces, moral forces. The essential elements of which it is made are *borrowed from conscience*' (1913b: 2.50–51). Here Durkheim explicitly refers to a passage in *Les Formes élémentaires* (1912a: 599/ 422). The mistranslation of '*emprunter à conscience*' by Swain in 1915 as 'borrowed by conscience' has obliterated Durkheim's logic and modality of social reality here and its reflexive foundation in conscience (1912a/ 1964: 419). Further, force has a connection with human power: 'The first thing which is implied in the notion of the causal relation is the idea of the efficacy, of productive power, of *active force*' (1912a: 519/367).

The analogy with thermodynamics implies that there is a mechanical 'push' to the forces which are central to social reality – which is in effect to deny agency and the possibility of autonomy. Yet for Durkheim force is 'actualised power' (ibid.): 'Society is . . . a system of acting forces' (ibid. 638/448).[7] Force in the first aspect of its double nature 'can only come from our inner experience' (ibid. 521/369). The meaning of moral force is tied to that of inner experience: it 'can only have been borrowed from our psychic life' (ibid.), and this power is 'actualised' and 'projected on to things; this logic is central to religion and its symbolism' (ibid. 599/422).

Comtean positivism establishes logically an externalist account of knowledge, as does empiricism. The dominant interpretation of Durkheim as a realist, a positivist and as the founder of empirical sociology stresses the logic of externality. But for Durkheim, 'If this externality is only apparent, the illusion will disperse as science advances, and we will see the outside return to the inside (*le dehors rentrer dans le dedans*)' (1895a: 28/70).[8] Indeed, he claims that 'We start from the outside because that alone is immediately given, but it is to reach the inside' (1897a: 356/315).

This axis of internality/externality is central to the modality of social action: 'The springs of action are internal to us' (1925a: 149/178). It matches the definition of the habitual: 'Habits are forces interior to the individual. It is from the activity accumulated in us which is unleashed by a sort of spontaneous expansion. It goes from the inside towards the outside' (ibid. 24/28).[9] There is a modality of social experience which involves habit: functions understood as 'definite ways of acting which repeat themselves . . . [and] become habits' (1893b: 357/302). Further internality is central to his supreme concept – solidarity (ibid. 351/297). Solidarity, which 'comes from within and not from without' (1886a: 212), cannot be adequately understood on an externalist model. Indeed, the active factor in social life is the 'internal social milieu' (1895a: 111/135). The whole conception of internality and its connection with science and action has been overlooked in Durkheimian scholarship. But through this, despite his analogies, it can be maintained that the logic of the constitution of the social for Durkheim does not *per se* deny agency or human rationality.

A central scientific concept for Durkheim is that of law. He praised Comte for extending law to the social realm, but does it follow that he is using it in the same sense as Comte? Newton's law of gravitation was the model for the Enlightenment conception of law which was handed on from Condorcet through Saint-Simon to Comte. For Comte, 'Positivity is invariability' (1975: 1.363). And continuity and a unidirectional momentum combined with natural necessity and determinism are central to this. But such a conception of law allows for neither action or intervention.

Against Lukes, I suggest that Durkheim's interest in law does not *per se* exclude contingency (Lukes 1973: 58): experience demonstrates both contingency and uniformity (Durkheim 1912a: 38/26). He acknowledges both determinism and a degree of contingency;[10] and argues that it has not been finally decided if causality must exclude contingency (1895a: 140/ 159).[11] He insists on the 'relative indetermination of conscience' (1898b: 15/3) and 'the flexibility and contingence of superior forms of reality' (ibid. 45/30). Likewise, I suggest that he is not opposed to Boutroux here, as Lukes suggests (1973: 58). To neglect contingency is to reinforce the view that Durkheim neglects the individual – for he agrees that to reconcile individuality and society is to reconcile contingency and necessity (Durkheim 1913aiv: 674).[12]

I suggest that Durkheim's view of law stems from the compositional view of reality, and thereby expresses the complex interrelated character of social reality, which has its own momentum and drive. This is connected with the 'mechanical theory of society' – which Durkheim argues does not reduce 'the human being to being an inactive witness of their own history' or exclude the 'ideal' (1893b: 331/279). Law so understood is not incompatible with intelligent intervention or even domination by collective effort – how else can Durkheim consider that 'we rise above things' to 'lay down the law to them (*leur faire la loi*)' (ibid. 381/321)?

The compositional and the mechanical together are central to determinate law. 'Because things happen in accordance with laws, it does not follow that we have nothing to do' (ibid. 331/279). But how can it be that Durkheim argues for civilization having 'necessary causes' and at the same time being an 'end' and an 'ideal' (ibid. 330/278)? There must be in his thought a reconciliation between the interests of science and those of action – in other words of the necessity of determinate law and freedom. 'The sciences at the same time that they declare the necessity of things, put in our hands the means of dominating them' (1888a: 143/75).

The reconciliation of freedom and determinism is fundamental to Durkheim's thought (and is associated with the compatibility of contingency and determinism). 'The objection will be raised regarding the existence of freedom. But if this fact really does imply the negation of any determinate law, it is an insuperable obstacle not only for the psychological and social sciences, but for all sciences. Since human volition is always linked to some external movements,[13] this renders determinism just as unintelligible for what lies outside us as for what resides within us' (1893b: xxxvii/xxv).[14] In other words, determinate law does not *per se* entail a determinism that denies action. What concept of freedom allows Durkheim to argue that we can 'rise above things'? And what definition of reality and of 'things' allows this?

In the sociological tradition, however, Parsons opposes Durkheim's positivism to a voluntary theory of action; Tiryakian opposes Durkheim's sociologism to existentialism; Nisbet argues that Durkheim overturned voluntarism in favour of the non-volitional (Nisbet 1966: 82); for Lacroix, Durkheim is an absolute determinist (Lacroix 1981: 102); Lukes says he is an extreme social determinist (Lukes 1973: 23); Hirst's analogy with Claude Bernard, for whom 'indeterminism is not scientific' (Janet 1872: 254), reinforces this tendency, and the accusations of determinism are continued by Lehmann (1993: 48). None of these commentators would doubt the significance of the ideal for Durkheim, but for this to be more than a mere possibility, Durkheim argues, 'Our wills . . . alone can make it a living reality' (1911b: 112/89). Uniquely, Watts Miller (1996) acknowledges the importance of Durkheim's reconciliation of freedom and determinism and the role of will. This is crucial to understanding Durkheim's theory, for it is central to the relation between agency and structure, to the reconciliation of the practical and theoretical aspects of science, and to the possibility of a science of ethics.

The neglect of his account of freedom of thought and action is at least partly due to a tendency to identify Durkheim with thinkers who not only have no theory of will or freedom, but glory in this as a theoretical advantage and badge of scientific authority and rigour – Comte and Althusser (Hirst 1975). But Durkheim argues that freedom's importance is such that it must have a more solid base than a 'metaphysical' one (Durkheim 1888a: 84/48). It is connected with the choices made by a 'personal conscience' (1893b: 399/335), the 'indetermination' shown in the deliberations of conscience (1898b: 15/3); and freedom of action as an 'initiative' (1925a: 100/118). But, most importantly, he has a quite unrecognized – even by the most recent commentators – radical theory of epistemological freedom as a necessary condition of science: 'Science, here as elsewhere, requires complete freedom of mind' (1893b: xlii/xxix).

This leads to more profound questions: what conception of science does not just allow, but can express, autonomy and the concept of will? 'It is science which is the source of our autonomy' (1925a: 98/116). And this autonomy is not received from nature; it is we who make it (ibid. 100/119). Autonomy is only possible if there is will – 'thought liberates the will' (ibid. 100/119). And what conception of science accommodates the concept of right? Rights can be seen as the political 'trumps' held by individuals (Dworkin 1978: ix): an individual has a right when there is a reason for assigning him or her some liberty or opportunity (Waldron 1992: 17). To overlook Durkheim's theory of freedom and the sphere of action appropriate to the individual misrepresents his theory of rights. Durkheim associates freedom and right. 'Once we have made use of freedom, we acquire the need for it . . . A right to a greater autonomy is founded' (Durkheim 1893b: 285/240). But it also theoretically undermines his account of individualism, which has a concept of free thought at its heart, and how his science expresses the reality of the person and their sphere of action and the primacy of human interest: to hold the 'human being is the sacred thing par excellence' means they have 'a right to respect' (1925a: 91/107).

In what sense of science and theory of reality can the human person be both the subject and the object of a science? In modern individualism, humanity is both 'object and agent' (1898c: 267/48). The support for practical humanism as it develops in the modern world is central to Durkheim's practical aim: 'This cult of man has the autonomy of reason as its first dogma and free thought as its first rite' (ibid. 268/49). These questions are not trivial, and are not answered by pointing to natural science or Comtean positivism. They go to the heart of Durkheim's doctrine: how are his humanism and individualism compatible with his theory of science? Indeed, how is it that rational and scientific thought and intellectual individualism mutually imply each other (1955a: 185)? Comte's 'Religion of Humanity' with its cult of the 'Great Being' cannot answer these questions, for it is anti-individualist, and relies on the dominance of the affective over the intellectual and the control of feelings by sacerdotal authorities.

## The compatibility of science and society

Society is real for Durkheim – it has a reality *sui generis* and it is available to science, but what is the sense of reality and of science that Durkheim is using? The fundamental question for the social sciences is still with us – how is society available to science? Despite the interminable critiques of Durkheim for his inappropriate science of facts and things, it is clear that for him there is a fundamental compatibility between the nature of society and that of science. 'To explain is to connect things one to another; it is to re-establish between them relations which we make appear as functions of one to another as vibrating sympathetically according to an interior law founded in their nature. Now sensation, which we can only see from outside (*dehors*) cannot discover these relations and internal connections for us; the mind (*l'esprit*) alone can create the idea of them' (1912a: 339/ 239). Thus, for Durkheim, to explain 'is to establish relations between things' (1955a: 84). Relation is central to Durkheim's rationalism: solidarity, together with association, responds to a science of relations. The core concept of sociological rationalism responds to the logic of relation.[15]

Further, for Durkheim social life is made 'entirely of representations' (1895a: xli/34). It is clear that there is a homology between the nature of the human being and the nature of society: 'A science is a discipline which, however one conceives it, always applies to a given reality' (1912a: 99/66). Not only is the human being 'a system of representations' (ibid. 325/229), so also 'collective life, like the mental life of the individual, is made of representations' (1898b: 14/2). The science that Durkheim espouses is, in a fundamental sense, a science of representation: 'Science begins when the mind, setting aside all practical concerns, approaches things with the sole object of representing them' (1900b: 113/4; 1895d: 15/ 60). Recent scholarship has stressed his constant concern with representation (Schmaus 1994; Meštrović 1988). But how can his identification of science with representation be explained?

What has further not been explained are, first, the distinctive features of representation – 'Intermittence' characterizes 'all complex representations' (1893b: 352/298);[16] – and second, its distinctive logic – 'Every time we unite heterogeneous terms by an internal link, we necessarily identify contraries' (1912a: 341/240).[17] How does the logic of contraries relate to representation? And what is 'the representative' – as seen in the 'representative life of nations' (1893b: 269/227). It is clearly part of his explanatory logic, as is 'the represented (*representé*)' (1912a: 162/114).

So, how is the reality of society connected with representation? And if all is representation what is exteriority and interiority? What is the connection between the psychic and representation (1898b: 25/12)? Where is the person, and what are the objects of reference in this representational view of reality? And if all is representation, how can there be a social being and a collective personality (1925a: 56/65)? Comte may have connected humanity and science, but he did not show how there could be a collective personality in a representational world; nor did he show how this is available to science. And most importantly, how does belief relate to representations – how is it that representations can stem from belief? This is logically connected with one of Durkheim's most famous claims – that science and philosophy stem from religion.

Further, if all is representation, why does he use 'thing' in the manner he does? And why does he then reject the 'thing-in-itself' as incompatible with the reality of representation (1898b: 29/15)?[18] The tendency to ally Durkheim with scientific realism overlooks his rejection of realism (1895a: xl/34) and a reflectionist view of representation, the rejection of which entails the practical force of representation (1893b: 64/53) – seen in their 'efficacious force' (1908f: 1.61/247). How does passion relate to representation? The repetition of representation and its emotional colour 'warms the heart and sets the will in motion' (1925a: 194/229). Further, not only are representations forces, they are also causes: 'Undoubtedly they are caused, but they in their turn are causes' (1898b: 16/4). This concept of representational causality is crucial to social explanation, for it connects both to social causality and to the springs of action in the human being.

The centrality of concepts which are 'impersonal representations' to society is clear, for it is through them that human intelligences communicate (1912a: 619/435), and conceptual organization implies signs. There is a clear connection between representation and sign, but what? Signs are evidence of 'that which is representable to the mind', and through them science 'goes from the outside (*le dehors*) to the inside (*le dedans*)' (1898b: 33/19). The whole theory of communication and of science depends on this theory of signs and communication, but, certainly in relation to the internal/external axis, so far remains unexplored. But signs are central to religion – 'The cult . . . is a system of signs by which faith translates itself outside (*au dehors*)' (1912a: 596/420) – and to society – 'objective signs are necessary to . . . all social organisation' (1912a: 631/443).

The concept of conscience has been acknowledged, but has been ignored as a term of theoretical significance. However, representation cannot be conceived without conscience (1898b: 37/23). And 'collective representations presuppose that consciences act and react on each other' (1912a: 330/232). It is clear that representations exist in conscience. 'Conscience at this stage is only a continuous flow of representations' (1903ai: 398/7).

Conscience is closely tied to the fundamental concepts of Durkheimian thought: not only with force, but also solidarity and rules come from the communality of 'states of conscience' (1893b: 78/64; 205/172); social cohesion results from the 'conformity of all particular consciences to a common type which is nothing but the psychic type of society' (ibid. 73/60); it is connected with personality (ibid. 74/61), function, belief, relation, contingency and indetermination (1898b: 15/3), religion and morality and the concept of duty (ibid. 68/49). Particular consciences (*consciences particulières*) are the necessary condition of society (1895a: 103/129).[19] Why does he use this phrase, and what is the significance of it for the interpretation of his thought?

Conscience is central to the practical interest of his thought: 'The more conscience is obscure, the more it is unwilling to change' (ibid. 15/14).[20] An obscure conscience is associated with the unconscious (1898b: 36/22). The neglect of this concept has fuelled a widespread misapprehension, even amongst experts (Pickering 1984: 293), that Durkheim has no theory of the unconscious. Conscience is connected to the '*psychique*' (Durkheim 1893b: 341/286),[21] and is central to the *conscience collective* which results from a 'plurality' of consciences (1895a: 103/145) or a synthesis *sui generis* of 'particular consciences' (1912a: 605/426). Why is the *conscience collective* the 'highest point of psychic life', since it is the 'conscience' of 'the consciences' (ibid. 633/445)?

Indeed, in a most important yet overlooked statement, Durkheim insists that 'To discover the laws of the *conscience collective*, it is necessary to know those of the individual conscience' (1888a: 86/50). The theoretical neglect of 'conscience' by his commentators is matched by the neglect of 'the communion of consciences' which is 'implied in all social life' for Durkheim (1913b: 2.57). Through this concept, Durkheim acknowledges a form of 'communicative action' in his theory of society, and Habermas is wrong to accuse him of not paying sufficient heed to it 'as a switching situation for the energies of social solidarity' (1992: 2.57).

Conscience is central to a rationalist definition of truth: 'Even what is collective in it [truth] only exists by the consciences of individuals; truth is only realised by individuals' (1955a: 196).[22] It is central to thought and action: 'Thought is a hyperconcentration of conscience. . . . Action on the other hand is a discharge (*faite de décharge*), to act is to exteriorise oneself, to spread oneself (*se répandre*) outside' (ibid. 166). He uses it to show that pragmatism has misunderstood the conditions of thought and action and the definition of being. Conscience is not a function which directs the movement of the body: 'it is the self-knowing organism . . . and through this one can say something new is produced'. Conscience becomes aware of itself through the 'holes' (*trous*) in action (ibid. 170).

The neglect of *conscience particulière* as a necessary feature of society by his sociological commentators has probably been inspired by Durkheim's infamous statement that social facts are, and must be treated as, 'outside' (*en/du dehors de*) each 'individual conscience' (1895a: 4/28, 52/70). I will show that the two statements are not incompatible (chapter 7). But this neglect has fed the view that for Durkheim consciousness is simply a reflection of structure. The real picture is much more complex, and does not entail the over-determined view that is ascribed to him.

There is place for a constitutive theory of consciousness in Durkheim's thought: it is not merely a reflection of being, but central to its constitution, as the above statement shows. Further, it could be said that the sociological interpretation of Durkheim, in its neglect of conscience, commits the same error as does Pragmatism according to Durkheim – that is, 'to make it just a moment in a series of movements which composes the world and which loses itself in this whole (*l'ensemble*)' (1955a: 170).

So, just as the relational and representational nature of society are matched by a science of relations and representation, the centrality of conscience to social reality is matched by the nature of science. 'Science is nothing else than conscience carried to its highest point of clarity' (1893b: 14/14). It is surprising that this term, its associated concepts, and above all, its connection with science should have been overlooked as a term of theoretical significance; it certainly poses a problem for the positivist or realist interpretation of Durkheim's science. But the viability of his science and its application to the social hang on it. Despite its similarities to the French word '*conscience*' (Lukes 1973: 3), it is clear that 'conscience' is a term of theoretical significance: how else can he use it to oppose ontologism, realism and common sense and associate it with science (1895a: xi/34)?

On its significance and meaning hang many questions about the nature of Durkheim's science. Through it we can rebut the constant accusations of his positivism, the lack of a reflexive theory of consciousness, a theory of the person, individuation and the concept of right. The type of relation, and therefore of solidarity, which can be ascribed to Durkheim depends on the interpretation of this word: are they active or passive, theoretical or practical, compatible with individuality and freedom? Is Durkheim's science entirely theoretical, or does it entail a form of practical reason, concerned with the construction of solidarity? Since action and intelligence are aspects of conscience, it is central to the understanding of a human world: it allows access to the invisible, mobile and changing character of the relations of persons which are the fundamental unit of any social world. The consequences of ignoring this term for the interpretation of Durkheim's logic of reality are disastrous – it is no wonder that Durkheim is viewed as having no theory of agency or of meaning!

The analytic dimensions of Durkheim's conception of science are thus relation, representation and conscience. These point to a different logic of science and of reality from that provided by either Comtean positivism or natural science: they point to a rationalist science founded on a critique of empiricism, positivism, realism and ontologism; they point to a science of representation. But, above all, a science of conscience culminates in a science of practical reason.

### The question of the interpretation of Durkheim

Even allowing for inconsistencies or changes of emphasis on Durkheim's part, we must still conclude that something has gone badly wrong when major statements by an important theorist contradict the received wisdom about him. It would appear that he has been put in a theoretical and interpretive double bind: he has been interpreted in a certain way, and then accused on the basis of it. The neglect of central theoretical terms has fuelled a substantial misinterpretation of Durkheim's rationalist project, and has allowed for reading it through different or later theories.

As has been noted, most early Durkheimians were philosophers. Durkheim was putting a theoretical language, which he did not invent and which was well known to his audience at the time, to a new and original purpose.[23] So, whilst Parsons was the educator of a generation of sociologists, Durkheim, as we shall see, was not exaggerating when he said that Renouvier was 'the great master' who was his 'educator' (Maublanc 1932: 299); this is the basis of important theoretical misunderstandings. Whilst this relation has been frequently referred to, it has never been analysed.[24] Since the terms that have been neglected or misunderstood are largely Renouvier's, unravelling this theoretical influence is at the core of this reconsideration of Durkheim. Since this is complex and unexplored, my aim is predominantly expository and elucidatory. Of course, Durkheim's substantive sociological judgements are of primary concern to the subject he founded. But how he makes these – that is, his theoretical language – is equally important, for it is on this theoretical framework that he hangs his empirical work. This is my concern, and I will challenge assessments of his sociology only to the extent that they have been fuelled by misunderstandings of this.

In reconsidering Durkheim, it is important, at least initially, to set aside all elements of later theories that do not adequately reflect his thinking and through which he has been read: systems theory, functionalism and structural functionalism. To these must be added concerns with normative integration and moral order, laced together with unexpressed assumptions about the nature and meaning of social reality derived from common sense, realism, positivism and holism. Views of society which he would regard as 'unrepresentable absolutes' have been foisted on him, together with an inactive view of relatedness – incompatible with his cognitive and moral constructivism. He has answers to the critical questions for a social science: under what terms is knowledge of the social possible? what guarantees that reference to the social is successful?

The central interpretive problem is that his theoretical language has been treated as though it is either simply transparent or merely common-

sensical; certain terms have just been ignored – for example, 'compositional', 'passion' and 'tendencies'. (This is connected with problems of
translation.) But in relation to the invisible world of social reality, a
language of description and reference is crucial; his theoretical language is
deliberate and consistent. Central to these problems of interpretation is
that word 'thing' which seems to attach him simultaneously to materialism,
realism, positivism and determinism. For Adorno, Durkheim's 'chosism'
outstripped Weber in positivist sentiments (Adorno 1976: 118). Through a
particular reading of this, the conception of reality and science that
Durkheim actually adopts, which focuses on the internal and the external,
on representation, relation and conscience, is replaced by a positivist,
realist or empiricist model of external relations.[25]

So in general the problems in the interpretation of Durkheim that have
arisen in the history of sociology are as follows: he has been assigned a
static version of function in place of a relational, dynamic and cognitive
one and a type of holism which he rejected; in place of a conception of
law which is compatible with a relational and representational science, he
is credited with law on a Newtonian positivist, historicist model which is
not only incompatible with freedom and the diversity and heterogeneity
of social life, but excludes the conception of possibilities in history; the
logical account he uses to indicate change – becoming – is ignored, and
replaced with a Comtean account of development; his accounts of power
and of discontinuity, indetermination and contingency are neglected; the
logic of representation is ignored – as is his logic of pluralism; and his
account of *conscience particulière* as the necessary but not sufficient
foundation of the social world is neglected.

He is falsely identified with thinkers who have no theory of rights,
individuation or freedom, and his conception of order, which is at least
partly an epistemological and scientific one, is given a deeply political gloss
through false philosophical and historical analogies; the concepts of constraint, sanction and discipline are defined independently of his accounts of
agency, autonomy and power, which not only makes them sound oppressive, but their location in a particular republican and philosophical context
is ignored and replaced by a timeless gloss of conservatism.

There is a complete exclusion of his account of freedom of mind and,
above all, of freedom as implied by science, and thus of the possibility of
critique. There is no account of how he reconciles freedom with determinism. The significance of a science of ethics for his overall conception of
science is ignored, together with practical reason. Force and synthesis are
given a scientistic mechanistic definition, which he specifically rejects.

The terms of his account of the nature and constitution of social reality
are neglected: the logic of pluralism, affirmation, belief, passion, power,
habit and the unconscious. (Only Schmaus (1994) and Cladis (1992)

acknowledge the importance of Durkheim's use of the habitual.) In this way his micro-logic of the social is neglected, and his macro-logic is perverted. This in turn threatens the internal coherence of Durkheim's thought and implies that, at best, it is eclectic; at worst, a syncretist conglomeration of inconsistent ideas: how many Durkheims are there? I suggest that there is a consistent theoretical language that runs through his works, even though each work calls on different aspects of it.

If any of the accusations with which I started chapter 1 were accurate, Durkheim would be the most unreflective and unphilosophical of thinkers. With no theory of change he would have to ignore the question of temporality, transformation and history; with no theory of meaning, he would have to ignore the question of consciousness and its relation to intentionality, choice and action; with no theory of the individual, he would have to have no theory of who it is that acts and who it is that thinks. Of course it is quite inconceivable that a philosopher of the Third Republic could have ignored these questions: clearly what has not been recognized in interpretation or in translation is the way in which Durkheim refers to and takes account of these questions.

Durkheim's science is a science of human and collective realities: it makes significant discoveries in a realm that is only postulated by philosophy. Nevertheless, it has affinities with philosophy in its conceptual foundation: there is a conceptual isomorphism with Kant and Renouvier that is never broken. It is the neglect of this conceptual foundation that has entailed the worst excesses of vulgar Durkheimianism. However, before this is examined in chapter 4, it is important to look at certain historical and political features of the extraordinary times in which Durkheim lived.

# 3

# Understanding Durkheim in his Time: Historical and Political Considerations

Durkheim's thinking and approach to the study of society were marked by the extraordinary nature of the early years of the Third Republic. The two streams which fed the nascent science of sociology were philosophy and politics: sociology in his time was a way of doing moral and political science (Lacroix 1981: 19). Both fields were united in the struggle for a republic; the historical background to both was the establishment of the Third Republic after the devastation of the Franco-Prussian War and the Commune of 1871. Out of these historical conjunctures developed three features which are essential to a full understanding of the nature and character of Durkheim's thought: first, especially in the early years, the fragility of republicanism and the strength of the right-wing monarchic or Bonapartist tendencies; second, the nature and character of indigenous French socialism, particularly as it developed after the Commune; and third, the problems of republicanism and the struggle for full democracy. Whilst what follows can only be the most superficial glimpse at the historical and political complexity of this period, it does stress certain features that are usually left out of account in the interpretation of Durkheim.

### Republicanism and the beginning of the Third Republic – a defining moment

'It was only after the war of 1870, that sociological reflection was awakened' (Durkheim 1915a: 1.112/379). The extraordinary early years of this initially fragile republic cast a long shadow over its subsequent intellectual and political development. Republicans faced 'profound demoralisation of a nation, the bitter separation of the classes, the obscuration of the republican ideal, and the opportunity open for caesarist tendencies' (Renouvier 1872b: 2.5). This conjuncture of historical and political events developed a unique intellectual 'mind-set'. After 1870, Durkheim said, all the citizens 'had but one thought': 'to remake the country. To remake it, it must first be educated' (Durkheim 1918a: 1.465). Republicanism was a question of work to do; this positive constructive spirit was inspired by the ideals of science and republican morality. This informed Durkheim's approach, and it contributes to the problem of interpretation of his thought now, since it is the antithesis of contemporary cynical, disengaged and relativistic attitudes concerned above all with critique and interpretation.

So, in the words of the song, Durkheim 'accentuates the positive and eliminates the negative'. This fault line runs through his entire sociology, and he has been frequently criticized for it. In the vulgar interpretation of his thought, this is understood as support for the *status quo*, and thus a form of conservatism; yet this positive attitude was characteristic of socialism at the time, which was 'future orientated, with a dynamic and optimistic vision of social becoming' (Charle 1994: 147).

In his passionate constructivism, there is, I suggest, a unique view of the significance of theory and its emancipatory role. This has been lost from view with the dominance of both hermeneutics and Marxism in social theory. Whilst the former would appear to ignore the social effects of theory, the latter assumes that change is reinforced theoretically through underscoring conflict and contradiction. Durkheim witnessed the near total collapse of society through war, siege and insurrection at the beginning of the Third Republic. 'The collapse of "the imperial façade" in the Franco-Prussian war led to the urgent question of the re-organisation of the country, and one which would be artificial but one which would be founded on the nature of things' (Durkheim 1900b: 123/12). In this context, for theory to support the positive trends of society and history is not merely to give it a positive role, but to help in the building of durable foundations for society. To elucidate societies' own ideals is to aid in their self-understanding and self-development. The 'hymn of praise' to society in Durkheim's thought, so apparently absurd now, in part reflects the 'ideological community' of republican hopes. But society also meant not only analytically the totality of social and historical relations, but also this totality as the forum for solidarity and human development; support for this runs throughout his work.

The central historical events of this period consisted, first, of the Franco-Prussian War. The devastation of this first of modern wars (Howard 1961) had a profound effect not just on the organization of French life, but also on its *amour propre*, and stimulated a patriotism – that might otherwise be unusual – amongst its intellectuals (Lukes 1973: 41). This devastation culminated in the Siege of Paris; although Bismarck believed that 'eight days without café au lait would break the French bourgeoisie', the suffering of the four months was extreme (Horne 1985: 221). This was almost immediately followed by the Commune in early 1871 – which was seen by some as civil war.

This conjunction of events led to an attitude of despair and ambivalence to republicanism among the Second Empire's intellectual leaders – Renan, Taine and Flaubert (Bellesort 1931: 25). By contrast, it was the socialists and republican leaders of 1848 who unequivocally supported the new regime. It has been argued that since the French revolutionary tradition was hostile to the republic, by implication, Durkheim's support for the regime was an indication of his 'liberalism' (Seidman 1983: 155). On the contrary, the socialist support for the republic was such that it was hard to distinguish the republicans from the socialists (Rébérioux 1972: 2.136). Thus the defenders of the republic after 1870 included the most militant – the Marxist Guesde and the anarchist Réclus (Vincent 1992: 152n.).

It has to be remembered too how narrow was the victory of republicanism: it was only through the failure of Empire and its disastrous war, together with the conflict amongst the monarchists, that there was a republic at all.[1] It was only recently that France was overwhelmingly Bonapartist (Brogon 1945: 109); the great popularity of Napoleon III must not be underestimated (Plamenatz 1952: 107). (Both empires in France had been accepted by the French in the name of order after a period of revolutionary 'disorder'.) It was only fear of what both the left and the right hated more than they hated each other – the Empire – that drove them to establish republican institutions – for this would bar the route to Napoleon IV (Brogon 1945: 109). The failure of Restoration and the fear of the Empire, in the words of Gambetta, meant that France entered the Republic 'backwards' (ibid. 106).

The victory of the republicans over the monarchists in 1877 must not be underestimated; even now, Furet regards this as completing the revolution of 1789, for it was the first regime to consecrate the principles of 1789, civic equality and political liberty (Furet 1988: 8). Durkheim, who entered the École Normale in 1879, celebrated in the streets for the rise of the republican left at the beginning of the Opportunist Republic; Gambetta was his 'idol' (Filloux 1977: 12). Gambetta was viewed as of the far left, and was regarded as a dangerous extremist for his sympathy for the Commune (Chastenet 1952: 19).[2] Durkheim's support for Gambetta at this time must undermine the suggestion of his early conservatism (Lukes 1973: 77).

The power of the right and the monarchist wing and the danger that both constantly posed to the nascent republic must always be borne in mind when reflecting on these early years of the Third Republic.[3] If the attempt at restoration of the monarchy was a failure, the power of the reactionary right-wing forces, which formed nascent French fascism in the

Action Française, remained active during the Third Republic right up to the Vichy regime and its collaboration with German fascism in 1940 (Thompson 1952). Behind the frequent changes of government there was a deeper form of instability which threatened the whole idea of the republic.[4] In each of 1877, 1888–9, 1892 and 1896 there was a possibility of failure of the republic, and France being dominated by the 'sabre and the goupillon'[5] – that is, by monarchists, aristocrats and the army.

Durkheim, together with Jaurès, was active during the 'Affair' (as the Dreyfus Affair became known) in support of the falsely accused army captain (Durkheim 1899g: 2.429). The great irony of the 'vulgar' interpretation of Durkheim's thought is that it places him theoretically squarely in the camp of those he opposed. The anti-Dreyfus forces were a rallying ground for the enemies of the republic. The Affair showed how powerful were the anti-republican forces – Catholics, militarists, Bonapartist and royalist partisans of autocracy and Boulangists. They shared a common view of the state, the safety of which was the supreme value, overriding all considerations of ethics, justice and individual right. Together with Boulangism,[6] the Dreyfus Affair was evidence of the anti-Semitic nationalism which was central to the right in France, of which both the royalists and the Church were sources.[7] Their racist and nationalist doctrine was presented in a populist tone, in opposition to the left, which in the 1890s grew more organized and adopted internationalism and pacifism.[8] As we shall see, the Dreyfus Affair also affected socialist thinking.

Although the political power of the right receded under the leftward tendencies of the republican regimes that started to develop after 1898, it remained a force that had to be ideologically combated and guarded against. Renouvier warned of the dangers of a *coup d'état* from the right provoked by 'the revolutionary method' (1879); Durkheim also feared this (Bourgin 1942: 76).

### Durkheim: conservative or liberal or socialist?

Durkheim, of course, aimed to establish a science of society that was above the 'fray' of politics; there is, however, a political vision that is a backdrop to this. Accusations or false characterizations of his politics still abound in the sociological literature: it is only in the context of the Third Republic and the history of nineteenth-century French society that the debate about Durkheim's political stance can be judged.

The lack of political parties in France meant that in the characterization of position there can be no simple reading from party to political stance. True political conservatism in France was Traditionalism for Thibaudet, and this incorporated an attitude which held the imitation and continuation of the past to be a good in itself. It never forgave the revolution for its systematic break with the past, and wished for a pre-revolutionary state in accordance with the forces of conservatism – that is, monarchy, nobility, family, acquired fortunes, the army and the Académie Française (Thibaudet 1932: 14). It demanded a solution to 'the social question' through inequality and hierarchy, by maintaining classes, the patronage of social authorities and the formation of an elite for culture. I have argued that it is quite fallacious to read Durkheim through this movement – as Nisbet has done – though this view is still widespread in sociology. Durkheim agreed with the father of French socialism, Saint-Simon, that this pre-revolutionary world had been rightly replaced (Durkheim 1900b: 115/6). Indeed, Durkheim opposed 'bourgeois traditionalism' (1998a: 226).[9]

The logical heart of conservatism is 'to conserve'. There are two senses in which this can be applied to Durkheim's thought. First, his passionate republicanism forms a political backdrop to his science of society: the attempt to conserve the republic was the goal of the socialists and the republicans; this must not be confused with conservatism in the political sense. Secondly, central to Durkheim's thought is the concept of the interest of society, found in his concern for its 'conditions of existence'; this must not be confused with maintenance of a hierarchy and inequality. The concept of the interest of society means in part that society as a totality of relations which surround the individual is a forum for the development of viable human life. To argue for the conservation of this opposes him to revolutionary socialism, but it does not follow that it is an anti-socialist position. Durkheim holds that society has its weight and specific gravity – the beliefs and practices of a people have a remarkable persistence – which it is dangerous to disturb. Indeed, he held that it is actually impossible to destroy this, and that revolutionary requirements for a *tabula rasa* are beside the point, for this old world will reappear through custom and habit.

So at this juncture of history, the republicans and those of leftist sympathies had to tread a narrow, risky path; the nascent republic constantly had to watch its back. Above all, its supporters had to oppose the arguments of Traditionalism and the forces of the right, and demonstrate that society left to itself without the traditional props of monarchy, Church, class and hierarchy could generate its own stability. Durkheim's apparent conservatism finds further explanation here.

## Liberalism: philosophical and political

For Lehmann, Durkheim is both a conservative and a liberal (Lehmann 1993: 8); whereas for Seidman (1983), Durkheim is a liberal in the context of the Third Republic. Undoubtedly there were elements of philosophical liberalism in Durkheim's thought: his defence of rights, his theory of freedom of mind, and his moral and political individualism. Recognition of these has been hampered by the political and epistemic positions falsely imposed on him and by the neglect of his theory of freedom of mind and of right. It is clear that he was influenced by the theorists of philosophical liberalism – Montesquieu, Tocqueville, J. S. Mill and, above all, Renouvier. He stresses the dignity of the individual, of individual rights, free thought, free democratic institutions and the essential liberal values of tolerance and pluralism, which puts him in the tradition of political liberalism thus characterized by Rawls (1993). However, to infer from this that he was a political liberal in terms of French politics is mistaken. Utilitarian liberalism was the prototype of European liberalism (Richard 1914: 112), yet the critique of this is central to Durkheim's work.

The term 'liberal' can be applied only with caution to France – there was no political party equivalent to the English Liberal party. It is said that to be a liberal in France means to be in opposition (Thibaudet 1932). There are three clear stages of French liberal thought. Germaine de Stael and Benjamin Constant establish the first stage: averse to both Jacobinism and the *ancien régime*, they believed that by defending constitutional monarchy and opposing divine right, they would regenerate as well as close the revolution. Whilst they opposed freedom to arbitrary state power, freedom is not freedom for all; it must be distinguished from democracy and equality. Although the limitation of power through a doctrine of rights was essential for them, these were negative rights (Soltau 1931: 40).

For Thibaudet liberalism was most clearly distinguished from Traditionalism under the July Monarchy. Guizot, after the downfall of the Bourbons, was one of the leaders of the government between 1830 and 1848. He held that political rights must be restricted: the property qualification must be the basis of the franchise, and power should be limited to the middle classes, for they would ensure order and liberty. Behind this lay the same belief in social order and the existence of classes as in Traditionalism. He held that the revolutionary principle of equality was a great danger: inherited inequality and property inheritance were foundations of civil society (Woodward 1963: 153). Like all liberals, he believed in *laissez-faire* economics: the government must not interfere in the free economic order. As Laski argued, the liberals could not acknowledge the seminal truth of Saint-Simon's recognition of the significance of property and its social effects: they believed that freedom must leave the property system untouched (Laski 1936: 242–3). They opposed democracy: 'all power to the people' was reminiscent of Jacobin tyranny – democracy and republicanism together meant revolution for them. So it was the socialists and the democrats who were in opposition to the liberals in the run-up to the Revolution of 1848.

The third moment of liberalism was clear in the opposition to Louis Napoleon after his *coup d'état* in 1852. Like the socialists and the democrats, liberals opposed the police state, censorship and centralization; they appealed to freedom, and opposed arbitrary authority. Yet, although they (for example, Vacherot, Jules Simon and Prevost Paradol) denounced the imperial system, their position was negative and defensive. Like Constant before them, they developed no positive theory of rights against the state, and like Guizot, they made order primary, particularly in light of the 'excesses' of 1848. They supported *laissez-faire* economics as a way of opposing socialism (Soltau 1931: 296); they denied the logic of economic justice, and expressed only 'thin pity' for the effects of huge economic inequality. In fact, liberal politicians in the 1870s and 1880s held out against legislation to improve the workers' lot (Collins 1982: 21). Republicanism, as it developed its leftward tendencies, forced them to choose between socialism and conservatism; through their fear of the masses, they resisted the full implications of a positive theory of rights and democracy. Liberalism thus became either a mere political empiricism or a blatant defence of bourgeois elitism through fear of the intellectual economic levelling effect of democracy (Soltau 1931: 299).

So, although Durkheim held to the supreme value of the person and the individual, he did not share the social and political aspects of liberal thought. Indeed, the original and central question of his thought is: under what social conditions do these values emerge, and what conditions support them? His support for the contemporary conceptions of human dignity – that is, 'respect for the human personality wherever it is found' (1893b: 395/332) – follows his argument for equality as the condition for the development of solidarity (ibid. 373/314). If we also remember his argument for freedom (ibid. 399/335), it appears that Durkheim held that the central value of liberalism results from the mutuality of liberty and equality within the historical possibilities of solidarity, which is a position similar to that later held by Rawls (1993: 3–16).

Yet, for the liberals of his time, the interest of freedom opposed equality and democracy. On the contrary, Durkheim argued, 'Social inequalities' are the 'negation of liberty' (Durkheim 1893b: 381/321), and countered the liberal argument that greatness requires inequality (1967a: 1.409ff./25). Unlike contemporary liberals, as we have seen, he argued that the conditions for the development of solidarity require 'absolute equality in the external conditions of struggle' (1893b: 371/313). Durkheim held that the social and economic exploitation of classes falsifies the 'moral conditions of exchange' and the determination of social value (ibid. 378/319). Such reflections do not place him in the liberal tradition: economic justice was the cry of the socialists at this time. It is false to argue that his 'neo-liberalism' supports capitalism (Lehmann 1993: 1). Whereas the liberal bourgeoisie held property to be a natural right, for Durkheim the question of property and its transmission is central to the social question: he argues against the hereditary transmission of wealth and the inequality it entails (Durkheim 1893b: 378/319).

Indeed, the originality of his thought is to undermine the central tenet of liberalism – understood as *laissez-faire* economics – by holding that this contradicts, rather than supports, real individualism. Nor did he believe that the individual must never be subjected to the community, as did Constant (Collins 1982: 7). Rights are real and positive for Durkheim, and not just defensive and negative as they were for the liberals: solidarity creates a system of 'rights and duties' (Durkheim 1893b: 403/338), not merely a forum for exchange.

So the acknowledgement of society as a system of rights and duties is central to moral individualism, and is the source of judgements of injustice (1925a: 17/16). Whilst the liberals set great store by charity, this has a lower value morally compared to justice for Durkheim (ibid. 71/83).[10] With the socialists, he argued for justice in economic relations – not pity or charity. Although Durkheim did not support the classic eighteenth-century liberal doctrine of natural rights (for it is unhistorical), he, like Rousseau, argued that rights are claims recognized by society, and held that the individual acquires positive rights of free disposition throughout history (1950a: 92/56); the positive rights which the individuals acquire against and over the state are to be protected by secondary groups (ibid. 97/61).

## The question of socialism

Through Marxism, the revolutionary tradition has dominated definitions of socialism; but 'revolution' as definitive of socialist thinking and action is precisely what is thrown into doubt by crucial historical aspects of the Third Republic. The Paris Commune of 1871 was a defining moment in this period of history: it led to between 20,000 and 30,000 deaths in its tragic, and bloody suppression. It has not been mentioned in assessments of Durkheim and the question of socialism, yet it had an important influence not only on the development of the Third Republic, as acknowledged by Réclus (1945: 22), but also on the development of socialist thought. Outside France, through Marx's 'Civil War in France', it entered the canons of revolutionary socialism. Its first socialist chronicler, Jellinek, endorsed Lenin's judgement of it as the first stage of the proletarian revolution (Jellinek 1937: 15).

Inside France, the reaction was rather different: it is more accurate to describe it 'not as the hopeful model for future political action but as the somewhat forlorn climax of the old French tradition' (Thompson 1952: 26). It spelled the end of the political hopes of Blanquist revolutionary socialism and its affiliation with Jacobinist statism – the French equivalent of Leninism. French history did not unequivocally support revolution as a successful model for the development of socialism. Revolution had become identified with the Terror which ensued during the first revolution and the reintroduction of dictatorship with Napoleon, just as the revolution of 1848 was finally overturned by the *coup d'état* of 1852. For Renouvier, aborted revolutions and authoritarian counter-reactions littered nineteenth-century French history without any achievement for republicanism or socialism in terms of freedom and democracy (Renouvier 1879: 177).

Memories of the Commune and its miseries determined the French people never to be exposed to anything like it again (Réclus 1945: 23). For Chastenet, it turned the people to the right; 'always patriotic', they ceased to be revolutionary. The Commune retarded the development of what it aimed for – socialism and a solution to the social question (Chastenet 1952: 30). Indeed, after 1848, the association of republicanism with socialism did much to discredit republicanism in the popular mind (Williams 1969: 25). Renouvier wrote in sympathy with the Commune (at a time when all public discussion of it was banned) and countered the conservative argument that republicanism meant radicalism, which in turn meant the Commune: it was the conservatives' fault for 'deceiving the people a hundred times and pushing them to the limit'. Indeed the 'great name' of the Commune – meaning 'association and autonomy' – needs 'a rational and normal constitutional foundation in a republic' (Renouvier 1875a: 229–30).[11]

It was Marxism's incorporation of the revolutionary tradition at its most dictatorial (Blanquism) that was, for Lichtheim, one of the reasons for its poor development in France; another was the low theoretical levels of its exponents (Lafargue, Guesde) (Lichtheim 1966: 9–10). Vincent (1992) points to the myth of Marxism as central to French socialism, and of French socialism as 'proto' or immature Marxism. For the French, France was the home of revolution: to continue 1789, without terror and revolution in the context of a republic, would be to achieve socialism. And given the parallel struggle to develop full democracy under the Third Republic, it made the revolutionary strand of socialism a difficult bedfellow for the republic. For Renouvier, Jacobinist authoritarian statist socialism shared in the 'heteronomous spirit' of monarchism and catholicism; it thus prepared the ground for dictators (Renouvier 1872b: 5). Historically, all that Jacobinism had in fact led to in France was a self-satisfied, rich bourgeoisie, which supported the 'party of order', which should better be called 'my peace at any price' in its desire not to share with the more numerous, and poorer classes (ibid. 3).

So the effect of the Commune was to stress the other tradition of French socialism, and lead to the development of its democratic and political nature; even the Blanquists and the Guesdists came to renounce violence. From 1893 onwards the socialists made strong parliamentary gains, and by 1905 Jaurès led the Unified Socialist Party, whose 'integral socialism' aimed to reconcile the reformist and revolutionary aspects of socialism. This libertarian and pluralist socialism, as opposed to the authoritarian and statist strand, was fostered and developed within the republican tradition. Opposed to the centralism of state and power, it was concerned with both decentralization and federalism.

At its heart lay the morality of fraternity, articulated in terms of the interests of the whole of society, as the forum for fostering the interests of humanity; even Louis Blanc saw society as the *'chef d'oeuvre'* of a human science (Michel 1898: 230). It focused on civic virtue, the importance of institutions, the socio-political consequences of untrammelled individualism and individualist economic interest (Vincent 1992: 108). The indigenous tradition of nineteenth-century republican socialist thought was much more important than Marxism, and it insisted on the interaction between political institutions and social mores. Republican socialism required virtue – the citizens must have a public morality. It opposed collective moral interest to private egoism, and held that the goal of reform was fraternity and justice.

So a distinctive feature of indigenous French socialism was its ethical nature: socialism appeared as ethically just, by contrast with the corruption of capitalism. This must contradict Gouldner, for whom Durkheim's 'moralism' is part and parcel of his 'conservatism' (Gouldner 1970: 122). It continued in the footsteps of the moral and humanitarian eighteenth-century precursors of socialism, as seen in the work of Morelly, Mably and Rousseau, for example. Mably identified politics and morality, happiness and virtue, in a manner reminiscent of classical Greek thought: politics concerns virtue. Collective moral interest and equality opposed greed and private interest.[12] However, through Saint-Simon, the conception of science entered the socialist intellectual apparatus; science and morality were two distinct strands of French socialist thought. The concept of a science of morality – the framework for Durkheim's first book – must be understood in this tradition.

However, a feature of the republican socialist tradition during the Third

Republic was the scientism which it espoused, in contrast to the romanticism of the socialists of the 1848 revolution – George Sand, Lamartine and Victor Hugo. Much as with the approach now in France to participants in the unrest of 1968, the activists of 1848 were mocked as '*quarante-huitards*'. The year 1848 'was the shipwreck of those celebrated utopias' (Janet 1878: vi). By contrast, a scientific approach to social questions, couched in statistical language, became a feature of socialism under the Third Republic. To be a socialist was to recognize the primacy of the collectivity over the individual; to be scientific was to base this on statistics (Rébérioux 1972: 1.167).

The question of work and social organization in terms of equality was a central theme of French socialism as it passed from the eighteenth to the nineteenth century. The revolution of 1789 marked the passage from thought to action. The question of subsistence and the right to work to some extent replaced the earlier moral critiques: the concept of equality led to the question of the conditions of existence in society. While the intellectual framework changed, there was a continuity in the concerns and demands of socialism: the right to work and the organization of work. Saint-Simonian socialism introduced the principle of association as central to its theoretical framework.

So the Paris Commune of 1871 posed a number of important questions, which became central to the problematics taken up by Durkheim's sociology: the nature of the state – centralist or federalist; the role of associations, especially of workers, and the forms of economic development that are possible within collectivism; the relationships between democracy and socialism; the relationships between spontaneity and organization in human action, and the relationships of science to both; and lastly patriotism and internationalism (Bruhat 1972: 533). Rather than it leading to the conception of a unified, authoritarian state controlled by a dictatorship of the proletariat, it led to a rethinking of the form of the state in a democracy with pluralist values. Most importantly, it led to the demystification of authority (Hitchens 1971: 16). It briefly showed that 'the human being is an active subject in search of his/her autonomy' (Rousset 1970: 113), that the ideal of communal self-government was a possibility, and that proper authority stems from the people. It thus contradicted the hierarchized, traditional systems of authority beloved of all authoritarian regimes in nineteenth-century France.

## Durkheim's relationship with Jaurès and Malon

Durkheim's sympathy with socialism is well known amongst Durkheimian experts: Durkheim 'never hid his sympathy for the socialist party and

Jaurès in particular' (Bourgin 1942: 73). Durkheim's friendship with Jaurès has been acknowledged; both were graduates in philosophy of the École Normale, and it is clear that Durkheim was a friend and associate of Jaurès from early on: it is said that Durkheim turned Jaurès from 'shallow radicalism' (Lukes 1973: 248).[13] However, what is not clear is the nature and character of the type of socialism they shared and the theoretical affinity between Durkheim and the movement of democratic socialism initiated by Benoît Malon, who influenced Jaurès and, through him, Léon Blum.[14] Jaurès held that it was Malon who converted him to 'integral socialism' in 1885 (Jaurès 1904: 177). When Durkheim told Mauss in 1899 that he would be ready to enter the political fray when socialism 'enlarged its formulae' and ceased to be simply preoccupied with class, this position was directly in line with Malon's 'integral socialism'.

The importance of Benoît Malon (1841–93)[15] was in intellectually accommodating socialism to the republic and, through his seminal influence on Jaurès,[16] on the political development of democratic socialism. In his late work *Précis de socialisme* (1892) he expounded his vision of socialism: the aim of socialism is to establish a new *order*; to throw a new civilization into the mould of history (Malon 1892: ix). (Even for Blanqui socialism is 'the belief in a new order' (Bruhat 1972: 512).) He argued against the revolutionary method, and outlined the dangers of 'romantic revolutionism', not only because of the misery it generated, but because of the danger of provoking a reaction. Like Gambetta, he said that the 'heroic times are over', even though he had 'gun in hand in tragic days'. (He was active in the Commune and in exile for nine years.) In the context of the Third Republic he held that the reformist method was the best one; the French 'have exhausted revolutionary policies – it produced 100,000 martyrs' (Malon 1892: 166). Only republican-inspired justice and fraternity can forestall 'future catastrophe'.

Durkheim's identification of the social question as a moral question that concerns the whole of society has been cited as evidence of his conservatism (Coser 1960: 217). Malon and Jaurès also held it to be a moral question: the social question, Malon argued, is not just a question of capital versus labour, but a means of determining a more rational and just social state. Socialism concerns the whole of society: the aim of socialism is to bring about a more rational social state – by focusing on the milieu, which is ignored by revolutionary socialism. Socialism for Jaurès also centres on the individual and the milieu, and he criticizes Marxist materialism and economism for ignoring justice and moral interest as inspiration for action. This 'more just social world' must be brought about by elevating and ennobling action through the human ideal and the ideal of justice. Moral forces, which are more important than class interests, can be forged in a synthetic vision, and are the focus for the development of a new order (Malon 1892: ix, 187). This line of argument continues that of his *Socialisme intégrale* (1890), which held that socialism not only concerns economic justice, but requires social and mental transformation.

Jaurès extended and developed these ideas: socialism is the realization of equality and justice in social relations – which Marx risked losing in the idea of class interest (Jaurès 1919: 15). Socialism must move beyond economic and historical 'fatalism'; like Durkheim, Jaurès held that revolutionary overthrows are childish dreams (*rêveries d'enfant*) (Durkheim 1905e: 286). This can never be enough to establish a new regime, for without institutional support, no such change can be effective: socialism cannot organize itself without institutions. In this sense socialists must focus on the 'reality of things': democracy is the form of all modern movements, and therefore the condition of socialism. Socialism must therefore concern itself with freedom and autonomy, which are only possible within terms of the totality.

In his introduction to Malon's *La Morale sociale*, Jaurès agreed with Malon that socialism is a morality, and that it means developing solidarity within a 'conscience', so that it can dominate egoism, and that this in turn is possible only within a united humanity. Socialism connects the welfare of individuals to collective organization: Jaurès rejected political economy's identification of the collective interest with self-interest. Socialism is future-directed; it is turned towards a new order, *l'ordre socialiste*, as the foundation of ethics. In this, humanity becomes 'a solidary whole (*un tout solidaire*)' which is the principle and end of conduct (Jaurès 1895: ii), and this is reconcilable with individualism, freedom and autonomy. Elsewhere he indicates the philosophical importance of the 'conciliation' or 'synthesis of contraries' which can bring solidarity and freedom together (Jaurès 1896a: 25).

The moral character of socialism meant that discipline was central to socialism: 'We are the party of discipline in action' (1900: 95).[17] But it was the Dreyfus Affair which confirmed the ethical character of socialism for Jaurès; he was the 'Victor Hugo' and 'Maigret' of 'the Affair' (Rébérioux 1972: 183). For Jaurès this was not a bourgeois quarrel, as held by the Guesdists, but a life-and-death struggle for socialism and the republic. It was through his famous *Les Preuves* that Jaurès demonstrated the trumped-up charges against Dreyfus and showed that the questions of rights and individual liberty were central to socialism, and not simply a bourgeois ideology (1898: 47). It showed that humanism must be central to socialism: Dreyfus was the symbol of 'suffering' humanity; he 'was nothing but humanity itself, in the highest degree of misery and unimaginable despair' (ibid. 48). Further, the Affair raised the question of 'reasons of state (*raisons d'état*)'; he argued that there is none that can justify the false accusations against an innocent person (ibid. 49).

He showed that, first, socialism does not concern solely the working class, and that there is a morality which extends beyond class – for Dreyfus was a 'son of the bourgeoisie'. Secondly, he confirmed the question of a morality for humanity which goes beyond the national question (ibid. 48). He was the first to oppose the anti-Semitism of many socialists, which had for a long time seemed the corollary of anti-capitalism and anticlericalism. This important historical conjuncture indicated the necessity of a theory of individual rights for socialism.

For Jaurès, socialism is concerned with the realization of an ideal in history (1894: 2.7) and this is central to the logic of critique and transformation, which for this particular movement of democratic socialism centres on the ideal versus the real. This was taken up by Léon Blum, through the influence of Jaurès (Lacouture 1982: 118); Lucien Herr also saw socialism as a moral ideal (Lindenberg and Meyer 1977: 65). For the latter, this was central to socialism as a doctrine of action – which justified science and prescribed human ends for it (ibid. 440).

In a number of ways, Durkheim shows affinities with these thinkers and this tradition of French socialism. This is especially evident in book III of *De la Division du travail social*: the interest in establishing a new order, based on a synthetic conception of the world; using and guiding 'the moral forces' of humanity by an ideal – the ideal of human fraternity; the implementation of an ideal in the real; the work of society as a work of justice; individualism reconciled with solidarity. The socialists also stressed the collective, the milieu and the importance of institutions, and they rejected utilitarianism and sought a solution to the problem of work. 'Let us use our liberties to search for that which must be done to soften the functioning of the social machine, so harsh on individuals, to put within their reach all the means possible to develop all their faculties[18] without obstacles, to work to realise at last a reality for that famous precept: to each according to their works (*à chacun selon ses oeuvres*)' (Durkheim 1898c: 277/56).[19]

## Republicanism

Durkheim's conception of science carries with it the polemical characteristics of republicanism and democracy: 'A society which aspires to govern itself, has above all need of intellectuals (*lumières*). Democracy would be unfaithful to its principles if it did not have faith in science' (1918a: 1.465). It is also connected with reason: 'It is from reason alone, that is to say science, that can be found the means of remaking the moral organisation of the country' (1900b: 121/11). Both science and democracy are central to the Durkheimian enterprise and to republicanism.

As we have seen, socialism was closely identified with republicanism – indeed, effective socialism was possible only within the terms of republicanism; thus, at this period in France, most political tendencies found their outlet in ordinary republicanism. In 1848 Tocqueville argued that the republic was the aim of socialism (Bruhat 1972: 501). This was true both of the early years and at the turn of the century (Rébérioux 1972: 136). Jaurès, in *République et socialisme*, citing Engels, argued that the republic is the form of socialism (Jaurès 1901a: 2.270). For Malon, the realization of socialism was inseparable from republican institutions (Vincent 1992: 102).

The achievement of full democracy was also the aim of republicanism and socialism. Durkheim was undeniably a democrat (Richter 1964; Lacroix 1981), but this has been obscured by the analogies made by certain commentators with profoundly undemocratic thinkers. Liberals had a tendency to see democracy as a 'disreputable force' associated with anarchy: 'In French middle class homes in the early nineteenth century the words democracy and republic were not considered suitable for use before the children' (Collins 1982: 12). Until the Third Republic, 'it became customary to think of democracy and government as two separate poles in politics, too far apart for the vital spark of democratic government to flash between them' (Thompson 1952: 14). It was against the background of a tradition of an absolutist monarchic state and an electorate, if not illiterate, accustomed to habits of deference to the Church and nobility, that both republicanism and full democracy were seen as ideals to be established. The volatility of voters and their conservative tendencies, unaccustomed as they were to long periods of democracy, must also be acknowledged as one of the problems in founding a stable republic.

Without a republic, there would be no possibility of either democracy or of socialism. The acute problem of establishing the legitimacy of a republic within the character of the French state, given its nineteenth-century history, has been shown by Nicolet in his classic *L'Idée républicaine* (1982). The republic had to replace the absolutist and undemocratic politics of the *ancien régime*, the July Monarchy and the Second Empire. To do this, it had to have a legitimacy and authority to replace that founded on tradition and *de facto* power. How can the republic proceed through authority without contradicting itself? (Nicolet 1982: 281). In the name of what does it govern, and in the name of what does it make change? It must create its own legitimacy – conceptually: in this context politics as an object of science was brought to the fore.

Democracy requires substituting one order for another; thus politics can no longer be simply a question of unravelling actual institutions: it is a question of judgement, not description, and this requires principles. Science opposed religion and the old basis of authority; in the context of the Third Republic, science was polemical, for it had to contradict the transcendent basis of authority and hierarchy (ibid. 287). The new political and social order must be based on a recognition of the rights of the individual and on free thought – but how can this be done scientifically?

All republicans believed that a science of man was central to the republic; the central question was: what kind of science can found a science of the human being and establish rights and freedom of thought? Against Nicolet, I suggest that positivism was not satisfactory,[20] and nor was Darwinism. Although both were adopted by some leftists in the struggle against theological politics, they were two-edged swords, for both were adopted by the Fascists Barrès and Maurras. Parodi, in *Traditionalisme et democratie* (1924), shows how the Action Française had married traditionalism and positivism.[21] Its ideas were formed by combining the ideas of Taine, Renan, Comte, Maistre and Bonald. It was precisely the reactionary, anti-revolutionary and anti-democratic features of Comte's positivism that attracted the Action Française; through these they developed a positivist, realist and historical approach.

Comte had shown that the interest in the conservation of society is bound up with the idea of being as subject to strict deterministic laws, and that this contradicted the ideas of freedom, will and the ideal, for it is based on common sense, not reason. The Action Française therefore rejected morality and individualism, which are opposed by the unity of society as a real being. It particularly admired Comte's later principle of sociability founded on the unity of being, which reflected Maistre's influence: the most essential of the conditions of existence and continuity of the group is its natural, unreflective nature. From Comte, it deduced the denial of rights from the authority of science and the realism of society. It used this to oppose the rights of the person: society is based on prejudice and instinct, on a collection of necessities foreign to reason. (Durkheim's statement, 'The progress of conscience is in inverse proportion to that of instinct' (Durkheim 1893b: 338/284) takes on added significance here.) To these considerations, it added the neo-Darwinian theory of the purity of the race: heredity is the biological basis of race, and is the condition of purity of the national type. Aristocracy by birth is the foundation of society; this and hierarchy alone can solve the social question.

The Action Française opposed this politics of fact, which admires instinct above all, to the politics of the ideal and reason. The 'facts' they wanted to preserve were inequality and all it supports – in capital, wealth and inheritance. Wealth comes from competition and free exchange; the Action Française supported *laissez-faire* economics. Inequality leads to war, which is good, for it is an expression of force, and force is good in itself. Whereas the Action Française supported social and political Darwinism, Durkheim opposed the moral use of Darwinism – for this is to ignore solidarity and altruism (ibid. 174/144).[22] So, against all doctrines of humanity, fraternity of people, communal organization, and against all that would make society more rational, it opposed the admiration of national energy, colonialization, love of the soil, hatred of the stranger. Indeed, Barrès argued that all questions of what is just, what should be, are 'foreigners in the interior (*étrangers à l'intérieur*)'.[23] Durkheim, on the contrary, opposed the 'brutality' and 'megalomania' of racial attitudes in European colonialization (1925a: 161/193). We can therefore see that interpreting Durkheim in terms of the combination of Traditionalism and positivism is, in effect, to tie him to this version of French fascism; but this is precisely what he opposes in *L'Individualisme et les intellectuels* (1898).

So Comtean positivism does not *per se* provide the type of science which is required for the construction of a rational politics centred on the democratic ideal – for this must allow for an account of freedom of mind, the autonomy of persons and agency. These were not developed by Comtean positivism, nor was a conception of right and freedom of mind: the politics of Comte's positive state were not democratic. Science may well require determinism, but what kind of science allows the reconciliation of this with freedom of mind, which is fundamental to a democratic politics?

Republicanism also had to break with history, with the historical dominance in France of absolutist and authoritarian governments which ruled in the interest of order. The past could not be the necessary and sufficient condition of what ought to be: it had to break with historicism. To go against the tendency of the past, republicanism had to show that 'our history is not our code' (Nicolet 1982: 290), and to break with Burkean conservatism and Burke's view that constitutions are not made but grow.[24] With Renouvier, the critique of historicism and of the philosophical continuum became the logical heart of republican philosophy. Further, what is cannot be the sole basis of what ought to be: reason, not expediency, should dictate politics – hence the political importance of the philosophical critique of empiricism. Politically, empiricism was associated with conservatism and with liberalism's stress on experience as the guide in politics. For Guizot, 'Experience is the suffrage of the centuries' (Woodward 1963: 113). There is a further consideration: the empiricism of Voltaire was accepted as one of the ideational causes of 1789. But this was a revolution that ran out of control (Joyau 1893: 8). The conception of reason as guide in the direction of humanist, republican values became a central philosophical issue.

It was in this context that Renouvier's scientific rationalism rose to pre-eminence. For Thibaudet, Renouvier was fundamental to the intellectual success of the Third Republic: 'Renouvier's speculative influence was profound for thirty years on about a hundred philosophers – that is to say on the form of thought' (Thibaudet 1930: 543). His thought was central to the pro-Dreyfus republicanism, for he outlined a theory of rights, and supported the concerns of justice in his *Science de la morale*. Justice, the correlation of right and duty, involves reciprocity or equal exchange (Renouvier 1872b: 11), and must be central to society.

From 1872 Renouvier declared himself one of the political workers of the republic which was in formation (Thibaudet 1930: 543). Republican action should lead democracy to find its rational principle; the false gods of the *ancien régime* – 'violence, cunning, intrigue and terror' – must be abandoned. He attacked the whole basis of 'reasons of state (*raisons d'état*)', which were the basis of repression and for him, merely a glorification of the interests of the *status quo* (Renouvier 1872c). In contrast to authoritarian statist politics, the new republican ideal must centre on 'a new feeling of respect, a clear strong sense of duty, which the Republic alone carries within itself'; only thus will there be 'an order, a legality' (1872b: 6). What must be established is 'a system of first principles of life' and a philosophy of 'man as associated with man' which focuses on the milieu for reform and education. Such ideals inspired a generation of republicans and philosophers. It is through Renouvier's scientific rationalism that we can understand not only Durkheim's theoretical language, but also how he hoped to reconcile science and democracy.

# 4

# Philosophy and the Republic: The Influence of Renouvier

Durkheim was educated as a philosopher at the École Normale, which he entered in 1879. 'Coming from philosophy, I tend to return to it quite naturally by the nature of the questions I have encountered on my way' (quoted in Davy 1973: 301). Although he considered the École Normale 'as still too closed to the scientific approach' (Davy 1919: 184), the crude scientism of the Second Empire and the philosophical failures of positivism were acknowledged there (Janet 1865). During this time he read Renouvier – who was viewed as avant-garde by the young philosophers (Andler 1932: 35). He 'fired him with enthusiasm', and 'marked him with an imprint that was never effaced' and which was reinforced by his great friendship with 'that other Renouvierist', Hamelin (Davy 1919: 186) (see Appendix). An examination of Renouvier's influence will elucidate Durkheim's theoretical language and some of its puzzles, which I outlined in the first two chapters.

Of the three distinct movements in nineteenth-century French philosophy – positivist-empiricist, spiritualist and criticist – the first has been over-emphasized, the second ignored, and the third underestimated in the interpretation of Durkheim. Yet he acknowledges the significance of spiritualism in the relative autonomy of 'psychic phenomena' from the organic (1895a: ix/32). This influence is also seen in the interiority which is a distinctive feature of his view of science, conscience and force. From Maine de Biran to Bergson, through Ravaisson, Lachelier and Boutroux, spiritualism opposed positivism and empiricism. Whilst Comte was resolutely opposed to the point of view of interiority (Gouhier 1948: 12), spiritualism stressed the reality and the value of interiority, the irreducibility of the human to the non-human and the reality of will and consciousness; in so doing it opposed materialistic reductionism.

For Maine de Biran force is an inner power which, when realized in action, is an 'acting force' (*force agissante*) which is also shown in 'effort' or 'willed action' (1812: 87). His influence on spiritualism was shown in a view of the self as active and aspiring; in this way he also uniquely raised the question of the person as a bearer of rights and as a free individuality (Janet 1872: 330). This self encounters reality as resistance; he initiated the definition of reality seen as an obstacle to will. So for this movement, unlike Comte and Spencer, force expresses not only mechanism, but above all will or tendency towards an end (Ravaisson 1867: 245).

A characteristic of the later spiritualist philosophy of Lachelier and Boutroux (Durkheim's teacher) was its evaluation of science: it aimed not to undermine science, but to demonstrate its ultimate limitation and to show that it rests on foundations that are non-scientific, thereby allowing room for spirit, creativity and freedom. Kant had demonstrated that science presupposes principles which mind contributes, and with mind we must acknowledge freedom and the moral and religious ideal (Boutroux 1933: xxxiii). Spiritualism questioned the value of science, its nature and its ultimate adequacy in terms of human life. The view of science prevalent in the Third Republic had moved beyond the Comtean or Baconian one of a simple passive account of external relations.

## The concept of a critical science and of scientific method

Durkheim nevertheless viewed sociology as a science. Science brings a 'spirit of criticism' (Durkheim 1912a: 613/431). His conception of a positive rationalist science, I suggest, comes from the Critical Movement, whose main proponents were Cournot and Renouvier, both of whom were influenced by Kant's reflections on the foundations of science.[1] An enquiry into the conceptual conditions of science is central to the meaning of 'critical': scientific philosophy is 'criticism' (*critique générale*), which Renouvier distinguished from the prevailing systems of university philosophy, particularly eclecticism. 'Critical' meant, first, the limitation of theory by fact – Kant's 'critical intention'. Secondly, the critical attitude involves the autonomy of reflection: he opposed a free scientific spirit to positivism and dogmatic scientism (Renouvier 1898a: 750).

Renouvier's concept of scientific method was opposed to positivism. Sciences are established only by the founding of a method. (Cf. Durkheim: 'There is only one way to make a science, that is to try (*oser*), but with method' (Durkheim 1893b: xlii/xxx).) For Renouvier, positivism neglected not only this, but also the Cartesian demonstration of the centrality of doubt to all question of 'evidence'. (Durkheim: 'We must rigorously submit ourselves to the discipline of methodic doubt' (ibid. xlii/xxix).) Positivism neglected the principles and postulates which sciences require (Renouvier 1875b: 403), and thus the higher epistemological principles which Kant had demonstrated as fundamental to the possibility of science and all question of certainty (1878a).[2]

Scientific method grasps reality – phenomena – without illusions or 'idols'. It discovers relations, which are fundamental to the interdependence and 'compositional' nature of reality. These relations have a relative permanence which is an 'order'. This logic supports the scientific study of the milieu. 'The milieu has a great power' (1872b: 7). The concept of law is tied to the compositional, and indicates the 'general communal connection' of phenomena (1875c: 1.78). 'Being' is a regulated phenomenon of any order (ibid. 1.106). A natural law is a function of different connected phenomena of *whatever* type (1876c: 49).

For Renouvier, function accounts for all relations of interdependence, and covers not just 'immobile' relations as in mathematics, but all dynamic relations. Both show what is essential to the concept of function: when the determination and variation of a phenomenon depend on those of others, then the first is a function of the second. Functionalism also includes the cognitive functions which belong to what he calls 'the internal objective order'. The supreme function of this order is 'conscience' – which covers all those intellectual and practical operations by which reality is disclosed; as such, it is supreme amongst the representative functions (1875c: 1.103).

A scientific approach to the mind, for Renouvier, is the study of '*psychique*' phenomena, which are conscious representations or consciences (1875d 1.11).[3] He affirmed the irreducibility of 'psychic facts' to organic facts (Milhaud 1927: 75), and criticized positivism for denying any truths of 'psychic origin' (Renouvier 1872b: 7). In so doing, it denied the reality and effectiveness of human consciousness and action; yet there is nothing in science to prove that the *psychique* cannot be the initiator of a series of phenomena (1876b: 17).

Concomitant variation is a 'law of nature' which covers the constant relations of phenomena diachronically and synchronically, and it applies to consciences which are constantly in relation and are thus in communication with each other. We have seen that the communion of consciences is 'implied in all social life' for Durkheim (1913b: 2.57).[4] It is a central tenet of Renouvier and means that a world of persons is related through communication. It follows that communication is central to the functional relations which occur between them: functional relations between 'psychic' phenomena testify to this communication and signification, especially through 'the signs' by which thought is expressed (cf. Durkheim 1895a: 4/ 51). Durkheim's concept of society as an '*être psychique*', and the social milieu as 'made of ideas and beliefs, habits and communal tendencies' (1897a: 339/302), and both as available to the method of concomitant variation are elucidated by this.

Concomitant variation allows for the variability and contingency of phenomena. Against positivism, Renouvier argues that science does not require absolute causal determinism: freedom indicates the limits of determinism. Whilst positivism presented events as entirely predictable, science must retain the idea of alternatives as possible within phenomenal reality (Renouvier 1876a: 7). Further to reflect on data, interpret evidence and formulate hypotheses, freedom of mind is required, yet positivism denies this. 'Scientific thinking requires freedom of thought and other freedoms which cannot be separated from the former in the social order' (Renouvier 1898b: 4.113). (Cf. Durkheim: 'Science here as elsewhere presupposes a complete freedom of mind' (Durkheim 1893b: xlii/xxix).) Science's interest in causality is satisfied by the idea of 'force', which does not require the denial of freedom or agency (Renouvier 1876c: 53).

So Renouvier opposed Comtean positivism in method and politics – just as he opposed the partisans of order. The influence of Renouvier so far must cast doubt on Gouldner's identification of functionalism with nineteenth-century positivism and conservatism (1970: 335). Whilst for Comte, function is central to social order (the 'Great Being') and its determinism, Renouvier shows how functionalism can be established without loss of cognitive, critical or transformational interest.

## Kantianism, the question of science and reality

Kant had both a scientific and a political importance at this time. In the context of the Third Republic, the significance of Kantianism was as 'a weapon against despotism and clericalism as well as a theme of meditation' (Krakowski 1932: 115). Renouvier's 'Néo-Criticisme' – a 'reformed' Kantianism – showed how it could reconcile the distinct movements of French philosophy: it satisfied the impulse towards positivity and scientific knowledge, whilst preserving the autonomy of reflection and the reality of interiority. Experience is central to knowledge, but not its foundation: the latter lies in the activity of understanding and its representative laws, which are interior and are the condition of knowledge of exteriority.

For both Boutroux and Renouvier, Kant had totally transformed the question of knowledge and reality, and hence of science: he had put the whole question of scientificity on a different footing from positivism, empiricism, realism and common sense, and had shown the impossibility of a presuppositionless approach to reality. There can be no unproblematic or direct reference to reality, as assumed by realism; a conceptual apparatus is necessary to the scientific approach to reality. 'The concept elaborated by science has the function of expressing reality' (Durkheim 1925a: 230/270).

Renouvier's *Traité de logique générale et de logique formelle* (1875c) was held to be the first fully scientific philosophy in France (Pyguillen 1970: 5). Renouvier was responsible for the 'scientism' of the Third Republic (Brunschwicg 1927: 2.522). It was an unusual science – Renouvier's phenomenalism 'derives in a straight line from Kant's *Critique of Pure Reason*' (Milhaud 1927: 69). His scientific rationalism was also a radical 'discourse' (Renouvier's term) of republicanism. His conception of free critical thought as a central condition of science did not undermine the democratic interest in self-determination and autonomous action, as did positivism. This central theoretical issue for democratic theory and its relation to science is linked with the question of how the human subject can appear in a scientific theory: 'What kind of science is it whose principal discovery is to efface the object with which it is concerned?' (Durkheim 1912a: 99/67). Kant's Copernican revolution was an achievement in method (Renouvier 1864a: 45).[5] Kant had allowed an approach to reality which does not deny the authority of mind or the reality of agency through its focus of representation, which he showed to be central to all questions of reality and science. Durkheim's use of 'conscience' and force within a system of collective representations is heir to these considerations.

### Representation, understanding and the problem of meaning

Durkheim's debt to Kant, like Weber's, is clear: Kant had shown that reality is accessed only through the understanding; for Weber this is leads to the method of '*verstehen*', whereas for Durkheim it leads to the focus on representations – which indicates the 'mental element' (Durkheim 1895a: xi/34). Representations are products of the understanding, which is central to both the orientation of the agent to reality (1893b: 69/56) and the activity of science (1895a: 34/74). Following Renouvier, the understanding is seen by Durkheim as one of 'our psychic functions' (1925a: 34/39), and is central to conscience. 'All knowledge, all analysis and science is produced, in fact, under the conditions of the states and acts of a particular conscience (*conscience particulière*): and no judgement, no reasoning, no proposition, no truth are given to us otherwise' (Renouvier 1875c: 2.362).

What does this term 'representation' mean? The way Durkheim uses it is connected with his conception of social facts: representations are 'ways of seeing' – that is, forms of consciousness which stem from the activity of the understanding in association with the data we receive through our senses. Together, these constitute 'reality'. So collective representations are shared ways of seeing that are central to a culture or a society.

Durkheim uses 'representation' in a significant way: it does not indicate the private, the subjective or an illusion. No thinker has put greater emphasis on the reality of society than Durkheim, but it consists 'entirely in representations' (Durkheim 1895a: xi/34; see also Stedman Jones 2000a). A representation is not a 'simple image of reality, an inert shadow projected in us by things' (1893b: 64/53). It is precisely to underscore the reality of representations that he rejects their identification with 'things in themselves' (1898b: 29/15). Why does Durkheim identify reality with representations, and what consequence does this have for his sociology?

Representation is fully adequate to define all aspects of reality for Renouvier; he establishes that, logically, there is nothing beyond representation – this follows from his rejection of the 'thing in itself' (Renouvier 1875c: 1.25ff). But representation must then accommodate both the person and the self, and nature and material things, to adequately express reality. Renouvier rejects both subjective idealism and materialism as foundations for representation (ibid. 1.59–60), which is a crucial step towards establishing its general and collective nature. Subjective idealism or 'egoism' starts with the self – but since representation is the logical term by which things are known, the self is not logically prior to it, and is not the source or basis of representation. Even though representations are characterized by a common characteristic, '*la conscience*', 'Conscience and I do not define me, but belong to all representation' (ibid. 1.17). Equally, we know material things and all of nature through representation; realism and materialism ignore this, and make the object logically anterior to representation. Through the rejection of the logic of materialism and of subjective idealism, he held that representation has a logical autonomy of both a material base and of the self.

This analysis of the logic of representation elucidates that complex term 'thing', which has caused so many problems in the interpretation of Durkheim. I will deal with this in greater depth later (chapter 7), but light must be thrown here on why Durkheim uses 'thing' whilst insisting that all is representational. For Renouvier, 'Representation is that which relates to things, separated or composed in whatever manner' (ibid. 1.6). Hamelin explains: 'Thought is defined by things and things by thought. This circle is broken when we establish representations' (Hamelin 1927: 45).[6] So 'thing' is not *per se* a material object, but part of a logic of composition – and indicates complex objects of thought. It is also an aspect of signification within terms of representation, for it indicates that which thought relates to. However, more generally, 'thing' means the real as discriminated within a framework of representation. 'Truth consists in the conformity of idea to thing and thing is the real ... that is the real external relation' (Renouvier 1903: 22). It thus indicates complex realities – independent of their ontological status (that is, whether they are material objects or forms of consciousness).

So 'representation is neither a projection, nor a reflection, nor an intermediary between a subject and an object. Representation is sufficient to itself' (Hamelin 1927: 49). But it has a distinctive character: it has a double face – the representative and the represented. The representative conditions are active in conscience, and their objects are the represented. For there to be knowledge at all, these must come into relation with each other – that is, subject and object must be in relation to each other. 'I am not the first to notice the utility of the word representation to express the synthesis of subject and object in a conscience, and thus to serve as the point of departure for all analysis of knowledge' (Renouvier 1875c: 1.8). Likewise, Durkheim argued: 'As the world only exists in so far as it is represented – the study of the subject envelops in a sense that of the object' (Durkheim 1909d: 1.186/238). This shows how misconceived is the characterization of Durkheim as an objectivist positivist who ignores the relation between subject and object (Walsh 1998: 276).

Now representation, if it is neither logically mine nor yours but ours, must therefore in a significant sense be general. This logical generality of representation is crucial to Durkheim's conception of social facts, to collective representation and to his conception of society as a sphere of relations. Kant had shown through his refutation of idealism that representation is not a private subjective experience (or merely 'inner'), but has an objective reality that is general (Kant 1781: 244, B274).[7] In this sense Kant had significantly influenced rationalism and moved it beyond the subjectivist implications of the Cartesian *cogito* as the departure for knowledge.

Renouvier extended this idea of the reality and generality of the representational sphere, and argued for it thus: it requires more than one being who represents for representation to be possible; if there were only one person, then the crucial distance between subject and object, whereby knowledge becomes possible, would not occur, and knowledge would collapse into solipsism. It follows that representation is not subjective, but is general, and that this is the condition of objective knowledge and of truth relations (Renouvier 1875c: 2.65). So this generality of the representational sphere underwrites a rationalist conception of truth and objectivity which, as we will see, applies to society as a sphere of general relations for Durkheim. It follows also that the method of science, observation, applies to the sphere of representation. This 'is the analysis of the data (*donnée*) of representation, considered in its greatest generality' (ibid. 1.115). (See also Durkheim 1898b: 16/4.)

So representation is general; but what maintains this generality? Renouvier argued that it is held in common by a plurality of beings; he thereby indicated a collective foundation for representation (Renouvier 1875c: 2.331). (This is a point made by Renouvier against both Hegel and Kant.) It follows for him that 'human representation is the only one of which one can speak with assurance' (ibid. 1.1).

So all aspects of reality are to be accounted for in terms of the generality of representation. Renouvier continued Kant's distinction between the inner and the outer aspect as a way of accounting for all aspects of experience within the logic of representation: the self logically belongs to the inner aspect of representation and nature, whereas material things and all external relations belong to the outer aspect. This logic underwrites Durkheim's sociological vision: he argues that the elements which compose the social milieu are 'things and persons' (Durkheim 1895a: 112/ 136).[8] He sees both as aspects of general social relations: the person as part of, and constituted through, a system of social relations, and material things as the repository of cultural and economic values.

So all external relations – that is, all relations other than the inner sphere and conscience – are logically 'outside'. But the internal and the external are always in contact, and mutually influence each other – there is a dialectical exchange between internal and external relations – that is, between persons and things. This helps to explain Durkheim's stress on external reality whilst insisting that all is representation – for society consists in the relations which surround the person and which are thus logically external. This must correct the view that Durkheim's account of society opposes the subjective *per se* (Walsh 1998: 278), just as it also explains Durkheim's comparisons of society with nature, for both, logically, are in the sphere of external relations.

## Representation and the categories

So we are part of a general system of representations which are held collectively; we thereby share forms of thinking. Durkheim's conception of collective representations indicates the diversity of these from society to society. It is precisely because our thinking is imprinted with collective forms of thinking that Durkheim can argue for the sociology of knowledge against classic rationalism. So, like Kant, he holds that the understanding implements certain fundamental rules of the mind – the categories – which prescribe the form that is given to experience; but unlike Kant, he argues that these reflect society in its various forms and its various systems of classification.

Durkheim's conception of collective representations has been taken to support relativism. However, his acknowledgement of cultural relativity does not entail the radical epistemological relativism that now abounds in the social sciences. The acknowledgement of difference does not require abandonment of the rationalist enterprise. (See below under 'Representation and quality'.) His support for relativism is reputedly through his theory of the categories, for these change through 'location and time'

(1912a: 21/14; see also Stedman Jones 2000b). How, then, can he hold that the '*fundamental* categories' constitute 'reason' (Durkheim 1912a: 19/13)? How can there be varying systems of classification and 'reason'? I suggest that reason is the totality of conditions which make representation possible, and that these conditions are the rules that belong to the representative aspect of representation.

This requires that we acknowledge Durkheim's use of the 'apriori', which he identifies with irreducible elements of knowledge (ibid. 21/14). The laws of the representative order are the apriori element of representation for Renouvier (Hamelin 1927: 87).[9] These are irreducible to the experience they govern,[10] and constitute the condition of any representation. They are thus the condition of all different types of classification – which we share as members of humanity; Durkheim argued that the concept of '*genre*' was formed in 'humanity' (Durkheim 1912a: 205/145).

The apriori is that which precedes experience as its foundation. This is what Renouvier called the 'skeleton' of representation, maintaining against Kant both that this is not dominated by pure reason, and that the key to its nature is not given through the table of judgements as formulated by Aristotle; the whole '*tableau humain*' must be consulted. So Renouvier broke with classical Kantianism and Hegelianism, and argued that this 'backbone' of representation was the result of 'long collective endeavours' (Renouvier 1875c: 2.203). In this way he showed Durkheim that the deepest and most abstract level of the formal structures of our knowledge is marked by social and historical factors.[11] Like Kant, however, he argued that these logically precede and form our particular experience; but, unlike Kant, he argued not for a pure rational apriori, but for one which accommodates the historical and the relative.

So now we can answer the question as to how there can be both reason and different systems of classification – through the concept of levels of irreducibility and levels of classification. That is, there are fundamental forms of conceptualization which make classifications possible and are thus at a different logical level to them. 'The fundamental relations which exist between things – the function of the categories is precisely to express these – are not essentially dissimilar in different realms' (Durkheim 1912a: 27/17). But these are represented differently in different societies: 'The primitive does not represent time, space, force and cause, in the same manner as the man of today' (1920a: 2.323). So all forms of classification involve the most irreducible levels of representation: 'everyone agrees with Kant' that thought has 'one or more sui generis functions, irreducible to experience' (1887a: 3.455).

All cultures, however differently they are conceived, share the following formal features for Durkheim: each is a reality and has a sense of reality which consists of interrelated elements (objects and persons). Although these are discrete, they are systematically related to each other through laws and classifications: a condition of the latter is that the elements can be grouped into kinds of things. Each culture is aware of the reality as temporal and spatial, and as changing; of events as brought about or caused to be; of action as a pursuit of some end. And it is a fact that our consciousness, however much it is collectively shared, is embedded in human agents; it is situated, social and historical persons who do the thinking – the representing. These formal features make representation possible and thus constitute 'reason'.

## Science and the categories

Parsons characterized Durkheim as an early positivist and a late idealist. This implies a polarization of facts and categories which is belied by Durkheim's constant concern with representation; it also implies that categories are a concern of idealism, rather than central to the practice of science. But just as there can be no facts without representation, so there can be no representation or science without categories. As we will see, Durkheim uses the 'fundamental categories' throughout his *oeuvre*.

So the 'fundamental categories' as the condition of all understanding are at the same time the conceptual foundation of science. Durkheim distinguished the spirit of science from positivism and evolutionism, and claimed that science is a 'superior' degree of knowledge (1895b: 3.432–3). Both Kant and Renouvier held that the fundamental forms of representation are the condition of understanding and knowledge of the world, and are thus the conceptual condition of science; Renouvier calls these the laws of the 'internal objective order of representation' (Renouvier 1875c: 1.77ff).

Durkheim's claim that representation, relation and conscience are fundamental to science, I suggest, can only finally be understood through Kant's logic of science as reworked and redefined by Renouvier. In contradistinction to the Newtonian science of nature which characterized Kant's account, Renouvier showed Durkheim how these representative laws can account for a social world with its relational, typified, plural and changing character.[12] This follows from identifying 'collective endeavours' as the root cause of the formal structures of knowledge; for these formal features of knowledge are the conceptual ossification of humanity's own experience. This is evident in the first and the most fundamental law of the representative order, which is relation.

## Relation and the question of holism

Kant's 'Copernican Revolution' established relation as the fundamental principle of science for Renouvier. This has a clear epistemological sense: 'What is thinking if not establishing (*poser*) relations?' (Renouvier 1875c: 1.69). But, most importantly, relation underlines the complex and the structural. It is central to the compositional view of reality for Renouvier (ibid. 1.73): composition indicates relational interdependence (ibid. 1.66ff). It is further associated with law (ibid. 1.78), and entails a definition of being as syntheses and determinate functions of phenomena (1898b: 2.14). Relation theoretically underlines the relatedness of social experience; the compound and complex nature of social reality responds to this first law of science.

We have seen that Durkheim's holism involves the logic of composition; Durkheim's conceptions of 'a composed (*composé*) order' which is a complex set of relations which have a relative duration (Durkheim 1895a: 86/116. 1893b: xxxii/liv),[13] and of the nation as 'composed of coordinated elements' (1885a: 1.373/110) reflect this view. Renouvier used the concept of social organism in his definition of society 'as composed (*composé*) like an organism of complementary and reciprocally interdependent elements' (Mouy 1927: 111). Compositional wholes are formed not only by aggregation but also by repetition for Renouvier (1875c: 1.165). ('Every social group ... is a whole formed by parts, the ultimate element, whose repetition constitutes the whole, being the individual' (Durkheim 1950a: 53/14).) We can see the family, for example, as a 'composed order', for it is a set of relations between persons, and the structure of society is a form of relational interdependence, each relation of which has a relative duration.

But relation is an active principle of consciousness which, as representative, has a relative autonomy of experience – that is, of the represented. To relate one thing to another is to synthesize them, and in this sense relation is a dynamic and constructive force which is central to the dynamic of social consciousness, to the 'creative syntheses' of Durkheim's thought, and to the practical moral interest in the development of new relations. It underwrites association – which generates the new (Durkheim 1895a: 102/128). Although Renouvier discusses 'chemical syntheses' in his *Principes de la nature* (1864b: 113), it is clear from his *Logique* (1875c) that synthesis is an active mental act central to representation. Together with becoming, relation is central to the dynamic of representation and its dialectic: these underwrite the fluid changeful nature of social relations and social consciousness.[14]

Relating as central to the synthetic nature of social reality can also be seen in mythical thinking and cultural activity which bring together elements which are not logically related – like Lévi-Strauss's '*bricoleur*'. 'Every time we unite heterogeneous terms by an internal link (*lien*), we necessarily identify contraries' (Durkheim 1912a: 341/240). Relation operates through contraries; the logical moments of *determining* a relation require that we first *distinguish* and then *identify* (Renouvier 1875c: 1.146). These logical moments of distinction, identification and determination characterize the contrary moments of all the laws of the representative order, for relation is implied in all of them.

## Holism and logical plurality

But we have seen that Durkheim's holism is also tied to a theory of plurality. The significance of wholes as 'logical pluralities' for Durkheim is that social complexity is compatible with the diversity and heterogeneity of phenomena. Society is made up of distinct persons and groups who act independently and in some sense differently from each other, but, as belonging to this society, they constitute a totality. Logically, pluralism guarantees that relational totality does not exclude the heterogeneity, autonomy or specificity of the parts: thus Durkheim rejects a monism which 'denies the heterogeneity of things' (Durkheim 1903c: 1.124/177–8).

Durkheim claims that 'totality' is the 'category par excellence' (1912a: 629/442) and that number is crucial to explanation (1893b: 241/330); it is central to how the elementary parts enter the 'composition' of society (1895a: 12/57).[15] 'Society . . . derives from positive and durable relations established between a plurality of individuals.' Its intensity derives from the 'exchanges between its composing units' (*unités composantes*) (1893b: 329/277).[16] This conception of unit is crucial to understanding the individual for Renouvier: 'Individuals are thus units (*unités*)' (Renouvier 1875c: 1.285).

Like Kant, Renouvier argued that a fundamental condition of our understanding of any world is that we can grasp it in terms of quantity: a world consists of many things. This is a judgement made through the law of number, which is Renouvier's reformulation of Kant's category of quantity. Its logical moments are unit (*unité*), plurality, totality. All totalities are logical pluralities: 'Unity cannot be conceived without plurality' (ibid. 2.293). We can see how this enters Durkheim's organicism: 'An organ is an association between a certain number of anatomical units (*unités*), united through a relation (*lien*) of solidarity' (Durkheim 1893c: 231/117).

But Renouvier draws significant consequences from this principle: it follows that knowledge must always be of determinate, numerable relations. Both positivism and evolutionism misuse the concept of the whole in Renouvier's view. The Comtean belief that the entire system of knowledge can form a unified, complete system is 'anti-positive' for Renouvier (1878a: 1.52). And the law of the three stages is an illegitimate construction (1864a: 163ff) which invokes 'the ontological continuum' in its linearity (see Durkheim 1906a(2): 1.198). The false whole enters into the absolutist holism and determinism of bad science (Renouvier 1876a: 6). So he argues that there is no science beyond the particular sciences which are limited to specific questions with a specific field (1873: 227). (Cf. Durkheim: 'a science is made of particular restricted questions' (1915a: 1.113/380).[17]) Thus a radical limitation of the whole by the particular follows: 'The general no more exists without the particular, than the particular is intelligible without the general' (Renouvier 1875c: 1.56). (Cf. Durkheim: 'The general only exists in the particular: it is the particular simplified and impoverished' (1912a: 617/434),[18] and 'The whole cannot change unless the parts change and in the same measure' (1885c: 1.352).).

The sciences which use false wholes found oppressive politics on false historical constructions (Renouvier 1864a: 156). Renouvier thereby rejected Comte's and Saint-Simon's organicism for logical and political reasons, together with Hegel and the 'metaphysics of the absolute' and all politics of 'order', including authoritarian state socialism. Pluralism is connected with republican and socialist interest in tolerance. (Cf. Durkheim: 'Tolerance must rest . . . on diversity' (1955a: 187).) False wholes justify terror, and deny the politics of autonomy and individuality for Renouvier. Pantheism is one such system. (Cf. Durkheim: 'A pantheist belief is impossible where individuals have a strong feeling of their individuality' (1950a: 94/59).)

Further, the law of number entails the critique of the 'ontological continuum' and the establishment of the principle of discontinuity and the complex, discrete nature of our perceptions. (Cf. Durkheim: 'Intermittence characterises all complex representations' (1893b: 352/298).[19]) It also entails the critique of infinitism (which is central to his critique of Hegel (Renouvier 1875c: 1.30)) and of the logic of the finite. It underlined Renouvier's critique of a necessary and inevitable law of progress running through history. And it underlies the classic Durkheimian theme that life is limitation. 'We continue to be limited (*borné*) because we are finite beings' (1925a: 100/118).

## Holism and realism

This account of holism was also, according to Durkheim, central to his own 'realism' (1913a(15): 326). Durkheim acknowledges the reality of society as realism in one sense, but also rejects realism and ontologism in another (1895a: xi/31). For Renouvier, realism or ontologism implies that persons are simply an effect of the world or a transcendent system, and this undermines the reality of action, choice and consciousness. This is not the case if we acknowledge everything as representation, and 'all representation as fact of conscience' (1901: 254).

This analysis also elucidates Durkheim's use of the term 'mystical'. Whilst contemporary social scientists tended to see race or nation in a realist sense (Michel 1898: 522), Durkheim called the nation an 'obscure', 'mystical (*mystique*) idea' (Durkheim 1903c: 1.148). Any idea that invokes 'unrepresentable being' is 'mystical (*mystique*)' for Renouvier, for it implies metaphysical entities which transcend the logical condition of knowledge – representation (Renouvier 1920: 236).

The question of right is involved here, for both realism and ontologism make individuals 'a subordinate organ' and a sacrifice to a higher end, thereby denying right. Against these, Renouvier argues that the social conscience (*la conscience sociale*) should be taken as the point of departure for the understanding of all human and political systems (1872b: 2.16/752). And in this logic of representation, the particular (*particulière*) expresses a real, indissoluble individuality, which cannot evaporate in a whole which threatens to absorb it (1869a: 1.301). The term *conscience particulière* thus has a cognitive and a moral dimension: the interests of epistemology and the possibility of right coincide.

## Representation and quality

Durkheim argues that the methodology, which is central to good philosophy, deals with 'kinds' (*genre*) and 'species' (*espèces*) (Durkheim 1895b: 3.427). He argued that 'the species presupposes kinds (*genre*)' (1912a: 257/182), and that fundamental to any characterizing of social phenomena are 'differences' and 'resemblances', which are central to the propositions of science (1893b: 355/300). He understands types of society through the logic of 'species' (*espèces*) (1895a: 76/108), and these are associated with interpretation (ibid. 89/119).

In so doing, he is using Renouvier's law of quality: 'difference', 'genus' (*genre*) and 'species' (*espèces*) (Renouvier 1875c: 1.279). Fundamental to any approach to reality is that we qualify it in some way, and this involves such questions as 'What is it like?' For example, 'Man is an animal'; whilst the latter is the kind/genus (*genre*), man is nevertheless 'different' from it. So this is a judgement which involves elements both of difference and of similarity; these correlative functions of judgement are brought together in species (*espèces*).

'No representation is possible except by this law' (Renouvier 1875d: 3.278). He held that it is an irreducible synthesis of the mind which is the basis of all forms of reasoning, propositional logic and, in particular, the relation between subject and object. It presides over the formation of all general ideas, and shows that conceptual organization is not an empirical accident. (Empiricism is irrational for it 'refuses all reality to logical life' (Durkheim 1912a: 20/13).[20]) It is the condition of all classification, and is the fundamental law by which we hierarchize and order things and therefore think (Séailles 1904: 98). So, for Durkheim, thinking is 'arranging ideas', and is the attempt to 'to classify' things (1912a: 107/73).

## Causality, finality, becoming and the personal

A fundamental condition of our approach to reality is the question 'Why did X happen?' The question itself is central to the possibility of explanation, and therefore to the intelligibility of a world. Durkheim held that 'efficacity', 'productive power' and 'active force' are implied in the idea of a causal relation (Durkheim 1912a: 519/367). This repeats Renouvier's definition of causality, which is understood through 'force' and which reconciles the contraries – 'act' (*acte*) and 'power' (*puissance*) (Renouvier 1875c: 2.53). Force expresses 'that which is brought about' as central to the meaning of causality, and revolves around power. This is not incompatible with causality as concerning the necessary and sufficient conditions of events. (See below under 'force'.)

Finality ('state', 'tendency', 'passion') is that through which we understand means and ends (ibid. 2.163). All life implies a movement from one state towards another: finality expresses this through tendency (*tendance*). (Cf. Durkheim: 'finalism is implied by existence' (Durkheim 1895a: 96n./144).) It is central to a dynamic view of reality. (Cf. Durkheim: 'A tendency (*tendance*) is ... also a thing' (1893b: 92/121).). It is that by which we grasp 'ends', and is required by the logic of change (Hamelin 1927: 156).[21]

Change for Renouvier is understood through becoming (*devenir*). The understanding of change is a complex intellectual operation which grasps that something that once was no longer is. It involves simultaneous acknowledgement of a present 'lack' and of what once was. So to say that society has become secular includes reference to its former religious state, together with its present non-religious condition. The moments of becoming are 'connection' (*rapport*) and 'non-connection' (*non-rapport*) which are reconciled in 'change' (*changement*) (Renouvier 1875c: 2.41).

We have seen that Durkheim uses the concept of personality (Durkheim 1920a: 2.323/86; 1912a: 13/8). Society is 'a being' (1885c: 1.351) which has a personality. He uses the concept of the personal which is part of science (1893b: 354/299), and through this will, freedom and individuality are understood. Although Durkheim rejects excessive 'impersonalism' in knowledge (ibid. 355/300), there is a tension between the personal and the impersonal, which are two aspects of our 'psychic life' (1914a: 318/152). Representation for Renouvier has the condition of its constitution in relation and the condition of its realization in personality (Turlot 1976: 81). Personality is the personal form of relation; its synthesis is 'conscience' which brings together 'self' (*soi*) and 'not-self' (*non soi*) (1875c: 2.177).

Personality indicates that it is persons who represent and are active forces in representation: all aspects of reality are marked by the personal and the human. Through its logical role in representation, we can see why humanism and science are not opposed, and why individualism and rationalism are associated for Durkheim. But, most importantly, this allows us to see why Durkheim associates science and conscience. Since conscience brings together self and not-self in the synthesis of conscience, it is the condition of the possibility of knowledge and of the relation of internal to external and subject to object (Renouvier 1901: 236).

All laws of the representative order are realized through conscience, which is thus the supreme law of the representative order and the condition for the understanding of reality. Yet there is another reason for Durkheim's association of science with conscience: each fundamental category founds a science (for example, mathematics is founded on number), even though each science calls on them all in different ways. Sociology concerns at least in part the social worlds formed according to a conscience collective: it thus significantly calls on conscience and its laws.

### The concept of rational psychology and the passage to a conscience collective

Durkheim was a rationalist, but did not deny the psychological nature of social facts, even though these are *sui generis* (Durkheim 1895f). It is association which differentiates this from individual psychology.[22] Renouvier argued that if the categories really are the fundamental forms of consciousness then this has implications for the subject of experience. Kant should have, but did not deal with the question of psychology. So Renouvier's *Traité de psychologie rationnelle*[23] gives an 'abstract anthropology' of the person (Renouvier 1875d: 1.202) through 'a classification of psychic phenomena' (ibid. 1.11). It rejects the conceptions of mind and soul of classic rationalism, and replaces them by functional states of conscience (see Durkheim 1897a: 25/61). It establishes a kind of 'formal psychology' (Durkheim 1895a: xviii/41), which can accommodate the formal interest of consciousness and action in explanation; it centres on the 'states of conscience which represent' the social world (1893b: 272/229).

It concerns the 'representative functions'; these are those mental functions in the agent that make representation possible and which, although 'irreducible' to each other, are indissoluble and inseparable (Renouvier 1875d 1.233). Thinking is a representative function for Durkheim (1899aii/ 157: 90) and the understanding is one of 'our psychic functions': it is 'a representative faculty' (1925a: 34/39).[24] Renouvier insisted that we understand the mind through the categories. 'The functions of the understanding and of reason are thus attached to the first six categories' (Renouvier 1864b: xii). This illuminates further Durkheim's association of reason with the 'fundamental categories' (1912a: 19/13). 'Intelligence is thus representation' (Renouvier 1859: 148). The 'representative functions' central to thought are indissoluble and inseparable (Renouvier 1875d: 1.233). These are central to the functions of conscience.

It follows then that relating is a central function of conscience. (Cf. Durkheim: 'it is *sui generis* relation' which establishes 'special combinations' of ideas (1898b: 27/14).[25]) This enters into attention, comparison and reflection. (Cf. Durkheim: 'The capital role played by attention' (ibid. 31/17).[26]) And it is central to the functions of analysis when ideas are analysed (*décomposable*) into the parts of which they are composed (*composé*) (ibid. 26/12).[27] (Cf. Renouvier: 'All language and science proceeds by composition and by decomposition' (1875c: 1.1).) Imagination, memory and the dynamic, changeful quality of thought – seen in the series of ideas – are aspects of these functions (Durkheim 1898c: 28ff/15). So we can see why Durkheim calls thought a hyper-concentration of conscience (1955a: 166). Reflection is the '*conscience de la conscience*', for it involves all the functions of conscience for Renouvier.

But reason specifically is understood through the law of quality: it is this that differentiates, generalizes and specifies. Linguistically it implies the subject and attribute which enter into all propositions (Renouvier 1875d: 3.281). Signification is a central function of reason, and this is central to all communication: 'Signification is the aid of reason. The sign represents the species' (ibid. 3.279). A system of signs is central to thought for Renouvier (ibid. 1.148). (Cf. Durkheim 1895a: 4/51.)

In addition to signs, reason requires symbols and symbolization (Renouvier 1859: 429). Although signs are, at first, symbolic, language develops through them. The sign is adopted in 'common', and through a natural convention and common associations is central to the communication of thought. So the functions of signification and symbolization are primary to conscience, and help to explain how social experience is generalized through communication between consciences for Durkheim and how social experience can be typified.[28] However, reason is even more necessary to signification than vice versa, even though these two powers develop together (1875d: 3.281). It follows, for Renouvier, that human beings have learnt to talk 'other than by tradition' (ibid.). Reflection and reason develop through the autonomy of 'attentive reflection' and through abstract general terms, and thus gain a freedom from conceptual conventionalism.

Lastly, Durkheim has a theory of the unconscious: it operates through unconscious representations: 'Outside of (*en dehors de*) clear representations, in the midst of which the scientist operates, there are the obscure ones which are linked to tendencies (*tendances*)' (Durkheim 1893b: 331/278).[29] He argues that the understanding 'is only the culminating and thus the most superficial part of conscience' and is not 'the seat of psychic life' (ibid. 267n./225). Conscience for Renouvier has degrees, stemming from the 'obscure' to its clearest form in free thinking and reflection. The 'obscure' relates to the unconscious: there are unconscious representations (1875d: 2.310).

There are clear consequences of this analysis for the interpretation of Durkheim. So, first, he has an account of the unconscious and its relation to both thought and action through 'obscure' representations, which, although not evident to the understanding, are nevertheless a potent source of social action. Second, given this view of reason and its relative autonomy (see below), we can reject the sociologism imposed on Durkheim through Nisbet's identification of his view with Bonald's theory of language. This required that reason should be subordinate to the linguistic forms imposed through the divine origin of language, and continued through tradition to oppose the revolutionary effects of 'reason'.[30]

Third, rather than Durkheim ignoring the problem of meaning and signification, it is clearly included in this wide-ranging account of the orientation of consciousness to reality – in attention and signification. Indeed, here conscience, representation and thing (*chose*) are the theoretical axes of a dialectic of reality. In this logic of signification, conscience is that which refers. It includes all those functions by which a reality is disclosed; it is dominant in the representative order. And that which is referred to is the represented; 'thing' (*chose*) covers all that representations refer to and belongs to the external order of the represented (Renouvier 1875c: 1.87). (The association of 'thing' and the represented (*représenté*) for Durkheim is clear: 'it is only on things that we have seen it represented' (Durkheim 1912a: 162/114).) In terms of a later discourse, they are the signifier and the signified respectively. (Signs and things are associated for Durkheim (1897a: 356/315).[31])

The advantage of this theory of signification, attached to a general theory of representation, is that it shows how a shared system of representations has its own referential logic; a general system of communications is central to cultural logic. The relationship between representative and represented allows the conception of cultural artefacts as forms of signification and repositories of value relative to collective consciousness. The representative element of the conscience collective (1893b: 144/120) is the means whereby it prescribes form to social reality. Through the general nature of representation, meaning and signification become diffuse through the system, as well as being an acts of orientation of conscience. In this sense the 'positivist' Durkheim, rather than being blissfully unaware of these problems, goes beyond to the problems of individual perception to a general theory of meaning and signification that is central to the understanding of society as a communicative system.

## The concept of action

Action is understood as a 'motivating or a practical function (*fonction motrice*)' for Durkheim (1899aii: 157/90). And we have seen that the passions 'are the motor forces of conduct' for him (1925a: 80/94).[32] Collective passions and what stimulate them are fundamental to his account of action and moments of effervescence (1893b: 75/62).[33] The logic of passion for Renouvier concerns the realization of ends: from an initial state we move through a tendency to passion, which is the synthesis of 'state' and 'tendency'.[34] It is thus the psychological version of finality, for action is the pursuit of ends and covers the logic of desire, aversion, aesthetic feelings and interest. The ideal functions as the supreme end of conduct for Durkheim, and is understood through the logic of passion.

There are different types of passion for Renouvier: possessive (*possédantes*), which covers sympathy, friendship, love and hate; there are passions which lead to development (*passions développantes*), seen in moments of 'enthusiasm' when conscience rises above itself. When desire is identified with will, then we get 'effort', which is a real principle of development, for it gives a power of action. So for Durkheim effort is central to change when it is concentrated and organized. 'A group effort is required to attack the ills of society' (1925a: 71/84). Effort is central to moral action for Durkheim (ibid. 84/99).

Habit is central to Durkheim's account of social action. Habits are 'forces on the interior of the individual . . . which goes from the inside towards the outside' (ibid. 24/28).[35] For Renouvier, habit is understood through the logic of passion; it is formed through repetition, and in this way becomes 'second nature'. Habit is 'the constant manner of being or becoming' (Renouvier 1875d: 3.289). The influence of Ravaisson was decisive: 'The universal law, the fundamental character of being, is to persist in its manner of being' (Ravaisson 1838: 2). And repeated actions become 'obscure' because they enter the sphere of the unconscious, and thereby the sphere of mechanism (Renouvier 1875d: 1.326). Mechanism is 'the power of habit to mechanically reproduce a series which anterior reflection has established' (ibid. 3.295).

Not all habits are passive and driven by the law of inertia; reflection can act contrary to habit through the acknowledgement of alternatives. So the function of reason for Durkheim is to oppose 'the blind passions' (Durkheim 1925a: 80/94). This turns the passive into the active. (Durkheim: 'That passivity becomes ... activity by the active part we take in willing it deliberately' (ibid. 100/118).[36]) Since the habitual is central to the structural for Durkheim, it is on this pivot that certain questions of transformation turn. 'When things continue in the same way, habit is sufficient for conduct; but when circumstances change ... habit must not remain the sovereign mistress. Only reflection allows the discovery of new practices' (Durkheim 1950a: 123/90). For Renouvier, 'The definition of habit implies the possibility of its change. With conscience and will the power to contract or to change habits grows' (1875d: 3.290). With the intervention of will, a new series of actions could be initiated to form new habits. Virtue would then be the rational, habitual pursuit of the good (ibid.).

## Freedom, action and causality: the question of force

I have argued against a scientistic and mechanistic interpretation of Durkheim's conception of force. This is incompatible with both its internal origin and as having a reflexive foundation in conscience (Durkheim 1913b: 2.51). 'The idea of force, such as is implied in the causal relation, presents a double character. In the first place it can only come from our internal experience: the only forces which we can directly reach are necessarily moral forces' (1912a: 521/369). The spiritualist influence on Renouvier is clear: 'The idea of force is mental in its origin and in its essence' (1878b: 1.86).

This scientistic interpretation makes Durkheim's thought riven with contradiction: how is the passage to morality effected? It appears to deny the possibility of consciousness and action as significant factors in social reality. Force, on the contrary, as the pivot of action and of practical reason, allows the passage to a science of morality. It is central to the constitution and modality of social experience. 'A representation is not ... a shadow projected on us by things; rather it is a force which raises up around it a whirlwind of organic and psychic phenomena' (1893b: 64/53).

But it is through the connection of 'active force' with 'productive power' and both with 'efficacity' (in the causal relation (1912a: 519/367)), that we can understand an aspect of Durkheim's thought which is otherwise inexplicable. That is how he can hold to both 'necessary causes' (1893b: 257/215) and 'freedom of mind' (ibid. xlii/xxix) at the same time and in the same book, one that is usually characterized as a work of positivism and determinism! Force is power, the power of agency: the power of action to realize a project shows that we can do something; it shows the reality of freedom at the same time as the power of agency.

But power in successful action also shows what is central to the meaning of cause: that something has been brought about by my action. In this I experience precisely what the intelligibility of the causal relation requires: direct knowledge of the relation between cause and effect. Thus, this power also founds causality. Knowledge of the connection between cause and effect and that of the power of agency are thus jointly founded. It follows that causality *per se* does not require the kind of determinism that denies the interest of action.

We have seen that freedom for Durkheim consists in 'the eminently personal power which is the human will' (1912a: 521/368), in initiative of action (1925a: 100/118), and in the relative indetermination of reflective conscience (1898b: 15/3). The power to do something and the reality of reflection and choice shown in deliberation regarding action require possibilities on which we can act. For Renouvier, the real debate about freedom centres on the 'ambiguity of certain futures' (1898b: 4.427). The significance of the critique of the continuum is clear here. If the series of events in reality were conceived of as unfolding along a smooth continuum, interconnected by a causal series, such that, as Renouvier argued, everything is an effect and nothing ever begins, then the intervention of action would be impossible.

The definition of law is crucial here: these are determinate and complex structures of events and orders in the world. This follows from the compositional nature of 'order' and law. But, when taken together with number, then possibilities can be found within complex events. It is through these that force as agency realizes itself. 'We must go higher up the chain of causes and effects to where we can find a point where action of the human being can effectively insert itself' (Durkheim 1895a: 91/ 120).[37] As we have seen, he argues that freedom does not require 'the negation of determinate law', since 'human wills' are connected to external movements (1893b: xxxvii/xxv). But action requires certain constant features of the world – 'laws' – which are the basis of my calculations and enable my decision to be realized. Freedom for Renouvier does not contradict law, but requires it; this is the significance of the reconciliation of contingency and law.

But there is another sense of freedom for Durkheim. I have asked how he can maintain that we rise 'above things' (ibid. 381/321). I suggest that 'necessary causes' relates to the sphere of mechanism which is the physical for the spiritualists, and that as we rise above this, we gain consciousness and freedom (ibid. 338/284). It also relates to unconscious habitual actions which can only be overcome by rational reflection and awareness of alternatives. Durkheim talks of a 'voluntary attention' which 'presupposes effort', and 'to be attentive we must suspend the spontaneous course of our representations' (1914a: 332/163). Freedom for Renouvier is a power to act belonging to representation (Milhaud 1927: 86). The self-determining character of representations (*automotivité représentative*) (Renouvier 1859: 482) is a representative power which is only clear when we call up or banish certain representations in the act of thought (Renouvier 1875d: 1.310–11). So Durkheim holds to the 'free functioning of our psychic life' (Durkheim 1893b: 65/53) whilst holding that all is representation.

But force as effort and power, especially through reflection, transforms the previous functions of conscience and particularly of habit. Together with becoming, they make a difference to what is meant by order and function (Renouvier 1875d: 1.309–10). It allows the development of new orders: 'The order of the world is only an order in process of formation' (Renouvier 1859: 482).

This analysis is important for understanding that mysterious conscience collective – the basis of accusations of Durkheim's mysticism and inordinate collectivism. It cannot be understood without a conception of freedom or of conscience.

## The question of the conscience collective

Durkheim holds that the conscience collective is part of 'collective psychology', and he identifies it with 'collective thinking' (Durkheim 1897e: 251/171). Certainly he was not the originator of the concept; it was a 'well worn' concept (1893b: 47/39); it was used by Espinas and by Schaeffle.[38] It was the logical conclusion of the historical and psychological movements of the 'last fifty years', said Durkheim (1897e: 250/171). I suggest, first, that it doesn't disappear from his thought: it is present when he talks of collective thought and syntheses of consciences (1912a: 635/637). And, second, it is not replaced *per se* by collective representations – indeed, he argues that the latter stem from it (1897e: 250/171). This is consistent with the logical point that 'conscience' is necessary for representation to be possible (Durkheim 1898b: 37/23).

The concept of the conscience collective has been variously associated with Rousseau's conception of the 'general will', Comtean consensus (Parsons 1974: li), the idea of a group mind, Hegel's conception of *Geist* (Gurvitch 1938) and the 'soul of the people' as used by Latzarus and

Savigny (Filloux 1977: 236). However, these ignore certain crucial factors which will emerge below. To begin with, however, I suggest that the issue of certainty, neglected by both Comte and Durkheim's commentators, is central to it. Here Durkheim acknowledges the influence of Renouvier (Durkheim 1955a: 201).[39] And among the elements of Renouvier's certainty 'there is a sort of *conscience collective*' (Milhaud 1927: 102).[40]

The problem of certainty is entailed by the freedom of mind: if there is an element of freedom in knowledge, then how can I be sure of what I know? For Renouvier, history and philosophy show such variability in claims to truth that we must finally admit that these are all really forms of belief: when I say I know x to be true, what I should say is that I believe x to be true. Belief entails a crucial, fundamental element of will for Renouvier;[41] he argues that belief and its collective nature – the *croyances communes* – are central to history (Renouvier 1864a: 2).[42] This shows that all forms of conceptualization, which are fundamental to social worlds, are supported by belief.

Nevertheless, this freedom to believe is hard to bear, Renouvier claims (1859: 543). Even the strongest find solitude difficult: all feel unhappy until they have communicated with others. A 'communion of hearts' is necessary such that a society is formed of all those 'who draw at the same water'. Thus 'a common voice calls them to share (*une pensée commune*)' (ibid. 544–5). In this way, Renouvier argues, societies, philosophies and religions are founded: they rule only in passing, but they establish a tradition, and thereby a 'shelter' for consciences (ibid.). 'The accord of ideas, the communication of hearts, the unity of practices, realises certainty in a visible manner' (1875d 3.83).

It is a great benefit to 'share a *thinking with* humanity' (ibid.). To do so requires effecting an agreement that must not appear temporary or passing: it should appear real, effective and affective. As a 'common voice' it establishes a reality, and is found in all systems of religion, philosophy and theories of reality. It is a kind of epistemological contract which answers the question, 'How can I be sure of what I know?' It answers the question of certainty, for it gives motives for belief, and founds cultural and religious activity, since it is attached to will and conscience. But further, it is a kind of contract which is a synthesis of authority and liberty. It is 'composed' of customs and traditions, and formulates itself into conventions and laws. Moreover, so as to have a sanction and constitute an authority, 'it abrogates power to itself' (ibid. 3.323).

As such, it forms and re-forms within society and history; 'it constitutes itself very slowly and modifies itself similarly' (Durkheim 1893b: 276/233). It is thinking about what counts as real and valuable: it operates for Durkheim at the 'highs' and 'lows' of culture and society. This is why philosophy is like the *'conscience collective'* of science (ibid. 355/301). Although Durkheim has been accused of positing a unitary *conscience collective* (Lukes and Scull 1984: 24), in fact, for him, there are 'several *consciences collectives* in us', since we are members of more than one group (Durkheim 1893b: 74n./67n.).

How can we understand the use of *'conscience'* here? The relationship between thought and reality is central to the *conscience collective*. Questions of reality involve conscience, for this is the concept under which reality is possible and is constituted, for it brings subject and object together. 'Conscience is an act inherent to all thought to establish an object for a subject' (Hamelin 1907: 271). Knowledge is itself a sort of conscience; thought is defined by conscience (ibid. 267).

As we have seen, Durkheim invokes the laws of conscience as central to the meaning of the *conscience collective* (1888a: 86/50).[43] On the basis of the foregoing analysis, I suggest that this means the *conscience collective* is a type of thinking supported by belief, which identifies and constitutes relationships within a determinate portion of reality; it symbolizes and postulates a realm of significations; it is a form of memory and imagination, is changeful and dynamic and postulates ends of action and it can also be unconscious (1908a(3): 1.209). Under the law of habit, it sinks to the 'obscure' levels of conscience, where, as an unconscious representation, it is a potent source of action and belief.

Crucial to its functioning is its representative component (1893b: 144/120). This collective belief system and definition of reality are active in representing, and order significations: they constitute a reality in the represented side of representation. In so doing, they govern the syntheses of relations and representations; but to synthesize representations and relations is to make a world, and this is the function of conscience. To make a shared reality, a conscience must be synthesized: thus the *conscience collective* is a conscience itself (1908a(3): 1.209). This requires the theory of the communication of consciences. 'The communion of a plurality of consciences is a conscience itself', and this is generated through a 'psychic operation' (1914a: 328/160).

The connection of the *conscience collective* with the communication of consciences, which all of social life presupposes (Durkheim 1913b: 2.57), in common with the laws of conscience, has been neglected in its interpretation. We have seen that communication is possible only through the signifying and symbolic functions of each conscience. The general nature of representation and psychic communication through these functions entails that the *conscience collective* 'is the psychic type of society, a type which has its own properties, conditions of existence and mode of development' (1893b: 46/39). Both the *conscience collective* and the communication of consciences lie at the heart of Durkheim's whole theory of solidarity and being: solidarity is an expression of social need and mutual dependence, but both communication and solidarity are possible through conscience – for relation is the first law of conscience.

Conscience *per se* indicates the set of functions by which any conscious experience is made possible; this attaches to the logic of representation, and does not itself indicate the individual. Only the addition of '*particulière/individuelle*' does that – by indicating the specifically individuated subject of experience, within a general system of representations. We have seen that representation requires the functions of conscience; shared representations – generated from association – require these functions as well. This is a logical and psychological point, and it is neglect of this that has led to accusations of a group mind.

But, further, the *conscience collective* cannot be understood without Renouvier's theory of the replication of the functions of conscience. All cognitive approach to reality presupposes conscience; reflection, for Renouvier, is the 'conscience' of conscience (Renouvier 1859: 218). 'Authority rests on conscience in general' (1875d: 3.323). So this collective epistemic authority which establishes certainty rests on 'conscience in general'. Authority is formed in this way, and the foundation required for 'the approbation of others' is the 'conscience of others more or less multiplied and generalised in the present and in the past' (ibid. 3.323).

Long-standing critiques of the *conscience collective* were initiated by Gurvitch (1938), who argued that the *conscience collective* is transcendent, Hegelian, absolutist and atemporal. The last accusation (which continues (Lukes 1973: 6)), specifically neglects the logic of becoming which applies to this shared thinking, as to all representation; it is not static. Through the above analysis, I have suggested that this infamous concept is precisely what Gurvitch suggested it should be: immanent, perspectival and plural.

Gurvitch ignored Durkheim's own strictures on the subject – his rejection of any 'unrepresentable absolute' and his insistence 'that conscience, individual or social, is not for us substantial, but only a collection, more or less systematised, of phenomena *sui generis*' (1895a: xi/34). Durkheim insists that although 'it is something other than the "*consciences particulières*", it is realised only through them' (ibid. 103/145). Hamelin confirms this.[44] Its support is that of associated consciences and the specific social and historical structures according to which they are associated (Davy, in Durkheim 1950a: 12/xlvi). The *communio rationis* between individual consciences precludes the promotion of the collective into a universal (Turlot 1976: 350). This inevitably focuses attention on the particular conscience as of primary theoretical significance. Between this and collective thinking there is a crucial tension: between freedom and authority; between the personal and the individuated, on the one hand, and the collective aspects of our experience on the other. Such tensions enter into the meaning of 'constraint'.

The accusations of hypostatization – which Durkheim specifically denies (Durkheim 1895a: 103n./145) – can be countered by the neglected logic of pluralism: the *conscience collective* presupposes the fusion 'of a plurality of individual consciences' (1914a: 328/335). As such, it is a plural totality at the mental level, established through the communication of consciences. The *conscience collective* indicates the collective thinking which develops forms of meaning holism, shown in 'ways of seeing', and thus a conception of shared reality which enters into all social and cultural activity, and is reinforced by being acted on. As a complex form of thinking associated with meaning, significance and constitution of reality, it can be 'diffuse' in society (1950a: 86/50).

In these ways Renouvier showed Durkheim how a human and collective world is available to a science. His rationalism underwrites the vision of the human being as '*l'être dans le groupe*' (Davy 1973: 25). To demonstrate Renouvier's profound influence on Durkheim is to show that Durkheim acknowledged a free critical science, based on a critique of positivism; questions of meaning, signification and communication and their collective nature within structured social reality; and the pluralist and changeful nature of this through becoming. With these philosophical and historical considerations, we must now turn to the works themselves, and see how they can help in their interpretation.

# 5

# Differentiation and the Problems of Modernity

Durkheim's *De la Division du travail social*, said to reflect his 'early positivism' and conservatism, is, on the contrary, inspired by socialism and articulated within the logic of reformed rationalism. It begins with the concept of a science of morality, which 'reconciles science and morality' (1893b: xli/xxviii), and ends with the practical conclusion of the necessity for making a morality. In between lie the substantial analyses of society – understood as forms of solidarity – accessed through different types of sanction. An autonomous science, sociology, was born out of the quest for a new route to morality: Durkheim, like Columbus, discovered a new kingdom whilst searching for new routes to old ones (Gurvitch 1938: 279).

Mechanical and organic solidarity are its central concepts; the demonstration of the distinct and autonomous reality of these forms of solidarity proves the discovery of the new continent – society. But behind the richness of sociological description are central philosophical arguments about the nature of human reality, the logic of change, and the role of action and critical thinking in history. These will be the focus of this chapter. They are not merely ancillary to his sociological task; they are central to the success of his argument, and it is the neglect of them which has contributed to false characterizations of this work.

An accurate translation of the title, 'The division of social labour', should have indicated the socialist provenance of the work: *travail* can mean either work or labour. Indeed, it was as a result of nineteenth-century French socialism that work was conceived of as a social function. For Proudhon, work was conceived as central to social organization: as intelligent action on matter, it is the motor of social development and the creative force of society. It creatively associates materialism and idealism functionally, where things and ideas are in a dialectical process (Proudhon 1967: 67).

In the nineteenth century it was not just liberal economists but also socialists who studied the problem of political economy (Malon 1876b: i).

The dominance of Marxism has supported the belief in the incompatibility of socialism and the division of labour, but for the original French socialists this was not so. Even the revolutionary Blanqui was concerned with the progress of the division of labour; and for Proudhon the specialization of functions became integrative of collective existence – it is central to the solidarity of the collective force (Proudhon 1967: 99). For Malon, political economy was important for social science; together with socialism, it can solve the 'social question' (Malon 1876a: ii). The division of labour should have been studied not simply in terms of wealth creation, but by the influence it could have on civilization through its relations with morality and social justice (1876b: 130). Durkheim's optimism about the course of modernism and what could be achieved within it contrasts with the dark vision of Marx, Weber and Tönnies. It reflects a socialist optimism about social becoming – about how society can be developed.

So indigenous French socialism developed the theme of work as a function of social relatedness and as central to solidarity. Jaurès saw Durkheim's book as supporting the concept of socialist organization in a decentralized society which calls 'upon the autonomy and spontaneity of groups and individuals – when society in its entirety enters into the sphere of action and of power'. Unity is established through the producers and syndicates which form corporations (Jaurès 1896b: 1.347). Indeed, Jaurès cited this work of 'his friend' as a work of socialism – important for university students – and as a support for his own ideas (1893: 1.140). Its famous second preface, argued to be evidence of Durkheim's proto-fascism, is, on the contrary, evidence of his socialist interest in organization.

## Modernity and its development

The development of modern civilization, its nature and causes, is the broad problematic of Durkheim's first book. Modernity is characterized by specialization and differentiation of function, autonomy of markets and, ideationally, by individualism, free thought and secularization. Its appearance is explained by transformation from the old world characterized by undifferentiated social forms, with the economy under the control of the domestic and social unit, and with the dominance of religion within its unified thought patterns. Although Durkheim broadly agreed with Tönnies's classification of two great types of society, he does not conclude that society becomes the 'mechanical aggregate' of *Gesellschaft* as *Gemeinschaft* is left behind; a collective life is possible within the later era of society. His argument also confounds that of Marx: socialism is possible within social and economic terms that Marx could not envisage; solidarity can be compatible with economic differentiation.

Solidarity and the *conscience collective* are the concepts used to provide the explanation of this great transformation. The old world, related through mechanical solidarity wherein law is defined through repressive sanctions, is characterized by the dominance of the *conscience commune/ collective* over the individual conscience; the intensity and determination of its states are such that no room is left for individual divergence (Durkheim 1893b: 124/105). Inversely, with organic solidarity, law is characterized by restitutive sanctions, and by greater indetermination of rules of conduct as individual differences and reflection grow with the retreat of the unified *conscience collective*. Solidarity expresses relations (ibid. 87/74). In mechanical solidarity, the 'links which attach us to society and which derive from the communality of beliefs and feelings are much less numerous than those which result from the division of labour' (ibid. 119/101). It is through the mutual dependence entailed by specialization that we are tied together in organic solidarity (ibid.); it is in this sense that differentiation can be integrative of social existence.

So it is through the examination of the relation between these two types of social relatedness, the disappearance of the one and the development of the other, that Durkheim addresses the main question – the division of labour. If, as Adam Smith and John Stuart Mill claim, this is 'the superior law of society' (ibid. 2/1), what is its function? Durkheim's famous answer is that this is to create solidarity (ibid. 19/17).

## Solidarity and differentiation

Durkheim's central argument is that solidarity is not only possible, but that it can be generated through economic differentiation. Much depends on the nature of solidarity: only if this is compatible with differentiation will his argument hold. This in turn requires a view of the nature of human and collective reality in which solidarity is a real and effective force. Social reality is associational and relational; his functionalist explanations include the 'psychic' and, with it, communication between consciences. These have been underestimated in evaluating the success of his argument. So I will concentrate on the nature of social reality: the logic of solidarity and of organic solidarity, the *conscience collective*; and the theory of change. But first we must look at how he confronts and confound the arguments of Comte and Spencer.

### The debate with Spencer and Comte

To establish his argument that the division of labour becomes the principal source of social solidarity, it is clear that Durkheim needs not only to mediate between the conclusions of Comte and Spencer, but further to distance himself from them theoretically. He thus requires, and in fact uses, a logic of reality and of change which is distinct from Comte's positivism and Spencer's evolutionism. This logic is that of Renouvier's scientific rationalism. Although Comte had showed that occupational specialization was central to a modern society, he had argued that a strong state is required to offset its dispersive effects. Durkheim opposed this latter conclusion – just as he opposed the vision of society rooted in political economy. To argue for the reality of solidarity as integrative of social life means opposing the political economist view of society as the free play of self-interest. That is, he needs to show that the solidarity which is compatible with differentiation is real and not merely contractual. So, against Spencer, he argues for the reality of society as associational and claims that this precedes, and is the basis of, any contract.

The logic of relation helps him in these arguments. This, together with number, underwrites the concept of society as a relational totality, which includes differentiation and plurality. So, against Comte, he argues that the relational nature of the whole can accommodate the differences on which organic solidarity is built. And against Spencer, he can show that interdependence is possible within the differentiation of the division of labour and the individualism of its social coefficient. Both mechanical and organic solidarity are relational totalities. He further qualifies them by the logic of quality: difference, kind and species (*espèce*). Whilst mechanical solidarity is built on resemblances, organic solidarity is built on difference (Durkheim 1893b: 100/85).

Although Durkheim acknowledges the importance of Comte's idea that the division of labour can be a source of solidarity, he argues that Comte did not recognize the nature of the new kind of solidarity that was developing in the modern world; this replaces that built on resemblances. Secondly, Durkheim insists that the development of this solidarity built on differences is not morbid (ibid. 356/301). Comtean logic has no theory of differentiation: solidarity is threatened by differentiation. Further, it has no account of action, or of this as the pursuit of differentiated ends; yet, as we will see, both are crucial to Durkheim's argument regarding action in a differentiated economy.

Indeed, Durkheim rejects the ideal of social and intellectual uniformity of the Comtean vision (ibid. 352/298). To express the spirit of the whole, a strong unified state is not required; what makes for the unity of society is 'a spontaneous "consensus" of the parts'.[1] Here an 'internal solidarity' is indispensable to 'the regulatory action of the superior centres' of society, and this must be 'continuously' represented so that each person acknowledges their dependence on the whole (ibid. 351–2/297). The Comtean state is incompatible with the democratic nature of modern societies.

These must rely on internal forms of integration, which focus on consciousness and autonomy of action within the whole (ibid. 399/335). He uses the ideas of representation, difference and the habitual to oppose Comtean conclusions.

But whilst the Comtean account preserves interdependence at the price of independence, Spencer's account preserves independence at the price of interdependence: he fails to show how 'autonomous individualities' move from perfect independence to mutual dependence (ibid. 263/220). Durkheim uses the theory of conscience and its central function of relatedness to demonstrate the real interdependence of consciences and to show that they are not merely temporarily connected through passing self-interest. The reality of human interest over economic self-interest is crucial to his rejection of political economy: the logic of conscience and the communion of consciences is central to the success of his argument against Spencer, for whom 'consciences are only superficially in contact; they neither penetrate each other nor are closely attached one to another' (ibid. 181/152).

So he rejects Spencer's thesis of contractual solidarity – that absolutely free exchange can establish a society. Solidarity cannot be based on the spontaneous accord of individual interests, for when interest alone reigns, nothing restrains egoism. Similarly, he rejects Spencer's theory of altruism as merely the 'ornament' of society; rather, co-operation is 'intrinsically moral' (ibid. 208/174). Society as a reciprocity of rights and duties brings with it acknowledgement that the value of the individual is not merely economic. The whole is 'composed' of individuals, whose dependence on it demonstrates the reality of the whole (ibid. 207/173).

Equally, he uses the rejection of a theory of progress, infinitism and of eudaemonism to refute the classic account of political economy of the progress of division of labour through the increasing search for happiness. And the quintessential Durkheimian argument – that life is limitation – makes use of the concept of the finite to argue that if humanity is not to become stationary, only moderate development is possible. Health requires a harmonic development of all functions: understanding cannot be developed beyond a certain limit without damaging the practical functions of consciousness. This balancing of internal functions of conscience (ibid. 217/183) is central to intellectual and moral life, but is damaged by the intense 'progress' required by political economy.

## Solidarity and the nature of social reality

It is only through understanding the logic of solidarity that we can understand that, theoretically at least, Durkheim achieves what he sets out to do. To recognize this, we must acknowledge that social reality is relational and associational, and that his functionalism accommodates the psychic and the communicative, which are central features of social reality.

## The problem of materialism

But Durkheim's account of the development of the division of labour has, from the beginning, been widely accused of materialism (e.g. Thompson 1982: 67). This overlooks his explicit rejection of materialism – 'the reduction of psychic life to being no more than an efflorescence of physical life' (Durkheim 1893b: 340/286). Solidarity is 'immaterial', and an 'entirely moral phenomenon' (ibid. 28/24). There is thus no covert base–superstructure model of explanation here. Equally, the accusation of positivism reflects the neglect of the concept of representation and the psychic in this work, which is associated with 'representations and actions' (ibid. 46/39).

Representation and conscience are the crucial intermediaries between matter and human action: it is through these that things become significant for human action. Matter is significant in so far as it is represented; it is only as such that it can lead to action (1925a: 189/224). So it is only in so far as they are represented that things count in social life. 'Social facts are thus signs or vestiges of the activity and ideation of the collectivity' (Davy 1973: 45–6). It is through the concepts of crystallization and exteriority that we must understand the concept of the material for Durkheim. 'Social life, which is thus as though crystallised and fixed on material supports, thus finds itself by this exteriorised, and it is from the outside that it acts on us' (1897c: 354/314).

The concepts of volume and density are not material. The definition of society as associative and relational (1893b: 337/283) establishes the reality of both solidarity and moral density. Within a relational view of reality they indicate the slackening of relations through distance or their intensification through contact. They establish the real meaning of moral density as the vitality and frequency of relations. Dynamic density is 'the degree of concentration of the mass'. Moral dynamic density may be inseparable from material density (ibid. 238/201),[2] but the formation of towns, and the growth in rapidity of communication and the aggregation of population are aspects of relations and not *per se* material forces.

Neglect of the concept of number and its connection with representation leads to the confusion about materialism here. Number is central to social mass (ibid. 248/209). The volume of a society is the *number* of social units (1895a: 112/136), which in turn is central to the 'composition' of society (ibid. 12/57).[3] This is a crucial aspect of Durkheim's explanatory logic. 'At the same time as societies, individuals transform themselves through changes produced in the *number* of social units (*unités*) and their relations' (1893b: 336/283).[4] As I have shown, number, which is central to pluralist logic, is central to his account of the constitution of society: 'All of social life is derived from positive and durable connection (*rapport*) established between a plurality of individuals. It is thus as intense as the reactions exchanged between its composing units (*unités composantés*)' are themselves more frequent and more energetic' (ibid. 329/277).[5]

Durkheim has a distinct view of social consciousness here; the neglect of the concept of 'attention' as central to it facilitates accusations of materialism. We have seen that this is central to the orientation of conscience to reality – but it also forms part of Durkheim's account of density. 'Collective attention', which is central to the pressure of opinion and to collective thinking, is affected by the frequency and continuity of personal relations (ibid. 284/239). Correspondingly, when these become 'rare and feeble', this leads to a 'mutual indifference' which releases the individual from 'collective surveillance' and allows the extension of the sphere of individual action (ibid. 285/240).

Another neglected concept which is central to density is that of vacuum (*vide*). For Durkheim, density is increased by diminishing vacuums (ibid. 241/203).[6] Renouvier argued that any theory of movement or action presupposes a concept of relative vacuum (*vide relative*) to indicate those spaces where no action takes place (Renouvier 1864b: 19). Logically, then, to increase density – contact and exchanges – means suppressing these vacuums (*vides*).

### Solidarity, its nature and its logic

Both the solidarists and the socialists talked of solidarity and its moral nature (Hayward 1961). Whilst for the former solidarity reaches across social and economic inequality (Zeldin 1984: 295), the socialists considered it possible only under conditions of justice and equality. This latter consideration, together with his rigorous logical use of the term 'solidarity', differentiates Durkheim's view from the conception of social debt and mutualism of Bourgeois's solidarist movement: he is quite clear that equality is the condition for the development of organic solidarity.

Social solidarity is a moral phenomenon – an 'internal fact' which can only be grasped by an 'external fact' which symbolizes it (Durkheim 1893b: 28/24).[7] This can be understood through conscience and its primary function of relatedness – in the epistemological and practical sense. So it is no philosophical accident that Durkheim associates conscience and solidarity: 'It is the result of this chapter that a social solidarity exists which comes from a certain number of states of conscience being common to all the members of the same society' (ibid. 78/64). This internal form of relatedness is in communication with the sphere of outer relations: solidarity and relation are coextensive logically (ibid. 87/74). Through its logical connection to relation, solidarity is a dynamic force in history and society. As we will see, it develops through the contrary forces which characterize the nature of social becoming.

Further, solidarity is connected to law through the compositional nature of the whole. Renouvier uses the concept of solidarity to mean 'A constant relation, a mutual dependence between the parts of a whole' (Renouvier 1880b: 150).[8] He maintains that as a 'a general law' it is reconciled with freedom – it is a link (*lien*) resulting from 'the motives of free action' connected to 'repeated and habitual actions' which lead to 'authorised maxims, institutions and customs' in a given society (1864a: 33). In this way Renouvier shows that freedom and solidarity are reconciled in a manner that Comtean positivism could not establish. We have seen that freedom does not contradict determinate law, or therefore solidarity, for Durkheim (1893b: xxxvii/xxv).

So solidarity is accommodated within terms of a rationalist science and responds to the logic of relation. This, together with the law of quality, allows for difference in relations. 'Difference' is 'indispensable for association' for Durkheim (ibid. 389/327). Solidarity in the modern era must be logically compatible with diversity: 'The more solidarity there is between the members of society, the more they maintain diverse relations one with another' (ibid. 28/24). The logic of relation which accommodates solidarity based on differentiation, and the pluralism of Durkheim's organicism, differentiate Durkheim's logic from that of Comte, who admits no pluralist logic. Solidarity for him is an aspect of Great Being – which tolerates no freedom of action, no differentiation or diversity of relation.

But this pluralism is essential to explaining organic solidarity; an over-identification with Comtean organicism has obscured recognition of Durkheim's claim that solidarity is 'organic' precisely because the individuation of the parts is more marked (ibid. 101/85). Organic solidarity requires differentiation, and this in turn requires a sphere of action, within conscience, that is free from the *conscience commune* where 'special functions develop'. The activity of each 'is more personal' (ibid.); the individuality of all grows at the same time as the parts. In contradistinction to Comte, sociological explanation and its interest in totality do not have to deny individuality and differentiation (ibid. 262/219).

Thus solidarity is compatible with individualism in a way not possible or even desirable on the Comtean model: specialization of function at the psychic level augments individuality and personality (ibid. 399/335). In this type of representational world, pluralist logic shows that the force of association is not diminished in the face of differentiation. It gives reality to a heterogeneous whole, whose parts are differentiated. In turn, this is crucial to Durkheim's opposition of his view of individualism to that of political economy: individualism does not have to descend into egoism and self-interest.

The significance of Durkheim's association of conscience and solidarity must not be overlooked (ibid. 78/64). It is the neglect of the concept of conscience and its theoretical association with solidarity which has facilitated the analogy with Comtean organicism. Social solidarity is a relation: the primary function of conscience is to relate, and this is also central to its active practical functions. Further, it is no accident that Durkheim denies realism in this context: realism is seen by him as denying the reality of human agency (as force) and the power of initiation and of maintenance of relations, and thus of solidarity, which is the active force of conscience (ibid. 64/53). Solidarity is not just to be discovered – it is to be made and to be acted on.

The concept of the 'relations between' consciences in a social milieu marks the passage from philosophical to sociological rationalism. In this way the principle of association – central to socialism from the Saint-Simonians through Fourier, Louis Blanc and Malon – is translated into the interest of science. Association is the primary and fundamental feature of society for Durkheim: it precedes and is the necessary basis of all exchange (ibid. 261/218). It responds to the logic of relation: the social milieu, as the totality of relations which surround the individual and the forum for association, enters the logic of science. This rationalism not only underscores association; it allows the theoretical expression of work as the synthesizing force of society which was central to French socialism: work creates solidarity through specialization and synthesis (Proudhon 1967: 293).

### The concept of organic solidarity

Organic solidarity is the central and most original idea of Durkheim's first book. Is it a thinly disguised apology for capitalism and the *status quo*? A weak substitute for *communitas* in a capitalist economy? I have argued that much depends on the meaning of both 'organic' and 'solidarity', but most importantly on whether organic solidarity can be fully realized under contemporary conditions. Book III of 1893b shows that the conditions for its full realization and consolidation were not present.

Durkheim's problematic of organic solidarity has been conceived above all as that of achieving integration within differentiation (Smelser 1993). This interpretation, however, does not acknowledge the conditions on which the full realization of organic solidarity depends, just as it does not acknowledge the significance of solidarity as a moral phenomenon, or the science of morality as the logical framework for the book. This is to misrepresent Durkheim's project. If, as Durkheim insists, organic solidarity is only possible ultimately on conditions of justice and equality, then its achievement goes beyond mere integration within differentiation; the obsession with integration above all else is a concern of later functionalist theory.

This approach operates with function understood only as integration within a system. Clearly, interrelation and interdependence, through differentiated work relations, are essential for Durkheim; this is why the division of labour contributes to interdependence. But we have seen that here Durkheim uses function to mean that which corresponds to the *needs* of the organism; solidarity as a wholly 'moral phenomenon' is compromised by social malaise.

So, although he is quite clear that 'morality is the minimum indispensable, the strictly necessary, the daily bread without which societies cannot live' (Durkheim 1893b: 14/13), he is quite clear that it is lacking in contemporary society (ibid. 405/339): 'Our first duty is to make a morality for ourselves' (ibid. 406/340). Solidarity is perhaps 'the very source of morality' (ibid. 1st edn, 10), but 'all external inequality compromises organic solidarity' (ibid. 373/314). It is thus quite clear that since solidarity is 'one of the conditions of existence of society' (ibid. 394/332), contemporary society is lacking in a fundamental way. The remedy to this 'evil', Durkheim says, is not to resuscitate old traditions; the only solution to anomie is to introduce justice in social relations by reducing the 'external inequality' which is its source (ibid. 404/340).

## The conscience collective and mechanical and organic solidarity

His 'Division of social labour' is a test case for explanation by the *conscience collective*. Indeed, his famous definition of crime is built on this: crime is that which offends the *conscience collective*. The nature of the *conscience collective* is to affirm itself when it is contradicted; punishment signifies collective sentiments, which are communicated by a 'communion of minds' (ibid. 77/63). The historical and social specificity of the *conscience collective* is central to his sociology: 'either the *conscience collective* floats in the void of a kind of unrepresentable absolute, or it attaches itself to the rest of the world through the intermediary of a substratum, on which it depends . . . what can this substratum be composed of if not the members of society as they are socially combined?' (1897e: 250/171).

The definition of this central concept is crucial to his argument. Parsons claims that Durkheim is 'seriously embarrassed as to how to connect the *conscience collective* with the differentiation resulting from the division of labour' (Parsons 1960: 121). Neither Hegel's conception of *Geist*, nor the conception of the soul of the people, the general will or Comtean consensus, shows how it can change with types of relatedness or how it is compatible with diversity and differentiation. My argument that it is subtle and complex thinking and believing about what is real and valuable is compatible with a *conscience collective* that becomes more abstract and more personal with differentiation. Further, it is compatible with Durkheim's claim there are several *consciences collectives* in a society, 'since we are members of several groups' (Durkheim 1893b: 74n./67n.).

The logic of Renouvier's concept of conscience as the set of functions by which a world is disclosed and which are attached to shared representations and relations is compatible with the relational and historical character of the *conscience collective*. It is also compatible with Durkheim's definition of it as 'the collection of beliefs and feelings which are averagely communal to the members of the same society [and which] forms a determinate system which has its own life' (ibid. 46/38).[9]

Conscience is central to the *conscience collective*: 'the conscience' of society is the result of syntheses between consciences (1900b: 128/16). Conscience is involved in the constitution of a human reality: as the synthesis which brings together self and not-self, it is the condition of a human world. It demonstrates a form of moral relatedness which is distinct from self-interest; so the association of consciences theoretically underwrites the possibility of collective moral interest. The possibility of the dominance of human interest over self-interest is central to Durkheim's critique of political economy; so the *conscience collective* can be central to the affirmation of collective moral interest over the laws of the market. But conscience, and therefore the *conscience collective*, is also central to the synthesizing and affirming of new realities: its connection with synthesis and becoming is central to the development of new forms of collective thinking.

So whilst in mechanical solidarity the *conscience collective* is characterized by a uniformity of belief based on resemblances, in organic solidarity, by contrast, it requires the differentiation and an individual sphere of action. 'It is necessary that the *conscience collective* leave open a part of the individual conscience, for special functions to develop which it cannot regulate' (1893b: 101/85). The activity of each is more 'personal', the more specialized it is. So gradually a society built on uniformity of beliefs and practices is replaced by one based on a system of differentiated parts which complement each other.

Initially Durkheim argues that this presupposes the disappearance of the *conscience collective*. However, it is clear that it doesn't disappear so much as change its nature through increasing differentiation; it becomes progressively undetermined (ibid. 267/226). The development of general ideas is the result of this in the ideational sphere (ibid. 275/232), and as it becomes more rational and less imperative, the *conscience collective* allows the free development of reflection and the development of the concept of individual truth (ibid. 276/232). Changes in the milieu bring about a transformation in the *conscience collective*, since, as a collective voice about the real, this complex form of thinking becomes identified with individualism and autonomy: 'The *conscience collective* is confining itself more and more to the cult of the individual' (ibid. 403/338).

So what begins as an account in which the *conscience collective* becomes 'progressively undetermined' and therefore weaker (ibid. 267/226) turns into one with a positive role for a new type of *conscience collective*, which is central to organic solidarity and which affirms the values of individuality, autonomy and difference. Its collective origin is much less obvious, for its voice is more diffuse and differentiated. It becomes more abstract – seen in the transcendence of the idea of God and the more rational character of civilization – in law and morality. But it still performs its unique function of affirming collective values and ideals. Indeed, Renouvier argued that his collective agreement becomes more reflective and voluntary as the autonomy of the person increases; and he held that this gave rise to revolutions in science and society (Renouvier 1875d: 3.324).

## The theory of change

Parsons initiated the fallacious, but widely held, belief that Durkheim has no theory of change. Durkheim's logic of change is distinct from a Comtean account of change (Durkheim 1895a: 98/125). Further, although there are evolutionary developments for societies, his argument is not that of evolutionism (ibid.). Although he admits that the 'struggle for life' is a cause of the division of labour (1893b: 253/212), Durkheim opposes Spencer's account of social evolution. He sees it as an aspect of 'cosmic evolution' and rejects its philosophical generality (1915a 1:112–13/379).

How can Durkheim use a Darwinian concept and oppose Darwinian conclusions? At least one answer is Renouvier's influence; he opposed Darwinism theoretically and politically, but admitted 'the struggle for life' as 'the great external cause' (Renouvier 1864b: 205). Although Durkheim saw evolutionism as a 'fruitful idea', it is not a science; it is a hypothesis which has neither a factual basis nor axiomatic foundation (1887c: 1.336). Certainly in an early essay he uses Renouvier's logic to argue against evolutionism: it reduces heterogeneity to unity and invokes the continuum and the infinite (1882: 16–17).[10] So, in contradistinction to the logic of Spencer's account, for Durkheim, 'Social evolution . . . is not directed from outside to the inside, but from the inside to the outside' (1885c:

1.352). Like Renouvier (1877: 18), Durkheim argued that evolutionary thinking involves Pascal's fallacy of thinking of humanity as a man who lives for ever and learns continually (Durkheim 1888a: 90/52).

Durkheim explains the development of the division of labour, and hence the change from mechanical to organic solidarity, by transformations in the relations of the social milieu. The division of labour progresses in so far as there are, first, a sufficient number of individuals who are sufficiently in contact, and who act and react on each other: it is 'the *numerical* factor' which is of primary importance (1893b: 328/277). 'From the moment that a number of individuals, between whom social relationships are established, is more considerable, then they can only maintain themselves if they specialise more, work more' (ibid. 327/276). The intensity of relationship is proportional to the number of elements, and through this relations change.

The argument for change through volume and density is not a materialist argument (Giddens 1974: 79). For Lukes, the misunderstandings of Durkheim's theory of change revolve around the neglect of social explanation by differentiation (Lukes 1973: 168). The logic of relation and of becoming support this argument. Durkheim differentiates between time and change: change is not necessarily produced as we move through time. 'Time in itself produces nothing: it is simply necessary for latent energies to appear. There is no other variable factor except the number of individuals in relation' (Durkheim 1893b: 330/278). Renouvier distinguished between time and becoming: variability and change are possible only through becoming.

The logic of becoming underlines this conception of the variation of relations provoking change. Differentiation is central to transformation for Durkheim: 'If all remains homogeneous, all will there be immobile . . . it is differences which provoke changes' (1885c: 1.351). Logically, differentiation specifically provokes change, for it requires new ways of doing things; in other words, what once was can no longer be maintained. This process and judgement are central to the logic of becoming. But becoming also operates on the totality of relations of society: differentiation of the relations of work transform the relational totality which is society. What provokes this is the struggle for life.

This view of change is clear when Durkheim discusses 'this becoming (*devenir*) of representations' and argues that the new in history and society is 'in a great part because of the grouping and combination of the old' (1898aii: 100). Durkheim argued that change in the whole requires change in the parts (1885c: 1.352). Totality as the synthesis of unity and plurality exemplifies the logic of correlation: a change in the relations of the units (*unités*) which 'compose' society will affect the plurality, and foster transformation in the totality. And in turn, transformation at the level of the totality will feed back into the parts – that is, the units. There is thus a transformational dialectic of reality, fuelled by the logic of correlation, which is central to the dynamic of society. But further combinations are not static: synthesis and becoming together underlie the dynamic and changeful aspect of society. But since society is also 'psychic' – that is, representational and relational – this change in relations central to the dynamic process of social reality affects consciousness, for society is a cognitive communicative totality.

For Durkheim, this dynamic of society involves what Renouvier calls the 'power (*puissance*) of contraries' (Renouvier 1875d: 1.307). This is effective both internally and externally in social relations. The internal logic of contraries can be seen in punishment. 'The representation of a contrary state is among the first rank of causes' (Durkheim 1893b: 64/ 53).[11] It causes a passionate reaction 'to maintain the integrity of our conscience' (ibid. 67/55). Here the contrary is a principle of change, for it causes the reaction which provokes action; it produces energy and active forces (ibid. 66/54). Representation as a 'force' of organic and psychic phenomena (ibid. 64/53) is central to the transformation of the internal social milieu and thus of change.

Internally, then, the logic of contraries – shown in correlative mental activity – is central to forms of representation and the communication central to social life. Without acknowledgement of this logic, no adequate account of collective effervescence as a principle of change for Durkheim can be given. A shared process of thought and feeling is central to collective effervescence: from the fusion which thus takes place, the possibility of development arises – for from this comes a 'new idea which absorbs the precedent' (ibid. 67/55).

But externally, the growth in the volume and density of societies releases 'contrary forces', one centrifugal, the other centripetal (ibid. 100/ 84). Individualism is a contrary force to mechanical solidarity, for it opposes the undifferentiated nature of mechanical solidarity. The resolution of these contrary forces leads to the development of a new form of social relatedness which acknowledges the values of individualism – organic solidarity. Jaurès (1894) also considered the dynamic of contrary forces to be a positive factor, both for society and in socialist thinking – particularly in envisaging the reconciliation of capital and labour.

## The perils of modernity

There is a peculiarity in the way in which Durkheim's argument unfolds in *De la Division du travail social*. It begins with what has been: namely, mechanical solidarity. But rather than proceeding to what is actual, it discusses what turns out to be only partially fulfilled, whose full realization remains only as a possibility – organic solidarity. It is clear that it is not actual, for Durkheim acknowledges contemporary inequality and how this compromises solidarity. The description of the actual, which is the pathological, comes in book III. The peculiar nature of this manner of presentation has contributed to the belief that Durkheim's account of organic solidarity is his view of the actual contemporary condition of society, and thus that he denies conflict and supports capitalism.

So all is not well with the world that has been ushered in by these transformations. If 'normally' it will produce organic solidarity, it has deviated from its natural direction and produced instead pathology. (It is already clear that the term 'normality' does not mean the actual order of society.) Nevertheless, he argues that the study of these pathological forms will elucidate the conditions of existence of its normal forms (ibid. 343/291).

## The pathological forms of society

The first of the pathological forms is the anomic division of labour, which is characterized by the conflict of labour and capital (ibid. 344/292).[12] 'Anomie' seems generally to be taken to mean 'disorder' (Lacroix 1981: 111). Besnard rightly holds that anomie is a critical concept, which in subsequent sociology has been turned into a conservative one indicating failure of adaptation to the social order (Besnard 1987: 13). He significantly differentiates anomie not only from this meaning, but also from indicating 'the meaningless of fragmented work' and from 'egoism' (1993: 169). He insists that the pure meaning of anomie for Durkheim must be separated from all subsequent glosses and redefinitions. It indicates the lack of contiguity and interaction – that is, lack of contact – entailed by the absence of co-ordination and organization. That is, only consistent and continuous contact will produce the solid forms of relatedness and rules of conduct which thereby establish the necessary regulation for the predetermination of functional integration (Besnard 1987: 33).

So anomie in its most important sense means lack of solidarity, and consequently lack of moral and social relatedness. It indicates a condition where there is a lack of sufficiently prolonged contact for habit formation to occur: relations, being rare, do not repeat themselves often enough, thus solidarity does not occur. The rules of conduct which predetermine action are not formed, since normally 'habits as they gain force are transformed into rules of conduct' (Durkheim 1893b: 357/302).

But why is this intermittent contact, which prevents habit formation, not 'normal'? That is, why should the division of labour normally rely on constant contact? The answer is that relations established by specialization require interdependence, and thus constant contact, whereas those of mechanical solidarity do not. So anomie does not occur when there is 'sufficient' and 'prolonged' contact in relations (ibid. 360/304). But when there is no work of such consolidation, then 'social life cannot have continuity where the different layers (*couches*) of social units (*unités*) are at this point discontinuous' (ibid. 282/237). This situation is exceptional, because habits have not been constituted: a disturbance in habits and a disturbance in relations mutually imply each other. Normally, then, habits will develop solidarity, because habits lead to the establishment of permanent relations. 'By itself the division of labour will make functions more active and continuous' (ibid. 387/326). This is his answer to Comte's argument that a strong state is necessary to overcome the dispersive effects of the division of labour. For Durkheim, on the contrary, recognition of our continuous mutual dependence through representation will lead to a spontaneous 'consensus' (ibid. 352/298).

So I suggest that the concept of anomie, rather than indicating a failure to adapt, actually entails a critique of capitalism for its failure to contribute to the stability of social life, because it generates instability and inconstancy, and thus a lack of effective social relatedness. It disturbs what Besnard calls the conditions necessary for the good functioning of a modern society: the continued existence of a system of relationships between solidary elements, the regulation which predetermines the way they function, and the consciousness of solidarity through interdependence (Besnard 1987: 32). That is, it fails to help with the proper organization and co-ordination needed for society. So even though the concept of anomie plays a limited role in Durkheim's work, as Besnard argues (1993: 170), I suggest that it is part of a central and continuing theme of Durkheim's thought: how society can be a forum for the viability and stability of human life.

The second case of abnormality is the constraining division of labour.[13] Durkheim uses the word 'constraint' (*contrainte*) in two quite different senses in his works. One is positive, where the normal regulation of social rules constrains egoism or the 'infinity of desires' and is productive of the stability and personal power of a personality. In this use he echoes Renouvier's argument that the constitution of habits is one of the main aims of a social institution, and that these must have a 'constraining force' (Renouvier 1869a: 1.231). But there is another sense in which constraint is used by Renouvier: it indicates conflict in 'the state of war', which is the actual state of social relations for Renouvier. It indicates the state of injustice and inequality, where association does not generate rights and duties.

It is thus no accident that Durkheim identifies the war of classes as the primary characteristic of the constraining division of labour. The unjust domination of one class by another 'through the resources at their disposal', independent of their 'social services', 'falsifies the moral conditions of exchange' (Durkheim 1893b: 378/319). So, for Durkheim, constraint is all kinds of inequality in 'the external conditions of struggle' (ibid. 371/313). Here regulation is maintained only by force (370/312), and individuals are not spontaneously attached to their function by natural talent; there is thus no harmony between individual natures and social functions.

So the conditions of the constraining division of labour – that is, all forms of external inequality, injustice and hereditary wealth – make the normal condition of the social body impossible. They prevent the spontaneity which the division of labour requires (ibid. 374/315). Renouvier argues that habits cannot be contracted 'When the existence even of the subjects becomes impossible' (Renouvier 1875d: 1.292); that is, when the things concerned have gone beyond 'the normal constitution of the subject'. So with 'constraint' the conditions of existence of the social body are threatened. For Durkheim, constraint in this sense begins when regulation can only be maintained by force (Durkheim 1893b: 370/312). And 'real constraint' is where even struggle is impossible (ibid. 371/313). Under this condition the very viability of the social body is threatened. Both 'anomie' and 'constraint' are thus critical concepts.

### The ills of modernism and the possibility of change

What can be done about the ills of modernism, where organic solidarity has not been, or has been only partially, fulfilled because of 'external inequality' (ibid. 373/314)? For the division of labour to produce solidarity, work must be divided 'spontaneously', and this occurs only when social inequality 'exactly expresses natural inequality' (ibid. 370/313): 'perfect spontaneity' is a consequence only of 'absolute equality in the exterior conditions of struggle' (ibid. 371/313). The actual progress of the division of labour, for Durkheim, implies 'an ever growing inequality' which is the contrary of the public conscience that equality 'rightly must grow' (ibid. 372/314). The tension between public expectations and reality is fertile ground for change through contrary forces.

I have argued that the orthodox functionalist account of Durkheim's sociological explanation overlooks his view of morality as something to be developed, and that it operates with only one view of function, meaning integration within a system. How can function and relation express development? 'It is the functions of relation, that is the representative functions, which are essential factors of human development' (1897d: 240/134).[14] These have a relative autonomy of the represented, and can activate change in the possibilities which these reveal. But the dynamic of this is the ideal – which expresses the logic of finality – and is uniquely able to realize the means–end relation central to action.

Thus the dynamism of change can only be grasped effectively through the ideals which activate people, and this requires a clarification of what is unconscious in social life. Thus representation can be a positive force for change, by clarifying the ideals and representations which guide collective action. In this sense sociology can be a mirror for society. By grasping societies' ideals as they are and as they develop, the dismal course of modernism can be affected. Modern humanism shows how this can be effective: 'the task of modern societies is a work of justice' (1893b: 381/ 321).[15] Its ideal is 'to continue to put more equity into our social relations so as the ensure the free deployment of our socially useful forces' (ibid. 381/321). It shows that collective effort can be directed towards the possibilities that history reveals.

In a differentiated economy and society with values of individualism, the final development of organic solidarity will depend on the representations which guide action. Indeed, more strongly, it depends on the *affirmation* of a new *conscience collective*, a new belief system, which asserts the full moral significance of the individual and the solidarity which makes individualism possible. And this will bring forth appropriate institutions – for Durkheim, aspirations precede institutional formation: egalitarian aspirations are an 'anticipation of the normal state to come' (1893b: 381/321; 1925a: 87/102).

So there is an 'only if' in Durkheim's thinking about modernity: only if there is a transformation towards equality and justice, can economic differentiation finally and fully realize solidarity. This argument depends on a logic of social reality which responds to the demands of a new *conscience collective* and the capacity of action to implement them – in a new institutional framework which supports egalitarian aspirations. But to understand this, we must look at factors that are essential to the success of his argument, but which are left out of account in sociological assessments of this work: first, the role of critical reflection and representation as a practical force, and second, the theory of action in history and the freedom it requires.

### Critique, representation and the possibility of transformation

Just as the spectre of a conservative functionalism, together with a false holism, has been cast over this book, so sociological assessments treat it independently of the science of morality, which seems to be regarded as an embarrassing relic of nineteenth-century thought which is unnecessary to either the argument or the interpretation of the work. But this is to efface its dialectic of reality and its logical structure of critique and transformation. Specifically, it is to neglect the role of practical reason as it interpenetrates and guides theoretical reason in the description and critique of relations. But for Durkheim the science of morality concerns action and the conditions under which it takes place. 'It will help find the sense in which we should orientate our conduct, and determine the ideal towards which we are tending confusedly' (Durkheim 1893b: xxxix/xxvi).[16] It focuses on the logic of representation, conscience and force, and concerns the possibilities of action and therefore transformation within the limitations of society and history.

The critique of actual economic social relations in terms of justice and equality is a marked feature of book III: the objective condition for just exchange for Durkheim is 'equal external conditions' (ibid. 377/318). Justice was central to Renouvier's conception of a science of morality: the association of agents establishes a community and a moral solidarity which leads to the superior form of moral obligation – the basis of right and duties – which is justice. And reciprocity, equal exchange, was central to it (Renouvier 1872b: 1.11).

For Durkheim, changes in work relations lead to shifts in consciousness: these release the powers of reflective consciousness, which are themselves effective in change. Differentiation at the level of work relations entails a difference at the level of representation: the division of labour entailed by the struggle for existence through the increase in numbers leads to the development of new relations and representations. Thus relational causality entails representational change: in the shift from mechanical to organic solidarity, a huge shift in consciousness has occurred. 'At the same time as societies, individuals transform themselves as a consequence of the changes which are produced in the number of social units (*unités*) and their relations' (Durkheim 1893b: 336/283).

Under mechanical solidarity, religion, 'the eminent form of the *conscience collective*' had absorbed the representative and practical functions' (ibid. 270/228), but these are now gradually released from communal imperatival control and become factors in social transformation. 'As societies become vaster and above all more condensed, a new psychic life is developed . . . A multitude of things which were outside of consciences because they did not affect collective being, become *objects of representations*' (ibid. 339/285). Now individuals become a source of spontaneous activity: particular personalities 'constitute themselves and become conscious of themselves; individual diversities develop' (ibid.). 'This growth of psychic life does not weaken, but transforms society. For as it has no other substratum than those of individual consciences, society becomes freer, more supple and more complicated' (ibid.). The social milieu becomes more human, and therefore more subject to human demands.

The crucial role of representation here is overlooked through accusations of his early positivism and the claim that representation is a post-1895 concept. But Durkheim insists that reflection intervenes in the course of historical evolution: 'Instead of letting causes engender effects hazardously ... reflection intervenes to direct its course' (ibid. 331/278). It can awaken aspirations and show in what direction efforts must be turned; it must deal with 'obscure representations' (ibid.). Thus representation becomes a practical force for change (ibid. 64/53). This goes together with the necessity of enlightening an 'obscure conscience' which is resistant to change (ibid. 15/14).

Thus change requires transformation of consciousness; unlike Comte, Durkheim requires a theory of consciousness that allows for choice and discrimination of ends within a differentiated economy. In a society not ruled by tradition, it is necessary for agents to see differences and not just resemblances/similarities. This autonomy of mind is functional in the sense that it brings around adaptations which the social organism requires. 'The more the milieu is subject to change, the greater the role of intelligence in life becomes' (ibid. 256/214). Freedom of mind, which is always possible for Durkheim, is reinforced within social differentiation because possibilities are structurally realized: representative freedom is reinforced as representations are released from communal control; freedom of choice and the logical basis of critique are strengthened at the same time.

The motor of change is the ideal which is central to the dynamic of critical consciousness and of practical reason (ibid. 331/279). For Malon, an ideal is central to economic relations, and for Jaurès, the ideal and the material are brought into indissoluble contact in the milieu: economic facts slowly translate the ideal of humanity (Jaurès 1894: 25). The relationship between the ideal and the real is synthetic and creative of new realities; for Malon, socialism is the creation of new synthetic order in the world (Malon 1892: ix). For contemporary democratic socialism, to realize justice for humanity is to forge the ideal in the real within association: to 'realise in the facts the ideal of human fraternity' (Durkheim 1893b: 401/336).

### *History and the logic of action: determinism and the problem of freedom*

*De la Division du travail social*, as well as being seen as a work of positivism, is also seen as deterministic. His 'absolute determinism leaves man helpless in the face of history', and through 'a universal causality, liberty loses its rights and action its meaning' (Lacroix 1981: 102). For Alexander, Durkheim is pushed by his logic into an anti-voluntarism (Alexander 1982). But the issue of freedom and determinism and their reconciliation (Durkheim 1893b: xxxvii/xxv) are central to Durkheim's account of historical action and its possibilities. 'Not only does a mechanist theory of progress not deprive us of an ideal, it allows us to believe that we will never lack for one' (ibid. 336/282). For Jaurès, history unfolds according to a mechanical law, but realizes itself according to an ideal (Jaurès 1894: 25).

Durkheim's use of 'mechanical' has been interpreted as meaning 'independent of will' (Lukes 1973: 69). However, the ideal is connected to will and action for Durkheim: 'It is wrong to accuse a mechanistic theory of society of reducing man to being an inactive witness of his own history' (Durkheim 1893b: 331/279). Indeed, without acknowledging a theory of action and a degree of freedom, how is it possible to argue that man can 'rise above things' (ibid. 381/321)? This is a necessary feature of Durkheim's definition of liberty as 'the domination of external forces', and therefore of the fight against 'the amoral' and the 'absurd' nature of things (ibid.).

How is mechanism reconciled with the ideal and action, and with a social reality defined as irreducible and 'psychic'? The Spiritualist movement saw mechanism and the ideal as at different poles of reality: mechanism belongs to the material and the bodily, but as we rise up through stages of being, we encounter more reflection and will, which is the sphere of the ideal. For Ravaisson, the repetition of habitual action becomes mechanical and obscure and a tendency, and thus the law of inertia applies to it; the tendency to persist in its manner of being is the universal law of being (Ravaisson 1838: 13). The transformation of mechanism can only be effected through effort against the resistance of inertia. And for Renouvier, mechanism in terms of action means 'the power of habit to mechanically produce a series of actions' (Renouvier 1875d: 3.295).

How is free will reconciled with scientific mechanism? For Renouvier, a sum of forces becomes mechanical through composition, which in turn becomes 'a solidary mass'; combination leads to an energy which exists throughout the system (1864b: 104, 368). Freedom understood as that which 'initiates' is incompatible with mechanism only if limited to a closed system (1874b: 168). In an open system, movement can be introduced without contravening this principle of mechanism: a force which engenders a huge amount of energy in a mechanical system can be so small as not to affect mechanism; the least force can be sufficient to break an equilibrium and release energy. A psychic force can be a cause of transformation of mechanism, without giving up the principle of mechanism.[17]

For Durkheim, 'the greater intensity of the struggle implies new and painful efforts . . . Everything happens mechanically. A rupture of equilibrium in the social mass gives rise to conflicts which can only be resolved by a more developed division of labour' (Durkheim 1893b: 253/212). So if we consider the totality of social relations, past and present, as constituting a system which is mechanistic, and action as a 'psychic force' which realizes itself through possibilities, then action can initiate changes within the totality of those relations. Action requires 'effort', which is a sign of will.

Durkheim discusses 'reconciling scientific mechanism with the finalism which existence ... implies' (1895a: 96n./144). Finalism is that by which means and ends are understood and action is possible: but how is this possible within a mechanistic conception of society? 'Although we only ever pursue definite and limited ends, there is and always will be, between the extreme points which we reach and the aim which we are tending towards, an empty space (*espace vide*) open to our efforts' (1893b: 331/ 279).[18] For Renouvier, historicism denies the reality of action, for it denies the sphere of the possible. Possibilities are the sphere of freedom: the logical continuum, for Renouvier, is the denial of possibilities (Renouvier 1875c: 2.268). The positive sense of the vacuum (*le vide*) demonstrates the possibility of action. (This demonstrates the significance of Durkheim's association of freedom of action with an 'initiative' which I have shown in the previous chapter.) For Renouvier, the plenum (*le plein*), infinitism and a system of total determinism mutually imply each other and, together with forms of realism or ontologism, deny the possibility of initiative or movement. Likewise, Durkheim uses the idea of 'a space' which is 'open to attempts and deliberations' (Durkheim 1893b: 368/310) and which is identified with contingency (ibid. 367/310).[19]

Renouvier argues that the modality of propositions which relate to the future is a problem for all necessitarian logic. Necessity applies only to what is past or what is actual: no necessary proposition can hold of that which is logically yet to be. All affirmations relating to the future imply possibility and contingency, which is real and not simply a matter of ignorance (Renouvier 1875c: 2.121ff). Nowhere is this clearer than with human action, where the fact of reflection shows that real possibilities exist.

So not only is Durkheim not the kind of determinist he is presented as being, he actually has a clear argument for freedom in his first book. His rejection of an 'impersonal' and 'metaphysical' theory of freedom is not a rejection of freedom *per se*, but an argument for the type of freedom which serves the requirements of personality (Durkheim 1893b: 399/335). He argues that freedom as an effective force requires a degree of individualization: it develops through history and above all with the individualization that is engendered through the development of the division of labour. Freedom is thus the reversal of the natural order made possible through social relations; as we have seen, it consists in the subordination of 'natural to social forces', 'to deprive things of their fortuitous, absurd, amoral character' (ibid. 381/321). It is physical and economic forms of inequality which are the denial of freedom for Durkheim.

Durkheim is often presented, by contrast with Marx's account of the conflictual nature of modern society and Weber's vision of the dark cage of modernity, as 'wrong' about the nature of modern societies. Although he acknowledged the reality of conflict as long as inequality continues, he showed that, despite this, there are forms of solidarity that can develop within a differentiated economy. Modern education and health services demonstrate this, and the solidary relation people have with these is formed not despite, but because of, specialization. There is no evidence that differentiation of function is going to disappear from history; although optimistic about its development, Durkheim showed that this requires a coherent social framework in which collective moral interest is paramount. Marx did not envisage these possibilities, just as he never mentions justice – the search for which is the central dynamic of modern societies for Durkheim. And, as we shall see in the next and following chapters, Durkheim approaches the whole question of the constitution and nature of democratic societies – through their 'psychic' and representational nature – and thus the nature of change available to them, in a way that is unavailable to Marxism. In all these ways, Durkheim's analysis still has a living *actualité*.

# 6

# Individualism
# Socialism

The initial question of *De la Division du travail social*, the relation between individual personality and social solidarity (Durkheim 1893a: xliii/xxx), is a reformulation of its original problematic: the relation between individualism and socialism (Lacroix 1981: 52). The structuralist reading of Durkheim, together with the theocratic and positivist interpretation of him as a thinker concerned to preserve an order which is threatened, specifically by individualism, hinders an understanding of his theory of individualism and how this can be reconciled with solidarity. And whilst he is seen as opposing socialism through his rejection of Marxism, not only is his account of socialism obscured, but so also is his account of the compatibility of individualism with socialism.

## Durkheim: the self, individuality and individualism

Durkheim's account of individualism is articulated within the terms of the paradox of modern society: how can the individual, whilst becoming more autonomous, depend more on society (Durkheim 1893b: xliii/xxx)? The sociological understanding of Durkheim unwittingly conspires with the theocratic and positivist interpretation through its neglect of his theoretical foundation of individualism.

In nineteenth-century France individualism was condemned not only by Catholic conservatives, for whom it was identical with the revolution of 1789 and thus with social breakdown, but by socialists harking back to Saint-Simon (and later by Marxists) for whom individualism was equated with the isolation of self-interested individuals of *laissez-faire* economics. Left and right conspired to identify individualism with incipient social disorder (Lukes 1973: 196). However, not all socialists opposed individualism: for Proudhon, true individualism was the opposite of economic liberalism, which served to reintroduce the rapacity of nature.

urkheim, 'Not only is individualism not anarchy, it is from now
e only system of beliefs that can assure the moral unity of the
ntry' (Durkheim 1898c: 270/50). He condemned the negative individu-
lism of political economists and rejected 'the moral misery' of Spencer,
the utilitarians and the economists for its 'ideal without grandeur', of
'shabby commercialism which reduces society to being no more than a
vast apparatus of production and exchange', whereas 'it is too clear that
all communal life is impossible if there do not exist interests superior to
individual interests' (ibid. 262/44).

How can he support individualism without supporting egoism, which is
the contradiction of solidarity? How can he retain the interdependence
which is central both to sociological explanation and to the reality of
society, whilst eulogizing the human person (la personne humaine)? To
analyse these questions, we must first look at what Durkheim reputedly
does not have: a theory of individuation, individuality and the self.

A number of theoretical questions must be asked, and distinctions
made: first, if all is representation, how is the individual represented? and
by what theoretical signs do we identify the individual? These issues
presuppose other distinctions: the self and the person must be distinguished – they are not the same; nor is individuation the same as the self,
although it is closely tied to it. Secondly, how is this connected with moral
individualism? Although individuation and individualism are distinct
issues, they converge in the historical emergence of individualism. A
theory of the moral value of the person which is central to individualism
logically requires a theory of individuality and of individuation. For
Durkheim, 'There is not only a parallel development between rationalism
and individualism, the second reacts on the first and stimulates it' (1925a:
17/20). How does rationalism account for these issues?

## The person, the self and the definition of individuality

Durkheim does have an account of who and what the person is: it is an
unusual account, and shows just how much his theoretical discourse
opposes common sense, positivism and realism. The person is associated
with conscience in De la Division du travail social: 'There is in each of our
consciences . . . two consciences: the one which is common with our entire
group . . . the other which only represents . . . that which is personal and
distinct in us, that which makes us an individual' (1893b: 99/84). Individual
personality is not only known through 'personal conscience', it is constituted through it (ibid. 74/61). Durkheim is clear that 'personal conscience'
represents our individual personality. 'A person is not simply a self-
contained being (un être qui se contient), it (c'est) is also a system of ideas,
habits, tendencies – it is a conscience which has a content; and one is that

much more of a person the richer this content is ir
73). The neglect of the concept of conscience in Du
is thus particularly unfortunate here, and must ha
view that Durkheim has no account of the individua

The person is identified through the personal asp
'the sentiment of personality which is at the root
(1920a: 2.323/86). Durkheim espouses a theory of the
of the personality, because it is made of parts, but th
with its unity (1912a: 386n./272). It is in terms of the transformation of the
collective personality that the 'individual' develops: 'The collective personality . . . can only become individual when the individual disengaging itself,
becomes a personal and a distinct being' (1893b: 155/130). For Renouvier
individuality is possible through personality (Renouvier 1875c: 2.183).

But does Durkheim have an account of the self? Comte claimed that *le
moi* is a metaphysical fiction given to modern philosophy by the theolo-
gians, without there being any corresponding reality beyond a cerebral
synergy (*synergie cérébrale*) which is always relative and incomplete;[1] he
opposed phrenology to metaphysics and psychology. Personality is syno-
nymous with egoism for Comte, and must be dominated by sociability.
The self (*le moi*) is constituted by 'the conscious personality' for Durkheim; this is the reflective part. But the self is also accompanied by
unconscious structures: we are not aware, however, of 'the multitude of
ideas, tendencies, habits, which act on us'. Besides the reflective conscious
part are the 'anonymous confused representations which are the substructure of our mind (*l'esprit*)' (Durkheim 1950a: 114/80).

We have seen that Durkheim identifies 'autonomy' with being a person.
And this is acquired 'only to the degree that there is something uniquely
their own, and which individualises them'. Freedom is an important part
of this individualization, for the power of the agent to undertake ends and
motives which are the agent's own, underwrite 'the concrete empirical and
variable personality of individuals'. Thus 'it is necessary for even the
materials of conscience to have a personal character' (1893b: 399/335).
Important here is the concept of 'personal energy' (1887c: 1.329); will, as
we have seen, is a personal power.

This form of individuation is developed through the social and economic
differentiation of the division of labour, whereby the particular conscience
(*conscience particulière*) detaches itself from the community and its collective personality. Individuation of a personal being (*être personnel*) is
reflected in the unique 'mark' which is imprinted on all that we do, which
is not only a constant feature of us, but distinguishes us from others
(1925a: 40/46). Against Wundt, he argues that there is a real pleasure in
the pursuit of 'individual ends' (1887c: 1.329).

In *Les Formes élémentaires*, Durkheim gives the body the role of uation. This has been treated as evidence of attachment to Comte, thus in effect as a denial of individuation. However, this ignores the psychic – that is, representational and relational – nature of society. Totemic societies have little economic or social differentiation, and thus little individuation at the level of representations; in this context the body alone is logically the factor of individuation (1912a: 386/273).

## Kant, Renouvier and the concept of the self

But why and how does he account for self and individuation in this manner? The influence of both Kant and Renouvier is clear. Kant acknowledged the importance of the Cartesian conscious self as reflected in the *cogito*: the subject in this sense was the formal logical condition of experience. For him, the I as an absolute subject is a logical function which is attached to representation, but does not fall under a category. Renouvier agreed with Kant, and developed the association with representation; however, he denied that there is a transcendental ego separate from representation: the self (*le moi*) is not anterior to, and separate from, representation. He developed what Kant did not – that is, the connection of the self with representation: the person is understood under the law of personality. 'The person is a conscience' (Renouvier 1901: 254).

Renouvier's rejection of the *cogito* and the transcendental ego of classical rationalism is a central step towards viewing selves as constituted by, and enveloped within, the relations of social and historical experience and towards seeing them as formed and developed through different representational structures. In this, Renouvier anticipates the de-centring of the subject of post-modernist thought: he does not, however, infer the death of the subject. He indicates both the possibility of different forms of selves and of greater or lesser individuation: 'the greater the development of the person, the more individuality is marked' (1875c: 2.184). Against such a philosophical background, Durkheim can argue that neither the self nor the individuality of which it is capable are primitive facts from which society is derived; rather, self develops through society.

Durkheim argues for the compositional nature of the self: 'We know today that the self (*le moi*) is the result of a multitude of consciences without a self, that each of these elementary consciences is in its turn a product of vital units (*unités vitales*) without a self' (Durkheim 1897a: 361/320). This reflects Renouvier's arguments against unitary and absolutist definitions of self: the self is a complex whole, and 'this whole is the self (*moi*) [which] is a composition (*composé*) of phenomena . . . its elements . . . are representations . . . [which] are indicated by a common characteristic – conscience' (Renouvier 1875c: 1.16–17).

The human power to initiate, to determine events, is the real indication of individuation for Renouvier, and stands in contrast to habitual action, which is unreflective. It is with will, understood as 'force', that real individuation occurs, and all volition is an effort (1875d: 1.303).[2] For him freedom is the supreme principle of individuation – which he opposes to all monistic doctrines which deny autonomy and agency. Through will, the human being transcends nature, and in so doing becomes autonomous: the voluntary functions of conscience give them an energy (*énergie*), which is capable of modifying the habits of mind and action (ibid. 1.403).

### Rationalism and individualism

We can now see why rationalism and individualism mutually imply each other for Durkheim: rationalism is the 'intellectual expression of individualism' (Durkheim 1925a: 10/12). Representation is central to rationalism, and the person and individuality are understood through its forms. A fundamental aspect of individualism is freedom of thought. We have seen that Durkheim has an important conception of intellectual freedom. For Renouvier, attention and reflection are voluntary mental functions. Intellectual doubt is central to scientific thought; in turn, freedom is the principle of individuation and self-definition. For Durkheim, 'The history of the human mind is the history of the progress of free thought itself' (1897a: 430/375).

This identification of freedom of mind with individuality and with right enables Durkheim to distinguish his theory of individualism from eighteenth-century doctrines of natural right which imply that right is anterior to sociability. But is not freedom of mind equally anterior to sociability, and hence independent of sociological explanation and the social nature of right? Durkheim doesn't hold that freedom of mind is just an adventitious effect of modernism. But this freedom becomes socially real with economic differentiation, when real possibilities of action and therefore of choice, both of which in this form are unknown to undifferentiated societies, are established.

For Durkheim, unlike Comte, sociological explanation does not require the negation of individuality; rather, it implies that the two terms, individual and society, are inseparable (1906f: 1.57). The logical structure of representation allows him to reconcile the individual (the unit) with plurality in totality. In turn, greater differentiation at the level of relations in the division of labour entails greater differentiation of the person at the psychic – that is, representational – level (1893b: 140n./125). At the same time as it becomes more complex, it is more individuated: it is simultaneously interdependent and differentiated. Further, this operates at the level of the ideal: 'The personal ideal disengages itself from the whole social ideal, as the individual personality develops and becomes an autonomous source of action' (1912a: 605/425).

So the pluralism central to his organicism allows him, against Comte, to hold that individualism is real and available to science. It has been argued that for Durkheim solidarity is a danger for individualism (Isambert 1993: 113). If solidarity is defined on a model of Comtean or biological organicism, then this is indeed so. But plural holism – the heterogeneity within the interdependence of relations – in no way denies differentiation. And it allows Durkheim – against Marx – to hold that solidarity is compatible with pluralism, autonomy and individuation.

### Durkheim and individualism

Durkheim thus has a theoretical basis for his account of individualism as a central feature of modern society. Individualism is the system of beliefs which acknowledges the dignity and value of the human person (*la personne humaine*), which is a collective representation. Modern individualism finds its home in organic solidarity, but in so far as this has not followed its normal development because of the pathologies of modern society, it follows that individualism is not adequately developed. However, Durkheim's analysis of individualism is more nuanced than simply identifying it historically with modernism. 'Individualism, free thought does not date from our days, nor from 1789, nor from the reformation, nor from scholasticism, nor from the fall of greco-latin polytheism or oriental theocracy. It is a phenomenon which starts nowhere, but develops without stopping all along history' (1893b: 146/121). The deterministic reading of Durkheim has particularly marred this aspect of his account of individualism. So far, there is no sociological account that shows how he can identify individualism with free thought and stress the primacy of the 'freedom of thought' (1898c: 269/49).

As we have seen, it is the transformation of social relations and hence the conscience collective that generates modern individualism. As it develops out of mechanical solidarity, the *conscience collective* becomes characterized by general and indeterminate ways of thinking; but in relation to the individual, it is 'strengthened and precise' (1893b: 147/122). Whilst other beliefs become secularized, here the individual becomes the object of a sort of cult: it is collective in origin, but 'individual in object' (ibid.). It is an exceptional state of the *conscience collective* for society to turn all wills towards an object that is not social: society thus 'attaches us to ourselves' (ibid.). Whilst he here denies that this is not a true social link, later he holds individualism to be truly integrative (1898c). The Dreyfus Affair and the effect this had on socialist thought occurred in the interval. Jaurès, in his famous *Les Preuves* (which was a turning-point in 'The Affair') argued for the sacrality and the rights of the person as central to socialism (Jaurès 1898: 147).[3]

We have seen that although Durkheim maintains that the disappearance of the undifferentiated *conscience collective* is necessary for the development of modern individualism, he opens up a new role for a transformed *conscience collective* in individualism. If we take a definition of the *conscience collective* as a common thinking and believing about what is real and valuable, then it is entirely possible that it can be formed within a differentiated society, yet still express a common belief system about what is real and valuable which focuses on the individual. Its origin is still collective, but less obviously so, since it stems from differentiation and not from resemblance. It still fulfils the function of a *conscience collective* – which is the affirmation of a psychic type (*type psychique*), of a new psychic life (*vie psychique*) for society – that is, of a reality and system of values. Conscience, as the term under which what is real and valuable is constituted, is the necessary means to do this. Thus the making of a 'new conscience' is central to social regeneration for Durkheim (1897a: 171/169). Durkheim says that modern individualism is part not of 'speculation' but of 'practice' (1950a: 95/59). This exemplifies the logic of affirmation and, through it, of practical reason.

The value and dignity of the individual are fundamental to Durkheim's humanism: 'If the individual is not worth something, however little this might be, the rest is worthless, and evil is irremediable' (1887c: 1.330). However, he regretted the weakness of individualism in nineteenth-century France, which is shown by the ease with which 'authoritarian regimes' were accepted: old habits die hard.[4] But to institute an individualist morality, it is not sufficient to 'affirm' it, it must be based on an order of society which is durable (1950a: 95/60).[5] Yet there is 'no law better established ... than that the dignity of the person is growing'. The individual is acquiring rights and becoming 'an autonomous foyer of activity, an imposing system of personal forces (*forces personnelles*) whose energy can no more be destroyed than those of cosmic forces' (ibid. 92/57).

It is in *L'Individualisme et les intellectuels* (1898c) that he most clearly defines individualism. Durkheim differentiates individualism as respect for the human person from political economy (1898c: 263/44), for the egoism extolled by the latter renders solidarity impossible (ibid. 267/48). By contrast, in his definition of individualism, humanity is respected and made sacred. The human person is an ideal in this 'cult of man' in which human beings are both objects and agents (ibid.). This individualism is a glorification not of 'the self' (*le moi*), but of the individual in general; from this stems a sympathy for all human misery and a desire to combat it – for it entails a greater need for justice. This cult of man has 'the autonomy of reason as its first dogma and free thought as its first rite' (ibid. 268/49).

Central to the distinction between the negative, destructive individualism of political economy and the positive individualism which holds the human person (*la personne humaine*) as sacred is the distinction between the self (*moi*) and the person. The person as an object of belief of individualism is a 'collective representation' (Watts Miller 1996). As we have seen, Durkheim defines the person through conscience; as such, he or she is more than a self. Conscience is that mental power, initiated in each particular (*particulière*), which unites self and not-self. But it also implements the other functions, which show how persons can do more than narrowly pursue self-interest. The primary function of conscience is to relate, and this is the first and logical dimension of solidarity. But the other functions of conscience show that ends of action are pursued through passion, and, through force, action is generated. In terms of the logic of conscience, agency and consciousness can transcend egoism and self-interest, and focus on the ideal.

Durkheim maintains that in individualism we hold the person as an ideal: the peculiarity of individualism is that it attaches us to ourselves. But how is this possible in the logic of representation? The person as known through conscience belongs to the representative, and thus the inner logical foundation of experience: it is thus a condition of experience. How can it become an object of attachment and action? The logic of this discourse of representation allows the representative to pass to the represented side. The person, as conscience, thereby becomes an object for itself and an object of conscious reflection – that is, of the representative activity of the mind. It becomes an object of knowledge, and thus an object for itself: the logic of individualism involves a reduplication of conscience and its functions.

Renouvier's logic explains how the person can be held as an ideal. In his *Science de la morale* he argues that in moral reflection we distinguish between the empirical person we are and the ideal which we aim at in moral action. The person can be idealized as a worthy end of action, and 'here reflection duplicates (*dédouble*) the person' (Renouvier 1869b: 1.17). This involves, first, the reflexivity of conscience – that is, conscience always refers to the activity of its cognitive functions, which are presupposed in all experience. Secondly, conscience as the supreme signifier among representative functions can make itself a signified object of representation – as an ideal object. This ideal stands in judgement of the empirical person, and indicates that this is an object worthy of moral work. In this way the person as ideal can be an object of moral action for each person, and as such it invokes action in the same way as the symbols of religious belief evoke ritual practices; as such, the person enters into the sphere of the sacred for Durkheim.

It is in this sense that, for Durkheim, the human being can be both object and agent of the cult (Durkheim 1898c: 267/48). Copernican logic shows how this symbol of the person stems from conscience, and is reflected back on to it. The concept of thing (*chose*) as that to which representations refer is significant here, for in individualism the person becomes the *chose sacro-sainte* (ibid. 265/47). One of the meanings of 'thing' proposed by Renouvier is a synthesis of representations. In this sense, the person as believed in and acted on in individualism is a synthesis of collective representations, for it is constituted and defined by the *conscience collective*.

The 'religion of humanity' as the cult of the person reinforces this, and associates it with social action: the person becomes a symbol which evokes 'enthusiasm'. The individual as an end of action is, as Durkheim says, 'a passion' to be affirmed. It is an end of action, and as such what Renouvier called an 'interpersonal passion' in which the goal is the person. 'Man places ends (*fins*) in man and tends to effectively unite with him and thereby to pursue common ends' (Renouvier 1869a: 1.398). Here passion 'implies the union of persons' (ibid. 1.401). Renouvier allows the comparison between religion and morality, for just as passions are excited by objects of religion, so are they in human relations. 'Religious passions are similar to communal passions of human relations.' And the history of cults confirms this (ibid. 1.432–3).

### Philosophical background

Central features of Durkheim's account of individualism include the following: the identification of individualism and rationalism, and both with freedom of thought; the reconciliation of individualism with solidarity and equality (Lukes 1973: 327); the opposition to political economy, the distinction of the self (*moi*) from the 'human person'; and the person as an ideal. Whilst it is my contention that it is Renouvier's logic and theory of science that have most influenced Durkheim, it is undoubtedly the case that his moral, political and theoretical account of individualism was of great significance for Durkheim; it is this which allows us to account for the above features.

For Michel, Renouvier was the only thinker in nineteenth-century France who managed to give individualism a foundation by showing both its central concern with the dignity of the human being and the reconciliation of this with equality and the 'social idea' (*l'idée sociale*). In so doing, he rescued individualism from the negative philosophy of the liberals, who not only had no positive theory of right, but also supported *laissez-faire* doctrines (Michel 1898: 599ff). Individualism for him – together with the theory of right and the conception of human dignity – followed from the freedom of mind.

Renouvier, by arguing that the laws of society – understood as forms of solidarity – are the condition for all action, indicated that individualism is only possible within society. Society for him, ideally, consists in the synthesis of solidarity and individual liberty; the aim of society is freedom reconciled with equality. Society should extend freedom: the more we are tied to the state of nature, the less we are free. Progress consists in the self-determination of human beings, and this is possible only to the extent that they escape external forces of nature and obey laws which they give themselves (Foucher 1927: 162).

## Socialism

I have argued that Durkheim's critique of Marxism does not mean that he is anti-socialist. Indeed, Bouglé denied that the Durkheimians were *petits bourgeois* who wanted to block the road to socialism; rather, they were socialists (Bouglé 1938: 34). Part of the significance of Durkheim's critique of Marxism is its attempt to make socialism compatible with the central features of modern society: he sees the danger of 'despotic socialism' (Durkheim 1885a: 1.371/108). He criticized communism for allowing individuals 'no sphere of action of their own', and this is characteristic of all despotism and authoritarian governments (1893b: 171/142). He held that socialism must be compatible with democracy. It is now clear that this is what Marxism failed to do, thereby threatening the very survival of the socialist idea, given the growth of democratic states. Although there are many forms of socialism – in light of the effective collapse of states built around the ideas of Soviet Marxism, however distantly inspired by Marx, on account not only of economic but also of political failure – interest in Durkheim's version of democratic socialism cannot be without interest at the present time.

### The critique of Marxism

First, it is clear that Durkheim rejected Marxism theoretically. He disputes the central logic of Marxism: dialectics, materialism and the Hegelian view of history. The doctrine of historical materialism, the Marxist theory of value, the iron law of wages, and the pre-eminence of conflict are 'disputable and out of date hypotheses . . . which compromise the idea of socialism' (1899e: 3.163/50). He rejects the central tenet of dialectical thinking – the logic of contradiction: 'It is an error to believe that two contradictory judgements can co-exist without danger in the same con-science' (1885a: 1.376/113). Scientific socialism requires 'a complete system of society', stretching from the past into the future, but Durkheim denies that 'a system of such extent can be scientifically constructed' (1897d: 242/ 136). Searching for one law which dominates social evolution in its totality is equivalent to searching for the philosopher's stone – 'there is no cause which dominates all causes' (1903c 1.129/182).

Durkheim repudiates the logic of a base–superstructure model, which is central to the Marxist model of explanation and of change and also to its logic of power. And he rejects the identification of an objective conception of history with the doctrine of economic materialism: the concept of a base in explanation is 'too simplistic'. The concept of an economic foundation does not constitute hard data; for the economic is always interpenetrated by values, which are 'matters of opinion', established by the demands of moral 'consciences', and which vary socially and histori-cally (1908c(1): 1.221/231). Religion, rather than the economy, is the most primitive of all social phenomena (1897e: 253/173).

In his review of Labriola's *Essai sur la conception matérialiste de l'histoire*, he argues that the Marxist law of history is a law which 'pretends to be the key to history' (1897e: 252/172), yet provides no 'methodological series', and that its facts such as they are, are incapable of 'empirical representations' (ibid. 248/170). 'The marxist hypothesis is not only not proved, but it is contrary to the facts which can be established' (ibid. 253/ 173). History can become a science only through dealing with collective representations and the *conscience collective*, and only through the latter 'can sociology exist'. Moreover, he claims that he encountered both ideas before reading Marx (ibid. 250/171).

Here he admits the importance of 'profound causes which escape conscience' (ibid.). Durkheim is not thereby committed to a base–super-structure model. The concept of unconscious representation and the levels of conscience help clarify this: 'The course of our representations is determined by causes which are not represented to the subject' (ibid.). That is they can be represented 'obscurely' – not at the surface of the conscience or at the level of the reflective self, but at 'the foundations of psychic life' which can, nevertheless, still be potent causes of action (1893b: 267n./225).

For Durkheim, revolutionary socialism is logically tied to the doctrine of historical materialism; if this is false, then so is the logic of revolution (1897e: 249/170). He rejects both the logic of historicism and materialism, which are tied to the logic of historical materialism. Whilst there is no logical or political pluralism in Marx's thinking, there is in Durkheim's, and he rejects 'materialistic monism' for making human life a simple epiphenomenon of physical forces and denying 'the heterogeneity of things' (1903c: 1.124/177). Moreover, revolutionary socialisms want the impossible – a *tabula rasa* with which to construct the future (1928a: 160/171). Socialism must begin with the possibilities of the present, which, when tied to the logic of becoming, are the only forces which can achieve transformation without rupturing social continuity.

These theoretical arguments constitute one of the reasons why Durkheim, who recognizes the 'sad conflict of classes', does not believe that class conflict is the motor of historical change and development. Class war is not central to the definition of socialism for him (ibid. 53/58). Like Jaurès and Malon, but unlike Guesde, Durkheim did not see violence as a route to social transformation. Among the intellectual reasons for this is the critique of the logic of Hegelian Marxism: if there is no necessary historical law, with a dialectical momentum, then its progressive development cannot be fostered by the implementation of conflict. He questions whether socialism and revolutionary destruction are mutually implicative – is this not a route to the development of a new Middle Ages? (1905e: 284). He believed that since socialism follows the natural bent of modern societies, the latter do not have to be overthrown to establish the former (ibid. 292). The testimony of French history from 1789 through 1830, 1848 and 1871 does not support the unequivocal success of revolution as a means of social transformation. Indeed, it tended to strengthen the forces of reaction in post-revolutionary retaliation; and Renouvier argued that it had effectively served the interests of the bourgeoisie (Renouvier 1872b: 3).

For Durkheim, Marxism fails to analyse socialism in its real foundation – which is in 'the inside': socialism must address the question of what really moves us (Durkheim 1898b: 19/6). It is the totality of unconscious habits and tendencies of action that weigh on the present which must be dealt with if change is to occur – if the specific gravity of historical momentum is to be countered. Marxism's stress on the external severs contact with the 'foundation and substance' of socialism, which is 'the collective diathesis, that profound malaise' of which particular theories are an expression. Even though there are 'objective causes' of suffering (1928a: 266/284), to grasp this 'collective cry of distress' is not just to understand socialism, it is to grasp it on the inside. 'Passion' is the inspiration of such systems, and socialism is 'the cry of pain' of those who feel collective distress (ibid. 37–8/41). This was a view shared by Jaurès and Blum (Lacouture 1982: 55).

Durkheim's problematic, then, is to interrogate socialism as a doctrine in the context of the nature and values of society engendered by the division of labour and thus of economic and personal differentiation. Durkheim's challenge to Marxism is that, for socialism to survive, it must be compatible with democracy and individualism. For Filloux (1977) Durkheim's objective is to make a socialist vision coherent with democratic society; in so doing, he opposes authoritarian state socialism just as much as the reduction of socialism to the workers' question (Durkheim 1928a: 45/50). Democratic socialism requires a constant dialogue between the state and economic groups: in a properly organized democratic state there should be conscious and open exchanges between the organ charged with representing the total social body – the state – and the economic sector.

## The nature of socialism

'If it [socialism] is not a scientific expression of social facts, it is itself a social fact and of the highest importance' (ibid. 38/42). It must be treated as a reality – as a 'thing' (*chose*) (ibid. 40/44). Durkheim did not intend his sociology as a contradiction of socialism: socialism, rather, was at the origin of his sociological vocation, and was 'its travelling companion' (Filloux 1977: 260). It was in the spirit of understanding socialism that Durkheim provided a definition of socialism in his lecture course of 1896–7, which 'struck' the leaders of French socialism, Guesde and Jaurès, who were also in agreement with him, according to Mauss (Birnbaum 1971: 29); indeed, Jaurès 'glorified' the work of Durkheim (ibid. 15).

Socialism, 'if not the work of science, is an object of science' (Durkheim 1928a: 38/42). As a reality, the signs by which it is recognizable must be grasped (ibid. 40–1/44). Durkheim held that the definition of socialism must follow a study of what is common to all socialist doctrines, rather than the idea that any particular thinker has of it (1893c: 227/114). This approach is similar to that of Malon's *Le Socialisme intégral* (1890), which, by seeking what is common in socialist doctrines, aimed to strengthen socialism. For Durkheim, the shared characteristics of these tendencies will reveal what is common to the spirit of socialism (*l'esprit socialiste*) (ibid. 230/115). To be understood scientifically, it must be classified into 'kinds' (*genres*) and 'species' (*espèces*). In this way Durkheim insists that, first, socialism must be distinguished from the question of wages (*salaires*). 'We are amongst those who think socialism is above all moral' (ibid.). It is future-directed, and concerns 'what ought to be', thus, it 'is an ideal' (1928a: 36/39). This is a view he shared with Malon, Jaurès and Lucien Herr.

For Durkheim, a primary characteristic common to socialisms is their protestation against the economic state and the demand that it should be transformed (1893c: 230/115). Secondly, socialisms require the organization of economic functions through attachment of them 'to the directing and conscious centres of society' (1928a: 49/54). Durkheim stresses the importance of attachment rather than subordination here (ibid.) and believes that an amelioration of the condition of the workers must be thereby entailed (ibid. 54/60). For Bouglé, this subordination of the economic functions to the directing and organizing functions of society was central to the socialist aim: in this way the state can intervene in the organization of production and oversee education (Bouglé 1938: 34).

The influence of Saint-Simon is clear here: indeed, Durkheim holds that 'the essentials of socialism are to be found in St Simonian philosophy' (1897d: 237/132). In this he concurs with Engels (Lukes 1973: 252). Durkheim, however, criticizes both orthodox economists and most of the great theoreticians of socialism since Saint-Simon for neglecting the concept of discipline and for believing that a society is possible without it (Durkheim 1925a: 31/36). For Durkheim, a socialist revolution cannot be undertaken without 'profound moral transformations': 'to socialize economic life is to subordinate individual and egoistic ends ... to truly social therefore moral ends ... it is to introduce a higher morality. This is why ... socialism tends to realise more justice in social relations' (1893c: 233/119).

This definition differentiates socialism from primitive communism, and thus blocks the refutation of socialism by orthodox economists. Socialism, as opposed to communism, requires the division of labour and thus social differentiation (ibid. 235/120). The object of socialism is to achieve the highest degree of organization: Durkheim insisted on the social organization of economic activity – an idea initiated by the revolution – even late in his career (1917c). I have argued that organization is central to the meaning of 'order', and that Durkheim's conception of the 'unity of the organism' expresses this idea of interdependence central to organized solidarity. 'Socialism, far from being backward looking, socialism *as we have defined it* is implicated in the nature of advanced societies' (1893c: 235/120). Thus socialism is not defined by the negation of property or by the strict subordination of the individual to the collectivity – neither Fourier nor Proudhon requires this (1928a: 44/48). Nor is it the 'economic philosophy of classes which suffer'; it goes beyond the workers' question (ibid. 45/50).

### The influence of Malon and the relation with Jaurès

This analysis shows a marked similarity to both Jaurès and Malon, and in this it is central to the movement of democratic socialism (ibid. 44/49). In his *Question du méthode* (1901b) Jaurès questions Marxism's account of power: under a democracy the proletariat must be conceived of as an 'autonomous force', not as a rock (Lasselle 1901b: 2.243) who come to power by 'a supreme rupture' or by an 'authoritarian coup' (ibid. 250).

This Communist vision of political power fails to take account of democracy and the power of the bourgeoisie (Jaurès 1901b). The only sure method of transformation for socialism under a democracy is progressive organization, which centres on the relation between the individual and the milieu in the interest of transformation (1984: 67). Socialism must be critical, active and constructive (1901b: 2.264), and must be rooted in institutions and laws which carry forward the interest of humanity – which through its 'organic force' will dissolve the old.

Jaurès argues that the orientation of socialism is towards the future – towards a new social order: it is the realization of the ideal of justice 'in consciences' (1919: 5, 31). For Malon, socialism is the realization of justice and solidarity in social relations (Malon 1895: 373). And, although it must be concerned with social economy, socialism is the pursuit of moral ends: humanity as a solidary whole (*un tout solidaire*) is the principle and end of conduct in the socialist *order*. The issue of collective organization is central to socialism, for the welfare of the individual is connected to this (ibid. i–xi).

Malon criticizes Marx for over-emphasizing economic interest as class motivation: duty is a superior motivation for action, which Marxism despises; class interest is not sufficient motivation to overthrow oppression – moral forces are more important. Materialism is a falsification of history; feelings and ideas are crucial factors in history – religious revolutions are deeper and more lasting. The social question must not degenerate into 'the question of the stomach' (*la question du ventre*) (1892: 150). Socialism concerns the whole of society: bringing about a more rational social state is the aim of socialism.

In his *Précis de socialisme* (1892) Malon defines socialism as a pity for suffering, and he defines the socialist as carrying a wound open to 'universal suffering' (Malon 1892: 187). For Durkheim, 'Socialism appeals to those feelings of pity for this society which is suffering in all its classes and in all its organs' (Durkheim 1899c: 3.169/56). Durkheim concurs with Malon's view that socialism is not reduced to the workers' question or to 'the question of the stomach' (1928a: 55/61). It is concerned above all with the social question and the whole of society.

## Socialism, change and differentiation

What, then, is socialism – if it is not the war of the classes engendered by the necessary laws of history and leading to the dictatorship of the proletariat? In a democracy, freedom of mind and choice is central, and socialism cannot ignore this. It is only by engaging with this that it can become an active force in a democratic world, and it does so by appealing to action through representations – both of the nature of social reality and the terms under which action should be taken. Thus socialism was in part a conception of action, and for Durkheim must concern the whole of society: society is the 'postulate' of moral action (1906b: 70/52). The human being as 'sacred' is the stimulus to action, and humanity is its long-term goal (1898c: 272/52).

I have argued that for Durkheim a distinctive feature of the transformation of industrialization is the release of certain forms of understanding and practical activity; thus is created the real forum for change in the human world. Individuality and differentiation are made possible through economic differentiation as developmental factors of the social world: freedom of thought especially is more marked than at any other moment of history. It is through these factors that the problematic not only of socialism, but of action and change, must be addressed. What is neglected by Marxism – the problem of agency and its collective dimension – becomes crucial to change for Durkheim.

What is missing from even the most sympathetic accounts of Durkheim is the particular logic of reality which Durkheim uses. He denies a model of change implied by Comte (and by Marx), wherein historical events *predetermine* each other (1895a: 116/139). The theoretical terms in which he articulated the possibility of action and change are particularly important in relation to socialism. The 'necessity for change' (to which socialist doctrines respond) and the centrality of the public conscience in this have been recognized (Filloux 1977: 299, 305). But these are hard to explain on a classic functionalist model. A doctrine of action was central to socialism, particularly to that of Lucien Herr (Lindenberg and Meyer 1977: 43). For Durkheim, representation precedes action, and is its foundation. 'Socialism is above all the way in which certain strata of society, which are particularly tested by collective suffering, represent this to themselves' (Durkheim 1897d: 244/137).

It is in terms of a neglected logic of action that socialism and individualism must be understood. 'Individualism, like socialism, is above all a passion which affirms itself' (1928a: 37/41).[6] Action appears under the logic of representation through passion and force: it requires these representative functions for the discrimination of ends, whilst the practical functions of force engage what consciousness perceives or discriminates. Action for Durkheim is also directed by postulates; so when Durkheim 'postulates' society as the end of action, this must also be understood as a means of transformation towards a more just social order through action (1906b: 70/52).

The complexity of social development is to be grasped through the logic of becoming, for this is the law under which change occurs; within rational psychology it becomes the function of change in consciousness. Time may pass, but things can stay the same; if the 'same' continues without variation, then no change occurs. The diversity of relations brought about through differentiation thus not only facilitates change, but occurs when change is at its fastest. Of course, the perception of all change depends on the discrimination of conscience; but the function of change of conscience can be active or passive. When it is passive, the mechanism to make things continue in the same way can dominate becoming within the structure of human representation, through the unconscious levels of conscience. This keeps things going as they are, because its mechanism is outside the reflective powers of the rational structures of conscience. But when it is active, it engages will and reflection – hence the importance of challenging 'obscure' consciences – for reflection activates will and thus force in action. In this way there is a dynamic and transformational functionalism within the logical structure of representation.

At the same time, we are governed by finality: that is, the logic of passion which reconciles 'state' and 'tendance'. Passion, whilst indicating the way in which ends are pursued, also implies becoming, for it entails movement from one state to another. This is why change can occur when the passions are activated: they are the real principle of development, and the reason why change occurs in moments of effervescence. To engage with the real possibilities of action, socialism must represent the reality of social suffering and thereby involve the passions, which motivate conduct.

Practical representation also has another function: it brings before the mind the possibilities of action. Differentiation opens up an 'empty space' (*espace vide*) in which effort can be made (1893b: 368/310). Theoretical humanism centres on probabilities and possibilities of action. Herr was attached to possibilist socialism (Lindenberg and Meyer 1977: 54). This theoretical 'possibilism' is grounded in a foundational logic of action and change. The attack on conceptions of the whole and of unity as transcending representation becomes crucial to understanding Durkheim's practical logic. When things stay the same in societies governed by the habitual, with absolute social uniformity, then no differences appear, and no options are evident – there is no gap in social continuity and no possibilities of action.

There is thus more possibility of socialism under economic modernism, for at the very same time as it causes social suffering, it generates those movements which represent this as intolerable: that is, moral individualism. For Durkheim it is precisely the parallel development of individualism and rationalism that increases moral sensibility to unjust social relations (Durkheim 1925a: 17/20). Equally, it is the time when communication is at its fastest; this is central not only to awareness of the need for change, but also to democratic socialism.

## The reconciliation of individualism and socialism

Individualism was central to an important form of non-Communist social-ism. For Proudhon, individualism is fundamental, and must be fused with socialism: 'As individualism is the primordial fact of humanity, association is the complementary term' (Proudhon 1967: 227). This vision was inherited by Jaurès through Gambetta. Jaurès, for whom individualism and socialism mutually imply each other, praised Proudhon for being 'a great liberal as well as a great socialist' (Jaurès 1910: 172).

Durkheim insists that socialism must be compatible with individualism: he denies the pretended antagonism between individualism and socialism (Durkheim 1893c: 226/113). Individualism is the dominant set of values released through economic differentiation. Of course, this must not be understood as the egoism of self-interested conduct extolled by political economy, but as that which views the human being as sacred: this is compatible with socialism concerned with a moral solidarity. Durkheim stresses that the solidary nature of the whole is not incompatible with individualism; pluralist logic, fundamental to the nature of the totality, allows the reconciliation of individualism and socialism, for it does not negate the possibility of individuation. Solidarity is compatible with the differentiation and individuation which the modern economic world requires. It follows that the reconciliation of individualism and socialism must be effected within organic solidarity.

These ideas grew out of republicanism and socialism. Pierre Leroux is the man credited with introducing the word 'socialism' into France (Michel 1898: 230). Indeed, Leroux claims to have invented the word 'socialism', and he used it thus to oppose economic individualism.[7] Socialism in this pure sense as defined by Leroux means the belief in the social, but as reconciling freedom and equality; thus it focuses on the religion of humanity and the principle of fraternity. Through these ideas Leroux opposes those socialists who established authoritarian and state socialism.

The reconciliation of the sacredness of the individual with the fact of human solidarity is central to Renouvier's thought (Soltau 1931: 307). In the revolution of 1848 he collaborated with George Sand and with Leroux, who in his pamphlet of 1834, *De l'Individualisme et du socialisme*, argued for the reconciliation of individualism and socialism as the goal of social science. Renouvier's article *Introduction à un essai d'organisation politique pour la France* (1851), written during the short-lived Second Republic, argues for the reconciliation of autonomy with the relatedness of society. Individuals presuppose 'life in relation (*la vie en relation*) and stem from it' (Renouvier 1851: 525). The whole understood as transcendent denies the individual, whilst society understood as life in relation does not. The former underwrites a political fiction by which classes and casts dominate and thus tyrannize. This was, for Renouvier, the history of all oligarchies – indeed, of all history's oppression (ibid. 529).

Thus Durkheim's original aim for his first book – the reconciliation of individualism and socialism – has a socialist and republican history. But how can they be reconciled? As we have seen, both socialism and individualism are 'passions' which 'affirm themselves'. Socialism is the affirmation of a new order: it is the will to initiate a new series of phenomena in becoming. And individualism affirms that the human being is 'sacred'. This ideal of the human being as the 'sacred thing' becomes the symbolic focus, the ideal by which solidarity is realized. The realization of ideals is only possible through the 'anticipated representation of the end' (Durkheim 1893b: 331/279).

It is thus that moral individualism is the rational expression of the religion of humanity (1898c: 271/51). Durkheim believes that eventually the idea of the human person will be the only thing left to love and honour in common (ibid. 272/52). In this way the centre of moral life has moved from the 'outside' to the 'inside', and 'the individual is elevated into sovereign judge of their own conduct' (ibid. 273/52). This is the ideal which supremely evokes action and passion, and 'the tendency of our efforts is to develop it' (1906b: 66/48). The human being as the sacred ideal of modern individualism reconciles individualism and socialism through its role as 'thing' (*chose*) in representational logic. As a symbol of representation, it is in relation to the representative and practical conditions of action; it is thus that it evokes action through signification and symbolization. Central to individualism is the conception that the human being becomes a god for themselves (1898c: 272/52).

Further, the concept of the sacredness of the individual requires an egalitarian order: individualism and socialism can be effectively reconciled only in an egalitarian order based on the value of the sacredness of the individual. As we have seen Durkheim associates the inequality resulting from hereditary wealth with 'the negation of liberty' (1893b: 381/321). Thus, central to his individualism is the proper social recognition and value of work: there must be equality in the 'external conditions of struggle' (ibid. 374/316). If we take the latter to mean life chances and the external to mean, in Renouvier's logic, all that is 'logically external' (Hamelin 1927: 182) and that which extends beyond the inner space, then Durkheim's statement here implies a greater form of egalitarianism than is implied by the meritocracy often ascribed to him.

So it has been suggested that Durkheim's egalitarianism is more apparent than real, because of insistence only on the injustice entailed by inherited wealth; to be really egalitarian, his statement must be adjusted to: 'There are unjust contracts not simply if there are rich and poor at birth but rich and poor *tout court*.' Equality of opportunity means little if equality of conditions is not stressed (Cuin 1991: 25). However, this argument overlooks Durkheim's statement that: 'The principle according to which all occupations are equally accessible to all the citizens cannot be generalised to this point unless it has constant application' (Durkheim 1893b: 319/269). Since the constant and the habitual are part of the general for Durkheim, a constant equality of opportunity would require and help to generate a general and structural equality.

In *Le Socialisme* Durkheim argues that 'work must be appreciated and remunerated according to its social value' (1928a: 54/60). What prevents this is the 'capitalist' as 'intermediary' between worker and society, which must be 'suppressed' (ibid.). The injustice of capitalism is that workers are dependent on the capitalist, and not on the total body of society; and the capitalist pays them not according to their social value, but at the cheapest rate (ibid. 53/59). In this respect Durkheim's socialism argues for a form of Rousseau-like equal dependency on the social body as central to modern egalitarianism. The significance of stressing the whole is that it reminds people of their need of, and dependency on, each other, and the point of making this a matter of representation is to affect action and thereby to make this a virtue of society: by becoming rooted in the tendencies of conduct and thus becoming a habit, acknowledgement of our mutual dependence will become a moral need which will tend to be structurally realized.

Much, however, depends on what Durkheim means by social value. It is clear that this can only be evaluated ultimately in terms of both the whole, understood as social interdependence, and the significance of each part as contributing to the viability and continuity of the social whole. In this sense there is a moral functionalism at the heart of the religion of humanity, which for Filloux harks back to the Saint-Simonian conception of merit. But social value is also accompanied by the conception of the equal dignity of each human being, which is central to modern individualism, and the egalitarianism which this requires. It is thus no accident that in *L'Individualisme et les intellectuels* Durkheim argues that to make a reality of 'the famous precept: to each according to his (their) work' is to enable individuals to 'develop their faculties without obstacles' (1898c: 277/56).

I have argued that central to the synthetic view of reality is the conception of how new realities are formed: syntheses are the source of the new: 'all creation ... is the product of a synthesis' (1912a: 637/447), and association is 'the cause of new phenomena which characterises life' (1895b: 102/128).

The past does not create: it can only transmit what has been created. Its creations can only be the work of the living who are associates and are co-operative contemporaneously. All new efforts in life can only come from beings who are active in life. It is only thanks to them and through them alone that the past continues to live. Thus I have made the study of these *creative syntheses* part of my effort. These new things create the society of the living.' (1914b: 1.69)

Central to synthesis is the logic of correlation, which shows how contrary states can be not only reconciled, but brought together coherently. The full realization of organic solidarity will synthesize a solidarity encompassing individuality at the same time as the whole (1893b: 101/85) – that is, it will stress real interdependence at the same as difference and autonomy. It will thus reconcile the contrary forces of individuality and solidarity and hence individualism and socialism.

# 7

# The Science of Facts and Things: Methodological Considerations

Durkheim's methodological treatise of 1895 is reputedly the most positivist of his texts; he, however, undertook this work to 'correct' Comte's methodological errors (Durkheim 1900b: 127/16). His *Règles de la méthode sociologique* (1895) is possibly the most vilified of his works. Lukes sums up its failings. First, Durkheim is a Cartesian rationalist and a realist who holds to an absolutist conception of knowledge, which not only neglects the problem of relativism, but which aims at a knowledge of the social which is independent of the meanings it has for social subjects (Lukes 1982: 12). This approach is 'sterile' compared with the hermeneutic approach, for it aims at establishing generality, objectivity and externality, which are at odds with the internal and subjective character of social facts. Secondly, it neglects all micro-questions and questions of psychology – thus his macro-theory rests on 'unexamined and implausible foundations' (ibid. 1982: 18). Thirdly, through his false ideal of scientific detachment, he neglects the extra-scientific and political contexts of science. Fourthly, through its concern with the attachment of the individual to collective goals, it neglects the bonds between individuals and groups. And fifthly, it neglects the question of power understood as struggle and dependency (ibid. 22). With such a catalogue of errors, Durkheim's work on methodology can only have an arcane interest, instructive solely for the errors it commits, or so it seems.

The first accusation, however, neglects Durkheim's rejection of Cartesian rationalism as 'archaic and narrow' (Durkheim 1900b: 135/22), and as over-simplifed through its neglect of the complex and 'obscure' nature of things (1925a: 214/252). The scientific rationalism which Durkheim espouses rejects absolutism, and introduces the relative through acknowledgement of the 'difference' of relations of experience.[1] Durkheim rejects realism – understood as a reflectionist, objectivist view of reality (1893b: 64/53; 1895a: xi/34). All questions of meaning are covered by the logical structure of representation and the 'particular conscience' (*conscience particulière*). I have questioned Lukes's claim that since representation is a post-1895 concept, this consequently mars his methodology here (Lukes 1982: 7). But Durkheim says here that social facts consist in 'representations and actions' (Durkheim 1895a: 5/52).

Secondly, Durkheim acknowledges the importance of 'a formal psychology, which is common ground between individual psychology and sociology' (1895a: xviii/41); I suggest that through this the micro-logical aspect of human reality is approached. Nor is it the case that the question of the politics of theory is totally ignored in pursuit of a false scientific detachment (Lukes's third accusation). Behind such accusations lie first, the spectre of the word 'thing' which has caused so much trouble in the interpretation of Durkheim, and second, the neglect of his identification of science with conscience. Fourthly, he did not neglect the bonds between people and groups – this is the significance of 'association'. Fifthly, it is not true that he totally neglects the concept of power: this misunderstanding results from interpreting 'force' in terms of thermodynamics and electricity (Lukes 1982: 8).

There is a 'whole logic of science and doctrine of truth' behind *Les Règles* (Maublanc 1932: 298). In no other of Durkheim's works is the mark of Renouvier clearer, so let us see how this can help us clear up some of the critiques. Renouvier's neo-criticism was not only widespread among intellectuals of the Third Republic; it was particularly important to young philosophers at Bordeaux (Fonsegrive 1904: 3). Durkheim wrote *Les Règles* whilst at Bordeaux, and it was there that the socialist students demanded that Durkheim should be their teacher (Weisz 1983: 105). Durkheim's close intellectual companion during all his years at Bordeaux was the philosopher Hamelin, who was not only a disciple of Renouvier, but his main interpreter.

The idea of an objective knowledge of society has been under sustained attack for so long now in sociology that it is worth remembering that in the context of the Third Republic such a position was neither apolitical nor conservative. To maintain that society was a real object of knowledge was to oppose the Catholic Church, the forces of the right, who were 'viscerally' antisocial (Bordier 1994: 13), the conservative and inegalitarian tradition, and the passivity of the people. The central question of *Les Règles* – the possibility, the reality and the nature of social fact – was central to Jaurès's democratic socialism.[2] Indeed, Durkheim says that socialism is above all a 'certain way of conceiving and explaining social facts, their evolution in the past, their development in the future' (Durkheim 1897d: 237/131).

## How are social facts possible?

The question of whether there are or are not any social facts goes to the heart of contemporary debates in the social sciences. The new rules of sociological method stress the subjective and the interpretative nature of social reality, and in so doing, oppose Durkheim's 'positivist' approach, seen to understand social reality through an inappropriate science of nature which entails a concern with a fallacious externality and objectivity. However, if we understand his method, first, through the dialectic of reality, conscience, representation and thing (*chose*); second, through a logic of social truth, and third, through a relational view of reality, then we can repudiate not only accusations of a false scienticism, but also that he neglects the processes by which social reality is an emergent property of meaningful interaction, that is, 'sighs, gestures and language' (Walsh 1972: 37). To do so, we need to look again at what 'thing', 'externality' and 'outside' mean.

### Social facts – the question of meaning and the conception of social truth

Durkheim has been frequently accused of empiricism and materialism; yet he insists that social facts are 'non-organic', and consist in 'representations and actions' (Durkheim 1895a: 5/52). Although the concept of social facts originated in Comte's classic positivism, Kant had shown that facticity is possible only through representation: so if the empirical in nature is only finally approachable through a conceptual organization, how much more so is it necessary when the science involves cognitively active agents in relational structures?

*Les Règles* is a formal enquiry, and it is at this level that he approaches the question of the conceptual presuppositions for an empirical enquiry: his method, he claims, 'governs thought . . . and action' (ibid. 74/104).[3] The 'particular conscience' (*conscience particulière*) is the necessary but not sufficient condition of social reality (ibid. 103/129), for in terms of a formal psychology, it is the condition of the possibility of human experience.[4] A human world becomes significant through the representative and practical functions of conscience, and understanding is central to the former. Conscience covers the signifying functions of thought (ibid. 4/51) together with the typifying and unconscious (*inconscient*) functions of consciousness (ibid. 7/53). Further, passion and force cover the logic of feeling and action; passion is that under which ends are given and pursued – it is that under which tendencies (ibid. 8/54) and especially habits are understood. Thus *in toto* these cover the ways of thinking, acting and feeling which are central to Durkheim's definition of social facts (ibid. 4/52). Acknowledgement of these will help to answer Lukes's claim that Durkheim's conception of enthusiasm and effervescence lacks a micro-basis.

How does a doctrine of truth apply here? We have seen that relations of truth are formed between the representative and the represented for Renouvier: a true proposition, then, is one that is adequate to the reality found in the latter, but which is made possible through the epistemic functions of the former. So the relation between the representative and the represented is a type of truth relation; as such, it encompasses a sense of *true for* the agent, which accounts for the orientation of a conscience towards a reality. Since Durkheim argued that the *conscience collective* can never be 'hypostatised' independently of each 'particular conscience' (ibid. 103/145n.), at least part of the logic of social reality centres on particular consciences.

But social facts are facts which are true for the *conscience collective*; that is, these ways of thinking, acting and feeling establish a world which is *true for* the *conscience collective*. Collective thinking forms itself on the representative side of representation, and is imposed on its objects as the 'represented', as its signified objects. The shared collective thinking forges a type of meaning holism which is shown in how the group 'thinks, feels and acts' (ibid. 103/129). Central to this dialectic of reality are the concepts of communication and the degrees of conscience, which produces a system of representations and relations which are fixed in signs, crystallized in institutions and various forms of social morphology. Typification is implied in all conceptualization through the logic of judgement (*espèce*) (ibid. 89/119) – which is central to all questions of meaning and interpretation. Signification – central to cultural activity – is central to the generalization of social facts through the typifying functions of each conscience.

## Social facts and the sphere of the general

Social facts concern the structural reality of society and are thus *true about* general social phenomena: social facts are phenomena, he says, which 'express the unique life (*la vie propre*) of societies' (1903c: 1.121/175). This reality is forged through association, which is the sufficient condition of social life (ibid. 103/129), and is constituted through composition of the number and nature of elementary parts (1895a: 12/57). This associational and compositional totality is a structural whole: it is the level at which social facts properly belong for Durkheim. It is the level at which inequality exists.

This involves a relational view of reality which holds that a conception of truth and objectivity applies to the social as a sphere of general relations. So, for Durkheim, significant sociological descriptions apply to

the realm of the general. The thesis of the logical generality of representation as the condition of truth and objectivity helps to elucidate Durkheim's position – in particular why 'generality' is associated with
'objectivity' (ibid. 12/57), and why the latter is associated with 'external'
functional characteristics (ibid. 44/81). Social facts are general and, as
such, objective for Durkheim.

But the general is constituted through action and interaction. The logic
of plurality helps to explain how wholes or totalities are constituted out of
the units which form them: the associational and the compositional nature
of the group go some way to explaining why 'ways of acting and thinking'
are general and constraining.[5] It is, however, through *repetition* that they
come to constitute 'a reality *sui generis*, very distinct from the individual
facts which manifest them' (ibid. 9/54). As we have seen, repetition is one
of the ways in which wholes are formed for Renouvier: wholes exist
synchronically but, importantly, diachronically.

The 'collective habit' (ibid. 9/55) is central to this. The concepts of the
habitual and repetition are central to action, and feed his notion of
generality. Indeed, habit explains how 'the free currents' of social life
become structural: it is this which gives a fixity and relative consolidation
to the changeful nature of 'ways of doing (*manières de faire*)' (ibid. 12/
57),[6] which become 'ways of being (*manières d'être*)' (ibid. 13/58).[7] I have
argued that it is false to oppose action to the structural approach in the
interpretation of Durkheim. Through the concepts of a relational totality
and of the unconscious (ibid. 7/53), he shows how structural conditions
pass into the unconscious of the agents and become the habits and
tendencies of the agent: thus meaning exists at the unconscious level. In
this he shows not only how structure and action are connected, but how
systems persist.

It is said that Durkheim's arguments about the diffusion through
generality of social facts become tautological without a further variable
(Borlandi 1995: 142). The 'tendencies' of action answer this, for each
social fact has a tendency to generalize itself (*tendance à se généraliser*),
because it is obligatory (Durkheim 1895a: 12n./59n.). In this sense generality is not independent of the micro-level, because tendency is an aspect
of the logic of action and enters social evolution in 'an active sense', for 'a
tendency is a thing' (ibid. 91–2/121). Renouvier argued that through the
'tendencies' of action things are generalized: 'habit is the aptitude to
reproduce and repeat the same development an indefinite number of
times' (Renouvier 1875d: 1.287).

But, most importantly, this social totality is communicative – as such it
is supported through the communication of consciences, which is the
logical foundation of all communicative reality, and is therefore central to
understanding the generality of social reality. It is in this reality that the

'currents of enthusiasm' (ibid. 6/52) and opinion and 'collective habits' (ibid. 9/54) are immanent. This communicative reality is expressed verbally from 'mouth to mouth' (ibid. 9/54) and through education, and it is in this reality that meaning can be general. Since social facts are 'normal' only in a particular type of society, it follows that type is central to the generality of social fact within a society – for typification is entailed through the signifying functions of each conscience, and is therefore germane to understanding how social facts can be generalized. It is the misunderstanding about the communicative nature of the whole and its 'psychic nature' that has led to accusations of Durkheim's fallacious objectivism (Tosti 1898). (See below under 'Causality and sociological explanation'.)

Durkheim insists that the generality of social facts is explained by their collective and obligatory nature, and not vice versa. But obligation and the habitual are connected for Durkheim in a dialectical process of social reality. The habitual produces an ascendancy: 'Definite manners of action ... which are repeated ... become habits; then habits as they acquire force transform themselves into rules of conduct' (Durkheim 1893b: 357/302).[8] Habits are to be understood as a form of *tendance*: they are central to the micro-logical aspect of action. It is through repetition that actions become obligatory (1895a: 19/63). But repetition is central to diachronic generality – generality continues over time through repetition. This is one of the ways in which 'the past predetermines the future' (1893b: 357/302).

## Social facts and the problem of externality

Social facts 'have this remarkable property of existing outside of (*en dehors de*) individual consciences' (ibid. 4/51).[9] And this is associated with externality. This phrase *dehors de* has inspired critiques of Durkheim's epistemological errors: Lacombe (1926) asked how a 'way of thinking' can be outside a conscience?[10] Of course a social fact as representation cannot be literally 'outside' – for, as Durkheim argues elsewhere, representations are impossible without conscience (Durkheim 1898b: 37/23). Lacombe overlooks the connection between the inner (*le dedans*) and the outer (*le dehors*), and assumes that all consciousness is, by definition, private and subjective. He overlooks the logical generality built into the conception of a representational and relational view of reality; it is only within this that the terms 'outside of' and 'exterior' make sense.

The central question concerns how these concepts are compatible with the representational nature of social facts? It is clear that Durkheim uses outside (*hors de*) in an unusual way: when we are distracted, then psychic states which are nevertheless 'real' and active, are outside (*hors de*) conscience (ibid. 35/21). This phrase 'outside' (*dehors*) has a specific logical meaning in Renouvier's rationalism: it indicates logically external relations. To treat a phenomenon *du dehors* is to treat it as having 'external relations' (Hamelin 1927: 183). This is a logical point, and does not mean literally outside of as external in the sense of the material world (although obviously it could mean this). What it indicates logically is having relations with something other than itself. So in this second example from 1898, it is clear that *hors de* means that the conscious mind, the *conscience claire*, is affected by something other than itself. In the first example it means that ways of thinking and acting that we acquire through education and the family do not come from the individual, but from social relations – from the social milieu – which are thus logically external to each 'particular conscience'. But they pass into the inside, where they exist as tendencies of action and thinking which can exist unconsciously.

Unfortunately, since Durkheim is translated in ignorance of this logical point about external relations and as though he means that social facts are literally 'outside' the consciousness of the individual (1895a/1982: 51), the logical point about the external relations of each *conscience individuelle* is obscured. So, for example, the individuated aspect of our thinking, clearly in this logical sense, has external relations with the collective aspect of our thinking. This is the sense of the 'two consciences' within us: one which represents us 'personally', the other collectively (1893b: 74/61).

So now we can see this dialectic of reality in terms of internal and external relations. The person is logically 'interior' (*dedans*) to a social framework which is outside it and which exists as 'external' relations. This dialectic of social reality matches the passage of science where the 'exteriority' 'is only apparent' and 'disappears as science advances', when 'we see the outside (*le dehors*) return to the inside (*le dedans*)' (1895a: 28/70).[11] As we have seen, the representative conditions of scientific knowledge are logically internal, and are both an activity of conscience and the condition of knowledge of the external. In this sense the logic of Durkheim's science, rather than being based on an inappropriate science of nature, actually uses a logic which matches the processes of conscious experience.

So social phenomena are external, because they exist in a shared relational and representational reality – that is, one that is common to a number of consciences and their communication. Of course, such a shared world is logically external to each person, even though it is constituted by the association of consciences. A 'way of acting' can appear as general within representation, through the concept of type which applies to this general form of representation.

So, without a theory of this general epistemic totality, together with the unconscious (ibid. 7/53), this project of studying social facts 'detached from the conscious subjects who represent them to themselves' (ibid. 28/70) has unsurmountable problems. Unconscious representations (Renouvier 1875d: 2.310) operate without the rational surface of the mind being necessarily aware of them. But these, as tendencies of action, are real in social and historical reality, and have absorbed the significations which exist at the level of general representation. Thus, what is represented by each rationally conscious self will not necessarily be adequately true about this reality which has a truth at the level of general external relations.

This passage must also be read as a rejection of introspection, the old method of 'psychology' or of Cousin – the liberal philosophical 'dictator' whom the socialist republicans opposed, and who held that what is 'outside conscience' (*hors de conscience*) is as though it did not exist' (Billard 1999: 90).[12] It was conservatives who argued that only 'conscience' as the 'internal individual' counts, and thus that all questions of transforming the external conditions of life 'must be abandoned' (Jaurès 1906: 67). In this short phrase, '*en dehors*', Durkheim points in a formal sense to a social and political context as crucial in the examination of social facts.

## Constraint and social facts

Durkheim's conception of social facts as defined by the 'external constraint' that ways of acting exert on the individual (Durkheim 1895a: 14/ 59) has also caused great difficulty. First, it is clear that for Durkheim constraint is the sign by which we recognize the social, not its whole nature, and in this he differentiates himself from Hobbes (ibid. 122/146). Secondly, constraint becomes an 'internal tendency', and is no longer felt, since it slowly 'gives birth to habits and internal tendencies' (ibid. 8/54) which can also become unconscious. It can also be elucidated by the spiritualist conception of reality as an obstacle to will: the aspiring force of will encounters reality as resistance, which is thus a criterion of reality (Dauriac 1924: 43). Social reality for Durkheim comes from external relations which, through the passage to the inner from the outer, are encountered as constraining; there is a dialectic of powers here which is central to the dynamic of social reality.

But it cannot be adequately understood without the idea of communication and the tension between the internal and the external in society as a relational totality. It is in this reality that constraint becomes the sign by which we recognize the social. Durkheim argues that constraint is explicable only through the plural nature of the totality which is external to each of us (Durkheim 1895a: xxii/45). Through the association of the plurality of consciences, the synthesis which is the root of society as a combinatory epistemic totality is made possible. And this takes place 'outside' of us – that is, in external relations as so defined. In such a totality there is a tension not only between the internal and the external, but also between individuated and collective forms of thinking – between the two consciences within us, the *particulière* and the *collective*. It is this which is the logical basis of 'external constraint' – when understood in the logical sense explained above. Further, the logic of pluralism ensures that totalities are not formed at the expense of the reality of individuality; there is always a tension, a gap that is never finally closed, between the individual and the collectivity. This is one reason why Durkheim can maintain both freedom of mind and social authority, which coexist as permanent aspects of the social dialectic.

However, what must still be explained is why Durkheim holds that constraint is explicable through the prestige with which 'certain representations are imbued' (ibid. xxi/44). How can this be connected to the 'plurality of consciences'? I have suggested that shared 'ways of thinking' establish a meaning holism – in collective representations – which is central to a significant world. The prestige of representations then indicates which representations are central to a significant coherent world. We have seen that the creation of a common thinking, forged from the tension between freedom and authority, was central to the creation of significant worlds for Renouvier, and thus fundamental to all religions and philosophy; all collective life revolves around this signification and meaning.

But we must go further: why do only certain representations have this 'prestige' for Durkheim? Certainly for Durkheim a mere 'conventional arrangement' does not; rather, it is those which relate to 'collective being' and which come from 'the entrails of society' which have this, which is experienced as a 'force' which dominates the individual (ibid. 122/143). These 'entrails of society' are connected to the concept of 'condition of existence' (ibid. 92/121). Since the fundamental social relations which surround each person make individual life possible, it is they which are the 'condition of existence' for the individual, and this is the source their 'prestige'.

In this sense, for Durkheim there is always constraint *qua* prestige involved in the relations between individuals and society. He thus rejects Hobbes's account of the relationship between individual and society – for here the individual is always resisting social life (ibid. 120/142). Equally, he rejects political economy, which acknowledges only the free play of self interest – and here constraint occurs only when things are 'abnormal' (ibid. 121/143). For Durkheim, constraint is forged through the possibility of loss of attachment to the source of our being (our condition of existence), and expresses our dependence on social relations within the milieu – on solidarity. So for Durkheim, not all constraint is 'normal' – that which is founded on wealth or power is not normal, and 'can be maintained only by violence' (ibid. 122n./146n.).

But does the constraining power of social facts imply that they are independent of our will? It is indeed the case, as Watts Miller argues, that social institutions are resistant to change at will through the logic of laws, unconscious resistance to change and, thirdly, because they are rooted in the deep rational structures of societies (Watts Miller 1996: 48ff). However, if we remember the concepts of levels of conscience, change through enlightenment of conscience, and force as power, then it follows that independence of will is not total. We must remember the reconciliation of freedom and determinism here: although a sign of a social fact is that it cannot be modified by 'a simple decree of the will', he argues that 'to produce a change', a 'more or less laborious effort' is required (Durkheim 1895a: 29/70).

## Social facts and observation: that word 'thing'

'The first and most fundamental rule is to consider social facts as things (*choses*)' (ibid. 15/60). This has led to accusations not only of Durkheim's fallacious objectivism and mechanism, but also of his positivism and materialism; that he overlooked the difference between natural and social phenomena (Parsons 1937: 399); and the continuing and widespread claims that he founded his science on a science of nature. It has inspired the view that his account of reality makes conscience a dull reflection of things, rather than the constitutive force it is. It has been taken as evidence of a positivist attempt to reduce the human to the non-human (Walsh 1972: 37). (Yet no consistent positivist would use 'thing' *tout court*, unanalysed into law and phenomenon.) Because of it, Hirst praises Durkheim for his anti-humanism: yet, for Durkheim, individualism makes the individual 'a sacred thing' (*chose sacro-sainte*) (Durkheim 1898c: 265/46). *Les Règles* is the most infamous location, but he uses it later, to indicate 'sacred things' (*choses sacrées*) (1912a: 65/44). Categories are social 'things' (ibid. 627/441); a sign is a 'thing' (1897a: 356/315), and 'tendencies' are 'things' (1895a: 92/121). Why would a professed rationalist who repudiates materialism, reductionism, realism and ontologism use this term and in a scientific language which opposes common sense? The central question is how 'thing' is compatible with social life as 'entirely made of representations' (ibid. xi/34)

Durkheim does much to clarify his meaning in the preface to the second edition: his aim was not to reduce the superior to inferior forms of being, but to indicate a degree of reality for the social world equal to that ascribed to the external world. Social facts are not material things, but are things in the same 'title' as them. To treat something as a 'thing' is not to categorize in any particular order of reality; it is not an ontological but a methodological claim, for it specifies an attitude of mind which is characteristic of science. A thing is that which is opposed to an idea, just as 'that which is known outside' (*du dehors*) is opposed to 'that which is known inside' (ibid. xii/35). To be a thing is to be that which is not naturally penetrable by intelligence, but which we can understand only by 'going out of ourselves' and employing observation and experimentation (ibid. xiii/36). A 'thing' is that which is not modifiable by a 'simple decree' of will (ibid. 29/70).

There are certain distinct questions central to an understanding of his use of the term. The first and most important question is how 'thing' is connected to the representational nature of social reality. As I have shown above, 'thing' belongs to the dialectic of reality: conscience–representation–thing. Durkheim makes it clear that a thing is that which is observed. 'To be a thing . . . is all that is given to observation' (ibid. 27/69). I suggest that it is only Renouvier's logic of reality and science which can explain this, for here 'thing' means 'all that manifests, all that appears' (Hamelin 1927: 45). 'Thing' is thus central to a logic of appearance, and, when taken in relation to conscience, indicates the role of signification within representation. This logic of appearance must overturn accusations of Durkheim's neglect of questions of meaning: the orientation of consciousness towards an object of reference is the primary and most fundamental aspect of representation in the relation of conscience towards a 'thing'.

But how can Durkheim talk of sacred things? For Renouvier 'thing', when understood more profoundly, 'indicates a more or less complex synthesis of representations' (Renouvier 1875c: 1.6). On this basis, the sacred can be a thing, because it is a complex synthesis of representations, as well as being an object of thought. In these two senses the concept 'thing' is compatible with all aspects of Durkheim's thought and is not a particular oddity of the 'positivism' and 'scientism' of *Les Règles*.

The second question concerns why 'thing' guarantees a reference to reality in a world that is 'entirely made of representations' (ibid. xi/34) and why it underwrites a scientific attitude of mind. Durkheim says that 'socialism must be envisaged as a thing, that is as a reality' (Durkheim 1928a: 40/44). The method of reality, Durkheim argues, goes from thing to idea (1895a: 16/60). For Renouvier, science and reality can be satisfactorily defined in terms of representation and relation; to attempt to distinguish reality from representation is to create an 'idol' or illusion (such as the absolute – seen in 'substance', 'infinity' and 'things in themselves'), which is not only logically unknowable but potentially inimical to democratic and humanist interests. Nevertheless, a concept is needed to express reality within the logic of representation, and 'thing' indicates this. 'The word reality . . . generally . . . is a synonym for thing (*chose*)' (Renouvier 1875c: 1.64). So when Durkheim says that 'tendencies are things', he means that they are real.

This analysis shows that the definition of social facts in his first chapter does not contradict this definition of the nature of reality and science. Ways of acting, thinking and feeling are real on this definition of reality; they would not be real within a logic of either materialism or subjective idealism. They are forms of representation for the agent concerned, whether the agent is always consciously aware of them or not, and are real in a shared representational reality.

The third question is why 'thing' indicates a datum? To treat social facts like things, according to Durkheim, is to treat them scientifically and thus to treat them as data. How can this be done? We can understand this in terms of the representative and represented aspects of representation. The represented is what one calls the object; when we think about something in this logic of representation, it becomes an object for thought. Thinking is the totality of the representative conditions. To be known objectively, social facts – ways of thinking – must become objects of these representative functions. To do so, they must be treated as the represented – that is, as 'things'; in this way they become scientific data in an epistemological sense. Of course, the reflective and discriminatory functions of conscience are always presupposed, and without a doubling up of these functions can never be transferred to the objective pole. Thus, in this dialectic of reality, where all is representation, to treat a datum like a thing is an epistemological act which represents the scientific activity of reflection and observation, and the critical detachment without which there can be no science.

The association of 'thing' (*chose*), 'the represented' (*représenté*) and the concept of exteriority for Durkheim is clear: 'The totem is relatively exterior to man; because it is only on things (*choses*) that we have seen it represented (*représenté*)' (Durkheim 1912a: 162/114). The objective side of representation in the logic of representation is also the 'exterior' side of reality as representation. 'Thing = the objective side of representation' (Renouvier 1886: 1.26). This is associated with the method of reality, which moves from things to ideas: that is, we must start with what is given to observation, not with our ideas about reality. Social facts are ways of thinking and acting which stem not from the self but from the system of relations which surround it – in external relations. 'We must study [social phenomena] from outside (*au dehors*) like external things for it is in that quality that they present themselves to us' (Durkheim 1895a: 28/70). Durkheim's use of 'outside' and 'thing' in relation to the meaningful nature of 'ways of thinking' has always provoked protestations. But in this logic of reality, 'outside', as a logical term which indicates external relations, shows that Durkheim is treating meaning and action as arising not from the self, but from social relations.

Lastly, we must ask how he can use this term and logically maintain the humanism which is central to individualism and to the practical moral dimension of his thought. Again, Renouvier elucidates this: in his *Esquisse* (1886) he argues that only this doctrine of representation can guarantee the reality of the person as a living force in a world, and that this is contradicted by a doctrine which holds that behind the real – that is, representation and its laws – there is a nature which is more true or more real in ontological terms than persons and their forms of representation. It is no accident that Durkheim includes that rejection of 'ontologism and realism' in the preface to the second edition of *Les Règles*, for it is these which for Renouvier effectively deny the activity of the subject in the constitution of reality. Thus Renouvier differentiates his system from the philosophy of 'The Thing' (*La Chose*) and maintains that, nevertheless, the scientific meaning of 'thing' is the object understood within the objective terms of representation (Renouvier 1886: 2.175).

## The normal and the pathological

Durkheim's distinction between the normal and the pathological has been seen as a threadbare dichotomy concerned with conservatism and overridden with false biological values (La Capra 1985: 15). The normal is associated with order, and the pathological with anything which disturbs this (Coser 1960: 214). The difficulties are said to stem from equating the normal with the average and seeing the pathological as divergence from this (Lukes 1973: 29). It is clear, however, that the normal is a critical concept: 'our social state is abnormal' (Durkheim 1928a: 266/284); 'normal constraint' is incompatible with wealth and power for Durkheim (1895a: 122n./146n.). And as we have seen, egalitarian aspirations are 'an anticipation of the normal state to come' (1893b: 381/321). It is also clear that the general can be pathological, as witnessed by his conceptions of anomie and the constraining division of labour (1893b). 'The social malaise from which we suffer' is general for Durkheim (1950a: 138/106). This complex chapter of *Les Règles* demonstrates a tension between the normal as a critical concept and as a sociological way of understanding a process which occurs in all societies.

At least part of the problem in understanding it stems from interpreting Durkheim only through Comte. For Comte, normality is a conciliation between constancy and variation: the normal type is the average state, more ideal than real, around which existence revolves (1854).[13] For Gane, the normal equals the stages of society at their appropriate point of development, and pathologies are incomplete developments or residues of this (Gane 1995: 188). There are certainly elements of this in Durkheim's account (1895a: 57/92); however, he rejects the Comtean account both of type (ibid. 76/108) (which is central to the account of generality) and of historical momentum.

The Comtean account concentrates on the normal and pathological as a series of disturbances around an equilibrium (Lagrange 1996: 210). But I suggest that the normal is not simply a question of integration or of a science of structures; it is above all a question about action for Durkheim: science is connected with life, practice and with the ends of action (1895a: 48/85). 'The principal object of a science of life is to define the normal state' (ibid. 74/104).

When Renouvier talks of 'the normal order of things' (Renouvier 1869b: 1.283), he does not mean the status quo articulated in terms of a science of nature. For him, the goal of 'the science of life ... is to specify the connections of type, succession and the mutual conditioning of functions' (1875d: 1.356), which for a conscious reflective being must concern conscience and its milieu. For him, the normal cannot be understood without the theory of the conditions of existence, which generally states that nothing is produced, first, without its conditions of existence, and second, without the means for being to achieve its ends (1864b: li).[14] This first meaning of condition is that which renders another phenomenon possible – what gives it life. So the 'inferior functions of the body are the conditions of existence of the superior functions' (1875d: 1.354).

But the second meaning concerns the successful pursuit of ends, and thus implies the logic of finality; this involves the satisfaction of tendencies, which can be positive or negative (ibid. 1.252). Positive tendencies are objects of desire (ibid.) which seek to realize themselves in the functional structures which surround conscience (ibid. 1.251). Under this functionalist logic there is an expressive theory of action whose core is human energy, which, when balanced, is in a 'normal' state (Milhaud 1927: 85) and which requires the appropriate milieu in which to realize itself. In both senses the 'normal' can be a critical concept: society can fail as a 'condition of existence', and a milieu can thwart action.

### The argument

Durkheim rejects sciences which deal only with facts and teach us nothing about 'higher ends' (Durkheim 1895a: 48/85). The question of the normal is central to that of good and evil (le mal), and concerns the interests of practice (ibid. 60/94) and the rights of reason (ibid. 49/86); it is a question of what we should will (vouloir) (ibid. 47/85). He connects normality with the norm which should be the basis of 'our practical reasonings' (ibid. 49/ 87). These considerations have been neglected – as too has been the question of why the 'goal of humanity' and the question of 'effort' (ibid. 74/104) enter this chapter. I suggest that the normal, so understood, is concerned with questions of satisfaction of action in the milieu as the only sphere in which significant human life is possible. 'Normally, man finds happiness in realising his nature: his needs are in relation to his means', and this is central to 'the harmony between the constitution of each individual and his condition' (1893b: 369/312). Morbidity is shown in the constraining division of labour when this harmony between 'individual natures and social functions' is perverted (ibid.).

The normal is part of the project of developing solidarity and under-writing change through grasping possibilities – without revolutionary intemperance (1895a: 74/104). As such, it is a critical concept, concerned with the coherence and viability of social action and its reflexive founda-tion – 'every strong state of conscience is a source of life' (1893b: 64/53), which implements science as a form of practical reason.

### The meaning of generality

The force of the argument, as it develops, must rest on the meaning of generality which is tied to the norm of practical reason (1895a: 49/87). His argument that it is only what is general that can count as normal is strongly political. How is the general connected with the normal? First, the general involves the compositional nature of society (ibid. 86/115). It is associated with type: he acknowledges diverse forms of normality among societies and within societies over time – thus his descriptive sense of normality acknowledges the relative and the comparative. However, within a society the association of generality with type involves judge-mental factors – of typification and communication, which are central to how a norm can be produced and sustained in a community. To will the general, then, is to will the communicative possibilities of society – and anything which undermines this is pathological.

This is not to eradicate the individual or difference – for the general understood through type and composition underscores both individuality and sociality. Thus Durkheim argues that 'species' reconciles scientific unity and diversity, and nominalism and realism (ibid. 76–7/108). (And through this he rejects Comtean realism (ibid. 77/109).) For Renouvier, 'species' reconciles nominalism and realism: the truth in realism is that there are general relations which are as real as individuals and the truth of nominalism is the reality of the 'different' (*différent*) (Renouvier 1875c: 1.283).

The meaning of 'thing' is important here. 'For sociology to be really a science of things, the generality of things must be taken as a criterion of their normality' (Durkheim 1895a: 74/104). The meaning of thing as reality, and as associated with objective external relations, elucidates Durkheim's meaning here. Sociology as a science of realities deals with general relations, and it is these alone which establish normality – that is, the health of society. Further, generality characterizes normality *externally* (*extérieurement*) (ibid. 59/94); in a relational structure this means relations other than the inner sphere.

So the norms which should govern practical reason are general conditions other than this inner sphere – again, this is a clear rejection of Cousinian liberalism and conservatism. In this context the health of society can be seen to be a critical concept – the contemporary malaise shows that health is not actually general in society. Durkheim argues that if generality is 'founded in the nature of things', then normality *de facto* becomes normality *de jure* (ibid. 59/94) within the conditions of existence of society (ibid. 60/94). The goal of democratic socialism is to realize normality *de jure* within normality *de facto* (Filloux 1977: 322).

### Action, humanity and normality

This analysis helps us to understand why Durkheim argues for the goal of humanity and the terms in which it can be realized: it is frustrated by action where the term of effort is not specified and limited (Durkheim 1895a: 74/104). How do we successfully pursue the 'goal of humanity' without overturning our condition of existence? Solidarity is one of the conditions of existence of society (1893b: 394/332). The goal of humanity as the supreme end of conduct must be pursued without disturbing the sphere of relations that surround us – without precipitating revolution (1895a: 74/104). The Commune was seen to have retarded what it aimed at and to have produced stasis and political retrogression in turning the people away from socialism. The pursuit of normality, then, expresses the goal of democratic socialism – that is, progressive action on the milieu.[15]

The normal is also a question of what is 'desirable' (ibid. 47/85). Desire is the function by which human being 'realises its works (*oeuvres*)' for Renouvier (1875d: 1.255). He develops the Kantian position that the faculty of desire is 'the cause which realises objects of representation' (ibid. 1.238). Action concerns the realization of ends (shown in the logic of passion), and an end which is completely unassignable leads to ineffective action (ibid. 1.395). It is through the pursuit of ends that conscience is developed (ibid. 1.251). Normal action is successful action, where there is harmony between the functions of conscience and the milieu on which it depends, for this is 'the theatre' of the will (ibid. 1.334). So proposing humanity as the goal/end of action will focus and develop the *conscience collective* for Durkheim – for it is through the postulating of ideals that action is initiated, and the present transformed. This can only be done 'progressively' through the capacity to rise above the 'fortuitous and amoral' nature of things' (Durkheim 1893b: 381/321). 'Humanity' gives a 'term of effort' for collective thinking that looks beyond the present malaise.

## Normality, crime and the conscience collective

We have seen that the function of the *conscience collective* is the constitution of a social world. It is thus a crucial factor not only in the development and maintenance of normality, but in its change and development. The *conscience collective* is central to Durkheim's definition of pathology: crime is that which offends the *conscience collective*. He relativizes crime, and argues that it will always be present – even in a community of saints (1895a: 68/100), since it is central to determining the normal and helping the evolution of morality and law, and thus of change.

Normality is a dynamic process to which the logic of contraries is crucial. Every normal state has its contrary; the pathological is the contrary of the normal (ibid. 74/104). This is evident in Durkheim's account of punishment, which 'consists essentially in a passionate reaction' (1893b: 64/52). And 'the representation of a contrary state' is the primary cause of this; we react against that which is contrary to our feelings and beliefs. The *conscience commune* tolerates 'no contradiction' (ibid. 67/55). In this sense the contrary is a principle of development, for it causes the reaction which provokes action: it produces energy and active forces (ibid. 66/54).

## Normality and the question of conservatism

But is not the argument for normality within limitation a conservative argument, whatever Durkheim's motives? I suggest that it is, to the contrary, an argument for successful action in terms of the milieu. For Renouvier limitation and determinate ends are the conditions of effective action: limitation is central to optimism (Renouvier 1864b: 244ff). This, I suggest, is the thinking behind Durkheim's argument for finding a 'term for effort' and the rejection of 'infinity' (1895a: 74/104). Normal action is healthy action, and health 'implies a harmonious development of all our functions', which can only be the case under conditions of moderation and containment, for without these, illness begins (1893b: 216/183).

The condition for healthy action is, first, balance within – 'Conscience . . . is a set of functions which balance each other' (Durkheim 1893b: 217/183; Renouvier 1875d: 1.232). Secondly, it requires a coherent organization without. As we have seen, abnormality occurs when repetition and the formation of habit do not take place (1893b: 357/302). The habitual is the pivotal link between generality and normality (1895a: 55/92), and is tied to the functional coherence of society (1893b: 344/291). This critical view of the coherence of action is opposed to all those milieux which do not support healthy action. So normality has a dual foundation: externally, it consists in satisfied and consistent action, and internally, it is an integrated, balanced psyche.

So habit and its development through the logic of becoming and finality are central to normality; actions are fixed through repetition. How are 'the rights of reason' (1895a: 49/86) expressed here? Durkheim says that blind habits must be avoided: these are those where the end of action is not clearly represented and is pursued without reflection (Renouvier 1875d: 1.283). Reason is the 'voluntary function' which has an empire over habit, and can modify or change it; thereby the inertia of the mechanical nature of things is overcome (ibid. 1.325). In a wider sense we can see that, for Durkheim, the rights of reason will be satisfied when society is presented as the end of action – that is, when the ends of action are compatible with the generality and stability of the social relations which surround us.

Thus normality does not indicate the *status quo*, as Giddens rightly observed (Giddens 1974: 93). It is central to the dynamic development of society, which is why it is connected with goals of action. 'Society is always in movement, within it there are tendencies towards movement, germs of change, aspirations to be other than it is, ideals which struggle to realise themselves' (Durkheim 1907a(4): 583). It is these goals which must be considered when considering the introduction of the new (ibid.). Tendency (*tendance*) is that which connects the stages of proposed action in the pursuit of ends for Renouvier (1875d: 1.251). This is tied to possibility, and to hope and fear (ibid. 1.264). So grasping possibilities and orienting them towards the compositional being which surrounds conscience is central to the possibility of improvement (ibid. 1.251). Durkheim's argument for egalitarian aspirations as 'anticipation of the normal state to come' (Durkheim 1893b: 381/321) shows a dialectic of reality which moves from inner to outer, motored by the logic of the ideal.

So normality, rather than being central to the dialectic of order and disorder (La Capra 1972), is central to a dialectic of transformation and relative fixity within the logic of becoming. As part of the underlying dynamic of society, the normal bridges 'is' and 'ought', and articulates a complex relationship between structures and ideals (Watts Miller 1996: 19).

## Causality and sociological explanation

Fully adequate explanation in sociology, for Durkheim as for Weber, must be supported by causal analysis. He distinguishes two types of causality, which we can call the 'relational' and the 'representational': both apply to society as an irreducible, interdependent reality.

Against Comte and Spencer, whose conception of social explanation is 'finalist' and 'psychological', Durkheim argues that sociological explanation centres on the social milieu. 'The constitution of the *internal social milieu* is the origin of all social process' (Durkheim 1895a: 111/135).[16] The social milieu is that which generates, brings about, social facts; it is an example of plural holism, which is constituted through association (ibid. 102/130). The volume and dynamic density of society (ibid. 112/136) are established through its 'composition' (ibid. 119/141)[17] – that is, through the number of its social units (*unités*) – which forms a relational 'whole' (*un tout*) (ibid. 113/137).[18] As such, the social milieu is a general fact, which, through its generality, can explain a 'a great number of other facts' (ibid. 115/138). For Renouvier, general phenomena are established through the compositional nature of complex, compound realities, which are associated with the relative permanence of an order (Renouvier 1875c: 1.77).

This is causally effective, and thus invokes efficient causality: a cause is that which is necessary and sufficient; it is that which is effectively determining of the effect. In this, Durkheim (1895a: 126/148) echoes Renouvier and the latter's critique of Mill: to identify causality as the totality of preceding conditions is to deny the real meaning of causality (Renouvier 1875c: 2.77ff). So, for Durkheim, society as a relational whole has a relative permanence, and, through its precedence of individual actions logically and temporarily, can be seen to be a cause of social facts.

But since this social whole is constituted through association, its nature is relational. However, causality is also relational: 'a relation of causality can only be established between two given facts' (Durkheim 1895a: 116/139).[19] There is reciprocity between cause and effect (95/124); it is because there is concomitant variation between social phenomena that causality applies to a social system (ibid. 115/138). Concomitant variation underwrites a form of relational causality which Durkheim opposes to positivism (ibid. 117/140). Cause and effect 'links two terms' (Renouvier 1875d: 1.26); once the false ideas of an absolute continuum and intransitivity are rejected, then causality applies to a plurality of beings. Thus causality applies to the concept of *the relations between* – that is, the social milieu and society as constituting a relational structure; in so doing, it gives scientific rigour to social explanation.

But the significance of the method of concomitant variations for Durkheim is that 'it reaches the causal relation (*rapport*), not by the outside (*du dehors*) but by the inside (*le dedans*)' (Durkheim 1895a: 129/151). As we have seen, the law of concomitant variation applies to 'psychic' phenomena – that is, to the phenomena of conscience, and therefore to the relations between consciences (Renouvier 1876c: 52). Consciences, if not 'absolutes', are associated, and thus they modify each other through communication (1875c: 2.73). This is central to the meaning of the internal social milieu for Durkheim; the 'whole' is a 'psychic individuality' (Durkheim 1895a: 103/129). Causal communicative relations occur between consciences, but also at all levels of conscience; they can be unconscious, and enter into our 'tendencies' and habits. Communication can effect changes; since it effectively brings things about, it generates a reality. Thus the concept of causality applies to it.

But how can causality be both efficient and determining, and be logically applicable to social facts as ways of thinking and acting? The significance of the nature of social facts as representational and of the definition of causality as 'force' is central to the answer to this question. Although Durkheim sets aside 'questions of intention ... as too subjective to be treated scientifically' (ibid. 95/123), nevertheless his account of sociological explanation reconciles meaning, action and causality in a way that has not been clearly recognized. This is largely due to the neglect of representation in *Les Règles*, and to an insistence that 'force' has a mechanistic meaning. In his account, Durkheim straddles the distinct traditions of explanation and understanding (Von Wright 1971).

The existence of 'particular consciences' as the *necessary* condition of social reality means that understanding is central to the approach of the agent to reality. Signification, which is central to thought (Durkheim 1895a: 4/51) and thus to all judgemental, linguistic and symbolic concerns, is crucial to how things are represented, and how and why things are acted on. Religion, in its link between the symbolic and action, demonstrates that how things are signified is crucial to action – it is central to how things are brought about, or caused. It shows the connection between meaning and social causality.

We have seen that the *sufficient* and 'determining' condition of social reality is association (ibid. 111/135) and the 'internal social milieu' is the origin of social processes (ibid.). Although this consists in 'things and persons' (ibid. 112/136), it is the 'properly human milieu' which is the active factor. The volume and dynamic density central to this include the concepts of social attention and the *conscience collective*; the latter is generated out of the association of consciences (ibid. 103/129). As a complex form of thinking about the real and the valuable, this is formed within distinct and determinate 'external' social and historical relations and representations. The 'representations' and 'collective tendencies' have 'the conditions of the whole social body' as 'their generating causes' (ibid. 105/131). This argument calls on the autonomy and causal effectiveness of a general system of representations.

The *conscience collective* within this system of representations generates culture and religion. It is causally effective; but how can this be understood? The *conscience collective* is the result of both the necessary and the sufficient conditions of social life (ibid. 103/129). It is what was later called a 'conditionship concept'. This involves those conditions which are necessary and sufficient for other phenomena; these conditions are causal, without being nomic *per se* (Von Wright 1971: 38ff). So this complex shared intellectual and passional thinking logically precedes and brings about action at the individual level through a 'constraining power' which comes from 'outside' – that is, from relations other than the self (Durkheim 1895a: 101/127). But its necessary intermediaries are the believing, discursive, signifying and feeling functions of conscience.

But why does each conscience accept this? This common thinking represents a world: it brings about a culture, a realm of beliefs and significations, which are fixed in signs and symbols. Thus it forms a significant world, expressed in collective representations, which constitute a form of meaning holism. This explains why the 'determining cause' of social facts (as 'ways of thinking, acting and feeling' (ibid. 4/52)) must be found in antecedent social facts, rather than 'among the states of the individual conscience' (ibid. 109/134). Moreover, it is this which gives the 'authority' to these ways of acting and thinking (ibid. 102/128). These are significant because they are the basis of shared meaning and attachment; they are the crucial link to the action they bring about. The loss of attachment and meaning is devastating to passionate signifying agents who depend on relatedness – that is, on social being. This is, as I have shown, part of the 'prestige' of certain collective representations, and why for Durkheim 'the fact of association is the most obligatory of all' (ibid. 104/130).

So this relational structure on which we depend can generate action by means of the discursive and signifying functions of conscience through the need we have of significant worlds. And it is effective as social causality because it generates action from the level of the plural totality. The logical keys to understanding this are, first, the idea of representational causality – that is, the conception of representations as causes. 'They [representations] are in turn causes' (1898b: 16/4); and second, the ideas of representative force (*force représentative*) (Renouvier 1875c: 2.70) and of 'motor force' (*force motrice*) which relate to the springs of action in beings (1859: 573).[20]

So for Durkheim representation generates action through signification. As I have argued, this is part of the meaning of constraint and its connection with 'the entrails' of society (Durkheim 1895a: 121/143). It is thus that social facts are forces which dominate our own (ibid. 90/120); force here is not a mechanical push, but the 'prestige' of representations which generate action. And behind this, in turn, lies the power or energy of agency, which at the level of the general becomes a collective power. Thus it is for Durkheim that the association of active forces constitutes this form of social reality. There is a dialectic of powers which meet through the interaction of internal and external: agency is stimulated by signification, which comes from the 'outside' – that is, external relations. This is due to the communication of consciences, which leads to relational and meaningful constraints through signs within collective representation.

This argument uses a particular model of causality centring on power. For Renouvier causality does not *per se* contradict freedom or the interest of action: it is only the 'vulgar and idological' sense of causality which turns 'the author of life into a thing which has no life' (Renouvier 1875d: 1.26). Will and causality are only finally incompatible if causality is seen, first, as a universal causal chain such that everything which happens is an effect, and second, if this rests on an absolute continuum – such that no intervention is possible.

*Les Règles* is not such an odd book, inconsistent with both Durkheim's earlier and later works. When its apparently strange, and inappropriate, logic is unravelled, it is not without interest for contemporary debates on social methodology, in its concern with action, structure and signification.

# 8

# Society as the 'Coefficient of Preservation': The Question of Suicide

That the most apparently private and individual of acts has social causes is one Durkheim's boldest claims. The fundamental importance of *Le Suicide* has never been doubted, despite familiar and oft-repeated criticism: of his use of official statistics, his logically inappropriate use of scientific language of causes and currents to explain an act that is permeated by intention and significance; the lack of a micro-theory of suicide and lack of theory of the subject, and the relation of it to his social realism.

If, however, we bring to the interpretation of this complex work neglected concepts and overlooked statements, then at least some of the familiar criticisms can be seen to be misplaced: the concept of conscience and degrees of conscience, society as 'psychic' and as a representational, relational system, the concept of unconscious representation, the communication of consciences, representational and relational causality, the critique of the concept of progress, the neglected concepts of will and individuation, the relation between internal and external, and the concept of relational totality and solidarity. Through these, I claim that Durkheim does attend to the micro-level – through the concepts of tendency and of will and attachment; and that he does have a theory of the subject, and it has a connection to his social realism; and that the scientific language is only inappropriate because of the false gloss that has been put on it. Further, I claim that he develops the idea of pathology of action and the questions about the coherence of the whole into a critique of the moral failure of 'civilization'. It is clear that *Le Suicide* is a test case not simply for *Les Règles*, but for the fundamental ideas of his thought.

Behind his theory lies a dialectic of action which correlates optimism with limitation and pessimism with lack of limitation.[1] He notes 'the correlation of sadness with the feeling of the infinite' (Durkheim 1968d: 2.309). This is not a conservative doctrine; rather, it concerns effective action and the use of energy and power. 'In reality all absolute power

(*puissance*) is the synonym for impote
is central to will: 'The mastery of will
of need' (ibid.). We have seen that,
condition of knowledge; equally, the p
for action, energy and optimism (in a
to absolutism, infinitism and the do
(1864a: 244ff). So, for Durkheim, hope
40), the constructive use of energy, and
avoids both 'the cult of the self' and 'th
72) – are central to positive action.

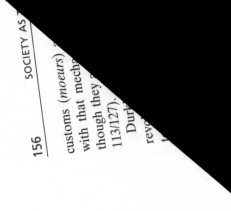

## Conscience, tendencies and t

Taylor (1982) rightly points out the unhelpful characterization of teaching
in this area: Durkheim versus Douglas, positivism versus phenomenolo-
gism. Of course, it must now be clear that Durkheim does not neglect the
theoretical issues of meaning and the orientation of consciousness to
reality. There is in *Le Suicide* an important theory of how consciousness
defines itself and establishes signification: 'All internal life draws its
primary material from outside . . . conscience . . . can only determine itself
through being affected by something other than itself' (Durkheim 1897a:
315/279). Further, the concept of representation and of 'psychic life' is
central to *Le Suicide*. Indeed, nowhere does he make so clear the centrality
of conscious cognitive activity to social life. We have seen that, like
Renouvier, he opposes the 'ancient' theory of the faculties of mind: 'We
no longer see in the different modes of conscious activity separate forces
which are not connected and only find their unity in the centre of a
metaphysical substance, but solidary functions' (ibid. 25/61).

The neglect of this in the interpretation of *Le Suicide* is matched by the
neglect of his view of 'ideation' which is central to his account of
consciousness and action even in his first book (1893b: 64/53). 'Conscious
centres' or 'psychic functions' are crucial to his theory of mind and, as we
shall see, to his theory of suicide, for representations and tendencies do
not have 'their own existence', they 'derive from' and 'express externally'
the general state of these 'conscious centres' (1897a: 25/62). The neglect
of these and their logical anteriority to representation – amongst even
those who acknowledge the centrality of Durkheim's concept of representation – is crucial to misunderstandings of Durkheim's epistemology here.

Against Tarde's theory of imitation, he argues for the reflective nature
of action. 'Between the representation of the action and its execution,
intercalates an intellectual operation, which consists in an apprehension,
clear or confused, fast or slow . . . The way in which we conform to the

...nd fashions of our country has nothing in common ...nical apish imitation ... The first has its reasons even ...re not expressed in the form of an explicit judgement' (ibid.

...heim's central claim for the social nature of suicide and its causes ...lves around his rejection of presumed motives of the agent as satisfac-...ory explanation – for the number of these stays the same, whilst the suicide rate varies (ibid. 144/149). His 'scientism' here is viewed as the explanation for the 'irrelevance of motives' (Pearce 1989: 144). However, the fact that motives are not *sufficient* to bring about suicide does not mean that they are not *necessary* factors. What it means is that there is a deeper cause – which is the general state on which they depend. To acknowledge that conscious motives of the agent are not causes, and that human volitions are complex (Durkheim 1897a: 144/148), is not thereby to exclude levels of consciousness as central factors in explanation by social causes.

The concept of degrees of conscience is crucial here. Durkheim argues that we have to recognize the profound depths (*les dessous profonds*) of 'psychic life' which are only reached with difficulty (ibid. 351/311). In his first book he argued that 'Every strong state of conscience is a source of life; it is a factor of our general vitality. Consequently everything which tends to weaken it diminishes and depresses us' (1893b: 64/53). The unconscious is crucial to his argument: it is in the psychic depths that dwell the passions, habits and tendencies that make up the substrata of each conscience. It is at this level that certain fundamental *tendances* exist; this is central to Durkheim's explanation of suicide, but, together with 'tend-ency', has not been analysed. He holds that the disposition to sacrifice one's life 'is an active tendency' (1897a: 320/284). In an important passage in *Les Règles* he argues that 'the tendency to suicide varies like the tendency to instruction'. But whereas instruction reaches 'only the most superficial regions of conscience; on the contrary our instinct for self-preservation (*conservation*) is one of our most fundamental tendencies'. So he argues that the weakening of religious traditionalism 'simultaneously reinforces the need to know and the penchant to suicide' (1895a: 131/152).

Hope is tied to the instinct for self-preservation and thereby to the 'relative goodness of life' for Durkheim (1893b: 225/190). And it is the instinct for self-preservation that gives us an 'energy' (1897a: 340/302).[3] In an important but overlooked footnote in *Les Règles*, Durkheim talks of 'the finalism which is implied by *existence* and above all by the *persistence of life*' (1895a: 96/144). This has implications for a theory of suicide, since this is a clear form of non-persistence of life! We have seen that action and ends are understood through the logic of finality (state–tendency–passion). Passion brings together state and tendency. Desires, hopes and fears are all forms of passion, and therefore are realizations of a tendency. So tendency is a crucial transitional state in the accomplishment of action; it indicates a movement from one state to another, which is implied in the pursuit of ends. These can be either a search for perfection or the satisfaction of need, and include the instinctive and unconscious realm of action. Tendencies are central to habit, and involve becoming, because all action involves some change – for it implies the movement from one state to another.

Successful action is the realization of an end, which is the satisfaction of a tendency. All passion without a counterweight, or without the conflict of ends, achieves its ends (Renouvier 1875d: 1.279). 'The development of being is the first condition of passion, not stability' (ibid. 1.267). Tendency thus implies a satisfaction in action – it moves towards a state which realizes it; frustration of this leads to a weakening of being. This deep impulse towards realization, if thwarted, is damaging to the instinctual make-up of the being. Joy and sadness (*tristesse*) are passions which involve the augmentation or diminution of power of action: this is the fundamental principle of development of being (ibid. 1.276–7).

Disturbance in the realization of ends leads to disturbance in feeling. This deeply affects the instinctual preservation of self; hope is central to the instinct of self-preservation and is given under finality (Renouvier 1875c: 2.169). So Durkheim argues that 'When desires can no longer be satisfied, suicide is the natural conclusion' (Durkheim 1968d: 2.309). When people have lost the habit of hoping, of turning towards the future, then hope loses its energy, and life loses its meaning (1893b: 225–6/190).[4] Then the instinct for self-preservation is undermined, together with all other tendencies in the deeper layers of conscience, which require satisfaction in coherent action. 'The tendencies which are not satisfied atrophy and as the tendency to live is only the result of all the others, it can only be weakened if the others are slackened (*se relâchent*)' (1897a: 272/246).

For Renouvier, a habit can strengthen or weaken a passion; it thus reinforces or weakens the tendencies which are realized through passion in action. A break in habitual action is a weakening of all these unconscious tendencies which are the unconscious bedrock on which reflective action occurs. Tendency implies a positive direction and determination for its satisfaction. For Durkheim also, any vacuum (*le vide*) as well as the infinite (*l'infini*) are enemies of this instinctive tendency of being, for they threaten the satisfaction of action. 'Those vacuums (*ces vides*) which separate consciences and which make them strangers one to another come precisely from the slackening of the social tissue' (ibid. 317/281).

### Social reality, collective tendencies and communication

The tendencies which concern Durkheim above all are the collective tendencies: 'Collective tendencies have their own existence; these are forces as real as cosmic forces, even though they are of a different nature; they equally act on individuals from outside (*du dehors*), even though this is through other routes' (1897a: 348/309).

The distinction of collective from individual tendencies (ibid. 350/310) relies on his definition of society as a 'whole' established through association (ibid.). It is a whole composed of parts, which is neither 'substantial' nor 'ontological' (ibid. 362/320). It is in this that the ground and cause of collective tendencies must be found. We have seen that 'representations, emotions and collective tendencies' have 'the whole social body' as their cause (1895a: 105/131). Since this social whole is a psychic reality, made of representations, it follows that collective tendencies and forces are representational. 'Tendencies or collective passions' must be regarded as 'things' – that is, they are realities which dominate particular consciences (1897a: 345/307).

The reconsideration of 'thing', exteriority and force must help to elucidate Durkheim's thinking here. I have argued that thing is compatible with representation and relation, and that its central meaning indicates a reality. To see a collective tendency as a thing is to argue that it has reality, but how is this exterior? This concept is central to Lukes's critique of Durkheim. I have argued that exteriority indicates logically those forms of reality other than the inner sphere. In this sense the totality of social relations is external to the self; collective tendencies are external to each conscience, for they come from a source other than the self.

The connection of exteriority to interiority in reality is most important to the understanding of the logic of suicide. I have argued that the reality formed through association is representational and relational. It is in a 'psychic' reality that the 'wind of sadness and discouragement blows', and this is connected with signification (ibid. 356/315). This reality is collective and general; as such, it is external to each particular conscience, yet it is not thereby out of touch with it, for its reality is representational. Collective representations are external to the self, but they pass from the external to the internal; this is central to the explanation of how the social affects the individual. We have seen that 'representations and tendencies do not have their own life'; not only do they manifest externally the general state of 'the conscious centres', they are in dialectic interchange with this centre. 'Consequently these cannot have a morbid character without this state becoming vitiated' (ibid. 25/61).

I have argued that this connection between representations and conscious centres and representative functions has been overlooked, and with it an important aspect of the explanation of suicide has been lost; for as collective representations become morbid, so do the conscious centres on which they depend, through the passage from the external to the internal. So, for example, 'the most cultivated societies are also those in which the representative functions are the most necessary and developed . . . at the same time, because of their great complexity, an almost incessant condition of change is a condition of their existence, it is at this precise moment that neurasthenics are the most numerous' (ibid. 45/76).

How are tendencies forces, and how are they transmitted? The ideas of the unconscious, representational force and social reality formed through association and the communication of consciences are fundamental to Durkheim's explanatory apparatus. Indeed, the constitution of this reality relies on this theory of the communication of consciences, and it is through this that tendencies are expressed. 'In a vital and coherent society there is from all to each and from each to all a continual exchange of ideas and feelings and a kind of mutual moral assistance, which makes the individual, instead of being reduced to its own force, participate in the collective energy which stimulates their own when it is exhausted' (ibid. 224/210).[5] It is through failure in this communication of consciences that morbidity in the 'will to live' arises. 'This is evident in anomic suicide', for in these conditions, 'does not the will to live become weakened?' (ibid. 282/253).[6]

An invisible world is expressed in these communicative relations, one that affects at a profound level our 'will to live'. Durkheim first raises this idea in *De la Division du travail social* where he talks of the will to live (1893b: xl/xxvii). In *L'Éducation morale* he discusses the concept of an energy which is attached to life: 'To live, we must face up to multiple necessities with a limited amount of vital energies . . . (this) is necessarily limited . . . by the sum total of forces which we have at our disposition, and the respective importance of ends pursued. All life is thus a complex equilibrium, whose diverse elements limit one another, and this equilibrium cannot be broken without producing suffering and illness' (1925a: 34/39).

The hitherto negected concept of 'hope' is central to Durkheim's account of action, and thus of suicide. 'If men have learned to hope, they have formed the habit of orientating to the future and there to find compensation for their present suffering' (1893b: 225/190). Hope plays a part in the instinct for preservation: its loss is associated with a loss of energy whereby life loses its attraction (ibid. 225–6/190). Hope alone, however, is not a sufficient explanation of the preference for life to death, for we learn to hope and to have a will to live only in the social milieu. The coherence and continuity of the milieu is central to viable human life: it is this which gives the terms and limits of action. 'If our efforts lead to

nothing lasting, why should we labour in vain?' (1887c: 1.329). A conception of the meaningfulness of action as central to a happy life is central to
Durkheim's critique of civilization for its suicide rate (1893b: 226/191).
Neglect of his view of action and its ends leads to the overlooking of this
point: 'an inaccessible end' leads to 'permanent discontentment' (1897a:
274/248); 'when our efforts are destined to end in nothingness (*le néant*)',
then our courage to live is lost (ibid. 225/210).

We have seen above that for Durkheim power and limitation are
connected: real power of the self goes with limitation, just as powerlessness
goes with lack of limitation, the feeling of the 'infinite' and a too
rapid progress. The concept of limitation, which is central to happiness, is
thus part of the explanatory apparatus of suicide, for it is this which gives
rise to 'the average contentment ... the feeling of calm and active joy; it
is this pleasure of being and living, which for societies as for individuals,
is the characteristic of health' (ibid. 277/270). Increasing suicide rates
attest to a decrease in the average (*moyen*) happiness, which for Durkheim is what is meant by the happiness of society. This is achieved
through the social milieu, when 'all are subject to similar conditions of
existence' and to a certain 'manner of being' and common happiness
(1893b: 228/192).

## Suicide and the problem of causality

Durkheim's argument regarding the social causes of suicide does not entail
neglect of the individual: Lukes's criticisms notwithstanding, Durkheim
does attend to a micro-theory within the terms of a general theory of
society. 'Thus in the common milieu which envelops them, there exists
some force which inclines all in the same direction, and whose greater or
lesser intensity makes for the higher or lower number of particular
suicides' (1897a: 343/305). He uses the concept of number to express the
circulation of ideas, feelings and tendencies: the intensity of feeling is
proportional to the number of consciences which feel in common – that is,
to the density of a group (ibid. 347/308).[7] Suicides are connected with
feelings sustained through the social milieu, so the strength of contact
established therein protects against suicide (ibid. 214/202). Thus suicides
increase when society disintegrates – for example, on the eve of the
French Revolution with the disintegration of the *ancien régime* (ibid. 215/
203).

We saw in the last chapter that relational causality applies to the
concomitant variation of relations in the internal social milieu, in the
communicative relations between consciences; it is here that the forces
which make up suicidal currents exist. Durkheim's explanation in terms of

forces is seen as crucial to the failure of his account: how can 'external forces' account for will or motivation? But the latter are definitive features of the consciences which are the necessary elements of the internal social milieu.

This communicative whole involves a dialectic of reality which involves the constitution of social reality as a system of forces. As we have seen, force is a power which is immanent in conscience, and which moves from the internal to the external and is developed, through association, into the semi-autonomous nature of social reality, which exists at the external side of representation. This social reality ideally feeds the individual through reciprocal exchanges of positive attachment and relationship. This system – as relational and representational – has its own life, however, and when the milieu is damaged, the collective force no longer provides the energy required by the will to live; it no longer feeds the individual 'force' – that is, the person's power and energy. The reciprocal connection between the inner and the outer and between collective representations and conscious centres means that the damage to social relations leads to internal damage to the individual, because of his or her dependence on social relations. There is a relationship between 'collective melancholy' and 'morbidity of conscience' (ibid. 424/370). The micro and the macro meet in suicidal currents: the cultivation of representative functions in advanced societies, seen in the development of neurasthenia, 'is a terrain on which very different tendencies can be born according to the way in which they are fed by social causes' (ibid. 45/77).

The concept of 'representative force' explains how these suicidal currents operate in a representational world; the connection between force and the mental is evident: 'The mental system of a people is a system of definite forces' (ibid. 446/387). The concept of a deep, unconscious representational cause, which is expressed as a force, is central to Durkheim's conception of the social causality involved here. 'The collective subject feels [the collective unhappiness] obscurely, whose action he or she submits to, but is not clearly aware of it' (ibid. 423/369).[8] That these forces can operate in the social milieu is because the latter 'is made of ideas, of beliefs, of habits of communal tendencies' (ibid. 339/302).[9]

Force stems originally from conscience, and is then transferred to society; so there is a dialectic of powers here. Failure in relatedness amongst social forces generates a macro-degree of non-attachment; the links that bind us are loosened and this has micro-results – in individual actions of suicide. It is in this sense that society as an active system of forces is the cause of the phenomenon of suicide; society has the power both to sustain and to destroy individual life through the strength of its forms of attachment. The tendencies of action and, with them, the will to live require definite terms under which they can be satisfied, and are reinforced or weakened by the nature and conditions of social relations. Thus a failure of relatedness at the macro-level is apprehended, albeit at an unconscious level, by each conscience. This is what is meant by the determinate amount of energy in the collective force which impels human beings to self-destruction. Here the logical relation between representation and relation is important, for morbid social representations enter conscience, and thereby affect its power of attachment at unconscious levels.

Suicide is thus a test case not only for the theory of solidarity, but also for the theory of social causality. Durkheim's definition of a relational causality in *Les Règles* is illustrated by his argument in *Le Suicide* – that suicides rise as the social milieu suffers.

## Solidarity and the will to live

'This tendency to suicide has its source in the moral constitution of groups' (ibid. 343/305).[10] What is it about the moral constitution of groups that gives rise to it? The central theme of *De la Division du travail social*, the relationship between individual personality and social solidarity, reappears in *Le Suicide*. It is in the relation between forms of individuation and solidarity that the causes of suicide in its egoistic and altruistic forms lie.

Theories of self, individuation and will are needed to explain this adequately, and it is these which are lacking from the interpretation of Durkheim so far. We have seen that Durkheim has a theory of individuation and of will understood as a personal energy. Normal action is a reconciliation of contrary tendencies of individuality and integration where the functions of conscience are in a balanced relationship with each other and the milieu in which they act; normal action expresses satisfaction in action and achievements of will.

By contrast, too much will or too little gives the wrong kind of energy for adequate integration. Egoism is that state where 'the individual self affirms itself (*le moi individuel s'affirme*) with excess in face of the social self and at the expense of it'. This results in an 'unbounded individuation (*individuation démesurée*)' (ibid. 225/210).[11] Here we no longer have the courage to live – that is, to act and to struggle – for when we have only ourselves as the objective of action, 'all our efforts are finally destined to lose themselves in nothingness (*le néant*)' (ibid.).

Altruistic suicide expresses a 'contrary' state: here there is insufficient individuation. Society prevents 'divergences', and the individuals cannot make their own 'milieu' which is unique to themselves (ibid. 238/238). There is too much 'impersonality' (ibid. 243/225), and the individual is deprived of reality. (Even so, acts of altruistic suicide are accomplished with 'enthusiasm', and are 'affirmed' in acts of a 'great energy' (ibid. 244/

225).) The army, which represents the chronic condition of altruistic suicide, has as its 'coefficient of aggravation . . . the states, acquired habits or natural predispositions which constitute the military mind' (ibid. 254/ 234). But these habits of 'passive obedience, of absolute submission are more and more in contradiction with demands of the public conscience' (ibid. 259/238).

Fatalist suicide occurs when there are no possibilities for the exercise of human power and therefore of will; the natural expression of the tendencies of action and, most importantly, of the will are blocked. Anomic suicide is different from egoistic and altruistic suicide, and reflects a breakdown in the overall coherence of relatedness and thus in 'the regulating action' of society; the anomic state of society 'weakens the will to live' (ibid. 282/253). A limitation of power is central to a healthy will and thus to the will to live. By contrast, the 'illusion of power' makes us believe that we are independent of others. Financial crises (both negative and positive) entail a 'rupture of equilibrium' which pushes the individual to voluntary death. The individual is weakened by extreme disturbances of wealth and poverty. Anomie here means lack of discipline of feelings and will as a result of disturbances in relations and thus in the continuity of contact (ibid. 281/253).

## Action and stability

Durkheim uses the theory of tendency and its centrality to a theory of action and the habitual in his concept of anomic suicide: the overturning of habits is central to anomic suicide (ibid. 322/285) and involves rupture of the equilibrium of the individual with his or her milieu (ibid. 326/288). Tendency is central to satisfied action, and a dissatisfied tendency atrophies: thus the will to live, which 'is only a result of all the others', is also weakened (ibid. 272/246). Satisfied action is balanced action; it is impossible if ends are inaccessible because they are infinite; this can only lead to a state of perpetual discontent (ibid. 274/248).

So for Durkheim limitation is central to effort and hope; passions lack restraint in anomic suicide (ibid. 288/258). All who make material prosperity the coefficient of industrial success fail to recognize this; this is true of both political economy and economic materialism. The apotheosis of the dogma of material prosperity leads to an unlimiting of desires, which translates into rates of anomic suicide (ibid. 284/255). The theories which 'celebrate this instability' are 'the passion for infinity' as 'a mark of moral distinction' and 'the doctrine of progress, the most rapid as possible' (ibid. 287/257).

The doctrine of continuous progress based on the excitement of new and more intense pleasures is destructive of the real conditions of effective action in human beings. The will to live is part of these tendencies of action, and disappears when the conditions of effective and realized action (satisfied action) are damaged. There is an important passage in *De la Division du travail social* which concerns action, habit and pleasure – that is, a crucial micro-theory of action – which is important for understanding Durkheim's account of action and his rejection of the doctrine of progress. Happiness is relative (as Comte recognized (Durkheim 1893b: 231/195)); it does not increase with progress.

But it is Renouvier's theory of action, habit and periodicity and the unconscious which informs Durkheim's theory of action in the social milieu. For Durkheim, happiness, like pleasure, disappears as it is repeated: continuous repetition makes happiness disappear, for it becomes unconscious. 'The needs of the mind are periodic, like the psychic functions to which they correspond' (ibid. 1893b: 234/197). Absolute continuity, which is the denial of periodicity, requires that we have new pleasures and new excitements. Discontinuous repetition, on the other hand, although it is habitual, is at well-spaced intervals; it is thus felt, and the expense of energy is repaired – whereas, if it is repeated without interruption, then each function is exhausted and becomes unhappy (*douloureuse*). Healthy action thus requires habits that are characterized by periodicity: these lead to a feeling of well-being. Here the pathological continuous need for excitement, which leads to a vacuum (*vide*) opening up, which needs to be filled, is replaced by a feeling of well-being. So Durkheim argues that there is a need for stability in our enjoyments (*jouissance*) and a regularity to our pleasures: it is on this condition that life maintains itself.

In this micro human world there is a dialectic of reality, between two contrary needs: the need for stability (because we attach ourselves to that which we like) and the need for change (ibid. 235/198). (Cf Renouvier: 'Every passion implies the feeling of contraries' (1875d: 1.267).) Change and stability as two contrary functions which are reconciled in a synthesis of regular, stable functions are the condition for effective action and happiness. At the centre of this is the logic of need. A 'complete need', Durkheim argues, requires two terms: a tension of will and a definite object. However, with 'incorrigible malcontents', this process is 'half representative' (Durkheim 1893b: 235/198).[12] Here the object is in the imagination, 'an intimate poetry', instead of being 'an effective movement of the will'. It does not take us out of ourselves, but is merely 'an internal agitation' (ibid.).

What he means by 'representative' is crucial to understanding Durkheim's theory of action and its satisfaction. For Renouvier, will is a representative function; effective action, such that the objects of will are realized, goes from inside to outside. That is, it goes from the representative side of representation to the represented, external side. In contrast to this, in ineffective, unsatisfied action, this energy is blocked half-way. This frustrates the tendencies which require that the movement implied in all action (whether of needs or of ideal) is realized in the new state aimed at.

So in general Durkheim's theory does not neglect meaning or action; indeed, it goes beyond a mere phenomenology of meaning, and points to the depths of the psyche and the bonds it has to society through attachments, feelings and tendencies. Durkheim thereby points to a subtle diffusion of meaning throughout a social system that goes beyond the attributions of meaning by one consciousness to what is invisibly shared in a society, and which transcends each person; this is the realm where solidarity is constituted and maintained.

The theory underlying *Le Suicide* is that it is solidarity which preserves us, which echoes the socialist interest in society as forum for the development and maintenance of human life. In societies characterized by sad suicide (*suicide triste*), the proper forms of autonomy and solidarity have not been worked out. It is the median relation of the person in terms of individuation and solidarity that is the life preserver. 'It is the action of society which raises in us feelings of sympathy and solidarity which inclines us towards others' (1897a: 226/211). The more we are detached from this, the more likely is suicide.

## The vision and the practical dimension

There is a whole philosophy of life here – a socialist republican vision – which revolves around not only certain analytic dimensions, but also a conception of a positive role for society. Society as the whole has duties to the parts: first, it must provide solidarity and communication and, through these, the energy to hope and live for each member; secondly, it should provide the regular conditions of life for effective and individuated action to be possible; thirdly, it must provide the forum for the proper relations between autonomy and solidarity, in which relatedness and individuation can occur; and fourthly, it should establish a system of relations where the deepest feelings that lie 'obscure' in our conscience, whilst contained and disciplined by the collective force, are not suffocated or contradicted, such that reflective will, which lies at the surface of conscience, is not denied by society.

The suicide rate demonstrates that these duties have not been performed satisfactorily – it is evidence of 'alarming moral misery' (ibid. 1897a: 445/387). 'It is the moral constitution of society which fixes at each instant the contingent of voluntary deaths' (ibid. 336/299).[13] The solution

can be found only through reflection, and intelligence is our only guide –
we must 'remake a *conscience* for ourselves' (ibid. 171/169) to reawaken
'communal things', thereby to effect a rebirth of solidarity. This must
involve 'uninterrupted communication', 'through a power charged with
representing the general interest' (ibid. 439/382). This power must be
decentralized, and for Durkheim, in the specific historical situation of
France, only a professional organization was capable of mediating between
an over-centralized state and a 'dust storm' (*poussière inconsistante*) of
individuals (ibid. 448/389).

# 9

# The Thinking State: Power and Democracy

'The essential function of the state is to liberate individual personalities' (Durkheim 1950a: 98/62). Acknowledgement of this view, so surprising for the 'vulgar' Durkheim, is marred, first, by the tendency to identify Durkheim with thinkers who hold an opposite or different view – Hobbes, Hegel and Comte – and, second, by the neglect of his account of freedom and individuation. Parsons's comparison of Durkheim with Hobbes casts a gloss of seventeenth-century statism over Durkheim's account of the state. Hobbes argued for 'Leviathan' as a unified and centralized state power against which there was no right of opposition: there can be no conflict between the individual and state if there are no individual rights. This view carried forward what Taine called the '*romain*' view of power of the state: all sovereignty, understood as unified and inalienable, is invested in the prince, whose power is unlimited; the first object of the state is the growth of power both internally and externally. This view of state power, which acknowledges no limitation on centralized power, is complemented by a top-down view of authority.

Durkheim, on the contrary, argues for a diffuse, not a concentrated, view of power: power comes from the collectivity, and is limited by the relations of the milieu; both constitute a check on state power. His account of the derivation of power attempts to satisfy jointly the interests of democracy and those of sociological explanation. Against both Hobbes and Hegel, who held that law and morality appear only fully with the state, Durkheim argued that they appear as soon as several individuals enter 'into relation' and live together (1886a: 200). His account of social power is compatible with individual liberty and rights: the interest of the modern state is to foster, rather than oppose, individual rights.

Nisbet's interpretation implies a theocratic account of the state, which continues the *de facto* realism and justification for established power of Hobbes. Both Bonald and Maistre opposed the individualism of the eighteenth century and the revolution of 1789, and denied its conception of rights. In society as established and necessary fact, built on hierarchy and subordination, there are no rights, only duties. The central idea of theocracy is that social order and its constitution infinitely exceed human power; it is beyond reason and human will, which the revolution had shown to be perverse and finally impotent. A power which does not carry the mark of the divine is illegitimate: papal authority, with its unified and inalienable sovereignty, is the model for all forms of state power. The power of the sovereign must not be limited even by a constitution. Durkheim, on the contrary, argues that the duty of the state is to both represent the authority which stems from the collectivity and to be the crystallization of rational thinking. 'For a democratic society, the people and the State are but two aspects of one and the same reality. The State is the people becoming conscious of itself, of its needs and aspirations, but through a more clear and complete conscience' (1915c: 54). Power must be contained, and authority must be compatible with democracy.

In this way Durkheim has been interpreted through thinkers who justify the use of *raisons d'état* ('reasons of state') against the person; yet he specifically repudiates this (1898c: 265/46).[1] False political analogies continue in contemporary accounts of Durkheim: Parkin (1992: 74) and Birnbaum (1976) draw a comparison between Durkheim's and Hegel's views of the state, the latter with its 'quasi-mystical properties'. One reason for this may be a misunderstanding of the *conscience collective* as absolutist and as akin to Hegel's idea of *Geist*.

### The critique of Hegel and the absolutist view of the state

Durkheim rejects the Hegelian view of the state: with its view of ends which transcend the individual, it is characteristic sociologically only of pre-industrial states which have a religious character. These have been replaced by the religion of the 'human person' (Durkheim 1950a: 91–2/55). Theoretically he rejects the Hegelian view for its 'absolutism' and 'hypostatisation' – that is, for its conception of the state as 'a transcendent being, superior to individuals and to laws' (1886a: 199). It is not an 'entity' or a 'substance', but 'a collection of organised individuals' (ibid. 200). His pluralist definition of the whole was partly constituted to oppose political absolutism, and it is not insignificant that Durkheim uses it in his *Leçons de sociologie*. A social group is 'a whole formed by parts: the ultimate element whose repetition constitutes the whole is the individual' (1950a: 53/14). The containment of power through its reciprocal relations is central to his democratic vision.

This is quite distinct from the political absolutism he confronted in *L'Allemagne au-dessus de tout* of 1915. Treitschke was the clearest theorist of the view of the state as 'absolute'. On this view, the state is above international laws, civil society and morality, and its proponents advocate a power of the state free from all limitation, which uses war as an instrument of its will (1915c: 20). Against this Durkheim argues for the relativity of sovereignty (ibid.), and for the internal limitation of state power. This must be complemented by an external limitation of the power of states, through their containment by other powers within terms of international laws. He argues that in this form of political absolutism, morality is only for 'little people', whereas for him, the object of morality is 'to realise humanity and to liberate it from servitudes ... to render it more loving and fraternal' (ibid. 45). Treitschke utters 'not a word on humanity', or the state's duty towards it (ibid. 44).[2]

The absolutist view of the state is characterized by a 'morbid' mentality central to which is a 'hypertrophy' of the will, which has a 'mania of willing' (*manie de vouloir*) and 'a morbid inflation'. By contrast, 'the normal and healthy will ... knows how to accept the necessary limitation of the milieu; to liberate themselves from this a vacuum (*vide*) must be created – which means to place itself beyond the conditions of life itself' (ibid. 84). The will to power, outlined by Nietzsche, is central to such absolutist conceptions of sovereignty.

Renouvier's doctrine of limitation is evident here, as is his attack on the Kantian conception of pure will. This he viewed as just as much a source of 'political terror' as Hegelianism; indeed, through its 'absolute' nature, 'pure will', like 'pure reason', leads directly to Hegelian absolutism and oppressive politics. Will can function only as one of the balanced and integrated functions of conscience, which finds its sphere of activity and limitation within the definite laws of the milieu which surrounds it; it cannot act in a vacuum (*vide*), but needs definite laws and conditions in which to exercise its personal power (Renouvier 1875d: 1.236).

A reading of this text should dispel any notion of Durkheim as a proto-Fascist. The optimism of his earlier views, however, is tempered, as he acknowledges future dangers posed by such a pathology of sovereignty and its mentality, forged between aspects of German idealism and Prussian politics. Significantly in terms of later historical developments, Durkheim argues that this mentality exists in the back of our consciousness (*l'arrière plan de conscience*) in the cultures where it was widespread (Durkheim 1915c: 13).

## The state as the organ of social thought

Although Durkheim begins an analysis of the state in his *De la Division du travail social*, it is in his *Leçons de sociologie* that he develops his positive theory of the state. This is developed through a critique of the 'mystical' and the individualist view of the state. For the latter, which he identifies with Kant, Rousseau, Spencer and the political economists, the individual alone is real, and society, being 'merely an aggregate', can function only negatively to prevent abuses. This view, he argues, is in contradiction of the social and historical facts: the functions of the state grow as history advances, and the state has other roles beyond caring for individual rights (1950a: 89/53). The 'mystical' view (which includes the Hegelian account) postulates an end superior to individuals to which individuals are simply a means of realization for the glorification of the state. But Durkheim supports contemporary democratic views, which specifically repudiate making the person an instrument subject to control by the state (1950a: 124/90). 'There is no "*raison d'état*" which can excuse an attack against the person when the rights of the person are above the state' (1898c: 265/46).[3] So the 'mystical' theory is not only false theoretically, but is morally unsound – indeed, Durkheim regretted signs of its contemporary renaissance.

Can Durkheim mediate between these two positions? Can he establish a positive theory of the role of the state without becoming 'mystical'? And can he maintain that the state's essential function is the liberation of personality without espousing the individualist theory of the state which he rejects? To fully understand his positive definition of the state, it is important to see how this in turn relies on certain theoretical positions. First, it requires rejection of the false view of the whole and of finalism, in contrast to which he uses the concepts of human ends and 'humanity'. He uses logical pluralism to underwrite the concept of diffuse power against the concentration of power underwritten by such false theoretical unification. Secondly, it requires a conception of human reality as representational and relational, whose focal point is conscience with its degrees. Thirdly, it needs the concept of habit and its role in social existence and its transformation through clarification of the unconscious *obscur*. And fourthly, it uses power as relational, and as contained and limited by the sphere of relations of which it is a part, and authority as stemming from the collectivity.

## Representations and the democratic state

His conception of the state rests on a definition of political society which is logically pluralist: 'A society formed by the union of a greater or lesser *number* of secondary social groups, subject to the same authority, which is not under the jurisdiction of any superior regularly constituted authority' (1950a: 82/45). In *De la Division du travail social* the modern state does not develop until mechanical solidarity has disappeared together with its unified *conscience collective*.

In *Leçons de sociologie* he defines the state as 'the organ of social thought' (ibid. 87/50). He uses the theory of representation to develop his earlier account of the state as an organ whose function is to co-ordinate the parts of the system. Since representations are elaborated in a milieu, they are necessarily collective (ibid. 85/48). 'The state is a special organ charged with elaborating special representations which are *of worth* for the collectivity' (ibid. 87/50).[4] This discussion of the state is located within terms of 'civic morality', and thus in terms of reciprocal obligations between state and individual (ibid. 84/48). As we will see below, this involves democratic communication, and the conception of 'psychic collective life', which is diffuse in society, is significant here (ibid. 85–6/49). In the context of parliamentary democracy, this becomes localized in 'a determined organ' (ibid. 87/50).

The state is 'a group of *sui generis* functionaries, within which representations and volitions which engage the collectivity are worked out'. It is not simply the instrument of 'canalizations' and 'concentrations' of the psychic life of the collectivity; it is in a sense 'the organising centre of the subgroups'. Since the *conscience collective* is diffuse in society and extends beyond the State, the latter is not the incarnation of the *conscience collective*. The representations of the state differ from those of the currents of psychic life in which they are grounded by 'being more conscious of themselves, of their causes and their aims' (ibid. 86/50). Thus the state is the organ of social thought: its essential function is to think. 'The whole life of the state does not proceed in external actions, in movements, but in deliberations, that is in representations.' These representations become practical, for the State thinks not just to construct doctrines, but 'to direct collective conduct' (ibid. 87/51).

## Different types of state

The definition of the state as the organ of collective thought allows a distinction between different types of state. Aristocracies and democracies are at opposite poles on a continuum between obscure and clear thinking: democratic states are more conscious, whereas undemocratic states rely on unconscious, unacknowledged habits and obscure feelings (ibid. 123/89), and instinctive and unreflective habits are resistant to change (ibid. 121/87). The positive value of democracy is that it brings all unconscious (*obscur*) aspects of social reality into the clear light of social conscience; and the more 'light' that is introduced into the depths of social life, the more change will be introduced. Democracy depends on 'deliberation, reflection and the critical spirit' (ibid. 123/89). By contrast, Traditionalism, feudalism and 'pseudo–democracies' require the 'maximum of obscurity and unconsciousness', and are incompatible with free critique (ibid. 121/ 88). 'The point of reflection and of the critical spirit is to oppose the dominance of habit' (ibid.); all 'habits are resistant to change precisely because they are obscure' (ibid. 117/84).

So the conceptions of free thought and critical reflection are central to the constitution of democratic states and their forms of authority. Communication becomes clearer, malleability becomes greater, and, because it depends on reflection, change is easier and more rapid. The moral superiority of democracy is that it is a regime of reflection. It must become more so, Durkheim argues, as European societies develop in the administration of justice, education and in the economic life of peoples (ibid. 120/ 86).

Durkheim elucidates the governmental 'conscience' with the analogy to the clear consciousness (*conscience claire*) of the individual in relation to the unconscious. Like the enlightened consciousness, it must bring the obscure parts of personality – habits and tendencies – to reflection. The central conscience is relatively clear by comparison with 'the anonymous, confused, representations which are the substructure of our mind' (ibid. 114/80). The state must not only think more consciously and more freely; it must be the centre for 'new, original representations' whose role is to encourage society with 'more intelligence' than when it is moved by unconscious feelings (ibid. 125–92). As I have argued, conscience means a 'thinking', which here the government must accept and clarify. But the duty of the state is not simply to represent this, but to develop new thinking to overcome the habit-ridden tendencies of the collectivity.

## Power, pluralism and democracy

Durkheim's definition of the nature of democratic government is complemented by his definition of absolutism in 'Deux lois de l'évolution pénale'. Absolutist power is characterized by a lack of reciprocal or bilateral relations: it is defined by the unilateral nature of relations (1901ai: 246/23). 'That which makes power more or less absolute is the more or less radical absence of any countervailing force that is systematically organised with the intention of moderating that power.' Indeed, in an anticipation of the dangers of 'democratic centralism', he continues: 'One can foresee that what gives rise to such a power is the unification (*réunion*) of all the directing functions of the state in one and the same hand' (ibid. 247/23). In contrast, through his logical pluralism, he underlines the importance of the reciprocality of relations to define power in a democracy; this theoretically limits any impulse to absolutism.

To understand his views of democratic power, we must look at what he means by both authority and power. In *L'Éducation morale* he argues that a large part of the problematic of authority is to examine the mental processes which are at the basis of it (1925a: 25/29). In *De la Division du travail social* he argues that the conception of authority stems from the conscience collective. 'Wherever a leading power establishes itself, its first and principal function is to respect the beliefs, traditions, collective practices, that is to say to defend the common conscience against all its internal and external enemies.' This power stems from the *conscience collective* through its 'force' and is 'communicated' (1893b: 51/42). We have seen that it is the communication between consciences which is central to this, and which at the same time prevents any absolutism for this collective thinking. This establishes a bottom-up authority, rather than a top-down one, for this indicates society obeying its own spontaneously established rules. In *Les Règles* he argues: 'To give a government the authority . . . it is necessary to address the only source from which any authority derives . . . traditions and common mentality (*esprit*)' (1895a: 91/120). And in *Leçons de sociologie* he argues that 'the only rational authority is the one with which society is endowed in relation to its members' (1950a: 107/73). There is here a reflexive and communicative model of power, whose foundation and legitimation are conscience and the *conscience collective* from which power stems.

Durkheim, in a review of Merlino's *Formes et essences du socialisme*, argues that the authority of the state must be 'controlled by collective power' (1899e: 3.171/57). Neglect of a theory of power and misunderstanding of the meaning of force in Durkheim's thought have contributed to neglect of his account of the democratic control of power. I have shown that, for Durkheim, power comes from society as 'active force'. It is through the power of collective agency that the power of the state, which has a tendency to grow, must be limited. Power stems from agency initially – the power (*puissance*) of the person – but is transformed into the power of society by collective association. The concept of force as a form of active agency and power carries the idea of productive power (1912a: 519/367). In *Les Formes élémentaires* the totem represents this collective power: it is collective force objectified and projected on to a material thing. A democratic government is constituted by collective power, but equally, is limited by it: it is charged with representing the collective force, as an agency of thinking and acting on behalf of the collectivity.

Power and authority stem from society; the concept of derivation is central to the sociological analysis of power: political power is derived from social power (Filloux 1977: 222). The state is a modality of the exercise of political power, involving a dialectic of power, which derives from the collectivity. In societies characterized by mechanical solidarity, political power is represented as the incarnation of the collective type: power is the derivation of the force immanent in the common conscience. The same logic is less easy to see in societies characterized by organic society, because of the heterogeneity of groups therein; but social power is still the root of political power, through the social forces which Davy characterizes as 'the globalising sovereign' (Durkheim 1950a: 33/lxvii). The logical pluralism of the definition of wholes theoretically underwrites the control of power by the constituting elements of any collectivity.

Filloux rightly rejects Coser's argument that Durkheim misunderstands the role of political power, for it neglects his articulation of social power (Filloux 1977: 221). There is a dialectic of powers in Durkheim's account, and this is supported by certain features of theoretical logic. I have argued that power, as *puissance*, exemplifies relational logic: theoretically, power is a form of relation. The logic of correlation confirms Filloux's conception of the triadic relation between the individual, the collectivity and the 'brains trust' which represents the latter (ibid. 238). Those who represent this power as 'a brains trust' (Davy) are contained by this power relation. Power, as I have shown, is bottom-up, rather than top-down, for the very reason that it stems from the collectivity. The power at the top of the triangle is contained in a dialectical relationship with the source of that power at the bottom of the triangle.

Power is not just diffuse and relational, but is at the same time contained. This reciprocal communication between civil society and the state avoids the twin dangers for a democracy: political anomie and despotism (ibid.). A balance of power and communication is the necessary minimum condition for the relation between the state and secondary groups in order for individual autonomy to develop (Müller 1993: 103). So Durkheim's theoretical model does not *per se* contain a gloss for the abuse of power by hierarchies; rather, it contains a model for the legitimation of power in a democracy. The reality of the abuse of power, of course, far exceeds any theoretical model. As a model for legitimate power, Durkheim's account does not necessarily whitewash any illegitimate use of force: is it not establishing a criterion for the legitimate use of power?

Further, there is a theory of political communication and expression involved. The state's first task is elucidatory – as interpreter of the 'conscience' of society. This involves a system of bilateral communications which is central to a system of equilibrium of powers (Filloux 1977: 247). It is the lack of this which characterizes absolutism. There is a circular process here, similar to cybernetics; this engages and elevates the social conscience, for all participate in the *conscience publique* (ibid. 230). But is there concealed here the possibility of an authoritarian power? Durkheim was certainly unwilling to admit this: he saw the duty of the state in *L'Éducation morale* not only to oversee reciprocal rights and obligations, but to constitute justice, morality and humanity (Durkheim 1925a: 65/77).[5]

## Individual rights and the state

The significance of Durkheim's rejection of the state as 'a transcendent being', superior to individuals, is evident in his treatment of the issue of rights. He rejects the moral consequences of this type of social and political realism, and repudiates the idea of a 'reason of state' (*raison d'état*) and the 'false antagonism' between the individual and the state (1899e: 57); indeed, the moral role of the state and the constitution of individuality imply each other. He argues that when the role of the state as fostering individualities is recognized, then the state can grow without diminishing the individual. History shows that the conception of the dignity of the person continues to grow: at the same time as the person is becoming 'an autonomous source (*foyer*) of activity and imposing system of personal forces whose energy cannot be destroyed' (1950a: 93/57), there is also an increasing role for the state.

There is only an unresolvable antinomy between state and individual if rights are held to be natural – that is to say, inherent in the individual; but if it is argued that rights are 'the work of society', then the antinomy is resolved (ibid.). Although the rights of the individual have not always been admitted, the 'further one advances in history ... the circle of individual life ... extends and becomes the object of moral respect. The individual acquires more and more extensive rights' (ibid. 92/56), because 'of the attribution of value to the individual' (ibid. 102/67). It is also because the state, which was formerly orientated towards the outside, 'is destined to turn more and more towards the inside' (ibid. 105/71). The more states renounce expansion and concentrate on the internal (*le dedans*), the more civic duties will be identified with the humanitarian duties of humankind.

I have asked whether Durkheim can reject an individualist account of the state, yet retain the individualist duty of the state; the conception of the *individu in genera* is central to the answer to this question. This is fostered by the moral interest of the state; it is a collective representation fostered as a human aim for the state, when this is understood as a thinking agent for society – that is, as the interpreter and agent for collective representations. The concept of the *individu in genera* has significance in the psychic – that is, representational and relational – life of society; it is through this that the conception of right and the conception of the person as a bearer of right has developed. And we have seen that the conception of right is associated with freedom of mind which is underlined by economic differentiation: in this way Durkheim can argue that the conception of the rights of the individual does grow through history.

So the state, without being either 'mystical' or merely negative, can neutralise all 'particular forces' which work against the individual (ibid. 100/65). The state is the agent of progressive liberation; as such, it must use its power for moral ends – for the development of individualities (ibid. 98/63). This positive end is not 'transcendent', but essentially human. The duty of the state is, first, 'to progressively call the individual to moral existence' (ibid. 104/69), second, to protect collective being. The state is destined to become neither, as the economists want, merely a spectator of social life, condemned only to negative intervention, nor, as the socialists want, simply a cog (*rouage*) in the economic machine.

Nevertheless, the power of the state must be contained. 'Every society is despotic, if at the very least nothing external contains its despotism' (ibid. 96/61). The political necessity of secondary groups follows from this, and these are a central feature of Durkheim's analysis of the relation of the state and the individual, and supplement the containment of power by triadic relations. 'What liberates the individual is not the suppression of regulating centres, it is their proliferation, provided that these multiple centres are co-ordinated and subordinate to each other' (1899e: 171/57–8). This concept was first introduced by Durkheim in the much debated second preface to *De la Division du travail social*. Durkheim's appeal to corporations to intercalate between the individual and the state is not evidence of fascism, but an indication of democratic socialism. His reference to the Commune as 'the corner stone of society' (1893b: xxv/xlix) and not simply an archaic relic should be noted; given the events at the beginning of the Third Republic, this was not insignificant. He argues that this 'union of corporations' (ibid.) can provide a 'communal solidarity' that will prevent 'the law of the strongest' from dominating industrial and commercial relations (ibid. xii/xxxix). The corporation facilitates communal utility and the subordination of individual utility to it, and this 'always has a moral character' (ibid. xv/xli).

In his *Leçons de sociologie*, he uses the concept of secondary groups as intermediaries which simultaneously prevent state despotism over the individual and prevent society from absorbing the state. Indeed, for Durkheim, the contemporary social malaise in France stemmed from the lack of secondary groups. In 'Deux lois de l'évolution pénale' he argues that absolute power is a lack of 'all counterweight' (1901ai: 247/23). It is this 'mechanism of counterweight' (Davy) which in Durkheim's view helps to prevent the state becoming despotic.

## Evaluation

What historical evidence was there that the strength of the state went hand in hand with liberation of individuals? As Durkheim himself noted, individualism was far from being profoundly rooted in France; France had accepted authoritarian regimes 'with great facility ... old habits survive more than we believe, more than we would have hoped for' (1950a: 95/60). Is this account of the state, given the clouds gathering over the twentieth century starting with the First World War, the development of Fascist and totalitarian states, and the contemporary domination of governments by 'the sinister interest' and global undemocratic powers, so optimistic that it would seem to be sociologically unimportant? For Filloux, Durkheim whitewashes the state of any domination or violent constraint (1977: 247). For Coser, Durkheim was so concerned with buttressing the authority of the republican state that he took no account of the violence of political power and corruption. 'What was a gain for the regime was a loss for sociological theory' (Coser 1960: 221–2). However much he ignores the shadow side of power, his account is sociologically true to the individualistic and humanitarian aspirations of democratic states as they developed in the twentieth century.

So, whilst it might be irrelevant to the mechanics of corrupt state power, Durkheim's account does anticipate the democratic ideal as it developed from the revolution of 1789 and is still with us at the beginning of the twenty-first century; his optimism reflects his reading of the tendencies of history initiated in 1789. It is clear that what Durkheim is not doing is giving an empirical description of actual states: his account represents not states as actually constituted, with their characteristic corruption, but states as hoped for, and sometimes realized, as governments are thrown out of office both for corruption and for being out of touch with the people. 'Social life is a perpetual becoming. It is therefore much more important to determine what society is in the process of becoming, what it should and can become in the near future' (Durkheim 1899e: 3.165/52). He was reading the positive tendencies of history and underscoring them. It is, as Parkin rightly observes, an attempt to outline a theory of the state consistent with the underpinnings of modern democracy and its forms of authority, a task which neither Weber or Marx attempted (Parkin 1992: 85).

For Giddens, Durkheim failed, where Marx succeeded, to reconcile 'sociological and political intervention in the interest of securing change' (Giddens 1986: 27). This accusation overlooks the conception of collective representation as an expression of collective practical reason and of this as a practical force for change in a communicative whole as it develops in social becoming. So this model accounts for how governments are, and

must be, controlled by the thinking of civil society, and how they can help
the process of change by the clarifying social thinking, but also how they
can initiate moral and political change through the practical force of
representation. In so doing, the state is the filter for determining the values
of the conscience collective. As such, the state oversees individualist values
within the context of equality: society must be based on the equality of both
chances and life conditions. As the filter for practical thinking, it encourages
the elucidation of values and ideals. As we have seen, the point of reflection
through representations is practical, to encourage new directions for effort
and the will. It is from the generalization of the ideals stemming from the
collectivity that real change is to be expected, for ideals are 'anticipated
representations' of the desired result (Durkheim 1893b: 331/279). In a
democracy, a government organ is needed to express these.

The difficulties with this model of the state as the organ for social
thought, however, are similar to the problems with Rousseau's conception
of the general will – that is, how is this social thinking to be grasped and
interpreted? A possibility of false representations exists: just as individuals
can be self-deceiving, so governments can and do deceive, whilst appearing
to represent society. Durkheim needs more than an analogy with states of
conscience to establish a criterion of adequate and inadequate representation of society, even though he argues that representation is clearest in a
democracy.

How can we account for Durkheim's highly optimistic view of the state?
For Giddens, he constantly shifts from the analytic to the optative (Giddens
1986: 27). For Filloux, his optimism stems, first, from his inability to imagine
that obedience to the law of the group could result in an apotheosis of the
state; second, his belief in consensus underwrote his belief in the individualist vocation of the state. However, his confidence cannot simply be the
hope of a socialist; he despaired at the effectiveness of socialist administrations (Filloux 1977: 250). I suggest that it is the intense constructivism
which informs his work, which came out of the unique concatenation of
historical, political and philosophical events, which explains this and which
forms the background to the development of his views. It is an ideal view
of the state conceived by a democratic republican; it is inspired by the
democratic and socialist traditions out of which his thinking emerged.
Through this, Durkheim as philosopher and political theorist to some
extent obscures the vision of Durkheim as sociologist.

## The philosophical background

This view of the state does not put Durkheim in the positivist tradition, as
Giddens and many others hold (Giddens 1986: 11). Nor is it to Tradition-

alism that we must look for the philosophical forebears of this view; a reflection on French history and philosophy holds a key. The revolution of 1789 was simultaneously statist and individualist, and the reaction to it produced strange bedfellows in terms of theories of the state: theocrats, positivists and state socialists were united in their condemnation of individualism and the demand for a strong centralized state. For Louis Blanc and Blanqui, just as for Maistre and Bonald, the centralized state must encapsulate a principle of authority to which individuals must submit. This is necessary for the state to intervene in the economy to oversee production and establish a moral direction for the country. Similarly for Saint-Simon, the state must encapsulate a new centralized power; he rejected the idea of right (of Kant and Rousseau), which he held to be central to individualism, which he also opposed.

Comte adopted a theocratic model of the state, albeit marked by elements of state socialism immanent in the Saint-Simonian model: the positive state must eradicate all traces of the metaphysical view of the individual and society – in particular, the doctrine of critical enquiry and free thought (and all institutions associated with it, such as sovereignty of the people and the concept of right). Scientific politics sees society as the only reality, and cannot tolerate the immoral and anarchic idea of right. There is room only for duty to the state; the principle of sociability must replace all elements of the critical doctrine. This social authoritarianism was reinforced by his later theory of a positivist pope. He admired unlimited power whenever he saw it – like Saint-Simon, he admired the Holy Alliance. In particular, he admired the *coup d'état* of 1852 – so hated by democrats and socialists – for steering the republic into its dictatorial phase (Michel 1898: 445).

On the other hand, there were the liberals and the economists who argued for the minimal state: whilst Adam Smith argued that state intervention was wrong in the economy, then, as now, his followers argued that it was wrong everywhere. The doctrine of *laissez-faire* was supported by both early and late liberal schools and, through it, they argued for a minimal state. On this basis they argued for a negative theory of right – that is, protection from interference – with no corresponding positive rights over the state. In particular, they attacked the principle of the sovereignty of the people dear to the democrats; for them, to limit the power of the state is to defend individual right. Tocqueville, on the other hand, argued that democracy must go hand in hand with political liberty, even though he saw a danger in individualism.

There were socialists and republicans, however, who did not espouse the logic of either theocracy or of state socialism. Durkheim's views grew out of libertarian and democratic pluralist thinking developed in the struggles of republicanism and socialism which opposed authoritarian

statism and which focused on a federalist vision and the containment of
power within and between states; this is the significance of political
pluralism. Proudhon called for political federalism in opposition to left-
wing Jacobinism, and for the limitation of the power of state by groups.
From this developed the idea of small groups mediating between isolated
individuals and centralized authoritarian power (Vincent 1992: 10).

Malon was influenced by this, but, unlike the anarchist element in
Proudhonianism he argued for a positive role for the state. In his *Précis
de socialisme* he claimed that a socialist view of the state must acknowledge individualist values and accommodate itself to representative democracy and republican federalism (1892: 297ff). Individualist values were
central to Jaurèsian socialism, especially after the Dreyfus Affair; for
Jaurès, the 'development of the individual is the measure of all things'
(Lacouture 1982: 55). Further, Durkheim makes central to the activity of
the state what Léon Blum posed as central to the democratic socialist
vision: 'Socialism is the result of a purely rationalist conception of society
... it tends to reduce more and more the obscure and evil forces which
escape from the light of consciousness and the influence of the deliberate
will' (ibid. 59).

To this must be added the influence of the democratic tradition of
Montesquieu and Tocqueville and their idea of secondary groups as a
limitation on central power. This conception of intermediate groups was
taken up by Renouvier in his theory of the state (Renouvier 1869b: 2.561).
He argued that purely political bodies working with majority rule will
produce little change. He placed great faith in freely constituted bodies to
establish social change; these can achieve what neither the individual
alone nor the mass can: real social progress, which he saw 'as victories
gained over general habits' (ibid. 2.354), is due to the initiative of free
associations. He acknowledges the socialist schools, especially that of
Fourier, as the inspiration for this idea (ibid. 2.355).[6]

Certainly it is through Renouvier that we can see why Durkheim called
the Hegelian view of the state 'mystical'. We have seen that infinitism
implies mysticism: for Renouvier, any idea that invokes unrepresentable
being is 'mystique', for this is to create metaphysical entities which
transcend the logical condition of knowledge – representation – and
thereby to underwrite the politics of terror. So the nation is for Durkheim
'a mystical unconscious idea (*une ideé mystique, obscure*)' (Durkheim
1903c: 1.148). In his *Introduction à la philosophie analytique de l'histoire*
of 1864, Renouvier defines a doctrine as mystical when it augments
personal belief and feeling beyond critical and experiential elements and
establishes 'arbitrary affirmations'. This adjective characterizes those
moral and metaphysical systems which absorb personality and life into

'the transcendent object of its faith' (Renouvier 1864a: 47). I have noted that he uses the word 'particular' (*particulière*) to qualify each conscience to indicate a real and indissoluble individuality (1869a: 1.301), which in turn gives a foundation to the idea of right.

This is one of the reasons why Renouvier accuses Saint-Simon, together with Hegelianism, of mysticism. Both involve a metaphysics which transcends representation and the freedom of conscience. Their logic establishes a 'raison d'état' which justifies oppression and the denial of rights and establishes a new ecclesiastical type of authority which denies not only freedom of mind and autonomy of action, but also the reciprocity of rights, and duties which justice demands. In this, Jacobin socialism and Catholicism reflect each other (1872b: 1.10): Jacobin socialism, as the 'party of order at any price', invokes a *raison d'état* and paves the way for dictators; this is the politics of heteronomy rather than of autonomy. In place of this, a form of political morality founded on practical reason must be instituted, which focuses on action in the 'milieu'.

For all his apparent rationalism, Hegel, like Maistre, privileges tradition, habit and instinct over reflection and deliberation. Moreover, the doctrine of absolute being entails a finalism in history which leads to oppressive and tyrannical politics. It follows for Renouvier that the state cannot claim any role in fulfilling the end of history. (Cf. Durkheim: 'The state without pursuing a mystical end . . .' (1950a: 100/65).) Such a conception of the state, he argues, is essentially 'Prussian' and invokes war as an instrument of its development.

His concern is with a state compatible with democracy: this, I suggest, explains the connection of representation with the conception of the state for Durkheim. Renouvier opposed all aggressive nationalism bent on conquest and colonialism, and identified a particular view of the state with this: that of the state as a person. Against this, he held the state to be 'a distinct society of persons with a constituted communal representation' (Renouvier 1869a: 2.430). A constant of his thinking, developed in and beyond the revolution of 1848, is the idea of the state as centring on the right of the person: the duty of the state is to establish the rational right of the individual (Picard 1908: 110). The reciprocity of rights, tolerance, freedom and equality will only obtain in a democratic republican state which is the most rational state. And real progress in terms of the state must consist in the degrees of reflection and freedom reached socially, which can only be finally achieved through overcoming customary habits.

His rationalist vision of the state opposed the concept of a natural state based on purity of race, blood and soil. He argued that in place of natural right, there must be rational right. The focus must be on the moral agent, whose morality develops in the historical relations of society. Here the idea of the irreducibility of culture and reason is crucial to seeing the state as 'the fruit of reflection and will' which subjects all the irrational and involuntary facts of human existence to the power of reflection (1869b: 2.286).

# 10

# Practical Reason and Moral Order: Morality and Society

Durkheim began the study of morality in his first book and his interest in it lasted to his last incomplete work, of 1917, 'La morale' (1920a). A constant of his thought is concern with the reality of morality and with the conception of a science of morality: the logic of this is central to this chapter.

Parsons cites Durkheim's science of morality as evidence of his positivism, which denied the difference between moral and natural phenomena, repudiated knowledge and action, and denied the element of choice (Parsons, 1937: 238). This overlooks Durkheim's unique view of science and reality and his central concern with representation and its relation to agency. Unlike Comte, Durkheim has a theory of the reconciliation of freedom and determinism and a theory of the reflexivity of consciousness and of intentionality, both being understood through representation and the states of conscience (Durkheim 1925a: 101/120). He is a reflexive moral thinker (Joas 1993: 238).

Durkheim's science of morality has been taken as evidence of his conservatism: first, through the assumption that 'ought' must be founded on 'is' and thus on the established order (Hinkle 1960: 281). Durkheim does indeed reject a radical split between 'is' and 'ought', but he argues that the logic of judgement, which uses ideals, is employed in both evaluation and description (Durkheim 1911b: 119/95). He cites the logic of the ideal to rebut the charge that his method of studying moral facts condemns him to the *status quo* (1925a: 103/122). Secondly, his advice to treat moral facts with a 'wisely conservatory attitude (*un esprit sagement conservateur*)' (1893b: xl/xxviii) has been taken in a conservative political sense and is so translated. But *conservateur* also means 'that which preserves'. So he argues that moral facts should be treated with 'prudence', as realities which are not revocable at will by the theorist (ibid. xli/xxviii). Respect for the reality of moral facts is connected with his holding 'traditions and the common spirit (*esprit*)' as the 'only source of authority' (1895a: 91/120). This is a democratic socialist respect for people's beliefs.

This 'conservatism' is reinforced by a Parsonian reading of Durkheim, which appears to make morality conform to role expectations in terms of the normative stability of the whole. But, on the contrary, Durkheim is concerned with showing the reality of collective customs and beliefs and their interconnectedness in a social totality. This is not to confirm an established order – indeed, Durkheim held that the *status quo* suffered from a lack of morality: 'Our first duty at present is to *make* a morality for ourselves' (1893b: 406/340). 'When morality has yet to be established . . . we must have recourse to the active and inventive forces of conscience, rather than to purely conservative forces – since it is not a matter of conserving anything' (1925a: 86/102).

Rather than being an apologist for the *status quo*, he is searching for transformation through the critical and active practical functions of conscience orientated towards society as the ground and end of practical reason: to generate 'a republic of persons' is the aim of Durkheim as moralist (Watts Miller 1996). To show that the totality of relations which surround the individual is the nexus within which individual life prospers or declines is to reject both negative liberalism and conservatism: moralization of the social milieu so that individuals can prosper is the practical aim of his science of morality. His project is that of developing new orders and a new morality of co-operation (Joas 1993: 238). Durkheim's position is in line with French socialist thinking: 'Solidarity is perhaps the very source of morality' (Durkheim 1893b: 1st edn, 10/2. 263).[1] For Jaurès, solidarity is socialist morality (Jaurès 1895: viii).

To understand his position, we must acknowledge, first, a new sense of order and its connection with practical reason; second, the logical basis of change through representation and becoming; and third the importance of agency, which is the key to change to new moral orders. So against a conservative, positivist, functionalist and scientific realist interpretation of Durkheim, I propose that the logical bases of his conception of morality be understood as *consciences in relation*. 'Moral relations are thus relations between consciences' (Durkheim 1925a: 51/59). First, relation establishes the logical connection with the social. 'There is law and morality when several people enter into a relation and come to live together' (1886a: 202). Secondly, conscience is the theoretical term which gives the reflexive, critical and practical functions without which morality cannot be understood. 'Morality which primitively was contained in the act itself . . . goes back closer and closer to conscience' (1925a: 101/120).[2] The concept of conscience makes a reality of the human world as a world of values and ideals: moral facts 'are evidently phenomena of conscience' (1920a 2: 331/93).

## Morality and social reality

Durkheim's classic account of the reality of morality and its social nature is given in the extended original introduction to the *De la Division du travail social*, and is no longer in print. Morality is historical and socially relative: it develops in history, and is subject to the same laws of variation as society. He opposes his method of observation and description to classic philosophical ahistorical procedures which ignore the reality of the social and historical milieu (1983b: 1st edn, 17/2.268). Lukes accuses Durkheim of an 'arch historicist and determinist' approach to morality (Lukes 1973: 421, 427). Indeed, he is widely accused of an early determinism.[3] But his reconciliation of will with determinate law is crucial to his whole project and to the reconciliation of autonomy with solidarity (1893b: xliii/xxx). If there is no possibility of freedom, there can be no account of choice, agency or motivation, for these are central to any account of moral action.

So Durkheim's interest in social causes does not exclude the interest of action or intervention: possibilities exist in history, and the role of contingency provides an opportunity for freedom. His recognition that 'morality in all its degrees is never encountered except in the social state' (ibid. 395/332) does not condemn him to an uncritical sociologism or functionalist determinism. Indeed, Renouvier argues for the necessity of a morality that takes account of the reality of history and society, and that not only acknowledges the laws of solidarity and habit, but is capable of dominating and judging history. The account of 'representative freedom' allows a reflection on morality that is partially distinct from history, and capable of dominating and judging it in terms of its own ideal.

## The passage to the sociology of morality

What is distinctive about Durkheim's approach to morality is his insistence on the centrality of the social. What enabled him to develop this fundamental insight? Durkheim's rejection of classical philosophical approaches to morality was initated by Renouvier, who, against Kant, recommended the study of solidarity in history and claimed that this is largely, but not completely, responsible for moral action (Renouvier 1864a: 33). Although Durkheim criticizes Renouvier for seeing solidarity as a source of corruption (Durkheim 1893b: 1st edn, 10/2.263) he follows him in locating morality in the concept of solidarity as found in social and historical relation.

Human beings are 'social in essence, since it is in society and by it that they develop their nature' (Renouvier 1864a: 93). Critical philosophy must take its departure in a 'truly human milieu', for it is only there that we find the origin of morality (ibid. 89). It is in the milieu that we find human association, which gives the 'superior sphere' of morality which is society; he initiated the connection between association and obligation which is so central to Durkheim's thinking (Durkheim 1895a: 104/130).

Indeed, before Durkheim, Renouvier criticized both the rationalists and the empiricists for their failure to show how a rational and positive science of morality is possible: the empiricists concentrate on the diversity of experience to the exclusion of any rational determination of action, and the rationalists treat 'good and bad for invariable absolutes of conscience ... in a word for treating the moral human being (*l'homme moral*) as though they existed without precedents and without milieu' (Renouvier 1864a: 134). That is, they ignore 'the historical nature of morality and any law of development of morality' (ibid. 133).

## Moral reality and the question of science

Morality is a reality for Durkheim; he stresses the social nature of this reality, and this is the significance of treating morality from 'outside' (*du dehors*) (Durkheim 1895a: 33/73). (This must be seen also as a rejection of liberalism, which sees morality as concerning only the inner self.) Without a reconsideration of 'outside', this seems a hopelessly inappropriate way of approaching morality. We have now seen that 'outside' and 'exteriority' mean the sphere of external relations. This is in dialectical exchange with the internal, and a dynamic interchange within the process of social becoming. This can be seen in his argument that solidarity, which is a 'completely moral phenomenon', must be grasped through the 'external fact' which 'symbolises' this internal fact. This external fact is, of course, law (1893b: 28/24).[4]

For Durkheim, any definition of morality must be adequate to the nature of its reality (1893b: 1st edn, 5/2.258). What is this? For Durkheim, moral facts are central to society as a sphere of relations which are determinate and particular (1893a: 1st edn, 15/2.267). These relations are diverse historically and socially: the diversity of moral facts is central to Durkheim's science of moral facts: thus he argues that there are duties, rather than duty (ibid.). So first, then, morality is 'a network of links (*liens*)' (1893b: 395/332), and this is shown in solidarity, which is fundamental to morality, and as an aspect of association and thus of society. But the phenomena of morality are not only shared, they are also internal, as is solidarity (ibid. 351/297).

Morality concerns action, and the modern form of action aspires to autonomy. There is unreflective action, as shown in 'habits and tendencies', which are at 'the root of moral life' (1925a: 228/269). And action cannot be understood except as orientation towards an end: 'Morality consists above all in positing ends' (1920a: 2.319/83). So the reality of morality encompasses agency. But effective action for Durkheim involves use of the 'limited vital energy which is central to life and living' (1925a: 34/39). It involves choice and therefore the possibility of freedom of mind, both of which are central to autonomy. So the 'agent' and the 'patient', together with the subject and the object, are part of the logic of morality (1893b: 395/332). Above all, morality concerns the reality of duty and acknowledgement of the good for Durkheim. These are real for the agent as understood through rational psychology, but they are part of the sphere of association, and hence are real at the level of the relational and so of totality (1925a: 53/61). This is the objective sphere of morality (1906b: 100/ 78).

These, then, are the features of morality. How are they connected to a science of morality, and what is its nature?

## The concept of a science of morality

Durkheim's 'effort to treat the facts of the moral life according to the method of the positive sciences . . . is . . . to make a science of morality' – which is not to derive morality from science or from any propositions borrowed from other 'positive sciences' (including sociology!) (1893b: xxxvii/xxv). It is an autonomous science which, it is clear from the original preface to his first book, understands morality through sign, symbol, representation and conscience, as well as through relation and function:[5] these are the theoretical terms of a science of morality. 'It was Renouvier's Science de Morale which showed him the way' (Davy 1973: 19).[6] Analysis of this should rebut accusations of Durkheim's 'intransigently positivist' approach to morality (Lukes 1973: 421, 427).

For Renouvier, positivism cannot account for morality, because of its refusal of all freedom to conscience and all psychological reality to agency and consciousness, which are central to action and choice. Only *criticisme* allows the foundation of morality as science, because it has already put the foundation of science 'in representations and critique' (Renouvier 1869a: 1.14). It involves the categories of causality, finality and conscience (1869b: 1.7). Morality as a science is founded on fact – an internal moral fact which is part of a science of morals (ibid. 1.223).[7] This is duty – more particularly the 'voluntary duty (*devoir être volontaire*)' and the 'active duty of persons' (*devoir faire des personnes*) (ibid. 1.7). The association of two agents establishes a community and a moral solidarity through reciprocity (ibid. 1.55). The social sphere is a 'composed order (*ordre com-*

*posé)*' of agents; it is the sphere of association which gives the objective form of morality (ibid. 1.59). Further, he introduced the concept of sanction to explain what engages human beings to observe moral law (ibid. 1.98). This is central to 'applied morality', which is morality in society; it is here that the concept of sanction becomes significant.[8]

Generally the science of morality indicates the domain of practical reason, which he calls 'moral order' (Renouvier 1872a: 2). This requires freedom; in this Renouvier follows Kant, who argued: 'By practical, I mean everything that is possible through freedom (Kant 1781: 632/A800 B828). Freedom for Renouvier gives the consciousness of power and action, and 'the power of free futures' (Renouvier 1859: 486). This is central to the formation of new orders of the world (ibid. 482); and it is effort that engages freedom. The real sphere of practical reason, then, is found in the possibilities of action within the discontinuities that open up in historical action.

The features definitive of moral reality can be accommodated by a science of morality. It is clear that since, for Durkheim, representation is central to morality and is crucial to action (1893b: 1st edn, 13/2.265), it is central to the possibility of a science of morality and to the complex issue of a moral phenomenon. Logically, only if moral phenomena fall under the fundamental categories can they count as phenomenal, for these constitute the logical condition of facticity. The science of representation, relation and conscience accommodates a science of morals.[9] It is thus no accident that Durkheim's statement that 'Science is nothing else than conscience carried to its highest point of clarity' is made in *De la Division du travail social* (1893b: 14/14), for the science of morality is its theoretical framework.

Solidarity is a relation, and responds to relation as the primary law of representation, just as the plural and discrete nature of these relations is accommodated through number. The diversity is founded logically on the *différence* which quality as species/type (*espèce*) establishes. The requirements of action, agency, choice and the determination of ends can be accommodated by the laws of personality, causality and finality. The ideal is accommodated in the science of representation through the law of finality, which covers the study of ends. 'By what reasoning can the ideal be said to be beyond nature and science?' (1911b: 112/89). Personality explains how Durkheim can acknowledge the 'personal factor' as essential to morality (1907a(9): 2.339). Productive agency is central to morality. 'Moral reality is a system of forces, surely not physical ones, but mental, moral forces, forces which derive all their power from action, representations and from states of conscience' (1910b: 2.373/65). Although 'force' is seen by Lukes as central to Durkheim's 'intransigent positivism', I suggest that, as agency, it is crucial to Durkheim's project of the science of morals.

It is central to understanding the power of the group, which is fundamental to the possibility of the transformation of the misery entailed by the economic organization of the state (1925a: 71/82). This requires 'effort' – that is, the moral energy central to will and moral action.

'Under the gaze of conscience' and in 'willed orders' we find 'energy' (1893b: 1st edn, 13/2.265). So force, together with passion, are central representative and practical functions of conscience under which morality can occur. These practical functions are the logical points of both the constitution and the transformation of moral reality; they are central to the dynamic potential of the 'creative syntheses' which are the focus of Durkheim's practical attention and which are implemented by the practical force of representation (1893b: 64/53). By the force of critique and transformation by the ideal, the development of the new is made possible.

The concept of a science of morality, then, is the theoretical foundation for the main features of morality for Durkheim, which are the ideal, duty, the good and autonomy.

## Morality and the concept of the ideal

The critique of the real by the ideal was central to contemporary democratic socialism, and was taken up by Léon Blum (Lacouture 1982: 118). Just as Lucien Herr saw socialism as a moral ideal (Lindenberg and Meyer 1977: 65), so the ideal is central to the concept of socialism as a 'regenerating faith' (Bouglé 1938: 34).

The science of morality 'will help find the sense in which we should orientate our conduct, and determine the ideal towards which we are aiming unclearly (*tendons confusément*)' (Durkheim (1893b: xxxix/xxvi). The concept of the ideal is a constant and central feature of Durkheim's account of morality. The ideal may be relative and historical, but it is no less central to every society; every society must have an ideal which it moves towards (1925a: 11/13). It is the dynamic of society, and the critical, practical, transformative interest of Durkheim's sociology relies on the logic of judgement, in which the representative and the represented and the meaning of 'thing' are central.

The ideal is 'sociology's own domain', says Durkheim (1911b: 120/96). He rejects the is/ought separation, for judgements of both 'existence' and 'value' employ ideals (ibid. 119/95). But those which aim to express reality are concepts, whilst those which aim to transfigure reality are ideals of value. Both relate ideals to 'things' (that is, to reality, the given), but ideals of value can transform reality, by 'adding' to the given (ibid. 120/96). Here judgement is not subordinated to the given (that is, by 'things'), but can dominate and change reality through its practical force. For

Renouvier, the practical functions dominate the represented: thus, logically, transformation occurs through them (Milhaud 1927: 83). This, together with his claim that all principal social phenomena are systems of values based on ideals, rescues 'positive sociology' from 'empiricist fetishism' for Durkheim (1911b: 120/96). The ideal is that by which reflection is transformed into action – it forms what is aspired to, and this is realized through 'anticipated representation' (1893b: 331/279).

For Renouvier, the ideal is what gives practical efficacy to morality; he criticized the empiricists for having no concept of the ideal, and the rationalists for having too abstract a concept. The ideal is the pivot of practical reason as normative science, concerned with relations 'which must be'. It is a judgement of conscience which evaluates the given in terms of that which is better. As a synthetic judgement, it is the active principle of human reality, for it activates the force of conscience and stimulates the power of production, of agency (Renouvier 1869b: 1.19).

So for Durkheim the ideal is the great motivating and dynamic forces of action – for they are 'motor' forces, behind which are collective forces (Durkheim 1911b: 117/93), which are central to periods of effervescence (ibid. 115/91). It requires a theory of will. 'Ideals, if not mere possibilities, must be willed' (ibid. 112/89). The ideal is the supreme goal of conduct: 'What is an ideal, if not a body of ideas which soars above the individual, energetically soliciting its action' (1925a: 103/123). It is central to the possibility of transformation. The function of ideals 'is to transfigure the reality to which they relate' (1911b: 120/95). In the creative periods of history, periods of effervescence, ideals are active in the constitution of new relations, through the more intense relations and feelings and the energy collectively produced (ibid. 114/91). The sacred is understood through the ideal: the sacred activates ideals. The contemporary ideal of humanism holds the person as sacred (1925a: 91/107).

The logic of the ideal is central to Durkheim's sociological theory of value. Here, he argues that we must recognize that value is not inherent in things. Only its collective origin can explain the nature of value; valued things represent an ascription of collective thinking and its force (1911b: 109/86). Collective thinking forms itself on the representative side, and is imposed on things – the represented. Through idealization and symbolization of conscience, collective thought transforms reality. 'It substitutes a different world . . . which is . . . the shadow projected by the ideals which it constructs' (ibid. 119/95). Morality can thus be compared to religion: the dialectic of human reality is the same in both cases.

## Duty and social relations

If the ideal is the dynamic of action and the point of transformation to the future, what are we to make of the notion of duty? The crisis of contemporary morality, for Durkheim, was characterized by 'anomie' and an 'artificial and superficial life' (1893b: 405/339). 'Our first duty is to make a morality for ourselves' (ibid. 406/340). Durkheim rejects the Comtean solution – the introduction of the intellectual rule of positivist thinking. 'Our malaise is . . . not of the intellectual order' (ibid. 405/339).

We must not misinterpret his conception of duty through Comte, for whom duty is submission to order: the principle of sociability requires submission to the positive state. So duty is duty towards its political priesthood, with no corresponding right for the individual. But for Durkheim, solidarity establishes a reciprocal system of rights and duties (ibid. 403/338). Equally, to read him through Traditionalism is to impose the politics of monarchic absolutism, which recognizes only the duty of obedience towards the reality of society as established fact with its inequality and hierarchy. Vulgar Durkheimianism sees duty as submission to order in terms of the stability of the whole.

Against such readings we must understand Durkheim's conception of duty as central to practical reason. We must locate its dynamics within the logic of representation and its practical force. As fundamental to the action which constitutes social worlds and to a morality of co-operation (Joas 1993), it is central to his interest in coherent, effective action within the limitations of the milieu and to his interest in the viability of significant human life within society.

Duty was central to democratic socialism. Malon's *La Morale sociale* focused on the triumph over egoism and the development of duty within a united humanity: it was concerned with the development of new orders and was future-directed (Jaurès 1895: iv). The Commune and aspects of its lack of discipline demonstrated the importance of disciplined action for effective socialism within a republic. There was a left republicanism orientated towards a form of Kantianism in morality. Renouvier's influential *Science de la morale* (1869) showed that the core conceptions of Kantian morality are not incompatible with interests of transformation towards a just and equal republic.

How is duty compatible with the recognition of the diversity of morals which the sociology of morality requires? It is clear that within his own contemporary moral world Durkheim searches for the foundation of obligation in the conditions of existence of society, and in so doing he lays a new 'groundwork' for social obligation. 'The duties of the individual towards himself are in reality duties towards society' Durkheim (1893b:

395/332). But if duty is prescribed action, who should prescribe, and to whom? The republican aim of replacing duty to Church, monarchy and established hierarchy emerges in Durkheim's thought as duty towards society. If society can be self-governing, it will prescribe rules to itself and be stable in its moral relations; then it will have no need of institutions incompatible with self-government.

So for Durkheim all moralities are characterized by duty: 'The domain of morality is the domain of duty, and duty is prescribed action' (1925a: 20/23). Certainly the importance of Kant and Renouvier for him inclines him philosophically in this direction. 'The domain of practical reason is characterised by the presence of commandments or by obligation' (Renouvier 1898b: 3.390). But what does he mean by 'duty'? It is not about a simple conformity to a particular order: it is a fundamental disposition, 'a moral force which is at the basis of all moral life' (Durkheim 1925a: 18/20). It is thus indispensable to any society, including the ideal of the good society (Watts Miller 1996: 145). Duty is the constituting force by which social worlds are built.

Duty is central to practical reason and to the way in which the practical order is made; in this sense, unlike Comte and the Traditionalists, duty is not independent of justice for Durkheim. Through the joint development of rationalism and individualism, our moral sensitivity and thus awareness of injustice grows (1925a: 17/20). To introduce more justice into social relations is to reduce 'external inequality', which is the source of evil (*mal*) (1893b: 405/339). For Renouvier, justice is a fundamental feature of the objective sphere of practical reason – the sphere of association, that is, reciprocal relations (1869b: 1.50). And the sphere of practical reason is that which must be created and constituted in social relations.

So duty is tied to action and rational agency: it is central to virtue ethics, the concept of individual flourishing, and self-mastery (Watts Miller 1996: 145). It is connected with discipline: Durkheim criticizes both the orthodox economists and the post-Saint-Simonian socialists for neglecting all question of discipline (Durkheim 1925a: 31/36). Discipline does not necessarily imply conservatism, as Lukes holds (1973: 78). 'We are the party of discipline in action' (Jaurès 1900: 95). To invoke discipline in social relations is not thereby to call in the social police and all aspects of the 'disciplinary society'. It is to do with harnessing human forces: discipline is a *sui generis* force, an energy, which must be used for constructive human ends. That is, it engaged the idealization functions of consciences.

So Durkheim argued that discipline should not instil 'resignation'; it concerns effective action in terms of 'an end of activity which is in harmony with our faculties and which allows us to realise our nature' (Durkheim 1925a: 43/49). It is tied to the idea of successful, satisfied action, which is limited action. 'We continue to be limited (*bornés*), because we are finite beings' (ibid. 100/118). Wills must not be orientated 'towards ends which are infinitely distant and inaccessible' (ibid. 43/49). Discipline, as a constitutive force of the moral world, is both creative of, and a limiting condition for, action; but it is 'a limit which is in perpetual becoming' (ibid. 45/51). It unites regularity and moral authority. The basis of authority lies not in hierarchies or established facts, but in the mental processes of agents; it is these which make the imperative force central to the moral power to which we give consenting obedience (ibid. 25/29). There is a dialectic between will and moral power in effective action.

This focus on agency and duty as part of the sphere of relatedness – in association – must entail a reconsideration of 'constraint'. It is clear that duty here is not the purely rational, reflexive, Kantian idea, but is constituted in relatedness. This is the sense of duty in which 'constraint' can be elucidated. Constraint for Renouvier, besides indicating conflict in the state of war of actual social relations, is also that which is generative of new social institutions (Renouvier 1869b: 1.231). Ideally, of course, it should be founded on consent. Durkheim uses it also in two senses: the constraint that precludes satisfaction of 'unregulated desires' 'must not be confounded with that which prevents just remuneration for work' (Durkheim 1893b: 377/318).

It is neglect of the concept of will, power and agency in the interpretation of Durkheim which leads to the accusation that constraint excludes 'the actor as conscious willing agent' (Giddens 1995a: 124). Yet, will and constraint can be seen as contraries which are productive of agency and power in action. Education and social rules are forms of constraint that lead to the production of active forces; the point of education is to develop internal effort into personal power and self-mastery, which develops through a tension between the internal and the external. The subject and the object, the agent and the patient, are accommodated in this moral dialectic of reality (Durkheim 1893b: 395/332). If discipline entails 'self-mastery' and all 'real power', then it is not a form of violence against nature, as it is for Bentham (1925a: 39/45). This form of human power is central to the 'creative syntheses' of society and history, and just as power is constituted through the dialectic of freedom and authority, so for Durkheim powerlessness results from lack of effective moral authority in social relations.

## The habitual and duty

The habitual and the moral are closely connected: morality is a 'collective habit', 'a common way of acting' (1887c: 1.275). 'It is habit which makes the force and authority of all discipline' (1886a: 195). 'Regularity . . . needs only habits which are strongly enough constituted' (1925a: 24/28).[10] Habits are strongly constituted tendencies of action established through repetition. 'A manner of acting, whatever it is, is not consolidated except through repetition and use' (1950a: 51/12). Duty, and therefore discipline, is the cultivation of the habit of virtue: it gives birth to the diversity of virtues on which moral life depends (1925a: 18/21). The conception of virtue ethics central to a flourishing society requires the constitution of internal habits through the authority of 'normal' moral rules, which is normal constraint. For Renouvier, through repetition, free action becomes habitual and is assimilated to the functions of instinct and the laws of nature: free will is absorbed in 'accomplished virtue' (Renouvier 1869b: 1.226). This is how action is grounded, and new rules – the moulds of action – are made.

The positive sense of habit is, for Durkheim, central to the constitution of normality: discipline, by giving habits to the will, constitutes normality. But this normal limit is 'in perpetual becoming', and must not be above critique and reflection, which 'are the agents par excellence of all transformation' (Durkheim 1925a: 45/51). Making new habits will break traditional habitual obedience to established hierarchies; the point is to make conscious orientation to the social – to the republic a continuous feature of action. To do this, old 'blind' habits, which have sunk to the level of *obscures tendances* of action, must be addressed through raising what is unconscious to the conscious level by means of critical reflection (which could be part of the significance of sociology (1893b: 331/278)).

Since all habits sufficiently consolidated become needs (ibid. 389/328), to do this is to shift the course of social evolution in favour of the needs of justice. Aristotle, Ravaisson and Renouvier inspire the idea of developing good habits, which become virtuous needs as they are grounded in conscience and become 'second nature'. This project, I suggest, is central to what Durkheim calls a 'rational operation' which 'transforms' the 'causes and effects of the past into rules of action for the future' (1895a: ix/33).

## Duty and the good

Against Kant, Durkheim holds that duty does not exhaust the concept of morality: it must be taken together with the 'good' (1906b: 52/36). Durkheim calls this 'good' (*bien*) a 'desirability *sui generis*' which characterizes moral action with its '*élan*'; it inspires an 'enthusiasm' which takes us out of ourselves and causes us to rise above ourselves (ibid.). 'The good . . . draws the will towards itself, which provokes the spontaneities of desire'

(1925a: 82/96). It is that which grounds the efforts of the will central to moral action and activates the 'active and inventive forces of conscience' (ibid. 87/102). This explains how morality can be transformed: the sacred reconciles duty and the desirable, and thus is an end of action which provokes passion. And the human being is 'sacred' in contemporary morality (1906b: 53/37). This is our ideal, and it is clear how it reconciles the tension between obligation and desirability – the characteristics of the ideal.

Renouvier argued that the moral law cannot be understood without an idea of the good (*le bien*) (Renouvier 1875d: 3.138). He criticized Kant for formulating his moral law independently of any end of action and of 'the necessary conditions for the maintenance of human society and the existence of beings' (ibid. 3.137). The good, for him, is an interpersonal passion central to sociability and a source of 'enthusiasm' (1869b: 1.76ff). 'The study of the ends of action is the essence of a moral and political science' (1859: 566). This, together with freedom, is among the central principles of practical reason. There can be no understanding of any action, moral action in particular, without a consideration of end: ends are the *forces motrices* of conduct (ibid. 573), and are central to the conception of the good as the foundation of moral action.

So, for Durkheim, effective action must have a definite end 'which is clearly represented' (Durkheim 1925a: 18/21). The ends of morality are found within society. If society can find its ends in itself, then morality has been founded without theology (ibid. 52/60); in this way morality has an objective foundation (ibid. 88/103). 'Society is the eminent end of all moral activity' (1906b: 73/54). But what are the proper ends for a politics of autonomy and democracy? For Malon, the proper end and the basis for a rule of conduct of a socialist morality is humanity itself as a 'solidary whole' (*un tout solidaire*) (Jaurès 1895: ii). For Durkheim, the pursuit of society as an end gradually leads to truly human ends which are distinct from 'ethnic particularity'; in this way, humanity as an end of conduct can gradually be achieved by approximating the ideal of each group to that of humanity in general. The state must serve as the realization of that ideal: it must constitute the ideal of humanity as the ideal of moral action (Durkheim 1925a: 64/77). A plurality of states is necessary to realize this; attachment to groups means, ultimately, attachment to humanity.

Ends of action are connected to the ideal. The individual must be attached to the great ideals of his or her time for Durkheim. 'In present conditions it is above all faith in a common ideal which it is necessary to awaken. New ideas of justice and solidarity are in the process of elaboration which sooner or later will bring forth appropriate institutions' (ibid. 87/102). In this way, morality is comparable to religion: God, like society, is an ideal which solicits action; it is society believing in, and reaffirming, itself as collectivity. This relational whole is the source of mental and moral life such that human life is rendered possible.

## The possibility of new orders?

We have seen that the question of how duty enables the development of new moral orders is crucial to the interpretation of Durkheim. How this is possible depends on the meaning of the concepts of order and discipline and on the logic of moral transformation. The ideas of the relational, the synthetic, constraint and the ideal show the way. Duty is not simply the blind following of moral rules in the interest of order. It is a 'force *sui generis*'; it is 'dynamic' and an 'energy' which is immanent to representation, 'which is expressed in consciences and which determines the will' (1914b: 1.65). The ideal and duty are connected: 'Morality obliges us to realise in ourselves an ideal type' (1925a: 74/87). The ideal for Renouvier is that 'which the human being must be and must do' (Renouvier 1869b: 1.215).

Further, duty is not tied to order or hierarchy. For Durkheim, 'We only have duties *vis à vis* "consciences"' – that is, 'to moral persons' (Durkheim 1906b: 68/49). In the contemporary morality of individualism, it is tied to respect: 'Following the Kantian formula we must respect human personality wherever it is encountered, that is to say in us and those like us' (1893b: 395/332). The human personality in the age of humanism is the sacred thing, it is the object of our 'efforts' and the 'ideal which we struggle to realise within ourselves' (1906b: 66/48). When this is opposed to injustices, then a tension of contrary forces is developed, central to which are passions, which are crucial to the development of new orders. The human being as 'sacred' is the dynamic towards the new morality – which can be achieved without overturning society as 'condition of existence', for this ideal is implied in contemporary social relations.

How can Durkheim claim both that we have duties towards moral persons and that society, so defined, is the objective end of moral action? This is tied to the collective personality: the idea of the moral person is not my or your empirical individuality; the objective of moral action can only be 'the subject *sui generis*' formed by a plurality of associated subjects – 'which is something else than the total individuals of which it is composed' (ibid. 70/51). So, where Kant postulated divinity, Durkheim postulated society as the end of action (ibid.). 'Postulates are born out of practical reason' (Renouvier 1874a: 130). In this sense society, understood as the totality of plural relations, is the goal of practical reason.

The significance of the plural totality as definition of the whole, the rejection of realism, and the attachment of duty to 'consciences' is clear here. For Renouvier, the fiction of realist metaphysics – society as a person, to whom we have duties, with no corresponding rights, is a great danger. 'A duty must always be attributed to someone in particular, or to several at the same time, but properly to each' (Renouvier 1869a: 1.162). The concept of right evaporates if it is not attached to definite persons (ibid.). The denial of rights follows from false – that is, non-pluralist – wholes, for this 'false being' can then ask for duties without rights (ibid. 1.161).

But can the ideas of sanction and constraint help this move towards new orders? Durkheim claims to have empirically rediscovered Kant's idea of moral obligation through the idea of sanction. As I have shown, obligation does not derive from the sanction, but is a symbol of it externally (Durkheim 1893b: 1st edn, 25/2.276). The interchange between the inner and the outer and the logic of becoming show that this can indicate a process of change. Sanctions are also synthetic links between acts and consequences, which are bound by social rules which change. Durkheim believed that the momentum for change – if governed rationally by societies' own ideal – through the logic of the ideal within representation, can be generative of a new moral synthesis.

## The autonomy of the will

Just as there is both a tension and reciprocity between duty and *sui generis* desire, so too for solidarity and autonomy for Durkheim. Like Kant and Renouvier, Durkheim argues that morality requires both duty and autonomy. He acknowledges the importance of the double necessity of the imperative, autonomous nature of morality, but criticizes the logic of Kant's account for undermining effective autonomy. Autonomy is a social and historical reality, and part of the movement of understanding which science gives us – of the 'relative liberation' it gives us over nature (1925a: 97/114).

Autonomy is the supreme principle of morality for Renouvier; through it he opposes the spirit of heteronomy present in Jacobin statist socialism and monarchic Catholicism, both of which see the human being as a 'subordinated' organ of a whole which makes it an instrument of its will (Renouvier 1872b: 1.10). Renouvier criticized Kant for failing to ground freedom in the real world of space and time. Unlike in this 'metaphysical' theory, will must be seen as a force of conscience – a type of personal power – which requires not only opportunities, but also coherent, consistent laws on which it can count for effective action.[11] This is the philosophical background necessary to understand Durkheim's argument that the solidarity of social relations is necessary for effective self-determination. This view of the reciprocity of society and autonomy is central to the politics of autonomy: Kant indicated the connection between autonomy and community through grounding self-determination in the 'kingdom of ends'.

Autonomy is effective self-determination, and cannot be understood without a definition of individuation, will and freedom, all of which are lacking from the sociological account of Durkheim given so far. But he has a clear account of reflective autonomy: 'Thought is the liberator of the will' (Durkheim 1925a: 100/118). Will and therefore freedom are shown in doubt and, practically, in the effort that morality requires (ibid. 84/99). But Durkheim pursues the conditions under which social relations establish the conditions for 'effective' autonomy: 'How is it that whilst becoming more autonomous, the individual depends more on society?' (1893b: xliii/ xxx). The argument of *De la Division du travail social* shows that autonomy is only really possible through solidarity. Durkheim's argument for a positive theory of freedom which guarantees autonomy turns the arguments of political economy on their head, for the latter requires a theory of rational agency, and, as Durkheim shows, the conditions for effective action lie in the social milieu: freedom, agency and the social relations of which they are a part cannot be separated. Effective agency does not just require internal clarity; since the conditions of effective action lie in the order of society, it follows that society either enables or disables. Thus the proper organization of the relations of society is crucial to effective action.

So the relations of society that enable the agent to have and to realize proximate goals are the real foundation for effective freedom. Freedom as a personal power requires the co-ordination of sets of relations in the milieu as the necessary conditions for the realization of action. But because of the interdependence of social relations, these are equally important for the realization of other persons' freedom. This totality of relations is 'order'. So, whilst political economy entails the idea of freedom as rapacity, Durkheim's idea of rational social organization argues for effective freedom within social relations. Personal freedom must be limited to a degree by the requirement of overall coherence in the totality of relations, for on this depends the viability of society.

So the relation between individual personality and social solidarity (1893b: xliii/xxx) points to a positive theory of freedom at the heart of which is autonomy: 'To be a person is to be an autonomous source of action' (ibid. 399/335). Autonomy can be seen to be effective self-determination; this is possible only in so far as there is a sphere within which self-realization is possible, and this requires overall coherence of the totality of social relations. People do not simply need protection from interference – the classic negative theory of freedom – rather, they require something positive that supports the possibility of action; this is something that only the relations that surround the person can provide. In this way autonomy and solidarity can be reconciled.

As we have seen, solidarity is compromised by all external inequality, and I have argued that 'external' means all relations other than the inner sphere of representation. So, if we become effective agents through the relations of solidarity that surround us from childhood, then autonomy – self-determining action – is the result of a stable character, which can use freedom in effective action and bears a personal and different, because individuated, mark. This is the result of the habitual relations of the social milieu; the great insight of Durkheim here is that it is the stability and differentiated integration of relations in society which make for autonomy of action: the 'normal' constraint of society develops the power of agency. It is in this sense that solidarity and autonomy imply each other. This argument also overturns political conservatism, for it maintains that it is in terms of just and equal social relations that we get stable relations and effective agency.

The association of science and conscience theoretically supports autonomy in a way that science understood as an external science of facts and things cannot: 'It is conscience which confers this autonomy' (1925a: 101/119). This is a reflexive acknowledgement of our power. But it involves acknowledgement also of our dependence on solidarity – that is, on the set of relations which constitute the possibility of effective agency – and on a coherent milieu. Our dependence on these is converted into a form of 'mastery of self' whereby real self-determination is possible.

## Durkheim as moral critic

For Durkheim, the point of a reflective critical science is to transform a conscience from being *obscur* to consciously aware. Reflection is the necessary condition of a moral science (1893b: xli/xxviii), and allows the discovery of 'new practices'. (1950a: 123/90). The practical goal of sociology is to clarify the unconscious, unclear ideal of collective thinking (1925a: 81/95). But, more than that, it is to underwrite the politics of autonomy by demonstrating that logically it is through conscience, in association and therefore in communication with others, that the proper ends of action will be found. But since these are found in the *milieu social*, there made general and normal, it is also central to the development of a moral republic. Locating things as a social reality is only the first stage of a sociology of morals.

Durkheim has a theoretical logic of critique: for him, the ideal by which the real must be evaluated must be found in reality. Thus to criticize the real is not just to undermine it negatively, but to positively point to forces developing in society. The moral failure of a society must then be judged in terms of how well it has realized its own ideal. It is in the immanent processes of the real that the effective basis of critique will be found. For contemporary European societies, the ideal has been that of humanism and of egalitarianism. Practical reason gives a non-instrumental end to the will – the human being as sacred – which must be achieved in the republic. The significance of representation as a practical force which initiates changes is clear; to act towards society is to both change and construct it. 'The primary role of collective representations is to make that superior reality which is society' (1955: 174).

But this critical reflection on the societal ideal aids transformation. In focusing on the unclear ideal which we pursue (1893b: xxxix/xxvi), science addresses the tendencies of conduct. This is to grasp the possibilities of history as they develop in becoming: the modality of action in becoming requires both necessity and possibility. Human effort acting on the discontinuities of history is central to practical transformation. If history is to be interrupted effectively, it is necessary to know what actually moves people. 'What really direct us are not some ideas which our attention is presently occupied with; it is the residues left by our anterior life; these are acquired habits, prejudices, tendencies which move us without us being aware of it, it is in other words, everything which constitutes our moral character' (Durkheim 1898b: 19/6).

# 11

# Belief and the Logic
# of the Sacred

Although Durkheim is widely viewed as moving to an idealism in his later thought, he argues for a *science* of religions in *Les Formes élémentaires de la vie religieuse* (Durkheim 1912a: 98/66). Given the importance of religion for Durkheim, the nature of the science which explains it is important. 'Religion exists; it is a system of given facts; in a word it is a reality' (ibid. 614/432). Religion is 'a system of ideas' (ibid. 98/66). The discipline of science 'applies to a given reality', and its theoretical terms must accommodate the object which it studies (ibid. 99/66). We have seen that representation is a constant theoretical tool of his thought, together with the concepts of conscience and the conscience collective. It is in terms of these that Durkheim accounts for religion, which involves forces, symbols, representations and the conscience collective, but, above all, beliefs. But this is not unique to the later work; in *Les Règles* he argues that social facts 'consist in beliefs (*croyances*) and constituted practices' (1895a: 6/52). These considerations must confound Parsons's characterization of the later Durkheim as an idealist, and the concept of an 'epistemological break' in his work.

But a distinctive feature of this work is his explicit introduction of the apriori: I have argued that the apriori appears throughout Durkheim's work in the neglected concept of the representative, and that the conception of a science which can accommodate this has not so far been analysed or demonstrated. Thus the science of religions must accommodate this also: the apriori is not characterized as 'innate', but as 'the irreducibility' of the 'distinct and superimposed levels' of knowledge (1912a: 21/14). Why does he do this, and how does he use it? I suggest that it enters his conception of religious phenomena as both beliefs and rites. The formal believing functions of conscience are 'sui generis mental functions, irreducible to experience', and are testimony to the importance of Kant (1887a: 3.455). So the representative and practical functions of conscience are the formal irreducible presuppositions of human experience and its availability to a science of description.

But in terms of the ritual aspect of religion, we can see another use of the apriori. Here it is a social apriori, seen in Durkheim's conception of the 'representative ceremony', which is central to the conception of rite (1912a: 546/386). The function of a rite is to have 'a general action, which while being always and everywhere similar to itself, is nevertheless capable of taking different forms according to the circumstances' (ibid. 552/390). Here he uses the representative to refer to the character of an institutional form which must remain the same, for it governs and anticipates particular circumstances; this is the characteristic of the apriori. Renouvier's concept of the representative function and his extension of this to the general sphere of representation, where it designates the character of a phenomenon 'suited to represent', allows this (Renouvier 1875c: 1.11). So in a philosophical sense the representative function is that which serves to represent; Durkheim uses it sociologically to show how a rite guides and anticipates social experience and governs the terms under which action is undertaken.

Another aspect of *Les Formes élémentaires* is the stress on practical reason: this is evident in the emphasis on the 'moral necessity' of the categories (1912a: 25/17). But it is evident also in the role of belief, which in the Kantian and post-Kantian tradition is a matter of practical interest. Belief is central to the moral constructivism of Durkheim's thought, for it has a constituting role *vis-à-vis* both religious and social reality. Recognition of Durkheim's argument for the constituting power of conscience in belief must repudiate all accusations of behaviourism and philosophical realism or of positivism as adequately characterizing his theory of religion, for each of these in different ways denies the constitutive functions of conscience and collective action in the formation of reality. 'The collective state which gives rise to (*suscite*) religion is the communion of consciences' (1913b: 1.40; see also 1912: 591/417). To overlook the latter constitutes a serious omission in the interpretation of what is the most important feature of society for Durkheim – for the communication of consciences is not only tied to the logic of the *conscience commune*, of which religion is the most 'eminent form' (1893b: 270/228), it is also the foundation of collective beliefs (*croyances collectives*).

For Comte, religion is logically tied to the long-outmoded theological stage of historical evolution: the scientific and the positive are, logically, at opposite ends of the intellectual and historical spectrum from the religious (despite his later theories and stress on fetishism). There can be no constitutive role for either belief or representation in his account of mind and of reality. Equally, realism cannot explain religion adequately in a sociological sense, for this logically acknowledges no reality relative to the believing functions of conscience: but this is precisely what must be accounted for in Durkheim's theory of religion.

Indeed, since religion is the quintessential social institution for Durkheim, it must be the testing ground for accounts of his theory of reality and science. I have argued that Copernicanism accommodates a view of reality relative to representation, and that a Copernican science is that which unravels the logic of relation and representation. It is this which accounts for the logic of the human microcosm, which, for Durkheim, is particularly evident in mythology as 'the way in which society represents to itself man and the world' (1912a: 536/379).[1] But mythology in turn is 'the collection of communal beliefs of the group' (ibid.). Beliefs are fundamental to the structure of a human universe as a realm of significations. Collective beliefs support collective representations, and are thus more fundamental than they are. It is on this logical axis that religion rests for Durkheim: a world relative to the structure of representation gives way to a world relative to collective belief. This demonstrates the distinctive circular logic of social experience, which Durkheim elucidates in the concepts of belief, symbol and force. It is this logic of social experience, which religion so clearly expresses, that positivism and empiricism cannot explain.

However much Durkheim developed the concerns of philosophy in the study of collective beliefs and actions in society and history, in distinction to the philosophical tradition he insisted on the institutional force of religion. This is fundamental to it, and it is where we must begin this analysis of his view of religion.

## The institution of religion

'For so long as men live together they will hold some belief in common.' For this reason, religion is the paradigmatic social institution for Durkheim (Poggi 1971: 252). To conceive of religion as an 'idealist popular metaphysic' which is concerned with the afterlife is to turn it into some 'voluntarily accepted philosophy' which 'is a simple incident in the private life and conscience of the individual' (Durkheim 1886: 196/22). An effective institution must be a 'collective discipline' which 'imposes itself with the overpowering authority of habit' (ibid.). For 'the power and authority of every discipline lies in habit' (ibid. 21). These reflections in the early review of Spencer indicate what is essential in religion: its integrative and socially expressive function in the reinforcement of group identity and in the direction of action. Central to this is regular repetition of action and habit, which are later central to his definition of the cult (1912a: 596/420).

In his early article 'De la définition des phénomènes religieux', he defines religious phenomena as 'the name given to obligatory beliefs as well as the practices relating to objects of such beliefs' (1899aii: 159/92). In his later works Durkheim tends to concentrate rather less on the obligatory and the habitual, and more on beliefs and practices as central to religion. But a constant feature of religion is stated early on: thought and action are so closely linked in religion as to be inseparable. It thus corresponds to a stage of social development at which the two sets of functions are not yet logically dissociated and separated from each other (ibid. 92). The same phenomenon occurs in 'the *representative* life' of nations as in the economic sphere: individual variation is impossible as long as religion, as an expression of the *conscience commune*, absorbs 'all the representative functions with the practical functions'. The first are only dissociated from the second when philosophy appears. But this is only possible when 'religion has lost a little of its empire' (1893b: 269/228).

The ritualistic and communal function of religion, evident through the influence of Robertson Smith, has been stressed in the interpretation of Durkheim's account of religion. But to over-emphasize this is to overlook just how strong is a reflexive theory of consciousness which is a necessary feature of the *croyances collectives*. This practical, constituting power of consciousness can be seen, first, in his account of the divine being.

## Religion is not defined by God

How does Durkheim arrive at his characteristic position – that 'divinity is the symbolic expression of the collectivity' (1925a: 89/105)? He opposed classical philosophical and theological definitions of religion which centre around the idea of God: not only do many religions not have a god (Buddhism, Jainism), but the concept of God does not universally have the omnipotence ascribed to it within the Western tradition. Durkheim underlined 'that state of dependence in which the gods are in relation to the thought of man' (1912a: 493–4/349). 'The gods . . . are conceived not perceived' (ibid. 617–18/434). Divinity is thus a secondary characteristic: it is the result of 'a special process' of 'concentration and concretization of religious characteristics made concrete in a definite individuality' (1899aii: 151/85). Religion originates 'not in individual feelings but in collective states of mind, and it varies according to these' (ibid. 94). 'The idea of the supreme being depends so strictly on the ensemble of totemic beliefs that it still bears their mark' (1912a: 418/295). The sacred beings who are the objects of belief are developed in the consciences of the believers. 'It is in human consciences that [religious life] is elaborated' (ibid. 462/327); 'sacred beings . . . can only live in human consciences' (ibid. 495/351).

This line of thinking has a philosophical history which goes back to

Kant. The significance of Kant's Copernican revolution in its practical conclusions was to reverse the traditional theological relation between God and the human being. The concept of God as a necessary object of moral belief implies a constitutive role for practical reason, which reverses the traditional dependence of the human being on God so characteristic of pre-Kantian theological thinking. After Kant, the concept of divine being is logically dependent on practical reason. This is central to the establishment of the politics of autonomy for Kant.

For Renouvier, the concept of God, and particularly its use, is the clearest example of the absolute. To subvert the absolute is to subvert theological politics: if there is no absolute, then there is no transcendent principle of unity which calls for subordination and hierarchy. 'We start with ourselves, with our passions and moral law and we establish what must correspond to this in the centre of the universe, so that there is harmony' (Renouvier 1859: 630–1). Kant's conception of practical reason thereby reappears as what the laws of conscience demand (ibid. 631). The concept of divinity within a scientific framework is anthropomorphic and is part of the sphere of the ideal (1876e: 135). Thus religion is freed from theology and enters the sphere of rationalism. This is consistent with Renouvier's aim of freeing rationalism from theology. 'Theism and the absolute reappear transformed in the ideal of moral perfection' (1859: 626).

Even though Durkheim extends this to the collective dimension, it is through this logic that he can argue that gods are 'ideal beings' (Durkheim 1912a: 602/423). Renouvier's theory of representative functions makes sense of how belief constitutes objects, in the represented, as symbols and ideals, which are made real by being believed in. The ideal is central to action and belief. 'The ideal . . . whose nature is not to be actually given, nor even actually to be thought, but is present to the mind by its elements' (Renouvier 1869b: 1.190). It relates to our intellectual, feeling and functions. Because it arises out of the gap between the 'is' and the 'ought', it is an unrealized object which possesses qualities relating to beauty and to goodness, and is a potent source of action.

Ideals, symbols and representations are part of the psychic activity which is central to social life, and especially to religious life for Durkheim (1912a: 603/424). Divine beings are closely associated with the processes of symbolization and idealization. The latter are necessary to flesh out the creatures of the religious imagination as it peoples the region beyond sense with sacred beings. 'What defines the sacred is that it is superimposed on the real; now the ideal conforms to the same definition: we cannot explain the one without explaining the other' (ibid. 602/424). We can understand the sacred ultimately only through the 'psychic mechanism' which produces the ideal. 'The human being uniquely has the faculty of conceiving the ideal and adding it to the real' (ibid.). 'What defines the sacred is that it is added to the real; the ideal responds to the same definition: one can then not explain the one without explaining the other' (ibid. 603/424).

Even if religion can be defined in logical independence of God, can there be a religion without the transcendent? Clearly the concept of what is transcendent to individual consciences is part of the sacred for Durkheim (ibid. 331/233), yet logically there is no transcendent for him; nothing transcends representation and its logic – which has no need of the 'thing in itself' (1898b: 29/15). The constitution of the ideal as the backbone of the sacred, understood symbolically, replaces the concept of the absolute and the transcendent (1912a: 331/233). Durkheim argues that the proposition that 'nothing exists except by representation' is 'doubly true in relation to religious forces' (ibid. 493/349): 'everything takes place in representations' (ibid. 536/379). The sacred, together with its opposite, the profane, is formed within the structure of representation: the sacred is constituted by human consciousness. The concept of divinity as the symbol of the sacred responds to the functions of end, passions, will and, above all, belief. For Durkheim the gods and sacred beings are not only the objects of belief; they are constituted by those beliefs.

## Belief or ritual?

'A religion is a solidary system of beliefs and practices relative to sacred things, that is to say separate, forbidden, beliefs and practices which unite all who adhere to it in the same moral community' (1912a: 65/44). With this final definition of religion in *Les Formes élémentaires*, phenomena are naturally arranged in two fundamental categories: beliefs and rites (ibid. 50/34). Pickering shows us that Durkheim postulated a relation between belief and action or ritual that has been debated ever since. Does ritual precede belief? Do rituals have equal explanatory value? Or does belief have primacy over ritual? Durkheim 'secretly awards first prize to belief' (Pickering 1984: 379). 'In short religion starts with faith, that is to say, with any belief accepted or experienced without argument' (Durkheim 1886a: 195/21). The point of ritual is to reinforce belief. 'The rite thus only serves and can only serve to maintain the vitality of those beliefs' (1912a: 536/379). Indeed for Durkheim, 'The true justification of religious practices does not lie in the apparent ends which they pursue, but rather in the invisible action which they exercise over conscience and in the way they affect the level of our mental state' (ibid. 514/364). A central conceptual condition of his sociological explanation of religion is the concept of a reality relative to belief.

The centrality of belief to religious experience is clear from the argument of *Les Formes élémentaires*. The definition of ritual presupposes that of belief, and this in turn presupposes the classification of things into sacred and profane: sacred things are a centre of organization around which revolve beliefs and rites. However, it is clear that these sacred things and rites are themselves the expression of beliefs. 'The rite . . . exists only in so far as it is believed in, and the effect of all these collective demonstrations is to support the beliefs on which they are founded' (ibid. 511/362). Cults and beliefs react on each other: 'Of course the cult depends on the beliefs, but it also reacts on them' (ibid. 424/299). But it becomes clear that beliefs are the foundation of religion. 'Mythological constructions . . . cover over a system of beliefs, at once simpler and more obscure . . . which form the solid foundations upon which the religious systems are built' (ibid. 289/204).

It is belief that is a constituting feature of religion, for, by definition, sacred things represent that which is believed in. 'The sacred character . . . is added to them by belief' (ibid. 492/345). Gods are constituted by, and thus depend on, the system of collective belief. 'Sacred beings are such only because they are represented as such in the mind. When we cease to believe in them it is as though they did not exist' (ibid. 492/349). Since objects of religious belief are thus constituted, belief plays a pivotal, foundational role in establishing the constitution of the reality that is believed in and its nature. Religion and its panoply of gods, rituals and cults could not exist without beliefs.

Thus, they underlie the collective morality and action so essential to the existence of society for Durkheim. As for Kant, so for Durkheim, there is a non-visible world which is not available to the senses. 'It is religious beliefs that have substituted for the world, as it is perceived by the senses, another different one' (ibid. 338/238). For Durkheim, the idea of God is real in the sense that it is the object of collective belief and expresses a reality – society. The failure of animism is that it makes religious beliefs 'hallucinatory representations without any objective foundation; on the contrary religious beliefs have a foundation in the real' (ibid. 97/65).

The stress on belief more than on ritual allows his comparison of individualism to religion, for this system of beliefs doesn't involve 'symbols and rites properly speaking', for 'this external apparatus' is only religion's 'superficial part' (1898c: 270/51). The cult of man 'has its first dogma in the autonomy of reason and first rite in free thought' (ibid. 268/49). Revolutionary moments and modern individualism share in the expressive power of religion: they are beliefs which focus on symbols and ideals that generate passion and action. Christianity, Buddhism, socialism and modern individualism are comparable, because they are all forms of belief which entail action and generate passions and moments of effervescence;

central to all these is belief, which plays a role in the constitution of the reality believed in.

Unravelling the psychic mechanisms that are essential to believing is part of sociological explanation for Durkheim. 'Social action follows ways that are too circuitous and obscure, and employs psychic mechanisms that are too complex to allow the ordinary observer to see whence it comes' (1912a: 299/211). Without the constituting, symbolizing functions of conscience, there would be no religions in this broad definition. The ideals, the symbols which are believed in socially, have no logical independence of the consciences which believe them, even though expressed in action and ritual. Belief is the result of a psychic process. 'This impulse towards believing, is just what constitutes faith; and it is faith which makes the authority of the rites, according to the believer, whoever he may be, Christian or Australian. The only superiority of the former is that he accounts better for the psychic process from which his faith results; he know it is faith which saves' (ibid. 515/365).

Belief enters the sphere of science because it is a representation. 'Beliefs . . . are states of opinion, they consist in representations' (ibid. 50/34). The integrated functions of conscience are essential to the activity of belief and the constitution of its objects, but will and passion are primary. 'For them to have the useful action on the soul which is their raison d'être, it is necessary that they are believed in. Now beliefs are only active when they are shared' (ibid. 607/427). This is possible because of the 'communion of consciences' (ibid. 591/417). Renouvier showed how shared beliefs enter into society and history. Collective beliefs (*les croyances collectives*) are the coefficients of 'human determinations' (Renouvier 1864a: 2).

However, belief plays a fundamental role in one of Durkheim's boldest claims: that it is from collective beliefs that the first system of representations stems. Through the logical force of this, Durkheim can claim that science and philosophy arise out of religion. This position implies that belief has primacy over cognition for Durkheim; this is to give belief not just a role alongside knowledge, but a foundational role *vis-à-vis* knowledge. 'The concept, which is primitively held to be true because it is collective, tends not to become collective except on condition of being held to be true' (Durkheim 1912a: 624/439). This 'holding something to be true' is belief, which for Renouvier, against Kant and classic rationalism, underlies all knowledge: everything that is 'known' is not thereby apodictic, but is in reality held to be true. By arguing that belief underlies all representation, he allows Durkheim to argue that science and philosophy stem from collective beliefs.

## Sacred things, force, symbols and the logic of representation

The division between the sacred and the profane is central to Durkheim's definition of religion. It is associated with the dualism of human nature: *homo duplex* has two irreducible components, the social and the individual. It 'is a particular case of that division of things into the sacred and the profane that is the foundation of all religions, and it must be explained on the same principles' (1914a: 327/335). Durkheim opposes Robertson Smith's naturalist definition of the sacred by arguing for its variation between societies. The sacred is therefore that which is decided by society (Pickering 1984: 131). The sacred is constituted by society, but how?

An analysis of the logic of representation elucidates certain features of the sacred and the profane. 'This duality is only the objective expression of that which exists in our representations' (Durkheim 1899aii: 157/90). The logical axis conscience–representation–thing (*chose*) elucidates this process by which things are rendered sacred. A realist or positivist account of 'thing' cannot explain how Durkheim uses the concept of 'sacred thing' (1912a: 487/345). The connection between representation and thing as the object of a representation is clear: totems, as sacred things, are symbolic expressions of totemic beliefs. Totems as physical objects, like any religious artefacts, symbolize belief: they are material representations of what is believed. Symbolization has been transferred to the 'external' side of representation – that is, to the side of 'things'. These nevertheless represent the 'internal side' – that is, the believing functions.

So sacred things are the material representation of beliefs: as such, they are objects of reference of beliefs. Representations have 'thing' as their object of reference. Believing is that act of mind by which the representative and the practical functions of conscience are brought together. When something is either held to be true or believed in by conscience, it becomes a 'thing' (*chose*) – that is, an object of the representative activity central to conscience. In this instance it is also subject to the idealization functions and, above all, the symbolization functions which are central to the logical structure of representation. As Durkheim argues in *Le Suicide*, 'Religion, definitively, is the system of symbols by which society becomes conscious of itself; it is collective being's own way of thinking' (1897a: 352/312).

The totem is an example of a sacred thing, as is the concept of God, and both represent what is *held* to be sacred. But what is actually going on in the complex psychic mechanisms here is the social state rendered objective. 'The religious force is nothing but the feeling which the collectivity inspires in its members, but projected outside of (*hors de*) the consciences which experience it and objectified (*objectivité*). To render itself objective (*pour s'objectiver*) it fixes itself on an object, which thus becomes sacred, but any object can inspire this role' (1912a: 327/230). This is central to human communication with itself, and thus to how religion is society worshipping itself: 'To express our own ideas to ourselves we need to ... fix them on material things which symbolise them.' Here, more than elsewhere, 'the idea makes the reality' (ibid. 326/229). The logic of positivism cannot explain this, but it doesn't follow that Durkheim's explanation is logically idealist – even though he argues for the 'essential idealism' of this ideal superstructure of religious belief. It is articulated within the logic of representation, and the passage from the representative side to the represented allows the expression of the realization, the symbolization of belief.

So sacred beings 'are nothing but the collective states rendered objective (*objectivés*)'; as such, they are 'society seen under one of its aspects' (ibid. 590/416). The understanding of the sacred, then, is to be partly explained by how collective states are *objectivés*. But what does this mean? It can only be understood, first, through the process from the inner to the outer, and the move from the representative to the represented. This is neglected, not only in the positivist-externalist account of Durkheim, but also in the insistence on his later idealism. Society is the totality of the consciences which make it up: its feelings, ideas and beliefs exist internally, but are externalized in symbols and objects of veneration, and so pass into the realm of significations – that is, external relations of representative life. They are collective states rendered objective because they have passed to the objective pole of representation.

It must also be remembered that for Renouvier too '*chose*' means a synthesis of representations – a definition which is independent of the material status of the object. A sacred thing can thus be an object of knowledge within the logic of representation; religious representations refer to the sacred: a totem represents sacredness. Through the symbolic functions governed by species/type, it represents all the idealization and believing functions brought together in one symbol: religious beliefs can create a synthesis for Durkheim (1950a: 219/194). 'The sacred character which clothes the thing is not thus implied in the intrinsic properties of the latter, it is added to (*surajouté*) ... it is superimposed (*superposé*)' (1912a: 328/230).

The concept of force is central to the concept of the sacred, and exemplifies this unique logic of argument. 'The force isolating the sacred being ... is not in reality in that being; it lives in the conscience of the believers' (ibid. 522/370). This logic of force shows how mistaken is a realist, empiricist or positivist interpretation of Durkheim. 'Religious forces are thus human forces ... In reality they have borrowed from conscience all the elements from which they are made' (ibid. 599/422). I have noted that Swain mistranslated this important passage, and renders borrowed *from* conscience as borrowed *by* conscience (1915: 419), thereby obscuring the logic of reality here.

Thus 'the totemic principle' is 'the collective force rendered objective (*objectivée*) and projected onto things' (ibid. 519/367). This is not derived from external senses: this 'internal process' escapes empiricism which is why the latter sees religions as 'mythological aberrations' (ibid. 520/368). Force 'is full of spiritual elements, which can only have been borrowed from our psychic life' (ibid.). Force 'is entirely psychic, for it is made exclusively from ideas and feelings rendered objective (*sentiments objectivés*)' (ibid. 521/369). In the first instance, it comes from our inner experience; but it is impersonal, and thus in the second instance comes from co-operation (ibid.). It is precisely because it is human power projected on to things that it is energy-giving: it is a symbolic way of stimulating energy. Force thus does not imply mechanistic or scientistic connotations, but refers to human power and energy. Through communal ritual expressiveness, Durkheim argues, 'they are really stronger because the forces which were languishing are now reawakened in their consciences' (ibid. 494/350).

Finally, there is no real mystery as to how the terms 'thing' and 'symbol' can logically coexist in Durkheim's thought. The objectivity of the symbol is translated into the exterior in material representation, into 'things', but its origin in the collective force is initially interior, rooted in 'states of conscience' (ibid. 331/233). I have argued that 'outside' has a special meaning in Renouvier's logic of representation, referring to external relation; thus the object pole of representation and the external coincide. Symbols for Renouvier are part of the grammatical logic of representation: they are of representation, and are fundamental to the possibility of language. We see this kind of logic in Durkheim's statement: 'Speech (*la parole*) is another way of entering into relation with persons or with things; it is something of us (*de nous*) which extends itself outside' (ibid. 435/309).

The symbol is different from the sign, however, although it shares the logic of signification. Whilst signs are purely conventional, the symbol understood as 'natural and primitive' includes personification and myth for Renouvier (1859: 111–12). It is 'poetry in image', which is lost as languages gain in logical clarity. 'The principle of [primitive symbolism] . . . is the necessity to personify the names of things, to attribute passion and will to all the subjects of discourse' (ibid. 1859: 112). This is covered through the logic of quality ('species') and typification under the laws of representation.

## Action, passion and moments of effervescence

The ideal, as the motivating force of action, tends to be neglected in the analysis of Durkheim's account of religion. But ideals are significant for his theory of action, for it is they which generate action. 'The ideal is a system of forces', and 'mental and moral forces draw all their power of action from representation, from states of conscience' (Durkheim 1910b: 2.373/65). 'What makes the sanctity of a thing is ... the collective feeling of which it is an object' (1912a: 590/416). 'Collective sentiments can only become conscious of themselves in fixing themselves on external objects' (ibid. 599/421). For Durkheim, as for William James, belief leads to action. The connection with action is one of the most important aspects of religion for believers. 'The real function of religion is not to make us think ... but to make us act, to help us live' (ibid. 595/419). Action and ritual are connected, and both involve the concept of periodicity. 'Group life is essentially intermittent', and even the most idealist religions cannot escape 'the intermittences of social life' (ibid. 493/349). Periodicity is central to action, and thus to ritual; the need for periodic assembly is to revive energies and strengthen beliefs. Regular repetition, central to the cultic, serves to reinforce the representations of the gods.

'A faith is above all warmth, life, enthusiasm, exaltation of all mental activity, a transport of the individual above himself' (ibid. 607/427). This is particularly noticeable in periods of effervescence: 'A state of effervescence ... implies the mobilisation of all our active forces' (ibid. 582/411). Here passion is significantly important: it is the passionate quality of belief that makes it so important for Durkheim, particularly in the periods of effervescence. Indeed, it is because of this theory of passion that Durkheim can compare modern individualism to a cult, and thus to a form of religion.

The relation of inner to outer demonstrates the logic of action and how symbols can activate action. Symbols are not simply allegories, but are closely related to action, and thus have a practical function. Symbolization of the sacred is the great source of collective action: as such, it moves forces which go from the inside to the outside. Representative and practical functions of conscience realize themselves in symbols which represent them, and thereby become sources of action. This is evident in cultic action, where sign and faith mutually interpenetrate, and is a means of periodic re-creation for the group (ibid. 596/420). In this respect Lévi-Strauss's accusation that Durkheim should have thought more clearly about how symbolic thought makes social life possible is somewhat beside the point (Lévi-Strauss 1945: 518).

Giddens has argued that to explain the existence of religion, the basis of the general energy which is the fount of all that is sacred must be discovered (Giddens 1974: 109). The relation between symbol and passion as part of the practical function of conscience, I suggest, explains this. Symbols are bearers of feelings: 'without symbols social feelings can only have a precarious existence' (Durkheim 1912a: 330/232). It is important to remember the role of the unconscious in religious life; symbols are powerful here, as are the tendencies of feeling (ibid. 493/349). For Renouvier, passions are 'the stimulants and the substance of life': the great intellectual facts of history cannot be distinguished from the passions (Renouvier 1864a: 2). Although he insists on the indissolubility of the functions of conscience as necessary for understanding or intelligent action, he nevertheless holds that passion activates both the will and the understanding. The 'development of being' is the first condition of passion, not stability (1875d: 1.267). Of the different types of passion, there are some that lead to developments (*développants*). 'Enthusiasm' is the clearest example of the latter type, and leads to a 'transport' of being (ibid. 1.271). 'The impassioned (*passionné*) man is eminently active and full of energy' (ibid. 1.278). These passions are activated by ends; passions of enthusiasm are dynamic, not static.

It is for this reason, I suggest, that Durkheim sees in moments of collective effervescence the great moments of change and dynamism for a society; for here the real principle of change in a human being, the dynamic passions, are activated. This is the heart of a 'dynamogenic' view of social reality which, although a reinforcement of solidarity and *communitas*, is not thereby a conservative enforcement of changelessness. As Pickering says, 'If religion generates power – if it produces social energy – it must be seen in the mode of activity and change' (Pickering 1984: 214). A 'communal passion' is central to collective assemblies (Durkheim 1912a: 299/211).[2] So passions of enthusiasm – the 'passionate energies' – are central to moments of effervescence; and this stimulating action of society, which gives an 'afflux of energy', comes from 'outside' (1912a: 301–2/213). Durkheim can thus argue that effervescent assembly gives rise to new actions and new ideas: in the heart of an assembly heated by a common passion, 'we become capable of feelings and actions of which we are incapable when reduced to our own forces' (ibid. 299/211). The Crusades and the French Revolution are examples of 'creative effervescence' (ibid. 301/213).

Various suggestions have been made about the source of Durkheim's concept of effervescence: Bergson and his '*élan vital*' has been suggested (by La Capra, Lukes and Pickering). Although I would not deny the importance of Bergson, this concept must be compatible with Durkheim's professed rationalism. Renouvier's account of the 'developing passions' seen in enthusiasm shows that effervescence is explicable through the logical structure of representation.

Thus action is central to Durkheim's account of society: 'Society can only feel its influence in action, and it is not in action unless the individuals who compose it are assembled and act in common' (ibid. 598/421). Collective action is an affirmation of collective reality, and is undertaken through symbols: the supreme symbol – of the sacred – induces action and feeling; the profane does not induce the passions and action in the same way as the sacred. The sacred generates moments of effervescence, and the enthusiasm which results from 'the communion of consciences' – the *sine qua non* of social communication. Thus there is a dynamic of expressive communication in the constitution of the sacred; this explains why the sacred is social, and why it is always present, yet takes so many different forms. The sacred, then, is the supreme example of the Durkheimian thesis that religion is society worshipping itself.

Pickering argues that there is a paradox between religion understood as a system of representations and the all-important action component (Pickering, 1984: 295). This is so only if representation is understood, first, in a realist way and as a reflection of a material reality expressed in 'things', and second, in a classical rationalist sense. I have argued that action is not antithetical to representation, but is accommodated through its active, practical, voluntary dimensions, especially through force. The word 'thing' is again confusing here: a realist or materialist interpretation disables understanding of Durkheim's definition of religion as beliefs relative to sacred things, and of why he insists that 'Social life in all its aspects and at every moment of history, is possible only through a vast symbolism' (Durkheim 1912a: 331/233).

### 'There are no religions which are false: all are true in their fashion' (1912a: 3/2)

For Durkheim there is no empirical coefficient for religious belief, for religion establishes a world distinct from the senses. There is, nevertheless, an objective reference of belief; there is a reality affirmed for believers. Like William James, he argues that religious beliefs are not illusory. 'Our entire study rests upon this postulate that the unanimous sentiment of the believers of all times cannot be purely illusory' (ibid. 596/420). But unlike James, Durkheim claims that the reality they have does not accord with the testimony of the believers. Gods do not exist because so many people believe in them; rather, their reality is social: the central element of the reality of religious belief is its collective nature. Religious beliefs have no transcendent object or empirical referent, but nevertheless have an objective reference in society; their truth lies in the human institution which they underpin. Religions are not false, for they point to a collective reality: it is human institutions that guarantee the reality of belief. Beliefs are objectified into symbols or gods; thus society worships itself. We have seen that beliefs are central to the affirmation and reaffirmation of collective identity, and that ritual action which expresses them supports collective action and morality, which form the cement of society.

Can Durkheim maintain his argument that religious beliefs, although lacking empirical corroboration, can still have an objective reference? I suggest that it relies on two positions: first, the conception of reality as affirmation, and second, the conception of the self-referentiality of belief. The first is Renouvierist, whilst the second is more clearly strictly Kantian. The concept of reality as affirmation is found particularly in the account of cultic action. In cultic, ritual action, Durkheim says, the group affirms itself, and strengthens itself through strong feeling. When the community comes together, he argues, 'The sharing of these feelings has, as always, the effect of intensifying them. In affirming themselves, these feelings are exalted and inflamed and reach a degree of violence' (ibid. 582/410). What does affirmation mean in relation to social reality? I suggest that it is implied by the cognitive acts of collective beliefs affirming a reality in collective representations.

I have argued that, for Durkheim, collective beliefs constitute a reality. By this I mean that non-material objects of reference become real because they are believed in: sacred things represent this reality and thus symbolize beliefs. This is real for the consciences which have constructed this super-sensible world through the psychic processes of idealization and symbolization; because this reality is believed in, it is affirmed by believers. That is, if, following Renouvier, we accept that all questions of reality involve the question of certainty, and that this is solved by the practical, believing functions of conscience, then it follows that reality itself is dependent on the practical orientations of our consciousness. By this he means that, at the deepest level, beneath all questions of evidence and necessity, underlying the most empirical of sciences, are cognitive acts of belief which affirm the reality in question.

In *Pragmatisme et sociologie* Durkheim says that theoretical certainty is another form of practical certainty, and that in this way 'we are in the Kantian tradition' (1955a: 202). Now, just as for Kant to deny that God is the object of theoretical knowledge is not to undermine but to save deism, so for Renouvier to go against classical rationalism and deny that the real is only the object of evidence and necessary theoretical determinations does not undermine the concept of reality; affirmation is the act of practical consciousness by which we relate to all reality.

This approach to reality is important for Durkheim: it indicates the human contribution to the concept of reality, and the practical, constructive spirit in which it is made. Affirmation is central to Durkheim's constructivism: it is central to the constitution of reality. It forms part of the Kantian concept of the primacy of practical reason and allows the passage from science to the supreme importance of morality. But its significance here for his constructivism is the affirming of human, and indeed moral, worlds through the practical functions of conscience. Renouvier establishes a connection between belief (*croyance*), affirmation and reality that Durkheim uses in his argument for the reality of religion relative to the *croyances collectives*. Belief is central to the constitution of a reality for it leads to affirmations of the real; indeed, any reality is ultimately founded on the practical necessity of affirmation.

The logical relation between belief and its objects is the backbone of Durkheim's sociological explanation of religion, and is central to the sociological argument that religion stems from the collectivity. Its beliefs are symbolized in sacred things or ideals, and are reinforced in action or ritual, which, as it were, boomerangs back on the collectivity and reinforces it emotionally and expressively in terms of solidarity. Thus Durkheim argues that it is only through acknowledging that human force comes from conscience and *sentiments objectivés* that we can understand the real significance of religion (ibid. 599/422). There is circularity of expressive communication here – the subject and object of this are the community itself. This helps us to understand how humanity can be both the object and the agent of the cult of man (1898c: 267/48). 'The rite thus serves ... to revive the most essential elements of the collective conscience' (1912a: 536/380).

There is distinctive logic to this claim. Just as a concept, as impersonal representation, is common to all, 'because it is the work of the community' (ibid. 619/435), so beliefs in turn act on the community from which they spring to reinforce action and the moral solidarity of society. 'It is this character of the ceremony which makes it instructive. It tends entirely to act on consciences and on them alone' (ibid. 537/379). A self-referentiality of belief systems lies at the centre of the logic of social reality: beliefs stem from conscience, are expressed in sacred objects, enacted in rites and cults, and flow back to, and reinforce, the social relations from which they came. I suggest that this is Kantian, because Kant showed that the most fundamental arguments involved in the constitution of reality are characterized by a form of self-referentiality.[3]

## Society as the womb of religion, or religion as the womb of society?

An ambiguity in Durkheim's thought has been noted by scholars: does he mean that religion is derived from society, or does he mean that religion is the matrix of all that is social? Giddens argues that Durkheim rejects the idealist interpretation that religion creates society. Rather, 'religion is the expression of the self creation, the autonomous development of society' (Gidden 1974: 110). Leaving aside the question of historical priority, it can be seen that religion and the social imply each other in a non-identical way. In arguing that beliefs spring from the community, it is true that 'all that is religious is social'. But in reacting back on the community through the symbols and idealized beings of religion, it is equally true that 'all that is social is religious' (Pickering 1984: 271). There is a circularity here, but it is not vicious, for symbols, and thus forms of the sacred, spring from the beliefs that are generated in social relations: everything in religion refers back to beliefs through the medium of symbolic expressive communication.

This kind of transcendental logic allows Durkheim to argue for the collective origin of belief systems; it is thus at the heart of a sociological explanation of religion. It further allows him to argue for the functional necessity of religion as affirming the collectivity in a way that no other human institution can quite match. I have argued that, in believing, human beings affirm a reality which is then a symbolic representation, in ideal and symbolic objects, of the beliefs themselves. The objects of these are ideal beings; but their reference, that from which they spring and to which they refer back in reinforcing rituals, are the 'consciences' which make up society. In affirming themselves thus symbolically, the latter create a world of ideals and values; because this world springs from society, it therefore represents society.

The republican problematic was to turn the object of faith from God to society: it was to harness the power of belief to make and underwrite society. So society can be compared to the gods; it too will die if no longer believed in. 'Were the idea of society to be extinguished in individual minds, were the beliefs, the traditions, the aspirations of the collectivity to cease to be felt, and shared by particular persons, society would die. One can then repeat for it what has been said above about divinity: it has reality only in the measure to which it has a place in human consciences, and it is we who make that place' (Durkheim 1912a: 496/351).

# 12

# Final Reflections: Durkheim contra Sociology

Durkheim is neither the kind of holist nor the kind of positivist that he is painted as; rather, he is a rationalist interested in the complex historical becoming of society. He is not concerned with the subordination of the individual in the interest of order, even though he acknowledges the profound interrelatedness of the sphere which surrounds and envelops the individual; the pluralism of this relational interdependence accommodates the autonomy of individual action. He is not an unreconstructed determinist who denies the reality of choice and reflection as central to both action and the power of agency at the heart of society. He insists that 'constraint' must be freely consented to, and that this is the only way its authority can be efficacious (1915c: 74). And, rather than ignoring the question of meaning, he makes the orientation of consciousness and understanding to reality and its unconscious features a fundamental, necessary feature of social life. Even though it is overlapped and interpenetrated by functional spheres of generality, this inner domain has its own individuality, partially distinct from the external relations which surround it. He accounts for the changing and complex forms of collective thinking that interpenetrate this, just as he underscores the contrary forces central to the dynamic of this changing reality. He uses a distinct logic and theory of science centring on representation, relation and becoming, to express this complex reality.

The theoretical and practical breadth and strength of this vocabulary stand in contrast to the present theoretical state of sociology. Whilst his science espoused an economy of concepts to achieve maximal empirical results, the opposite is now the case, which, as a 'battle field of . . . endless controversies', is reminiscent more of Kant's conception of 'metaphysics' (1781: Avii) than of a successful science rich in empirical results. 'The supposed guides to social reality (ethnomethodology, structuralism, structural Marxism, hermeneutics, phenomenology, phenomenological Marxism, functionalism, hermeneutics plus Marxism, linguistic philosophy)' are 'a desert of arid concept-chopping', whose 'theoretical extravagance scarcely advanced the subject at all' (Hall 1992: 1). Compared to the excitement of the founding fathers, this is not only 'awfully boring', but 'desperately innocuous' (ibid.). The latter is the more telling accusation: even the much maligned Comte was required to be silent by government. This is an accolade unavailable to much contemporary theory: there can be no danger to established powers if, ultimately, there are no facts, and all is interpretation or discourse.

To Hall's list we can now add post-modernism and post-structuralism. Much as ethnomethodology flourished in California during the Nixon era, so Foucauldian and post-modernist approaches came to flourish during the Thatcher years. Ethnomethodology, through its critiques of positivism and holism, initiated many of the highly relativist, subjectivist and interpretative movements that culminated in post-modernism and post-structuralism. It implied that all factual description of the general was a positivist illusion; it turned a minimal point (the indexicality of experience) into a maximal one, and through it nibbled away at the factual, the structural and the historical basis of theory. Whilst it developed no substantively informative account of social reality beyond the elucidation of the formal properties of accounting or practice, it opened up a theoretical vacuum in which post-modernism and Foucauldian theories could flourish.

It is significant that most of these developments in the new sociologies have been directed against positivism and conservative functionalism – that is, Durkheim! In fact, each manages to develop only a portion of the total theoretical vision which Durkheim generated. Phenomenology developed the intentionality of consciousness to the exclusion of the historical and the structural. Structuralism developed the latter without historicity, individuation or autonomy. Marxism developed the historical and the structural without a developed theory of consciousness or a theory of individuation or right. Similarly, post-Durkheimian functionalism proceeded without transformational and critical aspects to its theory.

While all this 'concept-chopping' was going on, Durkheim's warnings about the effects of political economy on social relations were lying moribund under a pile of misplaced critiques of his general theory. The intellectual, moral and social paucity of Thatcherism was scarcely touched by all the new sociologies – and the sphere of the social and the collective had no intellectual defenders when the political bandits arrived and sold off what remained of collective assets to the lowest bidder. It is tempting to dream – have a 'thought-experiment', as Durkheim would call it – of the effect of a substantial empirical work supporting the concept of structural and collective necessities that was widely read and accepted, and to speculate how different the political landscape in Britain might have been. If we wanted substantive empirical information about the state of the country at this time, despite honourable exceptions,[1] it was not to the dominant trends in recent sociology that we should have turned, but to the work of an eminent journalist, Will Hutton.

A significant feature of modern sociology is the influence of hermeneutics and linguistic philosophy; this has narrowed the subject to the dominance of interpretation and linguistic analysis as methods for approaching social reality. But social phenomena are not linguistic phenomena, even though they must reach the level of signification to affect action, as Durkheim was the first to show. Whatever the importance of language as a social institution for Durkheim, a linguistic or even quasi-linguistic method is not *per se* satisfactory for approaching the social. The net result of the dominance of the above methods for contemporary sociology is to stress the linguistic at the expense of the social, and literary over scientific values. So, for example, conversational analysis carries forward the limitations of linguistic philosophy – a narrow conventionalism in the conception of reality and in what counts as truth.

Durkheim showed that social phenomena are complex phenomena of relatedness. If this is a reality, why can there not be a science which accommodates this theoretically in all its diverse and specific social and historical determinations? However complex it is to interpret and measure, he has shown that this has a conceptual foundation that underwrites the collective sphere of relatedness – in the logic of relation. Durkheim also shows that meaningfulness is central to social life, and thus that the concept of representation is an unavoidable and irreducible concept for a social science. It forms the interface between human consciousness and the structured reality of which it is a part, and through the logic of signification, he shows its relation to action, and thus to the 'force' of agency. Durkheim used the philosophy of scientific rationalism as a springboard from which to discover this new continent.

Since much of modern sociology appears to have been inspired by philosophy, has not a philosopher the dispensation – like the fool of old – to ask forbidden questions of the king? What kind of philosophy adequately expresses the full reality of the social? This is apposite, given the current importance assigned to French philosophers of the 1960s and the character of philosophy at this time. Might this not carry the danger of 'eloquence' replacing 'vigour and method' (Durkheim 1918a: 1.464)? This philosophy was characterized by a broadly literary tendency, which, when applied to the social, led to the elision of the difference between social reality and text or discourse (Giddens 1987: 210). 'The interpretation of texts constitutes an art and not a science' (Durkheim 1888a: 99/66). Indeed, what is the justification for treating the social world as a text at all? Whilst interpretation, inspired by literary analogies, is now all, it is clear that without a grasp of the factual, of what is the case, no interpretation of society can begin. So the relation between knowledge of the factual and interpretation is still open; the latter cannot replace the former. Observation in the broadest sense involves interpretation for Durkheim, but cannot be replaced by it *in toto*.

These issues raise the question of what concepts adequately express the deep structural and historical reality of society. Durkheim warned that 'A purely aesthetic culture does not place the mind in direct enough contact with reality to enable it to create a sufficiently adequate representation of it'. For, in it, 'we do not acquire the feeling of the organic development of society, of our dependence on previous generations and on the milieux' (1890a: 222/40). His warning about philosophy can count for sociology itself: 'Philosophy, if it is not based on the positive sciences, becomes a form of literature' (1909d: 1.186/237). As this literary spirit grows, together with the fracturing impulse of post-modernism, is there anything that can prevent sociology from becoming what Durkheim called 'an anarchic dilettantism' (1895b: 3.418). Indeed, is there not a distinct danger that sociology is becoming what Durkheim characterized as 'a particular mode of speculation intermediary between philosophy and literature where a few theoretical ideas are trotted out across all possible problems' (1903c: 1.138/189)?

Against these tendencies, the value of Durkheim is that he offers an escape from the code and the discourse and its internal logic, through an outward-going epistemology which does not thereby neglect the issues of sign, signification and symbol, or even ultimately the discursive when understood in terms of representations and relations. It offers a conceptual, as opposed to a narrowly linguistic, approach, but one that constitutes the basis of an empirical approach to society as a historical and structural reality. The Durkheimian school was among the most productive of all research units, and in large part it owed its productivity to Durkheim's epistemological orientation to the concrete details of lived social life; underlying this were the Kantian critical imperative and Renouvier's insistence that the most abstract must always be grounded in the empirical detail of the concrete.

By contrast, modern sociology, particularly in Britain, has been dining on critique for so long that the possibility of a positive, factual theory of society seems to have long since passed from view. The endless critiques of positivism have finally dismembered the factual, and now we are told that reason itself is sexist and racist. And the Foucauldians tell us that the impulse to know is just another power game. Without any facts or reason or structure, we are now afloat on a sea of discourses, together with the rider that all discourses are equal. Whilst it is important to unmask all flawed pretence at fact and objectivity, the question remains: if, ultimately, there is no factual basis or rational justification for the subject, what is its point? If sociology is neither scientific nor generative of facts or *knowledge*, why should anyone bother with it? But this is the central question: is there, or is there not, knowledge of the social that is not so corrupted by power play and other prejudices that it is actually worth pursuing? Are there, or are there not, any social facts? If there are, then the discourse which establishes these is more adequate than those that do not.

Recent sociology is characterized by a constant search in diverse moments of modern French philosophy for concepts and glosses: it has found force, difference, becoming and desire, and of course from Foucault has derived discontinuity, the historical apriori and power. All are present in the theoretical model of explanation which Renouvier offered Durkheim, as are the critiques of Hegel, absolutism and progress so crucial to post-modernism. But given this obsession with philosophy, the question still remains: what philosophy provides adequate knowledge of the social?

Although post-structuralism, in contrast to ethnomethodology, at least attempts to get beyond the 'how' questions, and although it appears exciting, how coherent is it when examined closely? It is not a question here of its theoretical significance, but of its adequacy to the study of society, which, as Alexander (1982) rightly argues, requires a full presuppositional logic. It most clearly demonstrates the danger of applying a partial or one-sided theoretical vocabulary to the study of society. The concepts that have been taken from Foucault are, above all 'discourse' and 'power'. But, however important these are, they only apply to society when other more fundamental concepts and theoretical positions are already in place. Post-structuralism requires, but does not provide, answers to these questions: How is it that society is a system of relations to which power applies? And how does 'discourse' relate to consciousness, and thereby to action? The discursive is not lacking in Durkheim: the various historical forms of 'ways of seeing', which in turn rely on the formal functions of conscience, provide a discursive foundation for different social worlds; they engender action through its representative and practical functions. But how do the Foucauldians explain how social worlds relate to 'discourse'? Do social worlds emerge from discourse? If so, not since the first chapter of the Book of Genesis has the emanation of world from word been so clearly proposed.

Post-structuralism needs concepts which explain the slow constitution of significant worlds, and thus underwrite aspects of their causal generation, but it, like most of the new sociologies, has eschewed causality in explanation. Social worlds, for Durkheim, are built up out of types of action based on types of thinking and believing, which form complex significant wholes, and which are maintained and driven by habit and unconscious forces over a long period of time. None of this is available to post-structuralism, for it offers no explanation of how signification is engendered at the level of action or of how it is maintained in action.

Although it proceeds under the cloak of what Kant called the 'desperate expedient' of neologism (1781: A312/B369), it actually offers no explicit or positive elucidation of how realities are approached or how relations are grasped; these are simply presupposed by its own practice. So, whilst it eschews any justification of concepts, under its relativist patina it engages in an arbitrary dogmatism. This matches its narrow descriptivism, which culminates in mere social location and thus in a more extreme form of functionalist accommodation than was ever imagined by the 'conservative' Durkheim. Through its stress on the quasi-linguistic, it is limited theoretically to closed, conceptually impervious discourses. For Durkheim, the formation, interpenetration, transformation and development of cultures are explained logically through the synthesis and becoming of diverse forms of representation.

Although he does not stress power as dependency and struggle, the concept of power is not lacking in Durkheim's thought; indeed, in seeing power as central to 'force', he showed exactly what Foucault wanted: the constitution of power as productive (Foucault 1980: 119). His concept of society as a system of forces long antedates Foucault's conception of this as central to power relations. In fact, the concept of 'collective surveillance' was originally Durkheim's (1893b: 285/240); but, unlike Foucault, Durkheim can envisage an end to the social forms where this is dominant, whereas Foucault sees it, paradoxically, as a timeless feature of all institutions and forms of society. But is not the spirit behind Foucault's whole critique of power precisely that 'control' is judged to be 'intolerable', which indicates a greater autonomy in society (Durkheim 1893b: 286/240)? And just as power is only one aspect of social relations, albeit an important one for Durkheim, for Foucault, power is everywhere. Does this not call into doubt its significance as specific explanation? Whilst Durkheim tends to underscore the socially constructive aspects of power, Foucault appears to see only the negative aspects. Is there any possibility of a distinction between legitimate and illegitimate power, or of the limitation of power, within the Foucauldian perspective? This must surely be implied by its own critique of power. Durkheim can at least elucidate one aspect of the pathology of power in society – unavailable to post-structuralism – as a limitation on the possibilities of action for its members.

The Foucauldians make much of the resistance to power; but who is it that resists, and with what? Is it a discourse or a social construction which resists? Without a conception of agency or will, how can this resistance be accounted for? This is the contradiction at the heart of post-structuralism: for the early Foucault, human beings have been washed away on a post-structuralist beach, and for the late Foucault they are social constructions. Yet it is they who resist! An account of the person, and of the person as a power to resist, is not just an arbitrary element in a discourse of power, but central to any adequate account of social reality. Although Foucault maintained that power can be exercised only over free subjects, what clear conception of freedom is given within post-structuralism? Foucault's style condemns us to follow his gestural suggestiveness, without the final satisfaction of a definition. This is a considerable lacuna for a theory which presents itself as a kind of 'liberationist' sociology. By contrast, Durkheim shows how freedom is exercised as personal power, and how choices can enter into the structured relations of historical becoming.

Post-structuralism seems to generate a focus on cold discourses, where there is apparently no conception of need or of positive attachment. But how is it possible to describe a social, and therefore a human, world without these? Attachment to their 'normal' milieu and to 'home' is central to movements of nationalism, to displaced peoples everywhere, and is part of the unconscious background for all our actions, even when we are lucky enough to have a relatively stable milieu. Post-structuralism offers no account of this – just as it offers no convincing account of religion and the sacred. Nor is there an account of the search for justice – which activates so much social action – nor of the ideals employed in action; these lacunae are entailed by a lack of any coherent account of morality and practical reason.

Foucault's explicit nominalism underscores no collective concepts and thus logically neglects the structural: is it not thus a match for Thatcher's atomistic vision? The sphere of the social as a kind of totality, in synchronic and diachronic form, is the sphere for the development or the destruction of human life. Durkheim accounts for this through the concepts of relation and totality. Together with the relational, the disappearance of the functional has been disastrous for the social sciences, for without it there is no sense of interdependence or of the functional interaction of social conditions. We have seen that Durkheim accommodates these without loss of transformational or cognitive interest, and this rethinking of Durkheim must be of interest for the current development of 'neo-functionalism'. And whilst Durkheim shows the possibility of objective description of the general sphere of relatedness, the sphere of the general *per se* is discredited by ethnomethodology, post-modernism and post-structuralism. It is, however, implied by the globalization thesis, and it is crucial to ecological concern with the environment – the *sine qua non* of any viable community. In combination with this, Durkheim has the doctrine of limitation – so important to the exhausted environment and the exhausted people in the 'risk' society.

As the world grows more unequal, sociology, under the *i* post-structuralism, cannot say: 'What demoralises people i incredulity than the wealth of some and the poverty of others' (Durkᵢₑ 1887b: 2.154). The holistic perspective, from which equality and poverty can be judged, is crucial to social science, and is lost in post-structuralist sociology. This loss is not unconnected with post-structuralism's admiration, through its mentors, of philosophers who admire inequality – Heidegger and Nietzsche.[2] But critiques of systems which discourse 'in the void of totality' are not telling against Durkheim, for he had reflected on the foundational logic to any totality: this is the significance of his theoretical pluralism.

Equally, Durkheim's conception of the relative indetermination of mind allows for the variability and uncertainties of action and how it interweaves with social totalities and continuities. He does not suffer the fate of the great apostles of prediction, Marx and Comte, who failed to accommodate theoretically that great defect of human beings – that they can change their minds and not follow the laws of history! The breakdown of such visions expected of history has, at least in part, inspired post-structuralism and post-modernism.

Post-structuralism presents itself as the apex of critique – Foucault as the all-purpose subversive. But to actually be this, it needs what it lacks – a coherent logic of critique. But there is no clear sense as to how the critique of discourse is possible (Frank 1992: 113). Durkheim, seen by most as the architect of conservatism and positivism, has a coherent account of the freedom of mind – in relation to action and the evaluation of evidence – that is lacking from post-structuralism, and through it he can logically maintain that 'critique' and 'reflection' are the 'supreme agents' of transformation.

Do solidarity and all forms of positive human relatedness constitute just another discourse of power, as equally noxious as any other? If not, then all discourses are not equal and post-structuralism must invoke criteria; but criteria are precisely what it eschews, both in an epistemological and a moral sense. All distinctions dissolve under its own panopticon vision – and we can retain no sense of those forces which are beneficial in communities or of the importance of viable institutions. The sphere of relatedness and human interdependence really is crucial to the very nature of a society, and it is the basis of all significant description in sociology. Just as Durkheim underwrites this through his study of the historical forms of solidarity, so through the concept of the irreducible attached to solidarity, he points to the possibility of community beyond ethnic particularity. Post-structuralism cannot answer the question of how society is possible, or begin to formulate the conditions for social order – in the sense of viable social organization and its appropriate institutions. Current social disasters around the world show that it is the poor, the weak and the old who suffer first when these are lacking.[3]

So post-structuralism's theoretical lacunae are matched by its paucity of vision. In the world situation we face, which has been accurately described as 'the geo-politics of chaos', human beings are scuttling across continents through terror and need, not as the after-effect of a discourse. Just as we can ask whether there are any facts beyond interpretation, so it is important to ask whether there are any moral limits to difference and diversity. At the end of a century which has seen some of the worst crimes against humanity, and with the increasing racism and intolerance, can we afford to be complacent about the values of humanism, and see them as just another discourse of power?

Finally, at the end of this totalitarian century, can anything of Durkheim's optimism be justified? Even if we can look beyond the horrors of the two world wars and ethnic cleansing, we face global corporations whose trans-democratic power can bring a country to its knees and the possibility of environmental catastrophe. Yet, through the global marketplace and the power of communication, we are becoming a form of the communicative whole that Durkheim described. And whilst ethnic particularities face extinction with economic liberalization, we now face each other as members of humanity: we are thus reaching a stage 'where there is nothing left that human beings can love and honour in common but the human being itself' (Durkheim 1898c: 272/52).

So, whilst Weber's bleak vision offers no hope from the dark cage of modernity, Durkheim shows that humanity's belief in itself can generate new forms of relatedness and new institutions to carry us forward. He shows possibilities for change through the tension between new forms of collective thinking and established powers. And he shows that we need a sense of hope in the possibilities of the future, and how human action can build on these. This is significant now, with the sight of ancient cultures being ground under the boot of both economic liberalism and political oppression – the genocide and political and religious oppression in Tibet being only one recent example from the catalogue of twentieth-century disasters. Durkheim and his confrères in democratic socialism made the concept of humanity the central moral object of practical reason, just as he underwrote the concept of human rights as growing through history. So, paradoxically, given the interpretation imposed on him, Durkheim's thought may not underscore the logic of corrupt and oppressive states, but it does speak to the self-determination and autonomy of the modern consciousness and to the toiling masses and dismembered communities who aspire to live satisfying, self-determining lives within the limits of viable milieux.

# Appendix:
# Durkheim and Renouvier

There is no doubt as to the importance of Renouvier for Durkheim; he calls Renouvier the greatest contemporary rationalist (Durkheim 1955: 78). It is clear that Durkheim read Renouvier as an undergraduate (see Durkheim 1882). We know from the recently published *Lettres à Marcel Mauss* (1998) that he joked in 1916, 'J'ai dû ainsi prendre un diplôme d'études sur Renouvier!' (Durkheim 1998: 528). He also said that the influence of Renouvier 'preceded that of Comte' (1913a(15): 326). Maublanc maintained that, 'despite appearances', Durkheim owed far more to Renouvier than to Comte (Maublanc 1932: 299). It is clear that Durkheim had to re-establish the intellectual credibility of sociology after Comte (1895b: 1.73). The distinctive quality of Durkheim's work, I suggest, is that he reworks certain Comtean ideas on the basis of Renouvier's logic and theory of science. This is especially clear in relation to the conception of social fact, solidarity and organicism. It is possible also that he became acquainted with Spencer through Renouvier, who produced a sustained critical study of Spencer's evolutionism in his journal *La Critique philosophique*. Renouvier, of course, opposed his own scientific view to that of positivism and evolutionism.

It has to be remembered that at the time Renouvier's fame was such that he was identified with the spirit of science itself: his ideas entered intellectual culture. Lachelier, professor of philosophy at the École Normale until 1875, said that most of his students had become followers of Renouvier (Verneaux 1945: 5). Lachelier used the idea of the communion of consciences, which is a central concept of Renouvier's, in a debate with Durkheim (Durkheim 1913b: 2.57).

For Thibaudet, Renouvier was not only the ablest philosophical mind of his generation, he was responsible for the 'intellectual success' of the Third Republic and was the central thinker for the Dreyfusard republican intellectuals (Thibaudet 1930: 543). He was held to be the formative, definitive thinker for a generation of intellectuals. 'During a quarter of a century the thought of Renouvier directed the élite of French thought' (Prat 1937: 265). Ollé Laprune said in 1880 that Renouvier's 'criticisme is of capital importance ... which resumes and translates the spirit of the present epoch' (Verneaux 1945: 329). Louis Liard, the Minister of Higher Education, who did so much to help Durkheim found sociology in the university, was a follower of Renouvier, as were G. Séailles (who particularly admired his *Science de la morale*) and Henri Marion. It was said that Boutroux was more an admirer than a disciple (Prat 1937: 265); however, as I have shown above, Renouvier was held to be one of the major influences on Boutroux. The last three were Durkheim's doctoral examiners.

Durkheim's personal and intellectual friendship with Hamelin was such that he went through 'a moral diminution' away from his 'severe life' with Hamelin (Durkheim 1902g: 2.456), when he moved to Paris from Bordeaux. It is held that Hamelin was the 'disciple par excellence' of Renouvier, and that his system cannot be understood without that of Renouvier (Verneaux 1945: 5). Of course, such a relationship was not wholly uncritical, even though Hamelin simultaneously accepted and extended Renouvier's thought; I suggest that this is what Durkheim did, albeit in another direction. In this sense, Renouvier laid down the terms of the debate for both. Although Renouvier has become known in the history of philosophy as the founder of 'Personalism', a later development in his thoughts, he was known at the time as a scientific and logical thinker, and it is as such that he influenced Durkheim.

His intellectual influence does not mean that Renouvier was popular with either the republic or the university professors. He may have fought for republicanism, but he criticized the actual doings of the numerous regimes with frequent 'Un mot sur la situation' from his journal. In particular, he attacked the Opportunist Republic for its colonialism and racism: he repudiated the whole concept of race. He considered himself to be 'on the index' of the university in 1879, and he complained that those 'who dare not mention [his] name' use his ideas (Renouvier 1969: 107), citing Janet as one such. Paul Janet was the leading philosopher of eclecticism. Renouvier argued for a scientific viewpoint against the prevailing university philosophy of eclecticism, which he criticized for its lack of scientific rigour, method and political principles. Eclecticism was still the official philosophy in France, even in the 1890s.

I suggest, therefore, that it was not the liberal republicans that Renouvier influenced, as Lukes (1973: 55) and Scott (1951: 52) maintain. He argued for an egalitarian, libertarian republic, and was opposed by some 'liberal' professors. One can detect his influence on Jaurès and Malon. He was regarded as dangerous, not just for his stated sympathy for the Commune, but for his constant warnings that justice and equality are the only conditions for the stability of the social organism. His star rose in terms of a wider appeal as governments of the left emerged in the 1890s. Renouvier's thought was then subscribed to by many university professors. It was certainly very popular in Bordeaux, where an enemy of the republican left bemoaned the influence of *Néo-Criticisme*, especially Renouvier's journal *La Critique philosophique*, on young philosophers (Fonsegrive 1904).

In the text of this book I have done what Durkheim claimed he did with Renouvier. That is, I have pursued 'the analysis of a system into its most secret byways' (Maublanc 1932: 299). And I have shown what many have often suspected, that *Néo-Criticisme* is the theoretical springboard for Durkheim, and that Renouvier's influence goes to the foundational logic of Durkheim's thought. What might not have been suspected is how much this must shift the interpretation of Durkheim.

If further evidence of Renouvier's influence is required, we can see it in Durkheim's statement that good philosophy is not a discourse on the immortality of the soul, but as it feeds methodology – that is, concerns kinds (*genres*), types (*espèces*), organ, function, classification and mathematical reasoning (Durkheim 1895b: 3.427) It is shown when he identifies the problem of transcendent metaphysics as 'substantialism' (ibid.); and when he argues that 'Science has no knowledge of substance or pure form' (1898b: 23/9), translated as 'essence' by Pocock; and when he says that to admit the reality of representations, 'It is not at all necessary to imagine that representations are things in themselves' (ibid. 29/15).

It does not follow that he was uncritical of Renouvier: he argues against Renouvier's idea that solidarity can be a source of corruption but is the very source of morality. Equally, he doesn't hold to the concept of pure ethics. There are indications, however, that he was influenced not only by Renouvier's attack on political Darwinism, and on the racism implied by colonialism, but also – behind the rigorous scientific language – by Renouvier's passionate belief in the intellectual and moral freedom of the human being, which constitute the foundation of human moral and political dignity (see Logue 1993).

# Glossary

## *Apriori*

This does not mean armchair speculation: it has a rigorous sense of that which logically precedes sensory experience and serves as its foundation. Associated with the synthetic and thereby with the categories. For Kant the independence of the apriori from experience is total, but not for Renouvier – for the representative (the irreducible laws) and the represented are always in contact, and thus mutually influence one another.

## *Conscience*

This does not mean the same as the English 'conscience', i.e. that by which we feel guilty. Durkheim uses it in both a logical/scientific and a psychological sense, and also talks about the states of conscience. The latter, I suggest, are those particular feelings, thoughts, impulses to act, that are part of our consciousness. The logical/scientific sense must cause the most difficulty to understand. Broadly it indicates the formal set of functions by which any experience is made available to consciousness, and this is as much the condition of science as of ordinary awareness. The difference between the scientific and ordinary awareness is not only the ends to which these are put, but the degree of clarity attained. That is, all reflection and all action – conscious and unconscious – passes through these functions.

These functions anticipate sensory experience as the formal properties of the understanding; as Renouvier puts it, conscience is the supreme law of 'the representative order'. They are the functions by which any representation is possible – in this sense they are logically prior to it.

## Epistemology

The study of knowledge: of what knowledge is and how we acquire it. It involves evaluation of claims to knowledge and of the faculties by which we know; Durkheim's use of conscience and representation can be seen to address such questions.

## Holism

A doctrine which emphasizes the whole over the parts. Sociologically, individuals must be understood in terms of a network of social relationships which surround them. Durkheim's holism stresses the reality of interdependence and its effect on action, whilst attempting to preserve the autonomy and specificity of the parts. When it is said that wholes are logical pluralities, this means wholes are constrained logically by the parts which form them and thus cannot form an absolute. (See *Pluralism* below.) Durkheim's holism is, first, a logical/scientific claim: the grasping of general relations is central to both. Secondly, it has an epistemological sense, central to collective representations and the *conscience collective*. We think holistically when we think in terms of significant worlds, for this involves general signification, and hence the concepts of totality and type.

## Organicism

The claim that some systems – which are not literally organisms – are nevertheless like organisms, whose parts can only be understood in relation to the function they play in the whole. It is thus associated with holism.

## Pluralism

Political pluralism is the view that there is a real multiplicity of groups. Philosophical pluralism holds that the world contains many kinds of things – which have a uniqueness which cannot be reduced to one kind (monism). It holds to a real diversity, and is associated with concepts of 'heterogeneity' and 'discontinuity'. It involves the law of number for Renouvier – which answers the question 'How many?' A judgement of 'how many' is one of plurality, and requires both the identification of a single 'unit' and the concept of a totality. The latter is logically restricted by plurality, and cannot become real in an 'ontological' sense, and so serve anti-democratic interests in denying autonomy.

## Positivism

This says that positive knowledge (i.e. sure knowledge which is objective – of real phenomena) can only come from using the methods of science: it is opposed to metaphysics, intuition, subjectivism (see the biographical sketch of *Comte*). It founds knowledge (and thus all questions of epistemology) on science. Kant greatly complicated this picture by arguing that science is only possible through fundamental acts of mind: science is founded on our understanding. This, in combination with experience, allows for positive knowledge. It is the latter version of the 'positive' in knowledge that informs Durkheim's account.

## Realism

A view which maintains that reality (as states of affairs or things) is logically mind-independent. However, after Kant, the question of real existence, and thus of reality, became one of judgement, and thus of representation. Kant opposed realism by denying that we can know 'things in themselves', but supported knowledge of reality through empirical and scientific judgements which are mediated through representation. Durkheim's claim that society is real (as a system of representations and relations) but is not a reflection of a 'thing in itself' (1898b: 29) follows this logic. Durkheim is anti-realist in the latter sense, but a realist in the former sense. Renouvier attacked realism – i.e. the doctrine of the logical independence from representation of both the material object (materialism) and mind (idealism) – for it denies the reality of relations, which exist only in representation.

## Representation

Kant calls representations 'inner determinations of the mind' (1781: A 197/B 242). In his *Critique of Pure Reason*, representation indicates the activity of the mind in relation to the data received through our 'sensibility'. Our 'understanding' receives this input and orders it according to its rules – the categories – and 'reason' unifies it. All of these added together constitute knowledge. The association of representation with the activity of the mind was continued and clearly accepted by Durkheim (1895a: xi/ 34); however, he extended this to its collective dimension. Renouvier argued against Kant's faculty conception of the mind, particularly against the faculty of reason. This must be replaced with the formal functions of conscience; reason becomes one of the functions of conscience. These are the conditions for representation (see Durkheim 1898b: 37/23). Lukes argued that representation includes both the mode of thinking and that which is thought (1973: 7). The distinction between the representative and the represented and the logical priority of conscience to representation goes some way to clarify this.

## Relativism

With respect to morality, a relativist holds that there are no universal moral standards, and that all moral beliefs are relative to society or history. In terms of knowledge, a relativist would claim that all knowledge is relative to the person/culture/'conceptual scheme'. Two core elements of the doctrine, then, are, first, the rejection of absolutes, and second, the claim that all truths are 'true for' – i.e. 'are relative to'.

# Biographical Sketches

### Comte, A. (1798–1857)

Said to be the founder of positivism, even though, as Durkheim points out, most of his system came from Saint-Simon. He conceived of both society and the human mind as passing through the theological, metaphysical and positive stages. The movement from one to another constitutes progress, with Humanity or the 'Great Being' as the prime mover. In the latter stage intellectual unity – through the dominance of scientific method – will be achieved, and this should be the basis of social reform. Sociology, which is the application of scientific method to the study of social facts, is the last science to be born from the hierarchy of the sciences, and is intellectually dependent on biology.

### Parsons, T. (1902–79)

Founder of American structural functionalism, who held that societies are 'self-regulating systems', in which the parts or institutions maintain a balance so that the system has overall coherence and continuity; thus he stressed overall cohesion and hence 'consensus'. He subscribed to both the voluntarist element in action and the importance of role and common values in a social system.

### Renouvier, C. (1815–1903)

Philosopher and mathematician. Inspired by Descartes, his early 'Manuals of Philosophy' (1842 and 1844) show a Hegelian influence. He was active politically during the revolution of 1848 and the short-lived Second Republic. After the *coup d'état* by Louis Napoleon in 1851, he was forced to retire to the country and to restrict himself to philosophy. He then wrote the first version of his logical and scientific system (inspired by

Kant) in his *Essais de critique générale* (1854–64). Equally inspired by Saint-Simonian socialism, he nevertheless held that benefit for the 'people' could not come from false philosophies (including positivism). He came out of seclusion to fight for the Third Republic in 1870, and founded *La Critique philosophique* and later *L'Année philosophique*. A polymath of French philosophy, he was a shy and modest man (who refused the Légion d'honneur proposed by Louis Liard in 1899) whose stammer would have rendered him ineffective on the barricades in the early years. But he was nevertheless regarded as dangerous. He was kept out of the universities for his political views and his constant attacks on Cousin (the 'philosophical dictator' of France). He came to have such an intellectual dominance amongst the intellectual leaders of this strongly philosophical republic that his thought was regarded as almost the intellectual foundation of the Third Republic (Lukes 1973: 56).

### Saint-Simon, Claude Henri, Comte de (1760–1825)

In his reflections on science he carried forward the belief in progress of the eighteenth-century *philosophes*, the concept of the unity of science, and the view that the sciences must pass from a conjectural to a positive stage, which he applied to the idea of a science of man. He was concerned with the problems of European organization, and argued for an association between scientists and industrialists in government to replace the old social system. In proposing that this must act in terms of the interests of all, he introduced the idea of redistributive justice that became the hallmark of the socialism which sprang from his thought among the Saint-Simonians. Durkheim's statement 'To each according to their work' (*selon ses oeuvres*) (1898c: 277/56) is evidence of this vision of socialism.

# Notes

## Chapter 1 Questions of Interpretation

1 This is stated in the original detailed table of contents and was present in the Simpson translation of 1893b (1933), but is excluded from Halls's 1988 translation.

2 The Halls translation renders 'plurality' of individuals as 'number' here. This obscures the strict theoretical language of relational pluralism central to the dialectic of holism.

3 This assumption has been questioned by Merton (1949).

4 Since the original detailed table of contents is missing from the Halls translation of 1893b, so is this reference to functional activity.

5 *Attention* is translated as 'concentration' here.

6 The reference to *psychique* is eradicated in the Halls translation, and replaced by 'psychological'.

7 Halls again translates *psychique* here as 'psychological'.

8 *Conscience* is translated as 'consciousness'.

9 Translated as 'intellectual facts' by Pocock.

10 In both translations the reference to representative function is obliterated. Halls renders 1893b: 270 'functions of representation' (1984: 228), and Wilson renders 1925a: 34 as 'symbolic faculties' (1973: 39). The representative is associated with the concept of function in *fonction représentative*. These mistranslations significantly affect the interpretation and comprehension of Durkheim's thought.

11 Note that here 'not in the service of' is translated as 'not subordinate to'.

12 He repeats this in 1912a: 617/434.

13 So, e.g., *composée* (*une société composée*), is translated as 'made up' by Halls (1893b: xxxii/liv), and *le degré de composition* is translated as 'degree of organisation' by Halls (1895a: 86/115).

14 The Halls translation renders *ont pris l'habitude* as 'have become accustomed to', thus eradicating the reference to habit at this central point of the definition of structure.

15 The translation renders *conscience* here as 'individual mind'.

16 'Indetermination' is rendered as 'indeterminate state' by Halls. The latter is

not quite the same as the former, which expresses a philosophical/scientific conception.

17 The original *force agissante* is translated as 'active force' in both 1915 and 1995. The French equivalent to 'active' is *actif*, not *agissant*. In a subtle way a crucial reference to agency is eradicated.

18 Note that the translation of this article renders the frequently used term *conscience* as either 'reason', 'thinking mind' or 'thought'. No wonder the theoretical significance of this term is ignored!

19 The original has '*Ces normes impersonnelles ... elles dépendent de l'intelligence et de la volonté collective.*' Here this is translated as 'they tell the manner from which derive intelligence and collective will'. Here we can see how an organicist, functionalist reading dominates the translation, and makes collective will and intelligence dependent on structure – where what Durkheim says is the opposite!

20 Translated as 'individual human being'.

21 This crucial reference to *représentation* is transformed into 'conceives' in this translation.

22 *Psychique* is translated here as 'psychological'.

23 Note that *passion* is translated by Wilson as 'emotion' here.

24 'Soliciting action' translated here as 'stimulating behaviour'.

25 This is why the common translation of *milieu* as 'environment' is so fallacious.

26 Note that here, as frequently is the case, *psychique* is translated as 'psychological'.

27 Note that *représentation* here is translated as 'pictured ahead of time'.

28 The translation eradicates Durkheim's term 'unjustly' (*injustement*) and renders the phrase *faire la loi à*, which is 'to dictate to', as 'lord it over'.

## Chapter 2   Durkheim as Theorist of Order and Science

1 Social solidarity is itself 'a completely moral phenomenon' (1893b: 28/24).

2 This must cast doubt on Giddens's statement that Comte's interpretation of the decline of feudalism and the development of modern society is the 'principal foundation' of the whole of his writings (1971: 65). Durkheim rejects Comte's account of the positive final stage of society (Durkheim 1895a: 117/140).

3 The translation renders 'will' (*volonté*) as 'wants'.

4 Here, as elsewhere, the important term *milieu* is translated as 'environment'.

5 The *sociabilité* of the original is translated as 'sociology'!

6 Halls renders *leur extrême immatérialité* as their 'total lack of material substance'. This is to introduce a concept – substance – which Durkheim does not use and of which he says elsewhere: 'Science has no knowledge of substance or pure form' (1898b: 22/9). (However, in the 1974 translation of 1898b, 'substance' is translated as 'essence'.) His rejection of materialism in *Les Règles* has been obscured by the 1938 translation, which renders 'extreme immateriality' (90) as 'intangibility'!

7 Both translations render *force agissante* as 'active force'. Whilst this is not

false, it does eradicate the connection with action. *Agissante* is connected with *agir*, 'to act'. There is a separate word *actif/ve*, that means 'active'.

8   Neither translation does justice to the original, and each indicates the ontological prejudices of the translator. The force of *rentrer* is 'to return' and does not indicate 'to merge with' (Halls, 70). Halls also translates *le dedans* as 'the internal'. Solovay and Mueller's 1938 translation is: 'we will see our conception of social phenomena change as it were from the objective to the subjective' (28). This is false and gives a meaning that is incompatible with Durkheim's stance on science and objectivity.

9   Habit here is translated as 'custom'.

10  This proposition is not incompatible with Durkheim's claim that social phenomena are subject to determinism and that social phenomena are not *per se* contingent or arbitrary (1909e: 146/77).

11  *Contingence* translated here as 'chance factor'.

12  The conflict in nineteenth-century French philosophy between positivism and spiritualism was also conceived as the conflict between determinism and contingency (Engel 1988: 179).

13  Halls translates 'movement' as 'force' (xxv). The significance of Durkheim's argument that will leads to action and is realized in movement is thereby obscured.

14  Durkheim repeats this in 1909e: 143/75.

15  The concept of relation is central to the formation of wholes – which, mentally at least, are not formed by association of ideas (1903ai: 396/4) or by contiguity (1898b: 28/14).

16  Halls translates 'intermittence' as 'sporadic'.

17  His use of a contrary state, *état contraire* (1893b: 64/53), is obscured by the translation which renders this as 'opposing' state. Logically, the contrary is not one and the same as opposition, as will be clear.

18  This concept of 'thing-in-itself' – so infamous in philosophical history – is here translated as 'things having separate existence'.

19  The translation by Halls adds 'entity' where there is none in the original, and also turns *particulière* into 'individual'. The 1938 (p. 103) translation also renders *particulière* as 'individual'. But Durkheim differentiates, in the same passage, *individuel* from *particulière*.

20  Translated as 'unenlightened' by Halls.

21  The concepts *conscience* and *psychique* both disappear in Halls's translation: *conscience* is rendered 'consciousness', and *psychique* as 'psychological'.

22  Cuvillier notes that this will surprise those critics of his 'sociologism', but that this position represents the authentic thinking of Durkheim (Durkheim 1955: 196n.).

23  So, e.g., the *conscience collective* was a 'well-worn concept' (1893b: 47/39).

24  William Logue (1983) looks at the development of liberal ideas on nascent sociology, and identifies Renouvier as central to French liberalism. It is a welcome historical study of a neglected area. But it does not deal with the logical, epistemic and scientific links between Renouvier and Durkheim.

25  The exception to this is Schmaus (1994), who acknowledges the centrality of representation, but like others does not acknowledge the association of

science with conscience, and, although acknowledging the reality of relations to Durkheim's vision of social reality, gives a twentieth-century scientific realist interpretation of Durkheim. Meštrović (1988) stresses the role of representation through his comparison of Durkheim with Schopenhauer. Although based on rather slight evidence, this is a far more interesting interpretation than the classic reading through Comte. However, there are reasons to doubt this reading philosophically and sociologically. First Durkheim espouses neither the principle of sufficient reason nor 'the thing itself', which Schopenhauer retains and identifies with will and its unlimited striving behind appearances. Secondly, Durkheim's view of will as a personal energy which must be limited within the milieu, and there put to constructive social and individual ends, actually opposes the negativity, fatalism and 'infinitism' of Schopenhauer's view.

## Chapter 3   Understanding Durkheim in his Time

1   In the early 'République des Ducs', it was only the divisions between the monarchists – between the Legitimists and the Orleanists – that gave the republicans their chance. The early years, until 1875, were dominated by the question of the Restoration. The conflict between the Comte de Chambord and the Comte de Paris for the throne of France was finally settled when the former (who was a supporter of Maistre and Bonald) confounded monarchist hopes by refusing to accept the tricolour and what it symbolized.

2   He had defended Delescluze, one of the leaders of the Commune, and represented Belleville, the most radical working-class district of Paris. Indeed, the Paris Commune implemented Gambetta's radical Belleville programme (Gacon 1970: 13). Gambetta's preoccupations were the issues that were to dominate republicanism for the next thirty years: regeneration, clericalism and education. Against Catholicism, he extolled free thought and human science: nothing was higher than 'the study of man'. His intellectual sources were Proudhon, whose *De la Justice dans la révolution* was his bedside reading, and Comte, through the revival of his thought by Littré (Bury 1973: 37).

3   The vote for the first National Assembly of early 1871 showed the strength of the right–royalist wing: out of 650 deputies, 500 were royalists (Halévy 1930: 19).

4   The revolving door administrations and the political instability of the Third Republic are well known. Between 1871 and 1914 there were more than fifty governments, with an average life span of less than nine months each.

5   A '*goupillon*' is a sprinkler for holy water.

6   Histories of Boulangism have emphasized the peculiar character of the combination of support from both the left (particularly the Blanquists) and the right for the charismatic minister of war General Boulanger, who managed to appeal to the xenophobic working class with his spirited foreign policy and to the right in the interest of order. However, a recent study by Irvine (1989) shows the depth of the collaboration between Boulanger and the royalists

who supported the Boulanger campaign in the expectation of a restoration. The pretender to the throne, the Comte de Paris, was active in support from his exile in London. The appeal of a military *coup d'état* never died. It was revived briefly in 1892 with the Panama Canal scandal, which led to outrage against corrupt parliamentarianism. And in the Dreyfus Affair, royalists conducted negotiations with sympathetic generals.

7   There was, of course, a distinct movement of liberal Catholics whose views were distinct from this (Moody 1966).

8   For both the Jew was the symbol of the *parvenu*; the most anti-Semitic remarks were directed against Jewish republicans (Irvine 1989: 167).

9   He wished to help Jaurès and his friends 'to take hold of themselves' and to stop 'any equivocation which serves to maintain bourgeois traditionalism' (Durkheim 1998a: 226).

10   Thus, for example, the leading eclectic philosopher Victor Cousin expressed the liberal attitude in arguing that although one may have a duty of charity towards the poor and the hungry, they have no corresponding rights to financial help. For the liberal, rights and duties are not correlative. 'The worker has no more right to work than the poor have a right to assistance' (Krakowski 1932: 87).

11   Lukes argues that Renouvier had respect for bourgeois values (Lukes 1973: 56). His sympathy with the Commune must modify this opinion; Renouvier constantly attacked the bourgeoisie, not only for its greed and conservatism. He condemned 'base bourgeois positivism' which is attached to 'facts and interests'. The first revolution benefited the bourgeoisie, but it failed to share the benefits with the poor (Renouvier 1872b: 3). Lukes quotes J. Scott (1951), who misinterprets Renouvier as a political liberal. From the position of a type of Christian socialism, Renouvier attacked Victor Cousin, the archetypal liberal, for his ideas of sanctity and personal charity: a social republic has a strict obligation to help the poor (Méry 1952: 1.132).

12   Durkheim's study of Montesquieu and Rousseau as forerunners of sociology must gain a new significance in the light of socialist history: Rousseau was regarded as a dangerous revolutionary in nineteenth-century thought (as a result of Robespierre's admiration for him); and for historians of socialism, Montesquieu was regarded as one of the most important eighteenth-century precursors of socialism.

13   Charles Péguy, who influenced Lucien Herr, opened a bookstore as 'a bastion of socialism' which published and distributed two of the most serious periodicals of the time: *La Revue socialiste* and *Le Mouvement socialiste*. 'Around the bookstore gravitated the founders of the French school of sociology – Durkheim, his nephew Mauss and Lévy Bruhl' (Lacouture 1982: 59).

14   I am not suggesting that Durkheim was simply a follower of Jaurès: it is clear he took an active role in developing these ideas, although it is also clear that Malon was an original source of thinking here. It is apparent that Durkheim wanted to support Jaurès, and to help maintain a distance between Jaurès and Guesde (Durkheim 1998a: 225).

15   A worker and autodidact, he came to socialism through his factory work in the 1860s and the influence of Proudhon. He was active during the Commune,

although he opposed the authoritarianism of the 'Jacobinists'. After its suppression, he was in exile in Italy until the amnesty of 1880. He edited the *Revue socialiste* from 1885 until his death. Its aim was to reconcile the different factions of socialism by finding a common ground. Among his many works were his famous *Le Socialisme intégrale* (1890) and *La Morale sociale* (1876). It is said that he was the first to produce a history of socialism, in 1879.

16 As a young man, Jaurès regarded Malon with awe as the great man of French socialism (Vincent 1992: 2). In his *Socialisme et le radicalisme en 1885* he describes his walk towards the premisses of Malon's *Revue Socialiste* as that of a neophyte . . . inscribing in a temple' (Jaurès 1904: 177).

17 The issue of discipline became important for socialism, at least in part through the lack of discipline of the National Guard during the Commune, which was held to have contributed to its failure (Furet 1988: 500).

18 Translated as 'abilities' by Bellah (56) and 'capabilities' by Neyer (1960: 38). *Faculté* refers to forms of the mind, not merely ability – which of course follows from the development of mind. A philosopher has a precise use for faculty! But here the interest that Durkheim is underlining is the development of mind in and through work.

19 *Oeuvre* translated as 'achievement' by Neyer (1960: 38) and as 'labour' by Bellah (56). 'Work' is a direct reference to the preoccupation of French socialism. 'Achievement' implies that Durkheim is rather more meritocratic than is implied by this passage. See Filloux 1973 which stresses Durkheim's affinities with Saint-Simonian socialism.

20 Comtean positivism, of course, opposed transcendence and was useful in the struggle against the Church. Littré (1863), in his revival of positivism, attempted to ally it with democracy and disavowed Comte's later positive politics, seeing it as a return to the subjective method. However, the objective method for him was still a matter of fact and law, which does not accommodate freedom of mind or the ideal.

21 Parodi misinterprets Durkheim in this book, by identifying his thought with traditionalism and positivism. To do so, Parodi, in common with many of Durkheim's later interpreters, must ignore his statements about individualism, rights, ideals, freedom of mind and democracy (Parodi 1924: 77–97).

22 The fact that Durkheim admits 'the struggle for life' does not make him a social and political Darwinist. Renouvier, for example, admitted the struggle for life as 'the great external cause inseparable from existence' (Renouvier 1864b: 205), but opposed social and political Darwinism for its racism, and held that it is incompatible with justice (1875c: 2.308).

23 These theories received ideational support in the thinking of Renan and Taine: Renan deprecated reason and opposed science to it; Taine argued that opposing the ideal to the real is dangerous. Lukes points out that Durkheim had a distinctive antipathy to Renan and his elitism – all 'have a right to the life of the mind' (Lukes 1973: 72).

24 For this reason I believe that Lukes is wrong to say that Durkheim is Burkean through his respect for the wisdom gained through the 'struggles of humanity', and that this confirms his early conservatism (Lukes 1973: 77–8). Whilst

Burke was adopted by those Durkheim opposed – the monarchist right wing (Thompson 1952: 28) – his respect for the people's traditions was a part of the republican socialist tradition.

## Chapter 4    Philosophy and the Republic

1   Renouvier was one of the main influences on Boutroux (La Fontaine 1920: 76).
2   Durkheim discusses Renouvier's theory of certainty in the appendix to his 1955.
3   Note Durkheim's identification of function with 'psychic order' (1893b: 46/39).
4   We can see the logic of communication and of symbolization implied through 'conscience' and its association with others in Durkheim's discussion of the 'conscience commune' in 1893b: 51/43.
5   Durkheim cites Copernicus in *Les Règles* (1895a: 16/61).
6   Renouvier's concept of 'thing' responds to the same problem as Kant's transcendental object = $x$, which indicates that all representations refer to something (Kant 1781: 268, A251).
7   The proof of the objective reality of the laws of representation (the categories) revolves around the sphere of the outer in representation, and the generality of this for Kant is shown through the logic of 'relation' and 'community' (ibid. 254–5).
8   'Compose' translated as 'make up' by Halls (136), and by Solovay and Mueller (1938: 113). Whilst this is not false, it conceals Durkheim's theoretical use of composition as a manner of accounting for a complex reality.
9   The constancy of the representative to Durkheim's thought is one of the philosophical supports for what is known as the Giddens–Allardt thesis (Lacroix 1981): the fundamental continuity of his thought.
10  The categories are the fundamental laws of the representative order. As such, they are in touch with the represented, and are marked by the experience they rule in a way that is not possible for Kant. This may go some way towards explaining why categories 'recapitulate the real' rather than 'preform' it for Durkheim (1909d: 757/000). The social generation of the skeleton of representation also elucidates this. (See below.)
11  Schmaus (1994: 30) assumes that Durkheim is rejecting Renouvier in arguing for the social origin of the categories. On the contrary, he is following and developing the insight offered by Renouvier.
12  I will not examine the categories of space and time, since they are not so germane to the question of the interpretation of Durkheim as the others. Suffice it to note that it was Renouvier who made them categories, rather than forms of intuition as Kant held.
13  Note that *composition* is translated as 'organisation' in the first, 'made up' in the second.
14  This analysis of the dynamic and synthetic nature of relation lends support to

Pearce's *rapprochement* of Durkheim and Marx in *The Radical Durkheim* (1989).

15  The original *composer* is translated as 'constitute' here.

16  The original *composant* is translated as 'component' in both the Halls and the Simpson translations.

17  See Durkheim's critique of Comte on this point (1903c: 1.128; 1990b: 127/16).

18  *Appauvri* of the original translated here as 'stripped down'.

19  *Intermittent* translated as 'sporadic' here.

20  Schmaus argues that Durkheim's identification of meaning with representation makes the meaning of general concepts difficult, for these are 'Lockean complex ideas' which are progressively compounded (Schmaus 1994: 252). But Schmaus ignores *espèce* as logically central to representation, and it is through this that generality is established without empiricism.

21  This is nevertheless distinct from teleology and questions of final causes (Renouvier 1875c: 2.172ff).

22  He regretted a too strict separation of the logical from the psychic amongst German thinkers (1887a: 3.455).

23  The first edition was published in 1859.

24  As I noted in Chapter 1, *représentative* here is translated as 'symbolic'.

25  'Relation which establishes' translated by Pocock as 'relationship which is established'. This eradicates the active mental power that Durkheim is indicating here.

26  *Attention* translated by Pocock as 'concentration' here.

27  The reference to composition is cut from Pocock's translation.

28  The false view of the two Durkheims must be confounded by quality, which reconciles the symbolization of the later thought with *espèce* used in *Les Règles*. This is a constant of his thought, and is fundamental to the logic of representation and the logical basis of symbolization.

29  Note that Halls here translates *représentation* as 'idea' and *tendance* as 'trend'.

30  Durkheim's neglected theory of the rationality and freedom of the mind is in contradistinction to the sociologism of Comte, whose theory of language requires the subordination of the subjective to the objective – that is, the sphere of Great Being.

31  Although the sign and the thing signified must be distinguished, 'A sign is assuredly something (*quelque chose*)' (1897a: 356/315).

32  *Passion* translated by Wilson as 'emotion' here.

33  Note that *passions* here is translated by Halls as 'emotion'.

34  Note that Durkheim uses *passion* rather than Théodule Ribot's conception of 'sentiments' in his *Psychologie de sentiments*.

35  'Habits' translated by Wilson as 'customs' here.

36  The original *voulant* (from *vouloir*) is translated by Wilson as 'desire' here.

37  Renouvier never underestimated the significance of determinism. He talks of 'the immense sphere of determinism which from all sides envelops and contains desires and decisions' (1886: 1.230).

38  Most Durkheimian commentators hold that the conscience collective comes from Schaeffle. There is evidence, however, that Schaeffle was influenced by Espinas's *Les Sociétés animales*. Espinas taught at Bordeaux, where Renou-

vier's ideas were prevalent, and of course Hamelin, who was a follower of Renouvier, taught there. Renouvier developed this theory in the first edition of his, 'Deuxième essai de critique générale' of 1859. This does not mean that Schaeffle did not change or develop the concept.

39    Durkheim acknowledges the importance of certain features of Renouvier's account: his critique of the concept of evidence, the historically relative character of truth, its relationship to action, the practical underbelly of theoretical certainty and its collective nature (1955: 201–2). However, he criticizes a 'voluntarist' theory for ignoring the 'necessitating' character of a true idea (ibid. 202). Nevertheless, it is this account which entails a definition of the *conscience collective* – and thus introduces the authority of the collective into definitions of truth.

40    Renouvier didn't himself call this a *conscience collective* (as far as I am aware), but he did provide the peculiar logic of conscience through which this collective thinking is expressed.

41    This had a profound influence on William James – see his 'Will to Believe' of 1896.

42    The element of will in belief is central to the practical dimension, and this is shown in the logic of 'affirmation' (Renouvier 1859: 423). (Cf. Durkheim: 'Individual consciences ... affirm their autonomy' (Durkheim 1897a: 158/159).)

43    In 1893 he said he would not deal with the question of knowing 'whether it is a conscience like that of the individual'. It designates the 'collection of social similitudes', without 'discussing the category by which this phenomenon must be defined' (1893b: 47n./65).

44    Cuvillier says that Hamelin is clearly referring to Durkheim when he discusses the 'social conscience'. Hamelin insists that this cannot be established separately from each individual conscience – it only has as its support each of these consciences (Cuvillier, introduction to Durkheim 1955a: 11).

## Chapter 5    Differentiation and the Problems of Modernity

1    Durkheim uses the Latin *consensus* here, and it is thus translated by Halls. Willie Watts Miller has suggested that this more properly means agreement or cohesion.

2    Of course, in *Les Règles* he says that he was wrong to present material density as 'the exact expression' of dynamic density (1895a: 113/146).

3    Number is central to his first book (see 1893b: 78/64, 241/203, 248/209, 336/283, 342/287). And note the connection between his first and last books – supposedly far apart through the 'materialist positivism' of the one and the idealism of the other: both use the concept of number. He talks of the category of number (1912a: 13/8) and 'The concept of totality' (ibid. 629/442).

4    It is because number is a central feature of representation that statistical analysis is not incompatible with the logic of representation, and thus with the explanatory logic of the social.

5   Note that the Halls translation renders 'plurality' as 'number', and *composants* as 'components'.
6   Translated as 'vacuum' by Halls.
7   Simpson renders 'external fact' as 'index' (64), Halls as 'datum' (24). The 'index' thesis has led to accusations of Durkheim's legalistic positivism. But the translations obscure the relation between the internal and the external, which is important in the dialectic of social life.
8   Durkheim cites Marion's *De la Solidarité morale* (1880) (Durkheim 1893b: xliv/xxx). Marion in turn cites Renouvier as the inspiration for his work (Renouvier 1880b: 148).
9   The original is *communs à la moyenne des membres*. This is translated by Halls as 'common to the average member'. The meaning is slightly different, however: Durkheim is concerned with what members of the same society on average share in terms of communal beliefs, rather than with what the average person thinks.
10  Compare this with Renouvier's accusation that evolutionism invokes the continuum and the infinite (1877: 19).
11  Note that Halls translates *état contraire* as 'opposing state'.
12  I have argued that the exclusion of the original table of contents from the Halls translation is inexcusable, for it is here that Durkheim makes reference to conflict and the war of the classes.
13  Translated by Halls as 'forced'.
14  This is stated in Durkheim's review of Gaston Richard. Durkheim often uses reviews to develop and express his own views. Both authors, in using this concept, reveal their debt to Renouvier.
15  Note that Halls translates *oeuvre* as 'mission' here.
16  Halls translates this as 'we gropingly seek'. This eradicates the logic of finality shown in the 'tendencies' of action, just as it obscures the significance of 'confusedly', which shows the importance of the clarification of action for Durkheim, especially in relation to unconscious factors.
17  Boutroux acknowledges Renouvier's solution here in his *De l'Idée de loi naturelle* (1950: 56ff) – a course given at the Sorbonne, 1892–3.
18  Translated as 'vacant ground' by Halls.
19  Note that 'contingency' is translated by Halls as 'chance factor', space as 'field', and 'attempts' (*tâtonnements*) as 'trial and error'.

## Chapter 6   Individualism and Socialism?

1   See Comte 1975: i, lesson 45.
2   I have shown that the concept of will is central to Durkheim's idea of contract, as expressing an 'equilibrium of wills' (Durkheim 1893b: 376/317) (the translation here renders *volonté* ('will') as 'wants'). The enactment of new ideals requires that they are willed (1901aiii(45): 303). Moral action requires an 'effort' (1925a: 84/99).
3   Durkheim was in contact and active with Jaurès during The Affair in 1899 (1899g: 2.429).

4 Renouvier argued that monarchism and authoritarianism survive in habits of deference, which all politics of autonomy must combat (1872b: 2.2).
5 'Affirm' rendered by Brookfield as 'assert' here.
6 Note that 'passion' is translated by Wilson as 'ferment', thereby eradicating the link with action.
7 Durkheim claimed that the word 'socialism' was invented by Robert Owen in England in 1835 (1928a: 59/65).

## Chapter 7  The Science of Facts and Things

1 The compositional view of reality means that phenomena are related and are therefore relative to one another; for Renouvier, this relationism bars the route to absolutism in knowledge. Secondly, the acknowledgement of 'difference' is a judgement invoking consideration of the 'kind' of relations that obtain; this is made under the law of quality.
2 Jaurès reproached the Guesdists for their ignorance of social complexity – in making political struggle a simple reflection of the mechanical opposition of the classes. He also criticized Clemenceau and Radicalism for their refusal to acknowledge 'social fact' (Rébérioux 1980: ix).
3 Note that *régler* is translated as 'regulate' by Halls (1982) and in the 1938 Caitlin edition. This, of course, is the literal meaning of *régler*, but it doesn't make much sense in this context – how can a method 'regulate' thought and action?
4 Recognition of the centrality of this to social experience may be obscured by Halls's translation. Durkheim says the detail of social life '*débordent de tous les côtés la conscience*' (1895d: 18). *Débordent* is translated by Halls as 'swamp' (63), but *déborder* here, I suggest, means 'to extend beyond', and this is more compatible with the rest of the sentence. 'To swamp' is *inonder*! This mistranslation has implications for Durkheim's logic of social reality.
5 Borlandi (1995) argues that it is only in chapter 5 that Durkheim makes the argument for the associational nature of the group. However, as I have shown, he makes it also in chapter 1, with the concept of 'composition' of society (1859: 12/57).
6 This reference to action is eradicated, for *manières de faire* is translated as 'ways of functioning' by Halls (57).
7 *Ont pris l'habitude* is translated by Halls as 'have become accustomed to' (58). The habitual is central to how social facts becomes structural, yet this is eradicated here.
8 Translated as 'strength' by Halls. This eradicates a crucial reference to representational force, since habits exist within each conscience as forms of representation. One of the ways in which representations engender action is as forces. *La force représentative* is a crucial explanatory aspect of how things are brought about in Renouvier's account of representational logic.
9 Note that Halls translates this as 'outside the consciousness of the individual', as opposed to 'outside of individual consciences'. This significantly affects the interpretation of Durkheim.

10    The force of this argument underlies Durkheim's claim that psychic life is not limited by 'conscience' (1898b: 32/18).

11    I have already indicated the problems with translation here (70), where the force of science 'returning to' the inside is obscured.

12    It is interesting to note Durkheim's references to the need for a reform in sociology to match that achieved in psychology 'during the last thirty years' (29/71). The first edition of Renouvier's *Traité de psychologie rationnelle* was published in 1859. It opposed Cousinian introspection and liberalism, and located conscience within a framework of relations. This not only established concomitant variation, but also pointed to 'external' relations and the 'outside' as significant explanations of conscience.

13    This can be found in his *Système de politique positive* (1854), vol. 2, ch. 7.

14    Comte uses this principle, borrowed from the biologist Blainville. In lesson 40 of his *Cours*, he took this as meaning the 'necessary harmony' between the static and dynamic analysis of any subject (Comte 1975: 1.739). This revolves around sociology's dependence on biology, and establishes 'the order in nature' which Comte calls 'inevitable'. Even though he wants to argue that this necessity is modifiable, it is not clear that he has the modal logic by which intervention is possible. The theory of the conditions of existence for him is independent of the logic of desire.

15    For Jaurès socialism centres on transforming the milieu, rather than changing the individual alone, as conservatism postulates (1906: 68).

16    This internal social milieu – that is, consciences in association – shows that it is not the case that ideas and beliefs are derivative in *Les Règles* (Lukes 1973: 230). Durkheim's position is compatible with the later studies on representation and ideational structures in *Formes élémentaires* (1912).

17    'Composition' translated by Halls as 'constitution' here.

18    Hall's translation eliminates the reference to the 'whole' and renders *un tout* as 'an entity'.

19    This is why I believe that Halls's translation of *milieu* as 'environment' is not satisfactory (38), for it does not carry the force of this meaning of causality: milieu means the particular relations in which individuals are caught up, rather than those that surround them. Thus Durkheim talks about the 'internal social milieu'.

20    In his letters to Marcel Mauss, Durkheim discusses the 'idées motrices' of Renouvier, and suggests that they should have been more profoundly studied (Durkheim 1998a: 35).

## Chapter 8    Society as the 'Coefficient of Preservation'

1    This must further cast doubt on Meštrović's analogy with Schopenhauer.

2    See Hamelin 1927: 424.

3    The Spaulding and Simpson translation here eliminates Durkheim's reference to 'energy' relating to the instinct for self-preservation.

4    Durkheim uses the concept of 'the energy of the instinct for conservation'

against Quetelet's theory of the average man (*l'homme moyen*) (1897c: 340/ 302).

5   Spaulding and Simpson translate 'coherent' as 'cohesive' in this passage.

6   The 'will to live' is translated as 'desire to live' by Spaulding and Simpson.

7   Renouvier discusses the connection between the category of quantity (number) and quality (through which communication is possible) (1875c: 1.284–5).

8   Spaulding and Simpson translate 'obscurely' as 'vaguely', thereby effacing the link with the unconscious.

9   This passage above all demonstrates the drawback of translating *milieu* as 'environment'. It is one of the reasons why Durkheim is accused of materialism, as I have shown above.

10  *Tendance* is translated as 'inclination' here.

11  'Individuation' is translated as 'individualism' in this passage! This can only add to the misunderstandings – that Durkheim thinks individualism must somehow contribute to suicide!

12  Halls's translation renders this complex phrase *demi-représentative* as 'half representation' (198). If all is representation, how can something be half representation? This important phrase is retained in the Simpson translation of 1933 (255).

13  For Durkheim, a statistical theory of suicide does not deny freedom of will, (1897a: 368/325). 'Such a force does not determine one individual rather than another. It exacts a definite number of certain kinds of actions, but not that they should be performed by this or that person' (ibid.). Renouvier, in discussing the question of freedom of action and the status of general statistical laws in relation to the question of suicide, argues against the absolute determinism which characterizes social laws for both Buckle and Quetelet. Whilst it is right to maintain 'the prodigious effect of social laws', he argues (also against Cournot and Laplace) that the determinism of statistical generality can be reconciled with freedom of action through the concept of a 'partially indetermined function', which leaves statistical law and probability intact. The compositional nature of society, according to the law of number, entails this concept of partially indeterminate function. It also means that society is 'the slow work of human beings', and thus that there is always a dialectic between this totality and people's actions (Renouvier 1880a).

## Chapter 9   The Thinking State

1   These were invoked by those who believed that Dreyfus's conviction should stand, even given the problems of the evidence against him.

2   See Giddens (ed.), *Durkheim on Politics and the State*, 1986: 224–33, for selections from this.

3   Note that the translation renders *raison d'état* as 'political reason' and *la personne* as 'individual'.

4   The original is '*qui valent* pour la collectivité'. This is translated by Brookfield as 'hold good for the collectivity' (50). Before any accusations of elitism and

authoritarianism are raised, *valent 'valoir'* also carries the meaning of 'on account of' or 'of worth' or 'count for'.

5　Birnbaum (1976) claims that Durkheim's argument for a political role for civil servants implies a tyrannical role for functionaries. Durkheim's moral view of the state requires a conception of disinterested public service in overseeing justice and maintaining individual rights. Without a recognition of the power of the collectivity, and of Durkheim's rejection of the type of state which Birnbaum attributes to him, then it is not quite so oppressive as it sounds. However, the important question remains: can civil servants represent the thinking of the collectivity without themselves having political representation in a union? It is interesting to note that Jaurès (in 1909) also opposed certain rights to strike, but only under conditions of collective work contracts and acknowledgement of rights by the state. When the organization of work has become so vast, it is difficult for each element to be egoistical (Jaurès 1984: 82).

6　By contrast, Action Française's interest in corporatism is by analogy with the family as the basis of human societies (following Comte). They opposed this to liberalism, which leads to anarchy and socialism (Weber 1962: 247).

## Chapter 10　Practical Reason and Moral Order

1　I quote here from the first Alcan edition, for the original introduction has been excluded from subsequent editions, except for the Simpson translation, where it appears as the appendix (1964: 415).

2　The translation renders *la conscience* as 'knowledge' here, thus erasing the reflexive power of conscience, and renders *remonte de plus en plus* as 'depend more and more'.

3　For example, in Ashley and Orenstein's *Sociological Theory* (1998: 108) this passage is treated as an argument for determinism and against free will.

4　Note that Halls here translates *fait* as 'datum'. And Simpson (1933) translated *fait extérieur* as 'external index'. The concept of 'index' is thus added by translation.

5　Recognition of these critical and reflexive foundations of morality must cast doubt on the thesis of his early naturalism (Wallwark 1972).

6　The central concepts which Durkheim uses to define morality (duty, sanction, solidarity, constraint, coercive and repressive justice, the critique of utilitarianism, the concept of moral authority and the ideal) find their first philosophical expression in Renouvier's *Science de la morale* of 1869. It is held by some scholars of Durkheim's thought that his trip to Germany was a voyage of discovery in terms of the science of morality (Lacroix 1981; Jones 1993). However, he was ready with critiques of the ideas he found there; in this sense, it was rather more an extension of ideas he had already acquired. So, in contrast to the sociologists of the *chaire* and the jurists of the historical school, he argues that the relativity of milieu is compatible with morality as a science (1887c: 1.326). He rejects Wundt's idea of one law, one religious idea, one moral ideal (ibid. 1.331). Most importantly, he criticizes Wundt for denigrating the individual (ibid. 1.329–30), and for giving an inadequate account of obligation (ibid. 1.327). He also criticizes Wundt for arguing that morality in its superior form is not obligatory (ibid. 1.328). And he criticizes Jhering for neglecting a concept of end.

7  Durkheim also argues that morality is based on fact and that there are 'duties'; but he cites Janet as his source of this (1893a: 1st edn, 5/2.258). Now Renouvier claimed the same in 1869 (when his *Science de la morale* was first published). Is Durkheim being ironical or mischievous here, given Renouvier's undoubted unpopularity with eclecticism and liberalism, of which Janet was a representative in the university? Is Janet one of those who Renouvier accused of using his ideas, whilst not daring to cite his name?

8  For example, he treats a legislative external authority as a form of sanction (Renouvier 1869: 1.208), which is clearly important for Durkheim's treatment of sanction and law in *De la Division du travail social*.

9  The present unavailability of Durkheim's original introduction is a serious lack for scholarship, for it is here that the central feature of the sociology of moral facts, which acknowledges the historical and relative character of morality, is developed. It is here too that he shows that morality is to be understood through sign, symbol, representation and conscience. These concepts and their early location are central to the ongoing debate about shifts in Durkheim's conception of morality.

10  The translation renders 'habit' as 'custom' here.

11  These reflections may elucidate that strange thought-experiment wherein Durkheim argues that 'the first degree of autonomy' can be established through a complete 'science of things', which in turn establishes the laws, and hence the reasons, for everything (1925a: 97/114).

## Chapter 11    Belief and the Logic of the Sacred

1  Note that Fields translates *représentation* as 'imagine' here.

2  Note that *passion commune* is here translated by Fields as 'becomes worked up'.

3  Transcendental arguments characterize the rational determination of fundamental concepts of reality: see Kant 1781: 120ff. A84/B117ff.

## Chapter 12    Final Reflections

1  One exception that immediately comes to mind is David Lazar's *Markets and Ideology in the City of London* (1990). He, significantly, has now abandoned sociology.

2  Durkheim had of course read Nietzsche, but still concluded that a scientific approach to the real is possible. Was this simply a positivist delusion? Or did Durkheim see the limitations of Nietzsche's brilliant aphorisms to the serious business of knowledge and action? (1955a: 29ff).

3  This can be seen not only in the waste left after wars in Africa, but also in

Russia with its new 'medievalism' combined with gangsterism. Judge Louise Arbour, as a result of her investigation of the crimes against humanity in the former Yugoslavia, argued that it was the collapse or failure of viable institutions that left people unprotected (discussion on BBC Radio 4).

# References

## Primary Sources

### Durkheim

References to Durkheim's works in the text are by the date of first publication, and the designations follow Lukes. The first number after the colon indicates the page in the current French edition, the second the page in the translation, where available. I have made use of the current French editions of Durkheim's articles and reviews; thus, references are usually to V. Karady (ed.), *Textes*, vols 1–3, or to J. C. Filloux (ed.), *La Science sociale et l'action*.

1882a: *Durkheim à l'agrégation de philosophie de 1882*. Sujet: 'Exposer et apprécier la théorie moderne de l'évolutionnisme'. *Études durkheimiennes*, 5 (1993), 15–17.

1885a: Review. *Organisation et vie du corps social selon Schaeffle. Revue philosophique*, 19, 84–101. Repr. in *Textes*, ed. V. Karady, Paris: Les Éditions de Minuit, 1975, 1.355–77. Trans. in M. Traugott (ed.), *Emile Durkheim on Institutional Analysis*, Chicago: University of Chicago Press, 1978, 93–114.

1885c: La sociologie selon Gumplowicz. *Revue philosophique*, 20, 627–34. Repr. in *Textes*, ed. Karady, 1.344–54.

1886a: Les études de science sociales. *Revue philosophique* 22, 61–80. Repr. in J. C. Filloux (ed.), *La Science sociale et l'action*, Paris: Presses Universitaires de France, 1987, 184–214. Trans. of pp. 61–9 in W. S. F. Pickering (ed.), *Durkheim on Religion*, London: Routledge and Kegan Paul, 1975.

1886b: Review. *La Science sociale selon de Greef. Revue philosophique*, 22, 658–63. Repr. in *Textes*, ed. Karady, 1.37–43.

1887a: La philosophie dans les universités allemandes. *Revue internationale de l'enseignement*, 13, 313–38, 423–40. Repr. in *Textes*, ed. Karady, 3.437–86.

1887b: Review. *De l'Irréligion de l'avenir. Revue philosophique*, 23, 299–311. Repr. in *Textes*, ed. Karady, 2.149–69.

1887c: La science positive de la morale en Allemagne. *Revue philosophique*, 24, 33–58, 113–42, 275–84. Repr. in *Textes*, ed. Karady, 1.267–343.

1888a: Cours de science sociale. *Revue internationale de l'enseignement*, 25, 23–48.

Repr. in Filloux (ed.), *La Science sociale et l'action*, Paris: Presses Universitaires de France, 1975, 2nd edn, 1978, 77–110. Trans. in M. Traugott (ed.), *Emile Durkheim on Institutional Analysis*, Chicago: University of Chicago Press, 1978, 43–70.

1890a: Review. *Les Principes de 1789 et la sociologie*. *Revue internationale de l'enseignement*, 19. Repr. in Filloux (ed.), *La Science sociale et l'action*, 215–25. Trans. in R. N. Bellah (ed.), *Emile Durkheim on Morality and Society*, Chicago: University of Chicago Press, 1973, 34–42.

1892a: *Montesquieu*, ed. W. Watts Miller, trans. W. Watts Miller and E. Griffiths, Oxford: Durkheim Press, 1996.

1893b: *De la Division du travail social*. Paris: Alcan. 11th edn, Paris: Quadrige/ Presses Universitaires de France, 1986. Trans. W. D. Halls, *The Division of Labour in Society*, London: Macmillan, 1984. Also G. Simpson 1933, repr. New York: Free Press, 1964. An extract from the original introduction has been reprinted in *Textes*, ed. Karady, 2:257–88.

1893c: Note sur la définition du socialisme. *Revue philosophique*, 36, 506–12. Repr. in Filloux (ed.), *La Science sociale et l'action*, 226–35. Trans. in A. Giddens (ed.), *Durkheim on Politics and the State*, Cambridge: Polity Press, 1986, 113–20.

1895a: *Les Règles de la méthode sociologique*. Paris: Alcan. 23rd edn, Paris: Quadrige/Presses Universitaires de France, 1987. Trans. W. D. Halls, London: Macmillan, 1982. Also S. Solovay and J. Mueller, 1938, repr. Chicago: Free Press of Glencoe, 1967.

1895b: L'enseignement philosophique et l'agrégation de philosophie. *Revue philosophique*, 39, 121–47. Reprinted in *Textes*, ed. Karady, 3.403–36.

1895e: *L'État actuel des études sociologiques en France*, trans. from the Italian. Published in *La riforma sociale*, part II, 3: 607–22, 691–707. Repr. *Textes*, ed. Karady, 1.73–108.

1895f: The psychological character of social facts and their reality. Letter to Celestin Bouglé, 14 Feb. 1895. Repr. in *Revue française de sociologie*, 17/2 (1976). Trans. W. D. Halls in S. Lukes (ed.), *The Rules of Sociological Method*, London: Macmillan, 1982, 249–50.

1897a: *Le Suicide: étude de sociologie*. Paris: Alcan. 10th printing, Quadrige/ Presses Universitaires de France, 1986. Trans. J. Spaulding and G. Simpson, London: Routledge and Kegan Paul, 1966.

1897d: Review. Gaston Richard, *Le socialisme et la science sociale*. *Revue philosophique*, 44, 200–5. Repr. in Filloux (ed.), *La Science sociale et l'action*, 236–44. Trans. in M. Traugott (ed.), *Emile Durkheim on Institutional Analysis*, 131–38.

1897e: Review. Antonio Labriola, *Essai sur la conception matérialiste de l'histoire*. *Revue philosophique*, 34, 645–51. Repr. in Filloux, *La Science sociale et l'action*, 245–54. Trans. in S. Lukes, *The Rules of Sociological Method*, 167–74.

1898aii: La prohibition de l'inceste et ses origines. *L'Année sociologique*, 1, 1–70. Repr. in J. Duvignaud (ed.), *Journal sociologique*, Paris: Presses Universitaires de France, 1969, 37–101.

1898b: Représentations individuelles et représentations collectives. *Revue de metaphysique et de morale*, 6, 273–302. Repr. in *Sociologie et philosophie*, Paris:

Presses Universitaires de France, 4th edn, 1974, 13–50. Trans. D. F. Pocock, *Sociology and Philosophy*, New York: Free Press, 1953, 1–34.

1898c: L'individualisme et les intellectuels. *Revue bleue*, 4th ser., 10, 7–13. Repr. in Filloux (ed.), *La Science sociale et l'action*, 261–78. Trans. in R. N. Bellah (ed.), *Emile Durkheim on Morality and Society*, Chicago: University of Chicago Press, 1973, 43–57.

1899aii: De la définition des phénomènes religieux. *L'Année sociologique*, 2, 1–28. Repr. in J. Duvignaud (ed.), *Journal sociologique*, PUF, 1969, 140–65. Trans. in W. S. F. Pickering (ed.), *Durkheim on Religion*, London: Routledge and Kegan Paul, 1975, 74–99.

1899e: Review. S. Merlino, *Formes et essences du socialisme*. *Revue philosophique*, 48, 433–9. Trans. in M. Gane (ed.), *The Radical Sociology of Durkheim and Mauss*, London: Routledge, 1992, 50–8. Also in A. Giddens (ed.), *Durkheim on Politics and the State*, Cambridge: Polity, 1986, 136–45.

1899g: Letter to Celestin Bouglé, 17 Apr. 1899. Repr. in *Textes*, ed. Karady, 2.429–3.

1900b: La sociologie en France au XIXe siècle. *Revue bleue*, 4th ser., 13, 609–13, 647–52. Repr. in Filloux (ed.), *La Science sociale et l'action*, 111–36. Trans. in R. N. Bellah (ed.), *Emile Durkheim on Morality and Society*, 3–22.

1900c: La sociologie et son domaine scientifique. *Rivista italiana di sociologia*, 4, 127–48. Repr. in *Textes*, ed. Karady, 1. 13–36. Trans. in K. H. Wolff (ed.), *Essays on Sociology and Philosophy*, New York: Harper Torchbooks, 1964, 354–74.

1901ai: Deux lois de l'évolution pénale. *L'Année sociologique*, 4, 65–95. Repr. in J. Duvignaud (ed.), *Journal sociologique*, 245–73. Trans. in M. Gane (ed.), *The Radical Sociology of Durkheim and Mauss*, London: Routledge, 1992, 21–49.

1901aiii(45): Review. A. Fouillée, *La France au point de vue moral*. *L'Année sociologique*, 4, 443–5. Repr. in J. Duvignaud (ed.), *Journal sociologique*, 302–3.

1901b: De la méthode objective en sociologie. *Revue de synthèse historique*, 2, 3–17. Repr. as preface to 2nd edn of *Les Règles*.

1902g: Letter to Hamelin, 21 Oct. 1902. Repr. in *Textes*, ed. Karady, 2.455–7.

1903ai: De quelques formes primitives de classification (with Marcel Mauss). *L'Année sociologique*, 6, 1–72. Repr. in J. Duvignaud (ed.), *Journal sociologique*, 395–461. Trans. in Rodney Needham, *Primitive Classification*, London: Routledge, 1970.

1903c: Sociologie et sciences sociales (with P. Fauconnet). *Revue philosophique*, 55, 465–97. Repr. in *Textes*, ed. Karady, 1.121–59. Trans. in S. Lukes (ed.), *The Rules of Sociological Method*, 175–208.

1905e: Internationalisme et lutte des classes, extract from *Libres entretiens*, 2nd ser. Repr. in Filloux (ed.), *La Science sociale et l'action*, 282–92.

1906a(2): Review. A. D. Xenopo, *Sociologia e storia*. *Rivista italiana di sociologia*, 8 & 10; *L'Année Sociologique*, 9, 139–40. Repr. in *Textes*, ed. Karady, 1.197–9.

1906b: La détermination du fait moral. *Bulletin de la Société française de philosophie*, 6, 169–212. Repr. in 1924a, 51–101. Trans. in D. F. Pocock, *Sociology and Philosophy*, 35–79.

1906f: Remarques sur le problème de l'individu et de la société, extract from *Revue de métaphysique et de morale*, 14. Repr. in *Textes*, ed. Karady, 1.56–7.

1907a(3): Review. *Les Éléments sociologiques de la morale*. *L'Année sociologique*, 10, 352–69. Repr. in J. Duvignaud (ed.), *Journal sociologique*, 568–77.

1907a(4): Review. *En Quête d'une moral positive*. *L'Année sociologique*, 10, 352–69. Repr. in J. Duvignaud (ed.), *Journal sociologique*, 577–84.

1907a(9): Review. *Les Lois de la solidarité morale*. *L'Année sociologique*, 10, 382–3. Repr. in *Textes*, ed. Karady, 2.339–40.

1908a(3): Débat sur l'explication en histoire et en sociologie. *Bulletin de la Société française de philosophie*, 8. Repr. in *Textes*, ed. Karady, 1.199–217.

1908c(1): Debate on political economy and social sciences, extract from the *Bulletin de la Société d'économie politique*. Repr. in *Textes*, ed. Karady, 1.218–25. Trans. in S. Lukes (ed.), *The Rules of Sociological Method*, 229–35.

1908f: Remarque sur la méthode en sociologie. In *Enquête sur la sociologie: Les Documents de progrès*, Feb. 131–3. Repr. in *Textes*, ed. Karady, 1.58–61. Trans. in S. Lukes (ed.), *The Rules of Sociological Method*, 245–7.

1909d: Sociologie religieuse et théorie de la connaissance. *Revue de métaphysique et de morale*, 17, 733–58. First and second sections published as introduction to *Les Formes élémentaires*. Third section (754–8) repr. in *Textes*, ed. Karady, 1.184–8. Trans. in S. Lukes (ed.), *The Rules of Sociological Method*, 236–240.

1909e: Sociologie et sciences sociales. In *De la Méthode dans les sciences*, Paris: Alcan, 259–85. Repr. in J. C. Filloux (ed.), *La Science sociale et l'action*, 137–59. Trans. in M. Traugott (ed.), *Emile Durkheim on Institutional Analysis*, 71–87.

1910a(2): Review. *Soziologie des Erkennes*. *L'Année sociologique*, 11, 42–5. Repr. in *Textes*, ed. Karady, 1.190–4.

1910b: Débat sur les rapports entre les idées égalitaires et la rationalité de la morale. *Bulletin de la Société française de philosophie*, 10. Repr. in *Textes*, ed. Karady, 2.373–85. Trans. in W. S. F. Pickering (ed.), *Durkheim: Essays on Morals and Education*, London: Routledge and Kegan Paul, 1979, 65–76.

1911b: Jugements de valeur et jugements de réalité. *Revue métaphysique et de morale*, 19, 437–53. Repr. in Durkheim 1924a, 102–21. Trans. by D. F. Pocock in *Sociology and Philosophy*.

1911c(1): *Éducation – Nouveau Dictionnaire de pédagogie et d'instruction primaire*. Paris: Hachette. Repr. in Durkheim 1922.

1912a: *Les Formes élémentaires de la vie religieuse*. Paris: Alcan. 7th edn, Quadrige/Presses Universitaires de France, 1985. Trans. K. Fields, New York: Free Press, 1995. Also trans. J. W. Swain, 1915, repr. London: George Allen and Unwin, 1964.

1913a: Review. *La Synthèse en histoire*. *L'Année sociologique*, 12(2), 26–7. Repr. in J. Duvignaud (ed.), *Journal sociologique*, 674–5.

1913a(15): Review S. Deploige, *Le Conflit de la morale et de la sociologie*. *L'Année sociologique*, 12, 326–8.

1913b: Le problème religieux et la dualité de la nature humaine. Discussion, *Bulletin de la Société française de philosophie*, 13. Repr. in *Textes*, ed. Karady, 2.23–59.

1914a: Le dualisme de la nature humaine et ses conditions sociales. *Scientia*, 25,

206–21. Repr. in J. C. Filloux, *La Science sociale et l'action*, 314–32. Trans. in R. N. Bellah, *Emile Durkheim on Morality and Society*, 149–63. Also in K. H. Woolf (ed.), *Essays on Sociology and Philosophy*, 325–40.

1914b: Une confrontation entre bergsonisme et sociologisme: le progrès moral et la dynamique sociale, extract from *Bulletin de la Société française de philosophie*, 14, 26–9, 34–6. Repr. in *Textes*, ed. Karady, 1.64–70.

1915a: La sociologie. In *La Science française*, 1, 39–49. Repr. in *Textes*, ed. Karady, 1.109–17. Trans. in K. H. Wolff (ed.), *Essays on Sociology and Philosophy*, 376–84.

1915c: *L'Allemagne au-dessus de tout*. Repr. Paris: Colin, 1991. Selections in A. Giddens (ed.), *Durkheim on Politics and the State*, Cambridge: Polity, 1986, 224–33.

1916a: *Lettres à tous les français*. Extracts in A. Giddens (ed.), *Durkheim on Politics and the State*, 216–24.

1917c: La politique du demain. Originally published in *La Dépêche* (Toulouse), 17 Apr. 1917. Re-presented by J. Mergy in *Études durkheimiennes*, new ser., 5 (1999), 8–12.

1918a: *La Vie universitaire à Paris*, extract from a collective work. Paris: Colin. Repr. in *Textes*, ed. Karady, 1.453–83.

1920a: Introduction à la morale. *Revue philosophique*, 89, 79–97. Repr. in *Textes*, ed. Karady, 2.313—31. Trans. in W. S. F. Pickering (ed.), *Durkheim: Essays on Morals and Education*, London: Routledge and Kegan Paul, 1979, 77–93.

1922a: *Éducation et sociologie*. Paris: Alcan. 4th edn Quadrige/Presses Universitaires de France, 1993.

1924a: *Sociologie et philosophie*. Paris: Alcan. Repub, Paris: Presses Universitaires de France, 1951; 4th edn 1974. Trans. D. F. Pocock, *Sociology and Philosophy*.

1925a: *L'Éducation morale*. Paris: Alcan. Repr. Paris: Presses Universitaires de France, 1974. Trans. as *Moral Education*, ed. E. K. Wilson, New York: Free Press, 1973.

1928a: *Le Socialisme*. Paris: Alcan. 2nd edn, Paris: Presses Universitaires de France, 1974. Trans. as *Socialism*, ed. A. Gouldner, New York: Collier Books, 1962.

1950a: *Leçons de sociologie*. Introduction by George Davy. University of Istanbul Publications of the Faculty of Law, no. 111. Repr. Paris: Quadrige/Presses Universitaires de France, 1990. Trans. C. Brookfield as *Professional Ethics and Civic Morals*, 1957. Repr. with an introduction by B. S. Turner, London: Routledge, 1992.

1955a: *Pragmatisme et sociologie*. Paris: Vrin.

1967a: Le rôle des grands hommes dans l'histoire. Discours au Lycée de Sens, 16 Aug. 1883, *Cahiers internationaux de sociologie*, 14, 25–32. Repr. in *Textes*, ed. Karady, 1.409–17. Trans. in R. N. Bellah (ed.), *Durkheim on Morality and Society*, 25–33.

1968d: *La Morale*, Notes of lecture course 1908–9 by A. Cuvillier. Extract of Lukes 1968. D.Phil. thesis, 2.261–69. Repr. in *Textes*, ed. Karady, 2.269–312.

1998a: *Lettres à Marcel Mauss*, ed. P. Besnard and M. Fournier. Paris: Presses Universitaires de France.

## Renouvier

1848: *Manuel républicain de l'homme et du citoyen*. Paris: Pagnerre.

1851: Introduction à un essai d'organisation politique pour la France (with C. Fauvety). In *La Liberté de Penser*, vol. 7, Paris, 524–47.

1859: *Essais de critique générale: deuxième essai*. Paris: Libraire philosophique de Ladrange.

1864a: *Introduction à la philosophie analytique de l'histoire*. Paris: Libraire Philosophique de Ladrange, essay 4.

1864b: *Les Principes de la nature*. Paris: Librairie Philosophique Ladrange. References to 2nd edn. Paris: Librairie Armand Colin, 1912.

1869a: *Science de la morale*, 2 vols. Paris: Librairie philosophique de Ladrange.

1869b: *Science de la morale*, 2 vols, 2nd edn. Paris: Alcan (1908).

1872a: Ce que c'est le criticisme. *La Critique philosophique*, yr 1, 1, 1–3.

1872b: La doctrine républicaine, ou ce que nous sommes, ce que nous voulons. *La critique philosophique, politique scientifique et littéraire*, yr 1, 2, 1–16. Repr. in S. Douailler et al. (eds), *Philosophie France XIXe siècle* Paris: Librairie Générale Française, 1994, 727–53.

1872c: La raison d'état en 1872. *La Critique philosophique*, yr 1, 1, 177–86.

1873: Les prétensions de la science. *La Critique philosophique*, yr 2, 1, 227–35.

1874a: De la construction des postulats de la raison pratique. *La Critique philosophique*, yr 3, 2: 129–38.

1874b: Des fausses interprétations de principe de la physique moderne. *La Critique philosophique*, yr 3, 1, 161–74.

1875a: La Commune française. *La Critique philosophique*, yr 4, 1, 229–34.

1875b: De la méthode scientifique. *La Critique philosophique*, yr 4, 2, 401–4.

1875c: *Traité de logique générale et de logique formelle*, 3 vols. Paris: Au Bureau de la critique philosophique. References are to the 2nd edn (2 vols), Paris: Colin, 1912.

1875d: *Traité de Psychologie rationnelle*. 3 vols, Paris: Au Bureau de la critique philosophique.

1876a: De la méthode scientifique: les miracles. *La Critique philosophique*, yr 5, 1, 1–7.

1876b: De la méthode scientifique: les lois naturelles. *La Critique philosophique*, yr 5, 1, 17–21.

1876c: De la méthode scientifique: la cause et substance dans les sciences. *La Critique philosophique*, yr 5, 1, 49–55.

1876d: De la méthode scientifique: l'habitude et la volonté. *La Critique philosophique*, yr 5, 1, 113–18.

1876e: L'accord de la raison et de la foi. *La Critique philosophique*, yr 5, 1, 129–35.

1877: Examen des principes de psychologie de Herbert Spencer, IV: La formation de l'esprit par l'expérience héréditaire. *La critique philosophique*, yr 6, 2, 17–26.

1878a: La question de la certitude, I: le positivisme. *La Critique philosophique*, yr 7, 1, 49–53.

1878b: La question de la certitude, II: le matérialisme. *La Critique philosophique*, yr 7, 1, 81–7.

1879: Les dangers de la troisième république. *La Critique philosophique*, yr 8, 1, 177–86.

1880a: La liberté humaine au point de vue de l'observation. *La Critique philosophique*, yr 9, 2, 1–7, 33–41.

1880b: De la solidarité morale. *La Critique philosophique*, yr 9, 2, 148–60.

1886: *Esquisse d'une classification des doctrines philosophique.* 2 vols. Paris: Au Bureau de la critique philosophique.

1898a: L'attitude criticiste. In *Philosophie analytique de l'histoire*, Paris: Leroux, 4.750–6.

1898b: *Philosophie analytique de l'histoire: les idées; les religions; les systèmes.* 4 vols. Paris: Ernest Leroux.

1898c: La principe de relativité. *L'Année philosophique*, 2nd ser., yr 9, 1, 1–19.

1901: *Les Dilemmes de la métaphysique pure.* Paris: Alcan, 2nd edn, 1927.

1903: *Le Personnalisme.* Paris: Alcan (references to 1926 edn).

1969: *Lettres de Renouvier à Henneguy 1861–99*, ed. M. Méry. Paris: Éditions Ophrys.


## Secondary Sources

Aaron, R. 1960: Sociologie et socialisme. In P. Hamilton (ed.), *Durkheim: Critical Assessments*, London: Routledge, 1990, 6.75–97.

Adorno, T. 1976: On the logic of the social sciences. In *The Positivist Dispute in the German Sociology*, London: Heinemann Books, 105–23.

Alexander, J. 1982: *Theoretical Logic in Sociology.* Berkeley: University of California Press.

Alpert, H. 1939: *Emile Durkheim and his Sociology.* Repr. New York: Russell and Russell, 1961.

Alpert, H. 1941: Emile Durkheim and the theory of social integration. *Journal of Social Philosophy*, 6, 172–84. Repr. in P. Hamilton (ed.), *Durkheim: Critical Assessments*, London: Routledge, 1990, 2.28–39.

Althusser, L. 1965: *Pour Marx.* Paris: F. Maspero.

Althusser, L. and Balibar, E. 1970: *Reading Capital.* London: New Left Books.

Andler, C. 1932: *La Vie de Lucien Herr.* Paris: Rieder Éditeur.

Arnaud, P. 1969: *Sociologie de Comte.* Paris: Presses Universitaires de France.

Ashley, D. and Orenstein, D. M. 1998: *Sociological Theory: Classical Statements.* Boston: Allyn and Bacon.

Bellah, R. 1959: Durkheim and history. *American Sociological Review*, 24, 447–61. Repr. in P. Hamilton (ed.), *Durkheim: Critical Assessments*, London: Routledge, 1990, 2: 255–68.

Bellesort, A. 1931: *Les Intellectuels et l'avènement de la troisième république.* Paris: Grasset.

Beneton, P. 1988: *Le Conservatisme.* Paris: Presses Universitaires de France.

Berlin, I. 1991: Joseph de Maistre and the origins of fascism. In *The Crooked Timber of Humanity*, London: Fontana Press, 91–174.

Besnard, P. 1987: *L'Anomie.* Paris: Presses Universitaires de France.

Besnard, P. 1993: Anomie and fatalism in Durkheim's theory of regulation. In S. Turner (ed.), *Emile Durkheim, Sociologist and Moralist*, London: Routledge, 169–90.

Billard, J. 1999: Introduction to F. Ravaisson, *De l'habitude*. Paris: Quadrige.

Bilton, T., Bonnet, K., Jones, P., Shead, K., Stanworth, M. and Webster, A. 1981: *Introductory Sociology*. London: Macmillan.

Birnbaum, P. 1971: Preface to Durkheim, *Le Socialisme* (1928a).

Birnbaum, P. 1976: La conception durkheimienne de l'état: l'apoliticisme des fonctionnaires. *Revue française de sociologie*, 17, 247–59.

Bordier, R. 1994: Introduction to *Le Grand Débat: Jaurès–Lafargue–Guesde*. Paris: Les Temps de Cerises.

Borlandi, M. 1993: Durkheim lecture de Spencer. In P. Besnard, M. Borlandi and P. Vogt (eds), *Division du travail et lien social*. Paris: Presses Universitaires de France, 67–109.

Borlandi, M. 1995: Les faits sociaux comme produits de l'association entre les individus. In M. Borlandi and L. Mucchielli, *La Sociologie et sa méthode*, Paris: Éditions de l'Harmattan, 139–64.

Bottomore, T. 1984: A Marxist consideration of Durkheim. In *Sociology and Socialism*. Brighton: Harvester Books, 102–22.

Bouglé, C. 1938: *Humanisme, sociologie, philosophie*. Paris: Hermann et Cie.

Bourgin, H. 1942: *Le Socialisme universitaire*. Paris: Éditions Stock.

Boutroux, E. 1874: *De la contingence des lois de la nature*, 10th edn. Paris: Alcan 1929.

Boutroux, E. 1925: Kant. In *Études d'histoire de la philosophie*. Paris: Alcan, 317–411.

Boutroux, E. 1933: Témoignages sur Jules Lachelier. In *Oeuvres de Jules Lachelier*, vol. 1. Paris: Alcan, xxxi–xxxiv.

Boutroux, E. 1950: *De l'idée de loi naturelle*. Paris: Vrin.

Brogon, D. 1945: *The Development of Modern France*. London: Hamish Hamilton.

Bruhat, J. 1972: Le Socialisme français de 1848 à 1871. In J. Droz (ed.), *Histoire générale du socialisme*, vol. 1. Paris: Presses Universitaires de France, 501–33.

Brunschwicg, L. 1927: *Le Progrès de la conscience dans la philosophie occidentale*, 2 vols. Paris: Alcan.

Bury, J. T. 1973: *Gambetta and the Making of the Third Republic*. London: Longman.

Charle, C. 1994: Les normaliens et le socialisme (1867–1914). In M. Rébérioux and G. Candor, *Jaurès et les intellectuels*. Paris: Les Éditions de l'Atelier, 133–58.

Chastenet, J. 1952: *L'Enfance de la troisième république 1870–1879*. Paris: Hachette.

Cladis, M. 1992: *A Communitarian Defense of Liberalism*. Stanford, CA: Stanford University Press.

Coenen-Huther, J. and Hirschorn, M. 1994: *Durkheim et Weber – vers la fin des malentendus*. Paris: Éditions de l'Harmattan.

Collins, I. 1982: *Liberalism in Nineteenth Century Europe*. London: Historical Association.

Comte, A. 1854: *Système de politique positive*. Repr. Osnabrük: Otto Zeller, 1967.

Comte, A. 1975: *Cours de philosophie positive*, vols 1 and 2, ed. M. Serres et al. Paris: Hermann.

Coser, L. 1960: Durkheim's conservatism and its implications for his sociological theory. Repr. in K. H. Wolff (ed.), *Essays on Sociology and Philosophy* by Durkheim et al. New York: Harper Torchbook, 1964, 211–32.

Cuin, C. 1991: Durkheim et l'inégalité sociale; les avatars et les leçons d'une entreprise. *Recherches sociologiques*, 22 (3), 17–32.

Dauriac, L. 1924: *Contingence et rationalisme*. Paris: Vrin.

Davy, G. 1919: Emile Durkheim: L'Homme. *Revue de métaphysique et de morale*, 26, 181–98.

Davy, G. 1973: *L'Homme, le fait social, et le fait politique*. Paris: Mouton.

Dworkin, R. M. 1978: *Taking Rights Seriously*, rev. edn. London: Duckworth.

Engel, P. 1988: Plenitude and contingency: modal concepts in nineteenth century French philosophy. In *Modern Modalities*. Dordrecht: Kluwer Academic Publishers, 179–237.

Filloux, J. C. 1977: *Durkheim et le socialisme*. Geneva: Librairie Droz.

Fonsegrive, G. 1904: *Le Kantisme et la pensée contemporaine* (extrait de *La Quinzaine*, I/3). France: La Chape-Montigleon.

Foucault, M. 1980: Truth and power. In C. Gordon (ed.), *Power/Knowledge*. Brighton: Harvester Wheatsheaf, 109–33.

Foucher, L. 1927: *La Jeunesse de Renouvier et sa première philosophie*. Paris: Vrin.

Frank, M. 1992: On Foucault's concept of discourse. In *Michael Foucault Philosopher*. Brighton: Harvester Wheatsheaf, 95–116.

Furet, F. 1988: *La Révolution française 1770–1880: Histoire de la France*. Paris: Hachette.

Gacon, J. 1970: La Commune de Paris. *Europe*, Nov.–Dec., 6–17.

Gane, M. 1995: La distinction du normal et pathologique. In M. Borlandi and L. Mucchielli (eds), *La sociologie et sa méthode*, Paris: Éditions de l'Harmattan, 185–205.

Gehlke, C. E. 1915: *Émile Durkheim's Contribution to Sociological Theory*. Repr. New York: AMS Press, 1969.

Geuss, R. 1981: *The Idea of a Critical Theory*. Cambridge: Cambridge University Press.

Giddens, A. 1971: *Capitalism and Modern Social Theory*. Cambridge: Cambridge University Press.

Giddens, A. 1986: Introduction to *Durkheim on Politics and the State*, Cambridge: Polity, 1–31.

Giddens, A. 1987: Structuralism, post-structuralism and the production of culture. In A. Giddens and J. Turner (eds), *Social Theory Today*, Cambridge: Polity, 195–223.

Giddens, A. 1989: *Sociology*. Cambridge: Polity. 2nd edn 1993.

Giddens, A. 1995a: Durkheim and the question of individualism. In *Politics, Sociology and Social Theory*, Cambridge: Polity, 116–35.

Giddens, A. 1995b: Durkheim's political sociology. In *Politics, Sociology and Social Theory*, Cambridge: Polity, 78–115.

Gouhier, H. 1948: *Les Conversions de Maine de Biran*. Paris: Vrin.

Gouldner, A. 1970: *The Coming Crisis of Western Sociology*. Repr. London: Heinemann, 1973.

Gurvitch, G. 1938: *Essais de sociologie*. Paris: Sirey.

Habermas, G. 1976: The analytic theory of science and dialectics. In *The Positivist Dispute in German Sociology*. London: Heinemann Educational Books, 131–62.

Habermas, G. 1992: *The Theory of Communicative Action*, 2 vols. Cambridge: Polity.

Halévy, D. 1930: *La Fin des notables*. Paris: Bernard Grasset.

Halévy, E. 1948: *Histoire du socialisme européen*. Paris: Gallimard.

Hall, J. 1992: *Powers and Liberties*. Harmondsworth: Penguin Books.

Hamelin, O. 1907: *Essai sur les éléments principaux de la représentation*, 3rd edn, ed. A. Darbon. Paris: Presses Universitaires de France, 1952.

Hamelin, O. 1927: *Le Système de Renouvier*. Paris: Vrin.

Hayward, J. 1961: The official social philosophy of the French Third Republic: Léon Bourgeois and solidarism. *International Review of Social History*, 6, 19–48.

Hinkle, R. C. 1960: *Durkheim in American Sociology*. Repr. in K. H. Woolff (ed.), *Essays on Sociology and Philosophy*, New York: Harper Torchbooks, 1964, 267–95.

Hirst, P. Q. 1975: *Durkheim, Bernard and Epistemology*. London: Routledge and Kegan Paul.

Hitchens, C. (ed.) 1971: *The Paris Commune of 1871*, by Karl Marx. London: Sidgwick and Jackson.

Horne, A. 1985: *The Fall of Paris*. Harmondsworth: Penguin Books.

Howard, M. 1961: *The Franco-Prussian War*. Repr. London and New York: Routledge, 1998.

Irvine, W. D. 1989: *The Boulanger Affair Re-considered*. New York: Oxford University Press.

Isambert, F. A. 1993: La naissance de l'individu. In P. Besnard, M. Borlandi and P. Vogt (eds), *Division du travail et lien social*. Paris: Presses Universitaires de France, 113–33.

Janet, P. 1865: *La Crise philosophique: Taine, Renan, Littré, Vacherot*. Paris: Germer Baillière.

Janet, P. 1872: *Les Problèmes du XIXe siècle*. Paris: Levy Frères.

Janet, P. 1878: *St Simon et le St Simonisme*. Paris: Germer Baillière.

Janssens, E. 1904: *Le Néo-criticisme de Charles Renouvier*. Paris: Alcan.

Jaurès, J. 1892: Les origines du socialisme allemand. Repr. in *Études socialistes*, *Oeuvres de Jean Jaurès*, ed. Max Bonnafous, Paris: Éditions Rieder, 1932, 1:49–111.

Jaurès, J. 1893: *La jeunesse démocratique*, La Déphêche (Toulouse), 2 May 1893. Repr. in *Oeuvres de Jean Jaurès*, ed. Max Bonnafous, Paris: Éditions Rieder, 1932, 1:137–40.

Jaurès, J. 1894: Idéalisme et matérialisme dans la conception de l'histoire. Repr. in *Oeuvres de Jean Jaurès*, ed. Max Bonnafous, Paris: Éditions Rieder, 1932, 2:5–19.

Jaurès, J. 1895: Introduction to B. Malon, *La Morale sociale*. Paris: Librairie de la Revue Socialiste.

Jaurès, J. 1896a: L'idéalisme de l'histoire (debate with Lafargue, 12 Jan. 1896).

Repr. in *Le Grand Débat: Jaurès–Lafargue–Guesde*, Paris: Le Temps de Cerise, 1994, 19–49.

Jaurès J. 1896b: Esquisse provisoire de l'organisation industrielle. *La Revue socialiste*. Repr. in vol. 1: 1888–1897, *Oeuvres de Jean Jaurès*, ed. Max Bonnafous, Paris: Éditions Rieder, 1932, 338–72.

Jaurès, J. 1898: *Les Preuves*. Repr. Paris: Éditions de la Découverte, 1998.

Jaurès, J. 1900: *Les Deux Méthodes* (debate between Jaurès and Guesde 1900). Repr. in *Le Grand Débat: Jaurès–Jafargue–Guesde*, Paris: Le Temps de Cerise, 1994, 93–162.

Jaurès, J. 1901a: République et socialisme. Repr. in *Oeuvres de Jean Jaurès*, vol. 2, ed. Max Bonnafous, Paris: Éditions Rieder, 1932, 269–74.

Jaurès J. 1901b: Question de la méthode. Repr. in *Oeuvres de Jean Jaurès*, vol. 2, ed. Max Bonnafous, Paris: Éditions Rieder, 1932, 241–66.

Jaurès, J. 1904: Le socialisme et le radicalisme en 1885. Repr. in Jaurès, *Préface aux discours parlementaires*, ed. M. Rébérioux, Paris and Geneva: Ressources, 1980.

Jaurès, J. 1906: Discours à la chambre. Repr. in Gilles Candor (ed.), *Jean Jaurès 'L'Intolérable'*, Paris: Éditions d'Ouvrières, 1984.

Jaurès, J. 1910: Pour la laique. In *L'Esprit du socialisme*, Paris: Éditions Gonthier, Presses Universitaires de France, 1964, 126–79.

Jaurès, J. 1919: *La Justice dans l'humanité*. Le Forgerons: Librairie d'action et d'art de la Ghilde.

Jaurès, J. 1984: *Jean Jaurès 'L'Intolérable'*, ed. Gilles Candor. Paris: Éditions d'Ouvrières.

Jellinek, F. 1937: *The Paris Commune of 1871*. London: V. Gollancz.

Joas, H. 1993: Durkheim's intellectual development. In S. Turner (ed.), *Emile Durkheim: Sociologist and Moralist*. London and New York: Routledge, 229–45.

Jones, R. A. 1993: La science positive de la morale en France: les sources allemandes de la division du travail social. In P. Besnard, M. Borlandi and P. Yogt, *Division du travail et lien social*. Paris: Presses Universitaires de France, 11–39.

Joyau, E. 1893: *La Philosophie en France pendant la révolution*. Paris: A. Rousseau.

Kallen, H. M. 1935: *Encyclopedia of the Social Sciences*, vol. 6, ed. E. Seligman. New York: Macmillan.

Kant, I. 1781: *The Critique of Pure Reason*, trans. by N. Kemp Smith. London: Macmillan and Co. Ltd, 1963.

Krakowski, E. 1932: *La Naissance de la troisième république*. Paris: Victor Attinger.

La Capra, D. 1972: *Emile Durkheim Sociologist and Philosopher*. Repr. Chicago: University of Chicago Press, 1985.

Lacombe, R. 1926: *La Méthode sociologique de Durkheim*. Paris: Alcan.

Lacouture, J. 1982: *The Life of Leon Blum*. New York: Holmes and Meier.

Lacroix, B. 1981: *Durkheim et la politique*. Montreal: Presse de l'Université de Montréal.

La Fontaine, A. P. 1920: *La Philosophie d'Émile Boutroux*. Paris: Vrin.

Lagrange, J. 1996: *La Philosophie d'Auguste Comte*. Paris: Presses Universitaires de France.

Laski, H. 1936: *The Rise of European Liberalism*. Repr. New Brunswick, NJ: Transaction Publishers, 1997.

Lazar, D. 1990: *Markets and Ideology in the City of London*. London: Macmillan.

Lehman, N. J. 1993: *Deconstructing Durkheim: A Post-post-structuralist Critique*. London: Routledge.

Leroux, P. 1834: *De l'Individualisme et du socialisme*. Paris: J. Nétré.

Lévi-Strauss, C. 1945: French sociology. In G. Gurvitch and W. E. Moore (eds), *Twentieth Century Sociology*. New York: Philosophical Library, 503–37.

Lichtheim, G. 1966: *Marxism in Modern France*. New York: Columbia University Press.

Lindenberg, D. and Meyer, P. A. 1977: *Lucien Herr – le socialisme et son destin*. Paris: Calmann-Levy.

Littré, E. 1863: *A. Comte et la philosophie positive*. Paris: Hachette.

Littré, E. 1868: Préface d'un disciple to A. Comte, *Principes de la philosophie positive*, Paris: J. B. Baillière et Fils, 1–74.

Lockwood, D. 1992: *Solidarity and Schism*. Oxford: Oxford University Press.

Logue, W. 1983: *From Philosophy to Sociology*. Dekalb: Northern Illinois University Press.

Logue, W. 1993: *Charles Renouvier, Philosopher of Liberty*. Baton Rouge: Louisiana State University Press.

Lukes, S. 1973: *Emile Durkheim: His Life and Work*. Harmondsworth: Penguin Books, repr. 1988.

Lukes, S. 1982: Introduction to *The Rules of Sociological Method*. Trans. W. D. Halls, London: Macmillan, 1–27.

Lukes, S. and Scull, A. 1984: *Durkheim and the Law*. Oxford: Blackwell.

Maine de Biran 1812: Essai sur les fondements de la psychologie. Repr. in *Oeuvres choisies*, ed. H. Gouhier, Paris: Aubier Éditions Montaigne, 1942, 67–153.

Malon, B. 1876a: *La Morale sociale*. Lugano: n.p.

Malon, B. 1876b: *La Question sociale: Histoire critique de l'économie politique*. Lugano: n.p.

Malon, B. 1890: *Le Socialisme intégral*. 2 vols. Librairie de la Revue Socialiste. Paris: Alcan.

Malon, B. 1892: *Précis de socialisme*. Librairie de la Revue Socialiste. Paris: Alcan.

Malon, B. 1895: *La Morale sociale*, 2nd edn. Paris: Librairie de la Revue Socialiste.

Marion, H. 1880: *De la Solidarité morale*. Paris: Gerner Baillière.

Maublanc, R. 1932: La Chronique des idées. In 1932 edn of Durkheim, *De la Division du travail social*, Paris: Alcan.

Meadwell, H. 1995: Post Marxism, no friend of civil society. In J. A. Hall (ed.), *Civil Society*, Cambridge: Polity, 183–99.

Merton, R. K. 1949: *Social Theory and Social Structure*. New York: Free Press.

Méry, M. 1952: *La Critique du christianisme chez Renouvier*, 2 vols. Paris: Vrin.

Meštrović, I. 1988: *Emile Durkheim and the Reformation of Sociology*. Totowa, NJ: Rowman and Littlefield.

Michel, H. 1898: *L'Idée de l'état*. Paris: Hachette.

Milhaud, G. 1927: *La Philosophie de Charles Renouvier*. Paris: Vrin.

Moody, J. N. 1966: French liberal Catholics. In E. Acomb and M. L. Brown, jr (eds), *French Society and Culture since the Old Regime*. New York: Holt Rinehart and Winston, 150–71.

Mouy, P. 1927: *L'Idée de progrès dans la philosophie de Renouvier*. Paris: Vrin.

Müller, H. P. 1993: Durkheim's political sociology. In S. Turner (ed.), *Emile Durkheim Sociologist and Moralist*, London: Routledge, 95–110.

Nagel, E. 1968: *The Structure of Science*. London: Routledge and Kegan Paul.

Neyer, J. 1960: Individualism and socialism in Durkheim. Repr. in K. Wolff (ed.), *Essays on Sociology and Philosophy*, New York: Harper Torchbooks, 1964, 32–76.

Nicolet, C. 1982: *L'Idée républicaine en France*. Paris: Éditions Gallimard.

Nisbet, R. 1952: Conservatism and sociology. *American Journal of Sociology*, 18, 167–75.

Nisbet, R. 1965: *Emile Durkheim*. Englewood Cliffs, NJ: Prentice-Hall.

Nisbet, R. 1966: *The Sociological Tradition*. London: Heinemann.

Parkin, F. 1992: *Durkheim*. Oxford: Oxford University Press.

Parodi, D. 1924: *Traditionalisme et démocratie*, 2nd edn. Paris: Colin.

Parsons, T. 1937: *The Structure of Social Action*. New York: McGraw-Hill.

Parsons, T. 1951: *The Social System*. Repr. Chicago: Free Press, 1967.

Parsons T. 1960: Durkheim's contribution to the theory of the integration of social systems. In K. Wolff (ed.), *Essays on Sociology and Philosophy*, New York: Harper Torchbooks, 118–53.

Parsons, T. 1974: The life and work of Emile Durkheim. In *Sociology and Philosophy*, trans. by D. F. Pocock, New York: Free Press, xliii–lxx.

Pearce, F. 1989: *The Radical Durkheim*. London: Unwin Hyman.

Picard, R. 1908: *La Philosophie sociale de Renouvier*. Paris: Rivière.

Pickering, W. S. F. 1984: *Durkheim's Sociology of Religion*. London: Routledge and Kegan Paul.

Pierce, A. 1960: Durkheim and functionalism. Repr. in Durkheim et al., *Essays on Sociology and Philosophy*, ed. K. H. Wolff, New York: Harper Torchbooks, 1964, 154–69.

Plamenatz, J. 1952: *The Revolutionary Movement in France 1815–1871*. London: Longman.

Poggi, G. 1971: The place of religion in Durkheim's theory of institutions. *EJS* 12, 229–66.

Prat, L. 1937: *Charles Renouvier, philosophe, sa doctrine, sa vie*. Ariège: Labrunie.

Proudhon, J. 1967: *Textes choisis*, ed. J. Bancal, Paris: Gallimard.

Pyguillen, G. 1970: *Charles Renouvier: membre de l'institut*. Conférence au Lycée de Prades.

Radcliffe-Brown, A. R. 1952: On the concept of function in social science. In *Structure and Function in Primitive Society*, London: Cohen and West, 178–87.

Ravaisson, F. 1838: *De l'habitude*. Reprint of the original essay by *La Revue de métaphysique et de morale*, 2 (1894).

Ravaisson, F. 1867: *La Philosophie en France au dix-neuvième siècle*, 5th edn. Repr. Paris: Vrin, 1982.

Rawls, J. 1993: *Political Liberalism*. New York: Columbia University Press.

Rébérioux, M. 1972: Le socialisme française de 1871 à 1914. In J. Droz (ed.), *L'Histoire générale du socialisme*, vol. 2, Paris: Presses Universitaires de France, 133–90.

Rébérioux, M. 1980: Preface to Jaurès, *Le Socialisme et le radicalisme en 1885*, in *Préface aux discours parlementaires*, Paris: Ressources, i–ix.

Réclus, M. 1945: *La Troisième République*. Paris: Librairie Arthème Fayard.

Ribot, T. 1900: *Psychologie de sentiments*. Paris: Colin.

Richard, G. 1914: *La Question sociale et le mouvement philosophique au XIXe siècle*. Paris: Colin.

Richter, M. 1960: Durkheim's politics and political theory. Repr. in K. Wolff (ed.), *Essays on Sociology and Philosophy*, New York: Harper Torchbooks, 1964, 170–210.

Rousset, B. 1970: La commune – un fait philosophique? In *La Commune de Paris*, *L'Europe*, Nov–Dec, 107–14.

Schmaus, W. 1994: *Durkheim's Philosophy of Science and Sociology of Knowledge*. Chicago: University of Chicago Press.

Séailles, G. 1904: *La Philosophie de Charles Renouvier: introduction de l'étude du néo-criticisme*. Paris: Alcan.

Séailles, G. 1935: *La Philosophie de Jules Lachelier*. Paris: Alcan.

Seidman, S. 1983: *Liberalism and the Origins of European Social Theory*. Oxford: Blackwell.

Smelser, N. J. 1993: *Le Lien problématique entre différenciation et intégration*. In P. Besnard, M. Borlandi and P. Vogt (eds), *Division du travail et lien social*. Paris: Presses Universitaires de France, 259–78.

Soltau, R. 1931: *French Political Thought in the Nineteenth Century*. London: E. Benn.

Stedman Jones, S. 2000a: Representation in Durkheim's masters: Kant and Renouvier I: representation, reality and the question of science. In W. S. F. Pickering (ed.), *Durkheim and Representations*, London: Routledge, 37–58.

Stedman Jones, S. 2000b: Representation in Durkheim's masters: Kant and Renouvier II: representation and the question of logic. In W. S. F. Pickering (ed.), *Durkheim and Representations*, London: Routledge, 59–79.

Taylor, S. 1982: *Durkheim and the Study of Suicide*, London: Macmillan.

Thibaudet, A. 1930: Refléxions. *La Nouvelle Revue française*, 35, 524–54.

Thibaudet, A. 1932: *Les Idées politiques en France*. Paris: Librairie Stock.

Thompson, D. 1952: *Democracy in France*. Oxford: Oxford University Press.

Thompson, K. 1982: *Durkheim*. Chichester: Ellis Horwood.

Tiryakian, E. 1979: Emile Durkheim. In T. Bottomore and R. Nisbet (eds), *A History of Sociological Analysis*. London: Heinemann, 187–236.

Tosti, G. 1898: The delusions of Durkheim's sociological objectivism. *American Journal of Sociology*, 4, 171–7. Repr. in P. Hamilton (ed.), *Durkheim: Critical Assessments*. London: Routledge, 1990, 3.1–12.

Turlot, F. 1976: *Idéalisme dialectique et personnalisme: Essai sur la philosophie d'Hamelin*. Paris: Vrin.

Verneaux, R. 1945: *L'Idealisme de Renouvier*. Paris: Vrin.

Vincent, K. S. 1992: *Between Marxism and Anarchism*. Berkeley: University of California Press.

Von Wright, G. H. 1971: *Explanation and Understanding*. London: Routledge and Kegan Paul.

Waldron, T. (ed.) 1992: *Theories of Rights*. Oxford: Oxford University Press.

Wallwark, E. E. 1972: *Durkheim: Morality and Milieu*. Cambridge, MA: Harvard University Press.

Walsh, D. 1972: Variety of positivism. In P. Filmer et al., *New Directions in Sociological Theory*. London: Collier Macmillan, 37–55.

Walsh, D. 1998: Subject/object. In C. Jenks (ed.), *Sociological Dichotomies*. London: Sage, 275–98.

Watts Miller, W. 1996: *Durkheim, Morals and Modernity*. London: University College Press.

Weber, E. 1962: *L'Action française*. Stanford: Leyland Stanford Junior University Press. References given to French translation by Fayard, 1985.

Weisz, G. 1983: Republican ideology and the social sciences. In P. Besnard (ed.), *The Sociological Domain*. Cambridge: Cambridge University Press, 90–119.

Williams, R. 1969: *The French Revolution of 1870–71*. London: Weidenfeld and Nicolson.

Woodward, E. 1963: *Three Studies of European Conservatism*. London: Frank Cass and Co.

Zeldin, T. 1984: *France 1848–1945: Politics and Anger*. Oxford: Oxford University Press.

# Index